Lieber Peter,

In Dankbarkeit für deine Freundschaft und Hilfe.

[Unterschrift]

Deining 13.05.2073

Person and Human Dignity

Augustine Ben Onwubiko

Person and Human Dignity

A Dialogue with the Igbo (African) Thought and Culture

Bibliographic Information published by the Deutsche Nationalbibliothek
The Deutsche Nationalbibliothek lists this publication in the Deutsche Nationalbibliografie; detailed bibliographic data is available in the internet at http://dnb.d-nb.de.

Zugl.: München, Univ., Diss., 2012

Library of Congress Cataloging-in-Publication Data

Onwubiko, Augustine Ben, 1968-
 Person and human dignity : a dialogue with the Igbo (African) thought and culture / Augustine Ben Onwubiko. — First edition
   pages cm.
 ISBN 978-3-631-62486-9
 1. Theological anthropology—Christianity. 2. Dignity—Religious aspects—Christianity. 3. Human rights. 4. Igbo (African people) I. Title.
 BT702.O59 2013
 233.089'96332—dc23

2013001085

D 19
ISBN 978-3-631-62486-9
© Peter Lang GmbH
Internationaler Verlag der Wissenschaften
Frankfurt am Main 2012
All rights reserved.
Peter Lang Edition is an Imprint of Peter Lang GmbH.

Peter Lang – Frankfurt am Main · Berlin · Bruxelles · New York · Oxford · Warszawa · Wien

All parts of this publication are protected by copyright. Any utilisation outside the strict limits of the copyright law, without the permission of the publisher, is forbidden and liable to prosecution. This applies in particular to reproductions, translations, microfilming, and storage and processing in electronic retrieval systems.

www.peterlang.de

Dedicated to my beloved father
Augustine Nwachukwu Onwubiko (*Ksm*)

Table of Contents

Abbreviations 15

Acknowledgements 19

Foreword 21

Part One 23

General Introduction 25
1. Background of the Study 25
2. Discussions on Human Dignity and Rights in Africa. 31
3. Statement of the Problem. 33
4. Research Questions and Thesis Statements. 38
5. Relevance of the Study. 38
6. Delimitation of the Study. 39
7. Methodology. 40
8. Sources. 42
9. Division of Work. 42

Chapter One
The Theological Framework 45
1.1 Human Dignity as an Anthropological Concern 45
1.2 Modern Anthropology as a negative Development 46
1.3 The Modern Anthropological Turn. 49
1.4 Human Dignity as Theological Concern 54
1.5 Religion as a Competent Interpreter of Human Dignity? .. 57
1.6 Summary 59

Chapter Two
The Problem of Human Dignity 61
2.1 Human Dignity as an Anthropological Key to Person 61
2.2 The Human Person 62
2.3 Human Dignity and Universal Human Rights 64
2.4 Heteronomy and Autonomy Interpretations of Human Dignity 65
2.5 Meaning of Human Dignity 66
2.6 Human Dignity as Philosophical History? 70
    2.6.1 Metaphysical Concepts of Human Dignity 71
        2.6.1.1 Logos as Dignity by the Stoics 72
        2.6.1.2 Early Christian View on Human Dignity. 75
        2.6.1.3 Rationalistic Natural Law as basis for Human
               Dignity 78
    2.6.2 Autonomy Concepts of Human Dignity. 80
        2.6.2.1 Free Will as basis of Human Dignity in
               Augustine 80
        2.6.2.2 Creativity as Human Dignity by Pico Della
               Mirandola (1463-1494) 82
        2.6.2.3 Kant's Moral Autonomy as Human Dignity 84
        2.6.2.4 Human Dignity as a dynamic Principle in
               Avishai Margalit 86
2.7 Dignity as Moral Value 87
2.8 Dignity as Principle, Concept and Norm of Rights 90
2.9 Human Rights as Rights from Human dignity 93
    2.9.1 The English Magna Carter, (15 June 1215) 95
    2.9.2 The English Bill of Rights, (1225-16889) 96
        A)   The Petition of Rights, (1628) 96
        B)   The Bill of Rights, (1689) 97
        C)   Toleration Act by John Locke, (1689) 97
    2.9.3 The Peace of Augsburg and the Edict of Nantes
        (1555-1789) 99
        A)   The Peace of Augsburg, (1555) 99
        B)   The Peace of Westphalia, (1648) 100
    2.9.4 The American Declaration of Independence and the
        Bills of Rights (1776) 101
    2.9.5 The French Declaration of the Rights of Man and the
        Citizen (1789) 103

    2.9.6 The Universal Declaration of Human Rights UDHR
           (1948).. 104
         2.9.6.1 The African Charter of human and Peoples'
                  Rights (1978)... 106
2.10 Universal Human Rights?.. 110
2.11 Summary.. 114

Part Two
Conceptual Analysis of Human Dignity among the Igbo (Africans).... 117

Chapter Three
Social Anthropological Survey of Igbo World View........................... 119
3.1 Introduction.. 119
3.2 Extant Works on Igbo (African) Socio-Cultural Anthropology.... 121
3.3 The Igbo Worldview: A Social-Anthropological Perspective 136
     3.3.1 The Igbo Cosmology. 140
           3.3.1.1 The Igbo World as "Spirit-Dwelt" 142
           3.3.1.2 The Spirit World "Ala Mmuo"............................ 145
           3.3.1.3 The Land of the Living "Elu uwa" 146
           3.3.1.4 The Igbo World as Real and Dynamic 147
     3.3.2 Morality in Igbo African Society:
           A Socio-anthropocentric Concept.................................. 149
     3.3.3 The Sense of Struggle and Egalitarianism among the
           Igbo 151
     3.3.4 Influences and Manipulation of Forces in Igbo
           Metaphysics 153
3.4 Life is Paramount "Ndu bu isi" in Igbo (African) Worldview......... 154
     3.4.1 "Chi bu Ndu" God is Life for the Igbo (African) 156
     3.4.2 "Ndu bu Ugwu" Life is Dignity for the Igbo 162
3.5 The Human Being in Igbo Anthropology 168
     3.5.1 Human Being as "Mmadu" the Beauty of Life................ 169
           3.5.1.1 The Constitutive Elements of "Mmadu-Ahu na
                  Nkpuruobi" (Body and Soul)................................ 171
     3.5.2 The Individual "Otu Onye" in Igbo African Society 173
3.6 The Igbo sense of Community-African Communalism 176
     3.6.1 Conflicting Issues in Igbo African Communalism 178

    3.6.2 The Structure of the Traditional Igbo African Community 180
        3.6.2.1 The Igbo African Family-Ezi Na Ulo 181
        3.6.2.2 The Kindred – "Umunna" (Children of the Father) 184
        3.6.2.3 The Umuada/Umuokpu Agnate (Daughters) 184
        3.6.2.4 Mother's Agnates-Umunne/Umune or Ibenne 185
        3.6.2.5 The Remote Kinsmen 186
        3.6.2.6 The Igbo Village-Ama or Ogbe 187
        3.6.2.7 The Igbo Town-Obodo 187
3.7 Summary 188

Chapter Four:
Human Dignity: A Socio-Anthropological Construct among the Igbo ... 189
4.1 The Linguistic Analysis of Ugwu na-Nsọpụrụ (Dignity and Respect) 189
    4.1.1 Ugwu (Dignity) 189
    4.1.2 Nsọpụrụ- (Respect) 193
4.2 Human Dignity and Personhood in Igbo (African) Social Anthropology 197
    4.2.1 Human Person: 'Onye' as Communally Structured 199
    4.2.2 Personhood as Process among the Igbo (Africans) 202
        4.2.2.1 The Person at Birth and Initiation 203
        4.2.2.2 The Age Grade System 204
        4.2.2.3 Marriage and Family Life 205
        4.2.2.4 Death and Traditional Burial as Symbols of Personhood 207
4.3 Dignity as Function among the Igbo 210
    4.3.1 Dignity and Status Placement among the Igbo 210
    4.3.2 Acquisition of Wealth and Titles as Dignity 212
4.4 Loss of Human Dignity and Rights in the Igbo Traditional Society 214
4.5 Summary 217

Part Three
Theology of Human Dignity 219

Chapter Five:
The Judeo-Christian Perspective on Human Dignity 221
5.1   Introduction... 221
    5.1.1   Historical Development of Human Dignity as Imago Dei.. 223
    5.1.2   Towards a Theological Interpretation of Human Dignity?. 225
5.2   The Special Position of Human Being in the Creative Plan of God.. 227
    5.2.1   The Summary of the Theological Statement on Evolution and Creation... 229
    5.2.2   Human Being, Every Human Being is created by God 232
    5.2.3   Every Human Being Partakes in the Image and Likeness of God.. 234
    5.2.4   Gender Equality: "Man and Woman He Created Them" ... 239
    5.2.5   Universal Brotherhood: The Goal of Justice and Human Socialization. 246
    5.2.6   The Human Being as created in Responsible Freedom......... 248
5.3   The Person of Jesus as the True Image and Likeness of God 253
    5.3.1   Human Being as Person in Christian Anthropology............ 255
    5.3.2   The Early Christian Thinkers-From Mask to Person 256
        5.3.2.1   Origen (ca 185-254 A.D).. 256
        5.3.2.2   Augustine (354-430 AD) 258
        5.3.2.3   Boethius (480-524 AD) 259
    5.3.3   The Medieval Era-Ontological Perspective 261
        5.3.3.1   Thomas Aquinas (1225-1274 AD) 261
        5.3.3.2   Francis Suarez (1548-1617 A.D.)......................... 262
    5.3.4   The Modern Era-Psychological Perspective..................... 263
    5.3.5   The Contemporary Era-Dialogical-Existential Perspective... 263
        5.3.5.1   Jacque Maritain 263
        5.3.5.2   Gabriel Marcel... 264
        5.3.5.3   Martin Buber 264
        5.3.5.4   Karol Wojtyla (Pope John Paul II) 267

5.4 Historical Documents of the Church on Human Dignity............ 270
    5.4.1 Selected Papal Documents.. 272
        5.4.1.1 Libertas Praestantissimum of Pope Leo XIII (1888) 272
        5.4.1.2 Pope Pius XI: Quadragesimo Anno...................... 273
        5.4.1.3 Pope Pius XII: Christmas Message Dec. 1942...... 274
        5.4.1.4 Pacem in Terris of Pope John XXIII 275
    5.4.2 The Declaration of Vatican II on Religious Freedom, Dignitatis Humanae 277
    5.4.3 Gaudium et Spes (The Church in the Modern World).......... 281
    5.4.4 "De Iustitia in Mundo" of 1971 283
    5.4.5 Working Paper of the Papal Commission Iustitia et Pax 1974 286
    5.4.6 Pope John Paul II Redemptor Hominis 1979 and Laborem Exercens 1981 286
5.5 Summary.. 289

Chapter Six
Dignity of Human Person: A Shared Heritage 291
6.1 Hermeneutical Approach to Differences in Cultures..................... 291
    6.1.1 Human Dignity as a Limit Concept among Cultures.......... 296
    6.1.2 Dignity as an Interpretative Principle of the Human Person 298
6.2 Social Moral Values and the Dignity of Human Person in the Society.. 300
    6.2.1 Igbo Religious and Customary Norms and Laws – "*Omenala*" as Sacrosanct. 303
    6.2.2 Taboos, Punishments and Sanctions protecting Human Dignity and Rights? 306
    6.2.3 Human Violations as Affront on Human Dignity............... 309
        6.2.3.1 Alienating Elements in the Igbo Polity 309
            A) The Resident Alien-Mbiambia....................... 310
            B) Ohu – The Slave 312
            C) Osu – the Outcast... 313
        6.2.3.2 Traditional Igbo Slavery and Transatlantic Slave Trade... 315
        6.2.3.3 Colonial Imperialism as Human Violation............ 316

6.3 Understanding Human Dignity: A theological Dialogue 317
    6.3.1 Religion: An Ambivalent Phenomenon 319
    6.3.2 Missionary Proselytism: The Scramble for Igbo Land 321
    6.3.3 "Imago Dei": A Standard Principle of Interpretation 322
6.4 Universal Declaration of Human Rights (UDHR) 1948: A Child of Circumstance 328
    6.4.1 Human Rights as a Case of Moral Dilemma 331
    6.4.2 Selective Interpretation of human Rights and Dignity 334
6.5 Interpretative Openness A Way out? 336
    6.5.1 Shared Heritage as the Basis for a viable Interpretation of Human Dignity 341

General Bibliography 345
    Primary Sources 345
    Historical Books 345
    Church Documents 346
    Encyclical Letters 346
    Secular Documents 347
    Secondary Sources 347

Abbreviations

AAS	Acta Apostolicae Sedis
AD	Anno Domino
AFLC	Abolition of Forced Labour Convention
ANET	Ancient Near East Text
Art.	Article
AU	African Union
BA	The Biblical Archaeologist
BC	Before Christ
bzw	beziehungsweise
CAT	Committee Against Torture
CCC	Catechism of the Catholic Church
CEDAW	Convention on the Elimination of all Forms of Discriminations against Women
CERD	Committee on the Elimination of Racial Discriminations
Cf	Confer
Ch	Chapter
CIWA	Catholic Institute of West Africa Port Harcourt Nigeria
C.M.S.	Christian Missionary Society
CPR	Civil and Political Rights
CPRAMWM	Committee on the Protection of the Rights of all Migrant Workers and Members of their families
CRC	Committee on the Rights of the Child
CRPD	Committee on the Rights of Person with Disabilities
DH	Dignitatis Humanae
Ed	Edition
ed./s	Editor/s
e.g.	For example/ for instance
ESC	The Employment Service Convention
ESCR	Economic Social and Cultural Rights

et. al	and others
et. cetera	and so on and so forth
f / ff	and the following/s
FAPROC	Freedom of Association and Protection of the Rights to Organise Conventions
GS	Gaudium et Spes
HD	Human Dignity
Hg/s	Herausgeber/s
Hgg	Herausgebers
HRC	Human Rights Council
HRCAC	Human Rights Council Advisory Committee
ILO	International Labour Organisation
LThK	Lexikon für Theologie und Kirche
NCE	New Catholic Encyclopaedia
No./no.	Number
NT	New Testament
OAU	Organisation of African Unity
OT	Old Testament
P.T	Pacem in Terris
q.	Question
ROCBC	Right to Organise and Collective bargain Convention
[sic]	Emphasis mine!
S. Th.	Summer Theologica (Theologiae)
ThQ	Theologische Quartalschriften
Trans	Translated by
TRE	Theologische Realencyklopädia
UBE	Universal Basic /Primary Education
UDHR	Universal Declaration of Human Rights
UNESCO	United Nations Educational Scientific and Cultural Organisation
UNHCHR	United Nations High Commissioner for Human Rights
UNO	United Nations Organisation
UPRWG	Universal Periodic Review Working Group
UNGA	United Nations General Assembly
u.a.	unter anderem

usw.	und so weiter
Vat. II.	The Second Vatican Council
vgl.	vergleiche
vis á vis	in comparism with
Vol./s	Volume/s
Völl.	Völlig neue Auflage
z.B.	zum Beispiel

Acknowledgements

The present book: *Person and Human Dignity A Dialogue with the Igbo (African) Thought and Culture,* submitted as a doctoral thesis to the theological faculty of Ludwig Maximilians-University Munich Germany owes its existence to God Almighty, the Ancient Wisdom – *Sophia.* I am sincerely grateful to so many for their contributions, some of whom I can only acknowledge here.

I am grateful to late Bishop V. A Chikwe of Ahiara Nigeria, he was a great Soul and a man of foresight for granting me this singular privilege of pursuing doctoral studies in Munich, Germany. God mercifully grant his gentle Soul eternal rest Amen.

Next I will like to express my immense gratitude to my experienced *Doktorvater,* Prof. Dr. Bertram Stubenrauch and my second moderator Prof. Dr. Armin Kreiner for painstakingly supervising this work. Their corrections, critique and suggestions coloured the taste of this work. In the same vein I am grateful to Prof. Dr. Konrad Hilpert for giving me access to his numerous works in this field of study. The late Prof. Dr. Dr. Hubert Filser was very kind to me. God mercifully grant him eternal repose. I appreciate the academic help from Sr. Ysabel Künsberg and the entire staff of the theology faculty LMU.

My unalloyed gratitude goes to Friedrich Cardinal Wetter Emeritus, the Archbishop of Munich and Freising Reinhard Cardinal Marx, for offering me scholarship. I am particularly indebted to the Generalvikar Prof. Dr. Dr. Peter Beer and Prelate Lorenz Kastenhofer director of the archdiocesan Korbiniansverein for making my stay comfortable and partly sponsoring the publication of this book.

The following deserve a special mention for their contributions towards the realization of this work. I remain grateful to a brother and colleague the Rev. Dr. Dr. Celestine Chibueze Uzondu, Dean Faculty of Philosophy Seat of Wisdom Seminary Owerri, Nigeria for inspiring the topic of this research through several heart-searching discussions. I was greatly supported and motivated by my relations, dee Canny, deem Ali, deem Apii, dee Brain, aunty Fide and deem Gera. I thank my beloved cousin Dr. Ugochi Izumma Obasi and brother priests Dr Jude Ike and Dr. Nicholas Mbogu, for painstakingly proofreading this work.

I should also like to acknowledge the contributions of the following, Dr. Martin Elekwachi, Dr. Michael Onyebuchi Eze, Msgr. Dr. Theo Okere, Dr. Justin Anaele, Dr. Sylvester Ihuoma, Dr. Kenneth Obasi, Dr. Austin Okigbo, Dr. Columbus Ogbuja, Prof. Dr. Benezet Bujo, Prof. Dr. S.S Nwachukwu Iwe, Sr. Fiat Uzoegbu, and Sr. Calice Idika.

I am no less indebted to my brother priests for their friendship and support, especially my bosom Fr. Erasmus Okere, and Dr. Walter Ihiejirika. I remain grateful to Dr. Peter Irrgang and Father Michael Kiefer, for being there for me always. I thank my cousin Sr. Dr. (med.) Vivienne Onwubiko and Sr. Dr. Mary Joan Iwenofu, Sr. Barr. Uchenna Ajaero, Srs. Maria Priscillia Ibe, Irene Ann Anyalewechi, Mary Ebere Ugwa, Mary Cordis Ahuzi and Claris Orji, for their love and friendship.

The following families both here in Germany and Nigeria have always been there for me, the families of Marczok, Palka, Greif, Falarowski, Tenfelde, Fischer, Galli-Krottenthaler, Onyeakarusi and the Ziems. I thank you all, for your love and support so far.

Last but not the least I appreciate in a special way the sincere love and support of my entire family, both nuclear and extended. Their love for me has surpassed every verbal expression. May God reward all abundantly.

Munich July 2012   Augustine Ben Chukwubuikem

Foreword

The dignity of human person is in every lip, but the meaning remains contestable and unclear. The danger of emptying the concept of its meaning will have a great consequence on the tenability of human rights, which are based on the doctrine of human dignity. Most often it appears as if human rights are human dignity translated into legal forms. In the current debate about human rights and human dignity, many different problems have been focused: Of particular relevance is the question of universal acceptance of human rights in other words, the application of human rights. In the first instance, the formulation of human rights seemed to have taken place in a particular historical context, so that one may ask whether its application any how must also remain dependent on context. Another related problem is the question of the interpretation of human dignity. Does it allow itself to be exclusively anchored on reason, or is there still the need, over and above this for a religious interpretation? The refuge taken under the cover of reason will only put a universal interpretation of human dignity and rights to chance. However, universal claims of human rights become increasingly suspicious in a post-modern and relativistic formed culture. A religious interpretation sees itself confronted with the problem of religious pluralism.

The present work *Person and Human Dignity A Dialogue with the Igbo (African) Thought and Culture* focuses these problems and other related questions. First and foremost, the author inquires whether there are thoughts and themes in the Western tradition linked with the concept of human dignity and rights that can also be found in the Nigerian Igbo culture and if they exist, what contributions these can make for an intercultural discourse and dialogue.

One of the central theses of the book asserts that, „human dignity is an interpretative open concept". On the one hand, this means, that no ideology, religion or culture can claim an exclusive right of definition. On the other hand, it means that it is only in an intercultural discourse, in other words dialogue, that what human dignity is in itself can be decided. The chance of a universal recognition of human dignity and rights depends on the fact, whether it will be possible to discover those basic pivotal issues in the non- European cultures and their history and to integrate their peculiarities in the discourse. Otherwise, the instrumentation of human rights would only instigate an uncontrollable suspicion of cultural imperialism and imposition.

Prof. Dr. Armin Kreiner
Lehrstuhl Fundamentaltheologie
Katholisch- Theologische Fakultät LMU.

Part One

General Introduction

1. Background of the Study

In recent times human dignity can be said to have found favour in the lips of modern and contemporary persons. Since its historical declaration as the sole basis for the universal human rights charter the belief in an indwelling dignity in every human being has become inevitable in every serious human discussions, whether religious or social. However this magic doctrine, once declared and enthusiastically celebrated in history as the most suitable designate for describing the sublime worth of every human being, at the same time runs the risk of being emptied of every meaning. The reason for this risk is no other than the inflationary use of human dignity at every occasion without any generally acceptable interpretation of what it is. In place of a generally agreeable interpretation of the concept as expected, differing conceptualities continue to emerge. So far the meaning of human dignity presents itself as inexhaustible, illusive and enigmatic. It is sad to note, that most dialogues on human dignity turn out to be unsatisfactory and frustrating as debates continually end in pitch battles. Nowadays, references are made incessantly to human dignity at occasions albeit, without any further effort to interpret exactly what it is just as Renzo Spielmann, a German journal reporter once expressed the enigma in the following words:

> Which human dignity? In the political speeches during the states pogrom she will be put in the forefront. In the court verdicts on the care of those with meagre income and those without jobs, or in the last questions of the beginning and the end of human life; the dignity of human person: Why does every one refer to it and no one can say exactly, what it is?[1]

---

1 Renzo Spielmann, „Welche Menschenwürde?", Die Tagespost, Dienstag 11. November 2008, Nr. 1369. „Welche Menschenwürde? In den Reden zur

The above situation suggests an inflationary use of the concept in the sense of it standing for almost every human problem. But at the same time the absence of a concise meaning and interpretation of human dignity reveals the nature of the concept as one that is inexhaustible and interpretation open. The nature of the concept as 'interpretation open' creates three subtle possibilities: 1 an invitation, to take advantage of this gap created by the opening to enrich the concept with different interpretations and risk its single universal interpretation, 2 a dilemma of giving up completely the idea of any form of interpretation since they are now many, and with possibilities of causing quarrels, and 3 a tendency of a veto over a single interpretation of the concept, as has been the case until date, with every suppressive measures and imposition on the 'weaker cultures', and or in the case of the contending parties to assume a relativistic position. Unfortunately in the above situations the danger of the concept loosing meaning and content is imminent to the effect that today, a discussion on the dignity of human dignity seems to be a wild goose chase.

As a way of escape from or to avoid the above quagmire, more recent debates on the dignity of human person have shifted emphasis from issues of interpretation and understanding, to its application as a universal instrument of democracy and globalisation. This instrumentation has become successful in the emphasis on the human rights as the protective measure of human dignity, which seems to have become the foundation of every human social life. An attitude of 'doing away with the problem of interpretation' was earlier entrenched by the fathers of the Human Rights Charter, who just made use of the concept of human dignity as the basis of Universal Human Rights without further clarifications on which dignity was been spoken about. Of course the concept of dignity has many different histories of interpretations behind it. Their preference to leave human dignity open to different interpretations in history was a conscious one. Perhaps, due to the cost and the foreseeable consequences of a single interpretation they did not want to limit the understanding of human dignity to any particular interpretation of philosophy, religion or

---

Reichspogromnacht kommt sie vor. In Gerichtsurteilen zur Abrechnung von Spesen in der Klage um Hartz IV, oder in den letzten Fragen vom Anfang und Ende des Lebens: die Menschenwürde. Warum beruft sich jeder darauf und kann doch keiner genau sagen, was sie ist?"

cultural milieu in the past. Rather they saw the confluence of the fecundation of humanism in all its paraphernalia in history as an intellectual harvest and wished to harness its riches for posterity. However the positioning of reason as the final arbiter of this obsequious neutrality has become questionable in the face of subsequent realities and events. Therefore, the dignity of human person, which in turn gave birth to a set of universal human rights that are universal, inviolable and inalienable,[2] would remain without any particular interpretation. Nonetheless, Tiedemann opines but rightly too that: "whether their wish of a universal human rights charter based on the dignity of human person comes to fruition or not depends largely on whether there can be a universally cultural independent understanding of human dignity".[3]

The belief in an indwelling dignity in every human person has historically supplied both the religious and anthropological basis for the insight into the ideals of the human person. These ideals are shared heritage of humanity in every culture and they include: rights, peace, equality, freedom, love and compassion, truth, justice, brotherhood and charity.[4] However, it is pertinent to note that, even though human beings have been engaging with perennial struggles for rights historically, the consciousness that every human being possesses human rights which are universal, based on the fact of being human is a recent breakthrough.[5] The belief in the inviolability of human dignity made its way obligatorily into the preambles of state constitutional laws as the basis of law after the events of World Wars I and II and the subsequent Universal Declaration of Human Rights (UDHR). Since then, the world social order and aspirations (Democracy and Globalisation inclusive) and human development have been based on the doctrine of human dignity and rights.

In the basic law for the federal republic of Germany it reads: "Human dignity shall be inviolable. To respect and protect it shall be the duty of

---

2 Cf. The Universal Declaration of Human Rights (UDHR) Preamble.
3 Cf. Paul Tiedemann, Was ist Menschenwürde? Darmstadt 2006 12.
4 Cf. Bertrand G. Ramcharan, Contemporary Human Rights Ideas, New York 2008 14.
5 Cf. UDHR Preamble.

all state authority".[6] It is pertinent to note, that before now natural law served as the basis of every positive law, but by a subtle replacement with the human dignity clause a new significance of a high import in law was struck. The juridical implications of such a paradigmatic shift cannot be underestimated. However, we are not going to be concerned with the various juridical implications of this replacement, for that will be outside the competence of this inquiry. Rather it will be more relevant to show in this inquiry that even though this clause has been inserted as basis of state constitutions, its interpretation has varied accordingly in the various different world views. This variance in interpretation should not be overlooked or suppressed by any form of imperialism or dictation.

The doctrine of *Imago Dei* believed to be the protective sphere of the human person, as the enthusiasts claimed has become more and more doubtful in the presence of differing world views. Gunda Schneider-Flume highlighted the controversy among theologians regarding the actual understanding of the concept in these words:"It is not something hidden that the situation of discussion is not made clearer by applying the concept of *Imago Dei,* in the sense that the concept of *Imago Dei*, the image of God is no less controversial than that of the dignity of human person".[7] Furthermore the separation of the doctrine of *Imago Dei* from human dignity in the latter development of the concepts that used to be twin concepts in the philosophical and theological traditions has created a serious conceptual lacuna in the understanding of the originally interwoven terms. Traditionally, the human being is said to possess dignity simply because he was created in the image of God. This dignity was conceived as unconditionally given by the creator God irrespective of his rational capacity.[8]

---

6 The Basic Law for the Federal Republic of Germany, (Grundgesetz GG), Art. 1. Human dignity.
7 Gunda Schneider-Flume, Die Geschichte der Imago Dei als Schutzraum der Menschenwürde, in: Ammer Christian (Hg.), Herausforderung Menschenwürde: Beiträge zum interdisziplinären Gespräch, Neukirchener 2010 37-60 here 38.
8 Cf. E. Herms, Würde des Menschen, II. Theologisch, RGG ^{4}8 (2005), 1737-1739 here1737.

The biblical statement, "Let us make man in our own image, in the likeness of ourselves (Gen. 1, 26-27) bespeaks the worth and dignity attached to human beings. However it is pertinent to note that this statement is not new but has its origin in the religious history of the Ancient Near East Tradition. In 1630 B.C in Egypt the image of God resided in the personality and office of the king.[9] Furthermore some other cultures would prefer to favour other biblical passages that deal more with life as the gratuitous gift from God or *'Chukwu'* in the Igbo terminology. In the above sense, human beings have dignity not simply because of the image of God motif or directly created by God in his image, but because every living being possesses life-*Ndu*.[10] In line with the thought that some cultures reserved the honours of God's image for their king and not to every human being it will be more reasonable in this sense to emphasis the Life possessed by all as the basis for human dignity. Further more it is remarkable to acknowledge the note of variance in some African peoples' creation myths, where this function of creation may have been shifted to a divine agent other than God. Life as a sacred gift from God as documented in the scriptures (Gen. 9, 5-6; Ex. 20, 13; Mt. 5, 21; Jn. 10, 10) receives the same worth of respect and preservation found in the different cultures of the world, especially among the Igbo Africans, where it is given a resounding accent. For the Igbo life is sacred. It is respected not just because it is a gift from God but more so because God himself, is this life *Ndu-Chibundu*.[11]

What is at stake here is not just the idea of the human being created in the Image of God or his having life from God as the case may be, but the need for a conceptual understanding of the uniqueness of this person and what informs his or her dignity in the prevalent world view, in line with the demand for universality. The bone of contention is the fact that there is no universal concept of human dignity hanging out there unattached to any form of cultural interpretation as Tiedemann's hypothesis points out. Rather, there are in reality many forms of interpretations and understandings of human dignity claiming universal recognition at the same time to

---

9   W. Gross, Die Gottebenbildlichkeit des Menschen im Kontext der Priesterschrift, ThQ 161, 1981 244-264 here 248.
10 Igbo word for life.
11 Cf. Theophilus Okere, Odenigbo Lecture-Chibundu. Owerri 1997 66- 67.

the effect that when human dignity is being discussed, theoretically the meaning seems to be unequivocal, but in praxis it varies.

The chance of a universally accepted human dignity and rights depends on the fact, whether it will be possible to discover the basic principles of the concept in non European history and cultures, with view to integrate their peculiarities in the discourse. Against this backdrop, scholars insist that the nature of the concept of human dignity remains inexhaustible; it is "interpretation open".[12] The purpose of interpretation openness is to enrich the concept, so that it becomes possible for other cultures to contribute their own quotas in the debate on human dignity. At the same time this would offer theology the opportunity of filling the gap created by this opening.[13] Theology identifies with the challenges of peace and unity of a global multicultural world, which depends on this universal principle of human dignity and rights. It is through a congenial theological reflection of the relatedness of the entire humanity to God and to one another that a genuine theology of human dignity is based[14]. Faithful to this noble enterprise Huber rightly asserts:

> Theology is however confronted with the question of how the existence of human rights idea in a particular religious and cultural traditional complex can be understood in relation to the need for its universality.[15]

Therefore, it is on the basis of the idea of interpretative openness that this research is carried out. It is an interdisciplinary venture on the meaning of human dignity historically, and an inquiry into the Igbo (African) thought

---

12 Konrad, Hilpert, „Idee der Menschenwürde aus der Sicht Christlicher Theologie", in: Hans, Jörg, Sandkühler (Hrg.), Menschenwürde. Philosophische, theologische und juristische Analysen, Frankfurt am Main 2007 41-55 here 49; cf. Elisabeth Gräb-Schmidt, „Würde als Bestimmung der Natur des Menschen? Theologische Reflexionen zu ihrem (nach-) Metaphysischen Horizont", in: Wilfred Härle, Bernhard Vogel (Hg), Begründung von Menschenwürde und Menschenrechten, Freiburg- Basel-Wien 2008 134-168 here 157.
13 Cf. Hilpert, „Idee der Menschenwürde aus der Sicht Christlicher Theologie" 48-49.
14 Schneider-Flume, Die Geschichte der Imago Dei als Schutzraum der Menschenwürde 47.
15 Wolfgang Huber, Art. Menschenwürde/ Menschenrechte, 3, 3.1, in: TRE 22, (1992) 577-602 here 585.

and culture with the view of setting the stage for a viable intercultural and theological dialogue.

2. Discussions on Human Dignity and Rights in Africa

Discussions on the dignity and rights of the human person in Africa are usually divided according to the historical event of colonialism into pre-colonial, colonial and post colonial Africa. Pre-colonial Africa refers to the early stages of African traditional innocence. A period in which, the traditional African society was still in tact and undiluted. While the colonial and post colonial Africa refer to the periods, during and after the colonial invasion onward. Alternatively, some times the postcolonial period can also be referred, as the 'modern Africa'. It has been a matter of debate among scholars whether there was any thing like human rights in the traditional African societies as we have them today. As a matter of fact, systematic discussions on the subject of human dignity and rights only ensued after the UDHR 1948 as a sequel to subsequent conventions.

After the independence of African states, discussions on the universal rights of the human person have taken place in different parts of Africa. Deliberations have ranged from regional levels such as the OAU (Organisation of African Unity), now AU (African Union) to the national levels in countries like Nigeria, Ghana, Cameroon, Togo and others. Patterns of discussion are usually dictated by the Western concept of human right namely, the right of the individual against that of the state, which runs contrary to the African communal spirit. For instance, in the case of Nigeria, on the occasion of her independence in 1960 the first Governor-General of Nigeria, Dr. Nnamdi Azikiwe, in his inaugural address emphasised:

> … We have inherited the idea of individual freedom, which is the scheetanchor of democratic institutions. The sanctity of person, the right of a person to fair and public trial… These are examples of the basic human rights which feature in our Constitution and which I have sworn to uphold.[16]

---

16 Cf. Nnamdi Azikiwe, "Respect for Human Dignity": An Inaugural Address delivered by His Excellency, Dr. Nnamdi Azikiwe, Governor-General and

From the above citation it becomes clear that the body of rights has been inherited from the West. These rights are based on the Western culture and tradition and not specifically on the African worldview. It was based on this conviction that the body of rights was simply an inherited foreign right's concept that some African states saw it necessary to change to what has been termed 'the African mentality'.[17] This so-called African mentality emphasises the sense of community than that of the individual. However it will be pertinent to note here, but quickly too that unfortunately the so-called change in mentality has not substantially improved the respect of human dignity in Africa, because the respect of dignity does not equate in any way with its discussion or interpretation. Respect of the dignity of human person remains paramount and it is on this that all rights should and must be based. The dignity referred here, is a concept of dignity culturally and historically interpreted, with the view of appreciating the divergent views of other cultures and religions. It is not just a matter of borrowing narratives of a foreign mentality. According to Hans Jörg Sandkühler, the nature of human dignity as a dynamic principle makes it difficult for the whole meaning to be exhausted by a simple definition.[18] It is quite unfortunate that, in Africa human rights have remained at the level of debates on foreign models and imposed political interpretations, while the African person continues to undergo several abuses in his dignity.

For a typical Igbo person as well as most Africans, *"Ndu bu isi"* (Life is supreme and paramount). In the Igbo order of values Life is dignity, while for the West dignity is life. Furthermore, for the Igbo (Africans) dignity of the individual consists in his or her being member of a community, while in the Western culture it is a lone individual in need of

---

Commander-in-Chief of the Federation of Nigeria, Government Press, Enugu, 16 November 1960 5-6.
17 African mentality refers to the African worldview, which sees the society as coming first before every other individual. Priority is placed on the community in any customary legislation. This mentality runs contrary to the Western individualism, where the individual rights rank first.
18 Cf. Hans Jörg Sandkühler, Menschenwürde und die Transformation moralischer Rechte in Positives Recht, in: Sandkühler, Hans Jörg (Hg.), Menschenwürde, Philosophische, Theologische und Juristische Analysen, Frankfurt am Main 2007 57-86 here 66.

protection from the tyranny of the community. This makes the concept of human dignity among the Igbo (African) a socio- anthropological construct. That means, man acquires this dignity through a process of social integration and maturity through a communal life and he can also loose it. It is not individualistic in outlook and content, even though the individuality of the person is never subsumed in the communality. Therefore, it is pertinent to understand this subtle conceptual difference between the African and Western cultures, which are based respectively on communalism and individualism. For the West, life is only meaningful when it is dignified for the individual (individualistic) and not necessarily through a community (communalistic), while for the African to belong to a community is the source of dignity.

3. Statement of the Problem

The problems associated with human dignity and its attendant human rights as universal concepts are not new. Issues on human dignity have been discussed severally from different perspectives namely, epistemological, psychological, juridical, social cultural, economical, political and even from religious perspectives. What is new in this inquiry is its interest in dialoguing with the Igbo (African) culture in the spirit of interpretative openness. The burden of an in-depth comparative analysis of different cultures with different worldviews cannot be underrated. According to Christian Thies human dignity as a concept has been conceptualised and interpreted by different epochs in different ways.[19] A cursory glance at this history of interpretation of the concept of human dignity reveals a myriad of understandings, which poses the question as to what is to be accepted as legitimate: Should one accept the religious interpretation instead of the philosophical; or prefer the metaphysical to the anthropological; or even prefer the historical to political; or ethical to moral? As a result of the above complexity, a variety of understanding and interpretation have always posed obstacles to the universal claim of the concept.[20]

---

19 Christian Thies (Hg.), Der Wert der Menschenwürde, Paderborn-München-Wien-Zürich 2009 7.
20 Cf. Thies, Der Wert der Menschenwürde 7.

Maximilian Forschner commented on the issue of the lack of consensus among experts on the issue of interpretation thus:

> Der Begriff der Würde des Menschen ist nach den politisch-rechtlichen und moralischen Katastrophen des 20. Jahrhunderts zu einem Fundamentalbegriff moderner Verfassungen und Rechtsvorstellungen geworden. Er dient allenthalben als Begründungsbasis für Grund- und Menschenrechte. Gleichwohl fehlt es an einer prägnanten und konsensfähigen Interpretation des Begriffs. Die juristische Kommentar-Literatur gibt sich in der Regel eher wortkarg und theorieabstinent;[21] die Philosophie ist wie immer vielstimmig; und zunehmend mehren sich hier Stimmen, die auch von der Würde des Tieres sprechen[22], damit zu einer gewissen Begriffsverwirrung beitragen oder die Rede von der Würde des Menschen explizit relativiert sehen möchten.[23]

Still on the point, Wolfgang Vögele has pointed out that, the high rate of contradictory concepts of human dignity supports the impression that what is at stake is just an empty formulary, a loosed construction. This is right, when one listens in many public political speeches and also in the sermons on human dignity as a no questionable axiom and a self- explanatory concept. Its conceptual problems, and its usage; its unclear demarcations, which lead to hefty disagreements, remain unmentioned.[24] Against this backdrop scholars prefer to speak from an interdisciplinary approach to interpretation. For instance Thies agrees that, the whole system of our normative orientation seems to hang on human dignity, so that the

---

21 Maximilian Forschner meinte damit, dass der neueste systemtheoretische Versuch einer rechtstheoretischen Begründung von Karl-Heinz Ladeur, Ino Augsberg, Die Funktion der Menschenwürde im Verfassungsstaat Tübingen 2008 diese Lücke nicht füllen kann.
22 See. Peter Kunzmann, Die Würde des Tieres – Zwischen Leerformel und Prinzip, Freiburg/München 2007.
23 Cf. Maximilian Forschner, "Die Würde des Menschen ist unantastbar" – ein Plädoyer für ein Tabu, in: Menschenwürde a.D.? Ein Grundwert im Wanken, Tagung 7/8 November 2008 Katholische Akademie in Bayern, München 1-2.
24 Cf. Wolfgang Vögele, „Die christliche Deutung der Menschenwürde im Kontext gegenwärtiger Debatten", in: Christian Thies, Der Wert der Menschenwürde, Paderborn, München, Wien, Zürich 2009 63-74 here 62.

contemporary debates on human dignity should become interdisciplinary and that no one discipline alone can suffice for an exhaustive interpretation of the principle.[25] Therefore, it will no longer be adequate to remain on the sidelines of the discussion on problems concerning human dignity that challenge our shared contemporaneous existence as human beings.

Another problem involved in the discussions on dignity and rights is that of distinctions. Getting involved in the issues of human dignity and rights is one thing and making the necessary distinctions and the limits within the two concepts is another. Most often human dignity is unconsciously and unnoticed replaced with human rights or even used interchangeably. Unfortunately, it has become difficult for People to make distinction between a culturally historically developed human rights idea and the human dignity in the heart of every human person without prejudice to religion, culture and epoch. It is not uncommon to hear people talk of human dignity when they actually mean human rights. The preference for human rights discourse can be seen in the number of literatures and reports dealing on rights as dignity

Further difficulties in the understanding of the term are caused by an inflationary use of the concept. Hilpert and Maximilian Forschner caution against such *"inflationary"*[26] use of the concept that, the tendency to posit dignity as well as the counter-dignity for every possible problem and at the same time borrowing the term and emphatically enforcing it in public discussions is responsible for its inflationary usage.[27] Human dignity as a concept is always applied too high as much as too deep. For

---

25 Cf. Thies, Der Wert der Menschenwürde 9.
26 Konrad Hilpert, „Theologische Begründung der Menschenwürde und der Auftrag der Kirche", in: Menschenwürde a.D.? Ein Grundwert im Wanken, Tagung 7/8 November 2008 Katholische Akademie in Bayern, München 3; cf. Maximilian Forschner, "Die Würde des Menschen ist unantastbar" – ein Plädoyer für ein Tabu, in: Menschenwürde a.D.? Ein Grundwert im Wanken, Tagung 7/8 November 2008 Katholische Akademie in Bayern, München 6ff. These scholars, caution on the attempt to reduce the concept to a mere natural scientific formulation, which will only make the concept difficult for a capable self and world philosophical abstract reflection.
27 Cf. Spielmann, „Welche Menschenwürde?" 9.

instance, in some cases, people talk of the dignity of animals and trees.[28] While some cultures and religions may restrict the usage of human dignity only to human beings for example in the West, where the concept is only limited to rational individual beings, in other non Western cultures dignity is extended to include groups or communities, animals, trees, deities and sacred objects of worship as indexes of dignity. According to John S. Mbiti, in African religions and philosophy human beings are not the only subjects of dignity. Thus some deities, animals, things, rivers, the living dead (ancestors) and special places may be accorded dignity due to the special functions they perform in the life of the community.[29] A recent legislation on the rights of animals in Switzerland is another surprising case in Europe, where the rights of animals and even trees have been promulgated in the national code of law.[30] Against this backdrop one may without contradictions talk of an inflationary use of the term dignity.

In the light of the above the fear of the concept loosing its meaning is not unfounded. Already in some countries the concept has been rejected in view of its obstructive tendencies in juridical formulations. Especially, the interpretation of human dignity becomes superfluous in the cases of terror attacks if the dilemma becomes acute in the decision to kill in order to save life or save the life of the terrorist and risk the death of many innocent souls. Extreme example of rejection of the principle of human dignity due to an inflationary application of the concept can be found in Great Britain where the human dignity clause has not been only regarded as irrelevant but also dangerous.[31]

Further more, a careless negligence of the historical development of the concepts of human dignity on the pretext of interpretative openness leads to a reckless instrumentation of the concept.[32] Right from the formative stage of the Charter on human rights voices were heard, especially that of the then president of Apartheid South Africa, who insisted on the approval of the term "personality" as against the more favoured "human

---

28 Cf. Spielmann, „Welche Menschenwürde?" 12.
29 John S Mbiti, African religions and Philosophy, London-Ibadan-Nairobi 1969 51.
30 Cf. Spielmann, "Welche Menschenwürde?" 9.
31 Cf. Tiedemann, Was ist Menschenwürde? 31.
32 Cf. Tiedemann, Was ist Menschenwürde? 36.

persons" thus pointing to the possibility of using the concept as a political instrument in the world.[33] On this note, there exist some ethical and moral dilemmas like selective interventions in cases of human suffering, which are often associated with generalised principles. Historically considered, human rights had always been the domestic concerns of national governments and not a universal concern as presented in the Universal Declaration of Human Rights (UDHR) 1948.[34] The process of universalising human dignity principle as a global political instrument of unity has lead to some abuses where human rights have been instrumental to imposing certain inhumane foreign policy agenda on the international landscape.

Finally, one can speak of the problem associated with the relation of human dignity as an absolute value of the human person to other relative human values. In the kingdom of values there are also other values that are known as very essential to the human person such as life, justice, freedom, equality, security and affluence, religion and culture. It will be pertinent to ascertain how values relate to one another. In other words: the stand of human dignity in relation to other human values as an absolute value. For Africans for instance, it has been argued time without number that life, *ndu* is paramount and absolute, as opposed to dignity, *ugwu* which is viewed as absolute in the West. The same is applicable in the case of "the individual" versus "the community". African individualism inheres strongly on the community, whereas the Western idea of individualism means: the individual versus the community, in this sense, the national or social state.

From the above problem areas of the subject, it is already clear that issues on human dignity are neither moral philosophical nor academic and interpretational concerns alone, but also have consequences for a just and peaceful order in society.

---

33 Cf. Tiedemann, Was ist Menschenwürde? 14-15.
34 Cf. Stephen Krasner, Sovereignty, Regimes and Human Rights, in: Rittberger, Volker (ed.), Regime Theory and International Relations, Baden-Baden 1997 139-169 here 139-140.

4. Research Questions and Thesis Statements

This research therefore, questions in the first instance, the meaning of human dignity and what chances the UDHR has as a universal concept and political instrument.

Second, it seeks to discover the idea of human dignity and rights in non-Western cultures, such as the Igbo (Africa) and to what extent the dignity of human person is protected in the Igbo culture.

Third, the research seeks to know whether there could be any possibility of a conceptual convergence among the different religions, cultures and traditions that can serve as a basis for a viable interpretation of a universal idea of human rights and dignity devoid of ideological semantics; and finally what role Christian theology can play in this discovery.

These questions will be addressed by defending the following thesis statements that;

1. Human Dignity is the anthropological key to the ideals of the person conceptualised differently in all cultures, which reveals the interpretative openness of the concept.
2. An abandonment of the historical and traditional interpretation of human rights and the positioning of reason as the basis for a universal human rights' idea by modern thinkers, has contributed adversely to the loss of the historicity of the concept and the difficulty in the realisation of its universality.
3. Christian theology with its interest in anthropology has the capacity to transcend barriers placed by the differences in cultures and religions, through honest dialogue among different religions, peoples and cultures based on the common human heritage: self transcendence of the human ideals in the *Imago Dei*, which is a viable foundation for any universally acceptable interpretation of human dignity and rights.

5. Relevance of the Study

The principle of human dignity presents an epistemological challenge with regards to the exact meaning and definition of the terms involved. However, the practical encounter of day-to-day experience brings the meaning very near to human understanding. As a result, many interpretations abound but from different perspectives. This leads to a suspicion of the concept as an empty one. The concept of human dignity has been often misunderstood and even some times mistaken for human rights. Even though the two are connected they remain separate concepts. While human dignity represents the worth of every human being, human rights represents a codified way of protecting the worth of every person. Without prejudice to the current arguments on the rights of animals and trees a holistic appreciation of the three dimensions of coexistence namely, God-Man-Nature is necessary for a proper understanding of human dignity today. More importantly, issues of political abuses, human cloning and genetic manipulations have become matters of concerns in the presence of a technologically inflamed society, with such an unlimited know-how. Therefore, a diligent explication of the concept of human dignity becomes very relevant to all and sundry, especially for policy makers in politics and the society.

Further more, the craving for an all-embracing idea of human dignity by all cultures and religions attests to the relevance of the interpretative openness of the UHDR. This can only be possible; through a diligent interpretation of human dignity in the various cultures of the world; and by unearthing the riches endowed in these cultures with a view to presenting them for a convergent dialogue at the global level. The Igbo culture is one of such rich cultures. Therefore, a theological dialogue with the Igbo (African) culture will create awareness and be a great contribution in making the concept relevant to the people. It will offer the opportunity to understand and at the same time, to appreciate the very nature of the universality, imbedded in the concept of human dignity. The interpretative openness of the concept of human dignity and rights is the nature of this acclaimed universality. Among others this analytical and theological inquiry will create a viable platform for highlighting some of the human abuses in the continent of Africa and beyond.

6. Delimitation of the Study

The area in focus is the Igbo land, Nigeria in West Africa. However, this research interests itself on a wider scope on Africa as a whole, because of the basic homogeneous features found among almost all the various tribes in Africa. For instance in all tribes of Africa, life is held sacred. Africa is noted for her deep sense of religion just as John S. Mbiti opined: "Africans are notoriously religious, and each people have their own religious system with a set of beliefs and practices".[35] Furthermore, the sense of community and less emphasis on the individual shine out paramount in all the tribes of Africa. Africans are person's oriented people.[36] This is evident in their love for relations and extended family system. Moreover, almost all the African tribes experienced slavery and imperialistic colonialism of the past two centuries, which exhibit a homogeneous social structure. Therefore, this inquiry on human dignity, even though limited to the Igbo of Nigeria can be prudently spread across the African continent with some reservations. The researcher makes this assertion, also with full responsibility and with a humble recognition and respect of the marked cultural differences existing among the various African tribes.

7. Methodology

The methodology of this research is indigenous phenomenology. Scholars have designed this methodology for the purpose of studying religions, cultures and worldviews different from the West.[37] It tries to invent originality in its approach to the study of relevant peculiarities found in cultures other than those of the West. The style is different because of its ability to handle reality in a particular culture as self emergent, that

---

35 John, S Mbiti, African *Religions and Philosophy*, London-Ibadan-Nairobi 1969 1.
36 Cf. Leonhard Harding, „Menschenbilder und Menschenrechte: Afrikanische Erfahrungen". 283. Harding describes traditional African communities as „*Personen Orientiert*", because the people usually submitted their loyalty only to the members of their small communities and explains that this fact makes the African society a communal conscious society in contra distinction to the individualistic Western society.
37 See Jonathan Harold Ellerby, Indigenous Integrative Phenomenology: Integrating Indigenous Epistemologies in traditional healing Research, Doctoral Thesis 2006 61-63. <Http//www.gtfeducation.org/academics/OTL_Ellerby.pdf 06.12.2011>.

means unique in its own genius and to allow the reality found in the culture to speak for itself and not just imposing any foreign prejudice on it. Indigenous phenomenology as a contextual method is best carried out by an indigene of the particular culture in which the research is made. This methodology leans on Edmund Husserl phenomenology (1859-1938),[38] which approached reality as that, which manifests, that which presents itself in a self- blossoming emergence. Sequel to Husserl it was Alfred Schütz, who provided the philosophical foundation of Max Weber's interpretative sociology/*verstehende Soziologie* applying methods and insights derived from the phenomenological philosophy of Edmund Husserl[39]. Even though this method aligned itself with Marx Weber's sociology it did not restrict itself to it. It was coextensive with other fields of human and social studies. Phenomenology has been said to be successful in the study of indigenous traditional religions, even though not without sharp criticisms.

Therefore, this research is not just an observer's ethnographic presentation, as has been the case for a long time now, but an indigene's study of his own culture; one who was born and bred in the culture; one who lives and works among his people. Personal experiences and careful descriptive analysis give the whole research a lively and vivid blend required of a study of this kind.

This research is interdisciplinary in nature, combining the fruits of researches in other fields of human endeavours for a rich blend for interesting discussions. It applies the modern concept of research through its interdisciplinary interest in inquiry. The research is necessarily analytical and comparative, especially in the discussions of the various worldviews. Person and human dignity: a theological dialogue with the Igbo (African) culture qualifies to a large extent as a virgin field of study, which achieves its purpose through a contextual study of the person and human dignity.

---

38 Cf. Edmund Husserl, The crisis of European sciences and transcendental phenomenology: an introduction to phenomenological philosophy. Evanston, Ill: North-western University Press 1989 5.
39 Cf. Alfred Schütz, Phenomenology of the Social World. Evanston, Ill: North-western University Press 1967 7.

8. Sources

Major works on the subject of human dignity, reference books, journals and historical books in the libraries form the basis of this research. Reliable works on Igbo (African) world view; archives of renowned libraries on African studies, such as the Institute for ethnology and African studies Munich, the London Institute of African Studies, the Nigerian Institute of International Studies Lagos and the American Research Institute Lagos. Others consulted includes; the Mbari cultural centre of the Imo state art and culture department, Imo state Nigeria, and Bishop Whelan Memorial Research Institute of the Archdiocese of Owerri Nigeria. Important references were necessarily made to experts in the field of human dignity and rights across the West and Africa. Prominent theologians and philosophers were also consulted, including authors with interdisciplinary interests. The fundamental sources of this research were the major documents of the church, especially those on human dignity (*Dignitatis humanae)* and the pastoral constitution of the Church in the modern world (*Gaudium et spes)*. Among these were also the various documents on the theme presented in the papal social teachings. Most importantly, discussions, life interviews, seminars, and outcome of symposia and colloquia on the theme played major roles in this research.

9. Division of Work

The research is systematically divided into three parts with six chapters. Each part tries to address a research question. Part 1 the general introduction deals with the first research question, on the meaning of human dignity. It articulates the stage of the discussion on human dignity in the statement of the problem; posits three major research questions and thesis statements, which guide the course of the discussions; points to the relevance of the research, especially for general readership, and delimiting the scope however to the Igbo of Nigeria, but not excluding the entire African Continent on the grounds of relative homogeneity. Finally, it discusses the method and sources of the research.

Chapter 1 deals with the theological framework of the study; presents the stand of the discussion on human dignity as a theological anthropological discourse, while chapter two deals with the problem of human dignity in a historical perspective through the review of relevant literatures on the interpretation of human dignity in the West. This chapter among others clarifies the operative terms involved in the study and reviews the etymology and meaning of human dignity. It explores the philosophical as well as the Religious interpretations of human dignity; reviews the historical turn of the concept to moral rights and how it became fundamental in constitutions and state laws; and its triumph as fundamental universal human rights. The review covers also the contemporary arguments on the viability of a universal human rights charter.

Part 2, chapter 3 addresses the thesis on the need to interpret human dignity and rights in non-Western cultures. Using the Igbo culture to prove the thesis that, the abandonment of the interpretation of human rights and positing reason as the basis of human rights by modern thinkers, with the pretension of preserving the secular and universal character of human rights contributed on the contrary to the fact of the difficulty in the realisation of its universality chapter 3 answers the second research question on the existence of the idea of human dignity and rights in other non Western cultures like the Igbo (Africa); and to what extent it has been able to protect the violation of the human person in this culture. By using an indigenous phenomenological method this part presents a contextual analysis of human dignity among the Igbo (Africans). Chapter 4 explores the meaning of the concept in the Igbo worldview, and seeks among others, to analyse the human image prevalent in the Igbo African culture. The chapter deals specifically with dignity as a socio anthropological construct among the Igbo of Nigeria; starting with a detailed linguistic analysis of the two operational words, dignity and respect; also personhood and human dignity in Igbo anthropology.

Part 3, chapter 5 addresses the thesis that modern Christian theology with its interest in anthropology has the capacity to transcend barriers placed by the differences in cultures and religions through honest studies on the different religions, peoples and cultures based on the common human heritage: self transcendence (*Imago Dei*). The belief that every human being was created in the image of God remains a viable foundation for any universally acceptable interpretation of human dignity and rights. However this interpretation must be open to dialogue with other different views. Chapter five goes further to discuss the human being in the Christian theological perspective and exposes the Churches teachings on the human person as image of God, where as chapter six discusses dignity and rights as shared heritage of humanity. It evaluates the different conceptualizations of human dignity and at the same time addresses some global issues on human violation particularly, in Africa and tries to reconcile them at the transcendental level. This chapter concludes the whole inquiry by recommending interpretative openness as a chance for a genuine and sincere dialogue, which can only guarantee a universal recognition and respect of human dignity and rights as shared heritage of humanity.

Chapter One: The Theological Framework

1.1 Human Dignity as an Anthropological Concern

In the first place, human dignity as a matter of fact is not per se a biblical word. It is most likely not to be found in the bible at all, even though by inference one could assume its presence in the old testament creation narrative, in the *Imago Dei* (Gen.1: 26), in the mystery of incarnation and in the whole redemptive work of Christ in the new testament. Although one can talk of the concept in the ambient of churches theology today it did not belong originally to the churches dogmas. Its origin in the churches social teachings is recent with a long and painful learning process.[40] For this reason, it will be of great help for a proper appreciation and understanding of the discussion, to go first of all, to the question of the theological basis of anthropology and ethics.

Accordingly, the discussion on the theological basis reveals how the human dignity as an ethical principle came to be a topic of discussion for theology in the light of developed epistemological principles, which Melchior Cano (1509-1561) referred to as a *"loci Theologicus aliene"*.[41] In this sense, such issues that relate to the anthropological aspects of the human person like, human dignity and human rights are being referred to

---

40 Cf. Konrad Hilpert, „Die Menschenrechte in Theologie und Kirche", in: Michael Durst und Hans J. Münk, Theologie und Menschenrechte, Freiburg Schweiz 2008 68-112 here 71; cf. Arnold Angenendt, Toleranz und Gewalt: Das Christentum zwischen Bibel und Schwert, Aschendorff 2009 4.
41 Cf. Hans Joachim Sander, "Die angetastete Menschenwürde – ein Ort der Gegenwart Gottes", in: Severin J. Lederhilger (Hg.), Gott verlassen Menschenwürde und Menschenbilder. 8 Ökumenische Sommerakademie Kremsmünster 2008, Frankfurt am Main 2007 33-51 here 33.

as: *"Ort der Theologie"*.[42] Henceforth, human rights and dignity as objects of inquiry began to have a place in theology in the sense of their being just instances for theological discussion and not the theology itself. Without prejudice to the interdisciplinary interest in the discussions on human dignity, it is therefore, pertinent in the first place to reaffirm from the outset, that human dignity is fundamentally an anthropological theme.

1.2 Modern Anthropology as a negative Development

The reaction of existential philosophy against the method and outcome of modern anthropology was negative. Existentialists saw the approaches and conclusions of modern anthropology as calculated dehumanisation of the human person and therefore decided on a counter attack to rescue anthropology from such a misfit. Their efforts have offered great insights into the ethical and anthropological discussions of our time. The leading proponent of this existential counter position was Martin Buber[43] who accused the modern anthropology of objectifying the human being, there by tampering with his dignity. It was against this backdrop that Buber reflected anew the statement of Kant when he asked: what is a human being? This question as it were, has challenged the past as well as the contemporary epoch. The success of the society at any time would depend on how important she takes the human question. Consequently, human sciences have dissected the human being in single parts, with intention of studying him thoroughly but could no longer assemble him back to his original nature. This is also true above all of empirical anthropology and statements, which tend to reduce the human being to a mere object. Structural anthropology has created theories that worked against the human person. Such structures, above all, try to organise the human being in such a way that the objectification of the human being becomes clear. For instance, structures against the human

---

42 Cf. Hanjo Sauer und Alfons Riedl, Die Menschenrechte als Ort der Theologie. Ein fundamental- und moraltheologischer Diskurs, Frankfurt am Main 2003 31.
43 Martin Buber in 1942 opined, that the human being knows from the earliest time that he is the most dignified creature, but he shies away to handle himself simply as an ordinary object.

person contributed to a large extent to the National socialistic agenda.[44] On the contrary, Heuser insists that human beings are mysteries.[45]

Against the backdrop of the above trend in anthropology, two major philosophical ideologies were prominent namely, Liberalism represented by the chief proponent, John Rawls, whose liberal theory sought to come out with a weak subject. For instance, in his attempt in the presence of cultural pluralism to concentrate on Justice and process questions and to do without the norms of individual or societal living forms. Certainly, one can link this liberalists' ethical model to the frontline thinking of Martin Buber. This model tries to remove all predestination tendencies to what the human being is, and provides a ready theory for such a position.[46] Communitarians represent another opposite philosophical movement. For the communitarians the togetherness of human beings has much to contribute in their integral development. Stefan Heuser compared the two currents thus:

> While the liberal theory did not say, what human beings have to do with humanity, the communitarian theory allows the humanity to be given up in the human societal models. The focus points of the liberal paradigms, that the human dignity portrays a negative anthropology and could not be associated with this form of life, human dignity risks to be lost completely in the case of the communitarians. Both theory models do not answer the question, wherein the human being as an undeterminable self is formed and found.[47]

The coming into existence of human beings is a mystery. It cannot be attributed to the human functionality alone. The otherness in the whole event cannot be swept under the carpet. Human beings owe their existence

---

44 The Nazi German Party (National Socialistic Party), based most of its anti human agenda on structural anthropology.
45 Cf. Stefan Heuser, Menschen würde, eine theologische Erkundung, Münster 2004 13.
46 Michael J. Sandal, refers to his liberalism as deontological liberalism, a form of liberalism which acknowledges the limits of Justice as an immutable basis of rights in the distribution of common good and the protection of individual rights there from. For further readings see, Michael J. Sandal, Liberalism and the Limits of Justice, Cambridge –New York – Melbourne – Madrid – Cape Town – Singapore – São Paulo – Delhi – Dubai – Tokyo 1982 1998.
47 Heuser, Menschenwürde 2004 14.

also to the togetherness enjoyed in the company of others. Becoming a human being is no work in the real sense of it, rather it simply happens. What a human being becomes cannot be claimed by any human being but always endowed. Something would be missing, that which belongs specifically to the human being, if human beings allow themselves to be deceived into engaging themselves into producing human beings as in the case of totalitarian ideologies.

According to Heuser, the question here is not how a new human being will be magically formed but where and how this human being shows himself and who he is before the judgement seat of God. This method of looking at the human being goes beyond ethical judgement and anthropological contingencies. It tries to uplift the Image of God formed already by the human being and tries to appropriate this by way of ontology. It goes beyond the empirical, has every thing about the present to take seriously but not abstract. The theological assignment of the discussion on human dignity is not, from the point of view of God to give judgement, but on the side of man to remain steadfast in the expectation and reflection of the Judgement of God.[48] A theological sensitivity of human beings and their dignity describes the contours of the events, in which the human beings remain in the expectation that God, who became man, will reveal himself to them in his dignity. In this expectation one can think of the abandoned and the dejected of the society. They can no longer be anthropologically identified rather they can be seen as beneficiaries of God creative bounties in Christ. Human dignity and justice will be ascribed to them, because God will turn His face on them through Jesus Christ.

Therefore, the above Christological thought of Heuser is born from the modern theological paradigm shift from Metaphysics to anthropology. It was a decision on the question whether theological discussions should begin from information on the human person or God, but more also on the question of what human beings by them selves can achieve or from what the human beings can achieve through the promises of God.[49]

---

48 Cf. Heuser, Menschenwürde 14.
49 Cf. Heuser, Menschenwürde 17.

1.3 The Modern Anthropological Turn

The recognition of the role of anthropology in modern theological discussions has far reaching implications in the development of Christian Dogmas. In the first instance, metaphysics as the first source of knowledge had to give way to anthropology, which has the human being as its subject of study. In the second instance, history and humanity became sources of dogma.[50] The modern anthropological turn placed the human being, who as it were is the knower and the inquirer of things in the first instance of knowledge. Hence to enquire the inquirer became logically necessary if any knowledge can be reliable. The Anthropological turn reached its peak in the philosophy of Kant, who defined dignity as that, whose value no equivalent can exchange.[51] Reason was the trademark of this human dignity.

However, this paradigm change was remarkable in the reformation theology of Martin Luther, whose theology of grace was like a wild fire that shook the peaceful slumber of traditional teachings of the Church. It is worthy of note here that Reformation theology contributed a lot to the understanding of the transcendental nature of human dignity which links the human person with every created being.[52] Consequently on no account should the government or any person deny a person of his or her dignity. In this sense, the Reformation insisted on the understanding of the person with or without his acts and it worn more recognition, so much because the freedom of the individual was protected from external coercion. As a result human dignity came to be understood as inalienable and inviolable. Thus, it contributed to a large extent to the respect of human freedom. This freedom according to Huber is not only individualistic, but also communal in character.[53] Sequel to Luther's modern anthropological revolution in theology Karl Barth, Schleiermacher and Bultmann made further contributions in this regard. More recently, on the Catholic scene it was the transcendental theology of Karl Rahner that championed this

---

50 Cf. Sauer, Riedl, Die Menschenrechte als Ort der Theologie. Ein fundamental und moraltheologischer Diskurs, Frankfurt am Main 2003 39-40.
51 Immanuel Kant, Grundlage zur Metaphysik der Sitten, 1785, BA 77; Werke, (hg.), W. Weischedel, Darmstadt IV, 1975 68.
52 Cf. Huber, Art. Menschenrechte/ Menschenwürde, 1.5, 1992 581, 582.
53 Cf. Huber, Art. Menschenrechte/ Menschenwürde, 1.5, 1992 582.

trend.[54] The modern theological epoch revealed that if theology must remain relevant, it must understand the human being as a historical being. Moreover, a vibrant and lively theology must interest itself with the study of the human being without fear or pretence, since human beings are able to understand themselves in relation to the world only if they presupposed God as the common author of both themselves and the world.[55]

Traditionally theology had concerned itself only with the classical frontline sources of theological theory of knowledge. Christian dogmas were drawn exclusively from the Holy Scriptures and Tradition as the, *regula materialis fidei*; then from the churches teachings on revelation in her *de fide* definitions as *principium regulativum fidei* vis a vis *regula formalis fidei*.[56] As a matter of fact, during this period humanity and history were not regarded as sources of dogma or principles of knowledge. However, in the course of time it became necessary to review afresh those areas of interest for the churches dogma to include the historical person and his environment in the modern world.[57]

It was the genius of the Spanish theologian Melchior Cano (1509-1561) in his land breaking work *"De locis theologicis"* in Spanish and *"loci theologici"* in Latin, which was posthumously published in 1563 that championed this new wave of change. This new theological insight, which could simply be translated as 'instances or issues for theology' became as it were, a new discovery in fundamental theology. A classical

---

54 Cf. Wolfhart Pannenberg, Anthropology in the Theological Perspective, (Trans.) Mathew J. O'Connell, Philadelphia-Pennsylvania 1985 11.
55 Cf. Pannenberg, Anthropology in the Theological Perspective 11.
56 Cf. Sauer, Riedl, Die Menschenrechte als Ort der Theologie 30.
57 Melchior Cano was a middle age theologian from Spain, who discovered a new epistemological theory that can discuss human beings, history and the society as relevant sources theological principle of knowledge and dogma. Before then, traditional sources of dogma were limited to sacred scriptures, tradition and teaching office of the church. Dogma was streamlined under those few themes such as creation, trinity, grace, Mariology, eschatology etc. Issues and themes touching on history, human beings and the society had no place in theological discussions as relevant to theology, but only noted as mundane – a Latin word meaning 'vulgar and worldly'. For further readings, See B. Körner, Melchior Cano. De Locis Theologicis Ein Beitrag zur Theologischen Erkenntnislehre, Graz 1994.

author of fundamental theology of the past centuries Albert Lang described it thus: "the first systematic attempt and at the same time a highpoint theory of knowledge for theology and methodology, that cannot be overemphasised in the centuries to come".[58] As a matter of fact, the work of Melchior Cano remains a genial programme writing for new theology[59], and Cano himself remains, "the father of theological methodology".[60]

Nevertheless, his dream was to be realized fully over the centuries, precisely in the Vatican II council in its pastoral constitution of the Church in the modern world, *Gaudium et spes* and the declaration of religious freedom, *Dignitatis humanae*. Since the articulation of the joys and sorrows of the modern world by the council fathers as that of the church, it has also become the responsibility of theology to discuss and to handle, without fetters, all issues and themes relating to the human person and his environment. Today areas such as behavioural sciences, sociology, history and anthropology have developed rapidly, so that a neglect of their contributions to the wealth of knowledge that shapes the human person in our time will be heating the head against the wall. Theology with its proper object as God and material object as the believing humans can no longer fulfil its tasks without a collaboration with other relevant human and social disciplines.

As a result of giant strides in the above areas, an interdisciplinary approach to issues concerning human life in general has become very necessary today. More importantly, giving the tension created by a world shaped by a long history of ideological controversies, which has left behind unforgettable consequences that continue to stare the face of every future generation in form of an enigma a broader view of life and reality seem to be the only reasonable way forward. There is no gain saying, that the human and social sciences are fast growing branches of knowledge, and many questions in these branches are soul searching, eluding possible proffered answers. Questions such as what the position of man in the

---

58 Cf. Bernhard Körner, Art. Cano Melchior, in: LThK 2,(³1994) 924-925 here 925.
59 Cf. Albert Lang, Die Loci theologici des Melchior Cano und die Methode des dogmatischen Beweises, München 1925 243.
60 Lang, Die Loci theologici des Melchior Cano und die Methode des dogmatischen Beweises 1925 243.

universe is, and that of the relationship between man and the society continue to reverberate. Answers to these basic questions have shaped the contemporary society leaving traces of inescapable dilemma situations thus: a world clamouring for globalisation, with a grave danger of swallowing the individual human person in a collective-pluralistic society and at the same time strongly agitating for a relativism that stands the risk of rekindling the past memories of a world once sunk in a polarization, which led to many years of untold cold wars and human abuses.

The question posited by the psalmist, "Lord what is man that you keep him in mind" has become a reference question from the earliest anthropological occupations. This basic object of human wonder has always received a spiritual approach in the attempts to propose answers. God has always been implored in the attempts until the time of enlightenment when Kant asked the question afresh but not in the light of the former Theo-centric form. He tried, this time to approach the issue of human person from a purely rational way and brought God in only as a moral necessity of duty. This duty according to Kant is subjective. The existence of God as the *summum bonum* can only be understood in terms of moral and practical reason.[61]

However, the new questioning could not overtake the same old question of the psalmist. The problem of anthropology bases itself on the fact, that the human being in relation to himself as an external observer remains hidden.[62] Whether the human being distances himself, as an observer in his existential question or gets directly involved, an objective definition of who he is remains a problem.

Therefore theology would ever have problem with its material object of study, man. For this reason of all the three questions posited by Kant as problems of philosophy namely, "what can I know? What should I do? What am I allowed to hope for? Then in connection with these three, the fourth one, "what is a human being?" Kant could answer the first three but the fourth one he couldn't hazard a guess. The reason for the incapacity is the nature of the human being as a mystery unto himself. The transcendental aspect of human being, the ontological propensity of human

---

61 Cf. Immanuel Kant, The Critique of Practical Reason, (trans.) Werner S. Pluhar, Hackett United States of America 2002 157.
62 Cf. Heuser, Menschenwürde 29.

being allows him to be both tangible, which is, empirical but at the same time not fully determinable or comprehensible. It is this transcendence that links him with his creator God. According to Stefan Heuser, the nature of the human being does not allow itself apriority to be conquered by any inquiry, without it getting lost with its attendant morality.[63]

Wolfhart Pannenberg is noted for his new insights in theological anthropology. He repeated the same old question: "What is the human being?" and tried to answer it theologically. He highlighted the change that has occurred in the contemporary anthropological inquiry, a trend that shows a drift from the former metaphysical emphasis in the modern age to a new human consciousness:

> The human being does not want himself to be joined any more in a structured world, of nature; rather he wants to conquer the world. Metaphysics had situated the rightful place of the human being in the universe, in the order of the totality of all creatures from the beginnings in the Greek philosophy.[64]

Pannenberg described the anthropological description of the contemporary human being as "world open". This world openness characterises the outlook we have of human beings in the new dispensation. The human being is open in his freedom. The human being is not trapped by the contingencies of his environment; therefore, he is world open. The human being is open for new things, fresh experiences, unlike the animals, which rely only on their programmed instincts. There are however certain characters which the human beings share in common, however the human being is far more world open, because the human being continues to question and search ad infinitum. The human being searches for God. No wonder, the biblical understanding of the position of the human being in God's creation plan presents him as the centre of all creation. God created man, in his image and likeness he created him (Gen. 1.26).

The modern interest in anthropology shows the development of new thinking of our age about God and His relationship with human beings. On this note, Pannenberg has this to say:

---

63 Cf. Heuser, Menschenwürde 38.
64 Cf. Wolfhart Pannenberg, Was ist der Mensch? Die Anthropologie der Gegenwart im Lichte der Theologie, Göttingen 1962 5.

The concentration on understanding of the human being in modern fundamental theology thus reflected both the general intellectual outlook of the modern age and the development of this outlook as it found its characteristic expression in the course of modern philosophy. The development of modern philosophy was itself one of the stimuli for the growing anthropocentricism of modern theology.[65]

With this optimism in modern philosophy, theology has a brighter future in the human questions of our time and will be able to defend the truth precisely of their assertions about God if they first respond to the atheistic critique of religion on the terrain of anthropology. Otherwise all their assertions, no matter how impressive, about the primacy of the Goodness of God will remain purely subjective assurances without any serious claim to universal validity.[66]

1.4 Human Dignity as Theological Concern

Historically speaking, Christian theology preoccupied itself with the formal epistemological sources of dogmas until the medieval era. During this period, dogma included only: *1. authoritas Sacrae Scripturae 2. authoritas Ecclisiae universalis 3. authoritas concilii generalis 4. authoritas epistolarum decretalium 5. authoritas concilii provincialis 6. authoritas sanctorum partum 7. authoritas scholasticorum 8 authoritas philosophorum gentilium, und 9. Ratio naturalis.*[67] Theology was practiced strictly under these nine dogmatic headings. There was no particular mention of "human rights or human dignity in the out-line, neither could one gain access to them by inference. However, the last two sources, scholasticorum and philosophorum could be imagined to have been a possible opening to scientific research, but then again they were purely metaphysical.

The later scholastic era was shaken by these challenges in different fronts. In philosophy it was the modern challenges on Aristotelian metaphysics, especially on the teaching on substance, which was as it were the bedrock of medieval philosophical and theological positions. In addition,

---

65 Wolfhart Pannenberg, Anthropology in Theological perspective 12.
66 Pannenberg, Anthropology in Theological perspective 16.
67 Cf. Sauer und Riedl, Die Menschenrechte als Ort der Theologie 35.

the theory of the natural law was gradually beginning to loose relevance as new waves of humanism and new epistemological theories were beginning to spring up. It was at this stage that the beautiful work of Pico Della Mirandola "Oration on the dignity of man"[68] surfaced. Pico's treatise stands as the Italian renaissance manifesto of the 15th Century. As a matter of fact, no other work more forcefully, eloquently, or thoroughly revises the human landscape to centre all attention on human capacity and the human perspective. Pico himself had a massive intellect and literally studied everything there was to be studied in the university curriculum of the Renaissance; the "Oration" in part is meant to be a preface to a massive compendium of all the intellectual achievements of humanity, a compendium that never appeared because of Pico's early death.[69] He argued among others, that there existed in different intellectual traditions a rich philosophical and theological basis for an integral appreciation of the wisdom scattered all over creation, which point to the dignity bestowed on the human person.

On the theological level, it was the noble work of Melchior Cano, the *"Loci theologici"* (1554). This work had reference to the aforementioned outline, but with an addition of the authority of history.[70] Human history was understood before Cano as a separate area of events and was handled with a relative distance as a "worldly" study.[71] This time with its inclusion in the outline of Cano's *Loci theologici*, history became an instance for theology.

Melchior Cano stressed the need for theologically addressing historical instances as a genuine source of dogma, under which anthropological and ethical instances can be theologically addressed and not be abandoned as profane. A theological reflection on the human person (including a future reflection of the concept of human dignity and its attendant human rights) became possible to reflect on, theologically. This theological stride received a wider acceptance in the modern era and was practiced as an authoritative source of theology. An emeritus professor of fundamen-

---

68 Giovanni Pico della Mirandola, Oration on the Dignity of Man, Washington DC 1999 1.
69 Cf. Giovanni Pico della Mirandola 8.
70 Cf. Sauer und Riedl, Die Menschenrechte als Ort der Theologie 36.
71 History as a subject matter did not pass as an object of theological Dogma before the period under review. It was always regarded as profane or vulgar.

tal theology, in the famous Türbingen School, Max Seckler made this noble idea of Cano a genuine Catholic theological resource.[72]

Later on, basing his instance on the successful work of Melchior Cano, Karl Rahner conceived his own epistemological theory to include method of ascribing theological knowledge and truth in a manner of self-reflection as source of theology. According to Rahner, in his 1969 lexicon article on theological epistemological principles,

> Epistemological theory of theology and doctrinal methodology is the part of theology, which reflects on the specific and methodology of the theological epistemology and declarations, through which theology makes itself an object of study.[73]

With his emphasis on methodological reflection in theology Rahner underlined the meta-theoretical character of the epistemological theory of theology, which the intellectual air of the 1960's took very seriously.

The emphasis on the relevance of tradition was decisive in Melchior Cano's *"Loci Theologicus"* of history. Nevertheless, it remains a huge task to comprehend theology when one does not understand the dialectics of the transcendental foundation of revelation and the redemptive manifestation of God's salvific grace. The question remains, how a historically oriented epistemology can be possible as an epistemological theory of theology.[74] This historical problem was not even a problem for Aristotle or Aquinas; not even for Kant, because it did not come into question for them. For instance, in the bid for Kant to understand history he landed in a form of idealism that formed a total worldview of the German intellectual atmosphere. His successors never escaped this ditch, not even Hegel. However, in the bid to turn away from this idealism Karl Marx turned the idea of history upside down and found another extreme namely "a materialistic society."

The historical importance stressed by Cano was not an abstract or speculative one, rather a place where theology could hook up as instances of God's talk. It is to be understood in the words of Vatican II as *"the signs of time"*.[75]

---

72 Cf. Sauer und Riedl, Die Menschenrechte als Ort der Theologie 36.
73 Cf. Karl Rahner, *Sacramentum Mundi IV* 885.
74 Cf. Sauer und Riedl, Die Menschenrechte als Ort der Theologie 39.
75 The word was first used in the biblical accounts of Matthew 16, 1-4 and Luke, 12, 54-56. It was latter used by Pope John XIII in his famous Encycli-

The researcher's interest in this intellectual history of the renaissance is to show that the leap from theology to anthropology was not an easy one. The dogmatic air of the medieval era was metaphysical. It preferred to start its theological concerns from God, rather than from Man. The effort of the European Renaissance was to make a paradigmatic shift from this abstract world to a human world. This was exactly, what Pico and Cano achieved with their bold erudite reflections on God and human beings. For instance Pico referred to the human intelligence and freedom as assets to transpose nature instead of mystifying it.[76]

Nowadays, theologians could theologically address human dignity and its attendant human rights as "a place of God's presence", "a place of theology." Hans-Joachim Sander referred to the timely intervention of the Vatican II as a demonstration of what he calls the "powerlessness of the Church before the modern world"[77] with which the medieval Church once acquired an authoritative voice to address the human violations in the modern and contemporary world. This powerlessness of the Church is her power to proclaim the gospel of Christ to the ends of the earth. This prerogative unfolded itself in the pastoral constitution in the modern world, *Gaudium et spes* and the declaration on religious freedom, *Dignitatis humanae*.

1.5 Religion as a Competent Interpreter of Human Dignity?

The above historical excursus goes a long way to show among others, the justification of religion as an authoritative interpreter of human dignity and human rights. However, I would consider that to be a naïveté just to presume that this religious approach towards the interpretation of human dignity will be simply accepted by all without obvious dangers. It is clear that the world is made up of atheists and theists, believers and nonbelievers. Therefore, one would ask under what prerogative religion can be well accepted as a competent interpreter of human dignity.

---

cal *"Pacem in Terris"* And thereafter used as a key leading concept of the Pastoral constitution on the Church, *Gaudium et spes and Dignitatis Humanae*.
76 Cf. Pico della Mirandola, Oration on the Dignity of Man 10.
77 Hans-Joachim Sanders, Macht in der Ohnmacht. Eine Theologie der Menschenrechte, Freiburg (a. u) 1999 166.

On the above worries, the first thing that comes to mind would be to look at what could discredit a genuine answer to a natural problem that affects every human being in the modern age. For Pannenberg such an obstacle is possible: "when religion or theology does not arm itself with foundation in general anthropological studies".[78] On the contrary, if the prerequisites for such a historical and anthropological discussion are met, we are no longer dealing in this case, with a position that one may or may not decide to accept. According to him, "individuals are not free to choose the problematic situation in which they prefer to play a part and make a contribution, whatever form this may take".[79]

Judging from the historical development of the society especially in the humanism of the past centuries religion has played great roles in the formation of the human society, without prejudice to the ambivalent nature of religion.[80] The rich Christian heritage has specifically coloured the course of human history, and generally it has been shown that Christian principles have not been antihuman development.[81] In line with this assertion, Pannenberg pointed out the chances of religion, especially in the case of Christian theology when it comes to anthropological issues that concern both the believers and nonbelievers alike:

> This explains how anthropology, or in any case the discussion of anthropological themes, became so fundamentally important to the public life of the modern age. For just as the Christian religion had been the basis for the spiritual unity of society …. It is understandable that not only Christians but also modern atheists who deny any and all religious faith should seek an anthropological basis for the universal validity of their claim.[82]

---

78 Pannenberg, Anthropology in Theological Perspective 15.
79 Pannenberg, Anthropology in Theological Perspective 15.
80 Religion is said to be ambivalent because of its propensity to manipulation. History reveals a catalogue of such abuses by the strong over the weak.
81 The researcher makes this assertion without prejudice to the position of the Church in the middle ages, especially over the issues of freedom and human rights. However, the commitment of the Church on issues of human rights in the contemporary era shows a great sacrifice in the learning process. See also, Hilpert, „Die Menschenrechte in Theologie und Kirche" 71.
82 Pannenberg, Anthropology in Theological Perspective 15.

In this vein, Konrad Hilpert outlines three major reasons for a Christian interpretation of human dignity. First, through a religious interpretation of human dignity it will remain in the consciousness that all powers, be it political, individual, ideological, systems, and states are limited. Second is the fact that it will not be enough for all human endeavours on the side of the various aspects of the society, especially justice, to arrive at the ultimate fulfilment by itself without a transcendental dimension. Third, is due to the fact that religious interpretation of human dignity and rights in the Christian ethos, will contribute towards strengthening the normative consciousness of future generation in the respect of human dignity. Hilpert concluded his argument with making reference to Jürgen Habermas who opined in the recent years, that it could be that the modern society may choose to be secular in outlook and by so doing reject the normative traditions of religion and this can mean so much there, where norms and values would have presented themselves as violable and distortable.[83]

From the above discussion it becomes clear under what pretext theology can assume authority in matters regarding the interpretation of human dignity. As a dynamic principle, the interpretation must remain "open ended."[84]

1.6 Summary

The theological framework on which this research is based shows a historical development of the relationship between theology and anthropology. Initially anthropological and ethical themes were not part of the core Christian dogmas. Moreover, history as a subject was relegated to the background as mundane subject. It was a metaphysical domination of the medieval theology whose theological methodology was strictly: God as dictating his holiness to this creature human being, whose sins and unreliability disqualified him as a genuine lasting theological reference otherwise enjoyed by dogmas such as the trinity, grace and eschatology. As

---

83 Cf. Konrad Hilpert, „Die Idee der Menschenwürde aus Sicht christlicher Theologie", in: Hans Jörg Sandkühler (Hg.), Menschenwürde. Philosophische, theologische und juristische Analysen, Frankfurt am Main 2007 41-55 here 50.
84 Hilpert, „Die Idee der Menschenwürde aus Sicht christlicher Theologie" 49.

at then, anthropology was not conceived as part of dogma but was later on rescued and received into theological discourse through the intervention of Melchior Cano and Pico Della Mirandola, and later through the influence of Martin Luther in the so-called anthropological turn.

In line with the spirit of the era, Martin Luther and Immanuel Kant played major roles in this event of the anthropological turn. Through Luther's teachings on grace and incarnation (Christology) and the Kantian autonomous subject the human free will became elevated as a standard for every moral action. From thence, theological anthropology developed to be recognised as an insight into an important aspect of creation – the human being. Its contributions in sensitive areas such as the dignity of human person have been enormous.

Today, if religion and theology will be relevant in the world at all times, especially as a competent interpreter of human dignity among cultures and religions, it must open itself to constant scientific assessment. It must be anthropologically founded, interdisciplinary, informed and at the same time informing.

Chapter Two: The Problem of Human Dignity

2.1 Human Dignity as an Anthropological Key to Person

The *'who'* and *'what'* of a person, has occupied the minds of thinkers through out the human history. Right from the biblical times, the psalmist had asked: Lord what is man? (Ps. 814; 144, 3) Consequently so many answers have been proffered from various perspectives, but none has succeeded in providing a precise answer to *'who'* and *'what'* of a person. Incidentally modern theology has discovered that it must depend heavily on the understanding of human person in order to perform its reflective functions on God and man. In the first instance, it is the belief in human dignity that offers a veritable key to the understanding of the human person and this has become the preoccupation of theology since the modern anthropological turn. The belief that every human being is endowed with dignity from birth, which ought to be respected no matter what race, colour, sex and religion, has remained a constant gateway to the understanding of the human person in history. However, a first-formal reflection and interpretation of the principle of human dignity would have to be historical. Traditionally, Western concepts of human dignity emerge from two main historical sources namely, philosophy and religion. The philosophical sources refer to its origin in the ancient Greek stoicism, in the *logos* and in the Roman *dignitas*, while the religious sources touch on the Judeo-Christian tradition, which is based on the famous Biblical assertion of the creation narrative of Gen. 1.26, *"created in the image of God"*. The early Christian tradition anchored its theology of human dignity on the theologomenon of the image and likeness of God- (*Imago Dei)* and incarnation. Early Church fathers like Justin the Martyr, Ambrose and Augustine of Hippo, taught a sound theology on the position of the human being in Gods creative and redemptive plan and accordingly gave the concept of human dignity a new Christological interpretation based on the mercy and incarnate love of God. Early Christian philosophy brought in the concepts of God's mercy and love into the nascent Roman humanism and by so doing was able to moderate extreme emphasis on law and justice. With the age of Enlightenment, Immanuel Kant based his insights on the earlier stoic tradition of the logos as reason, to affirm the autonomous subject as the self law-giver. This autonomy for Kant becomes the basis for human dignity. As a matter of fact, the whole of Western understanding of human dignity can be said to hang upon the Fichte and Kantian edifice.[85]

The declarations of human rights in history are always based on the basic convictions of the ideals of the human person. These ideals such as Freedom, justice, equality, rights, peace, self-preservation, respect, sense of community and security reveal what every human being longs for. Hence in the preamble of the UDHR 1948 it stands clear: "Whereas recognition of the inherent dignity and of the equal and inalienable rights of all members of the human family is the foundation of freedom, justice and peace in the world...."[86] In these ideals, the whole human race share the same heritage. However, if the human person is to be understood properly in his dignity and rights the historical and cultural realities that establish the differences amongst peoples and cultures should not be neglected.

2.2 The Human Person

The idea of human dignity bespeaks of a sublime value attached to the status of being human, which implies all the qualities, faculties, characters that make up the human person.[87] Consequently, the idea of the person occupies a central position in the discussion on human dignity. It is the

---

85 Cf. Georg Mohr, „Ein „Wert, der Keinen Preis hat" – Philosophiegeschichtliche Grundlagen der Menschenwürde bei Kant und Fichte", in: Hans Jörg Sandkühler (Hg.), Menschenwürde. Philosophische, theologische und juristische Analysen, Frankfurt am Main 2007 13-39 here14.
86 The Universal Declaration of Human Rights, *Preamble*, published by the United Nations Organisation (UNO).
87 Cf. Konrad Hilpert, Art. Menschenwürde, in: Walter Kasper u.a., LThK 7, (³1998) 131-137 here 133.

worth and meaning of the human person that we study in this context. The human person is both the subject and the object of this study. If the meaning and understanding of human dignity is so controversial then that of the person will be definitely more, because it is the person whose dignity is involved and talked about. It is not just an abstract person instead, this person. If one dares to study him, as a problem the risk of objectification is imminent he is substantially a subject. Moreover, when studied as a subject of value, the tendency is to moralise for he is invaluable. Therefore every attempt to study him is a risk. For this very reason the question, who and what is a person has remained a perennial one. Despite the above difficulties, the importance of answering these questions in history both to philosophy and theology has been evident in the multi-dimensional answers proffered by the different fields of human studies and yet no single answer has been able to capture the entire mystery of the human person. Answers remain hypothetical, making the definition of human person multifaceted, contextual and interdisciplinary in nature.

There are different human images as much as there are different cultures and religions. While some agree with each other, others agree partially or disagree. For example the West perceives the individuality of the human person over and above his or her communal nature, while Africans can only perceive the person not just as isolated individual but only in relation with the community.[88] For the Africans the community stands tall above every individual person. However, at the basis of these differences is the *humanness*.[89] Human images reflect the values of human person in the different cultures, which serve as anthropological key to his or her ideals. Consequently, human ideals such as freedom, law, equity and justice are common heritage of humanity.[90] They resonate and reflect the dignity of human person by constituting what and who the person is in all ages, cultures and religions.

---

88 Cf. Bénézet Bujo, Ethical Dimension of Community, Nairobi 1998 148.
89 Cf. Bernhard Vogel (Hg.), Im Zentrum: Menschenwürde, Politisches Handeln aus christlicher Verantwortung. Christliche Ethik als Orientierungshilfe, Germany 2006 12-13.
90 Cf. Ramcharan, Contemporary Human Rights Ideas, 8-9.

2.3 Human Dignity and Universal Human Rights

The subtle distinction between human dignity and human rights has often led to a misplacement of the two related concepts. While human dignity refers to the worth of being human, human rights are laws drawn from human dignity. They are not laws of human dignity but laws from it for the sake of ensuring that dignity remains inviolate. Even though both refer to human values, their origin and development in history remain remarkably different. Generally speaking, while human dignity or dignity of human person refers to the value attached to the human being as such, human rights are those legal protective instrument of the human dignity. Human rights emerge from the cultural and historical narratives of a people, which are in turn informed by their unique life experiences. Apart from the earliest recorded effort to articulate the rights of man in the famous "Magna Carter" (1215) and those of America and the French in1776 and 1789 respectively the UDHR of 1948 remains the greatest declaration of human rights so far in history. It was occasioned by the sin perpetrated against humanity in the World War II. Human rights are protective laws for human dignity, not laws of human dignity or human dignity per se but rights drawn from dignity itself.[91]

However, nowadays human rights enjoy so much popularity, so that many mistake them for human dignity they are meant to protect. The reason for this could be attributed to the heightened attention paid to it by all and sundry. Instead of going the memory lane to discover human dignity as a concept, many prefer to remain at the level of the Western historically invented human rights codifications. If references are made to human dignity they are often interfaced with human rights. For this very reason, Renzo Spielmann asks: "Which human dignity?"[92] As a matter of fact, the UDHR 1948 stands as the climax of the Western articulation of moral norms into what we have today as human rights. Incidentally human rights have become at the same time a veritable political instrument

---

91 Cf. Hans Jörg Sandkühler, „Menschenwürde und die Transformation moralischer Rechte in Positives Recht", in: Hans Jörg Sandkühler (Hg.), Menschenwürde. Philosophische, theologische und juristische Analysen, Frankfurt am Main 2007 57-86 here 58.
92 Cf. Spielmann, „Welche Menschenwürde?" 9.

of the West in its various forms of centralisation. Human rights thought as universal human rights stays under suspicion of imperialism since universalism itself as a concept is normative and can only fit human dignity as shared heritage. But human rights as laws coming from human dignity can only be understood against their historical cultural developments. The chances of a genuine universal interpretation and application can be gleaned only if the rights are left interpretative open with the view to dialogue and convergence.

2.4 Heteronomy and Autonomy Interpretations of Human Dignity

Opinions on interpretation of human dignity have always parted ways among those who lay claim to heteronomy as a concept on the one side and those for autonomy on the other. Heteronomy claims that dignity is infused into the human being through an external agent,[93] who becomes as it were the guarantor and the source of human dignity. On the other hand autonomy bases dignity solely on the will of the human person, in his capacity as an autonomous subject. According to Immanuel Kant, this autonomy is "the basis of every human and rational nature".[94] Both concepts claim universality in their conception of dignity.[95] Nevertheless, it is important to note that despite its historical development the variation in the idea of human dignity as a shared heritage is not ambivalent rather the word human dignity remains interpretative open. Human dignity as interpretative open concept has been underscored in the modern contemporary human dignity discourse, without minding from which historical ambient the interpreter chooses. It represents a nonexclusive and all-inclusive interpretation model.

---

93 Cf. Paul Tiedemann, Was ist Menschenwürde? Eine Einführung, Darmstadt 2006 39.
94 Immanuel Kant, Grundlegung zur Metaphysik der Sitten, in: ders, Werke in 10 Bänden (hg.), Wilhelm Weischedel, Bd. 6, Darmstadt 1983 (1786) 79.
95 Cf. Tiedemann, Was ist Menschenwürde? 66.

2.5 Meaning of Human Dignity

The perennial problem for different generations has been to determine the real meaning of human dignity. Human dignity as a concept finds acceptance in different cultures but its conceptualisation especially on the occasions of gross human violation produces results arguable among cultures. It is not uncommon to be confronted by conflicting and contradictory ideas of human dignity with each tacitly claiming validity. In order to quell these incessant discrepancies of meaning and the often-annoying incidence of people talking above the head of each other the necessity of a collectively acceptable understanding of the meaning of human dignity becomes not only obvious but also urgent. Such issues as those in the biological sciences, juridical cases in modern terrorism and other perturbing ethical issues in the society are not easy to be swept under the carpet or treated with obsequious silence as if they never existed. Moreover on the universal acceptance of human rights the agreement on the basis of rights – the dignity of the human person is very necessary. Stressing the need of a universal independent cultural meaning of human dignity Paul Tiedemann opines that, if there would eventually be a universal understanding of human rights depends principally on whether there could be a universal independent cultural understanding of human dignity.[96]

Therefore, chapter two enlightens on the meaning of our operational concept through the etymology and usage of human dignity among various world cultures, including the Igbo of Nigeria. In this chapter, the researcher will be concerned with conflicting conceptualisations and definitions of human dignity, which were postulated as values or positively projected as norms. In the opinion of Hans Jörg Sandkühler,[97] these interpretations were naturally dependent upon epistemological and practical interests of human and world images and the milieu in which they were formulated. The day-to-day discourses in philosophy, theology and jurisprudence provided the moral content of the interpretations. Whether the issues border on substantial metaphysics or functional pragmatic definition, from their plurality there must be an interpretation of human dignity

---

96 Cf. Tiedemann, Was ist Menschenwürde? 12,
97 Hans Jörg Sandkühler, „Menschenwürde und die Transformation moralischer Rechte in positives Recht" 57.

in the sense of what human dignity is, and when it is being violated. Its interpretation occurs neither from a unified clear existential status, nor from a self evident practical need, or even still as an analytical truth got from the concept in its double roles as an ethic-anthropological category and as constitutional rights concept.[98] Two major issues involved in the discussion of human dignity refer to the meaning of the concept and the source of human dignity. First of all, what is the etymological meaning of human dignity?

Etymologically, the term "dignity" was derived from the Latin word *"dignitas"* used to depict the sublime value of the human person. *Dignitas* means a quality or state of a thing deserving to be honoured, whose inner quality has the capacity also to be honoured.[99] It is connected with status, which is principally not to be put into question or doubted; and represents the value of a human individual, who is qualified in all its ramifications. This was how *dignitas* became a human value concept in the Roman literary genre.[100] While the word *"Pretium"*- price became a word for indicating what one can possess, that which one can avail of *"dignitas"* was only reserved to the roman aristocrats. As it were, only the aristocrats and the free men had *dignitas* while the slaves had *Pretium*.[101]

Among the Igbo of Nigeria the word *"Ugwu"* stands for dignity. It expresses a high sense of value attached to persons, events, situations and things. However, the value of human life surpasses all other values. It stands as it were as the first instance of every imaginable value. Life is dignity in this sense, hence the Igbo have as a proverb: *"Ndu bu isi"* meaning, life is paramount. The source of dignity is God as the giver of life and goodness. Dignity is associated with value, honour and respect, which can be given or acquired in the community but also, can be lost. *"Ugwù"* is related to another Igbo word, *"Nsọpụrụ"* meaning respect. They are most often used synonymously or concurrently to convey a

---

98 Cf. Sandkühler, Menschenwürde und die Transformation moralischer Rechte in positives Recht" 66.
99 Cf. Tiedemann, Was ist Menschen Würde? 69.
100 Cf. Helmut Wegehaupt, Die Bedeutung und Anwendung von Dignitas in den Schriften der republikanischen Zeit, Breslau 1932 7.
101 Wegehaupt, Die Bedeutung und Anwendung von Dignitas in den Schriften der republikanischen Zeit 7.

sense of worth or value. For the Igbo, what ever that is endowed with dignity deserves respect; hence they are commonly joined together in expressions like this: *"Ugwu na Nsọpụrụ"* meaning, dignity and respect. Even though the two can be used together or interchangeably, the Igbo know that dignity is an endowment from God, which the individual accepts and assiduously develops in the community. It is only in this ability to function and to develop these gifts that the community accords one respect and honour for a proper reception of the dignity from *Chi*-god.

Therefore the word *"Nsọpụrụ"* – respect is an attitude of recognition shown to the elder, titled men and women, who have distinguished themselves in the right sense of personhood in the Igbo community according to Igbo culture and tradition. The dead, who qualify while alive, are generally accorded respect. In the Igbo traditional religion, human life, *chi*, benevolent spirits, the ancestors, some animals and trees; shrines and town squares for gatherings and market places are accorded respect. Nevertheless this sense of respect does not speak of dignity as in the case of human being who is dignity himself. Hence in the Igbo culture *"mmadu bu ugwu"*- human being is dignity. For the above reason the Igbo world even though "a spirit dwelt world" remains albeit, anthropocentric. Chinua Achebe, a famous Nigerian literary genius observed, but rightly too, that the Igbo man though under the tutelage of his *chi* has always reserved some authority and respect to self and would not like to be left out in the order of things concerning his destiny. He (the Igbo man) is not prepared to leave such a unilateral decision even to his *chi*.[102] Again this self consciousness proves his recognition of the dignity of human person.

The English infinitive "to dignify"– *"ikwanye ugwù"* in Igbo language refers also to *i sọpụrụ*"-to respect some one in view of certain endowments and prowess bestowed in a person by *chi-god,* which one has taken up and through human efforts developed through mature personhood in the community and through acquisition of titles and wealth. It is therefore, an acknowledgement of fit attained in the community sense of the word and achievements in life. For instance, when respect is being used for the dead or the deities, *"chi or Chukwu"* it means simply to accord respect – *Nsọpụrụ* to a deity, god or *ndi iche* – the dead but still leaving

---

102 Cf. Chinua Achebe, „Chi "in Igbo Cosmology, in: Emmanuel Eze (Hg.), African Philosophy: An Anthology, USA 1998 67-72 here 69.

ancestors. Thus there is no significant difference when respect is applied in both cases, but only in the conceptuality of its application, in this case to a human person.

However, in all cases the society plays a major roll in their recognition, guarantee and protection. In Igbo linguistic usage, the word *"ugwù"* remains an adjectival noun. A qualification to a status in the society as in the case of the ancient Roman *"dignitas"*, Spanish *dignidad*, Italian *dignita*, French *dignité*, and Portuguese *dignidade* meaning to honour and to be honoured. For the German speakers, dignity means *"Würde"* in the sense of some one being worthy of honour. Linguistically seen, dignity and honour are closely related. Both has something to do with the status and recognition, which the individual enjoys in the society that he or she belongs and lives.[103] Traditionally, a person of dignity is respected and honoured because she consciously lives out virtues, which are highly valued in the particular society. A human being has dignity, if he has a value for the society.[104]

In the above etymologies, we notice a consistency in the line of thought of the different cultures. Traditionally, the meaning of dignity revolves around the human being; his values, his virtues and the recognition of these virtues; these virtues being honoured by the society or the community where he lives. But on a note of development and change Dunja Jaber distinguished three uses of the word today: a) Dignity in form of Hierarchy, status, position, office or title. b) Dignity as a value predicate for distinguishing behaviour and virtuous way of life. In all these, the recognition comes as a result of a peculiar virtue, quality or character. Dignity is accorded from the perspective of from "down" to "up" situation, whereby the junior or the weaker person as the case may be accords his senior or superior respect and dignity from a sheer reason of some exhibited profiles over and above him. c) Dignity as in the sense of putting oneself in the position of the other as a dignified person. This has nothing to do with high or low esteem.[105] Value remains the basis for

---

103 Cf. Tiedemann, Was ist Menschenwürde? 69.
104 Cf. Tiedemann, Was ist Menschenwürde? 69.
105 Cf. Dunja Jaber, Über den mehrfachen Sinn von Menschenwürde-Garantien. Mit besonderer Berücksichtigung von Art. 1 Abs.1 Grundgesetz, Frankfurt am Main 2003 11ff.

these uses of the term today. The value attached to being human as human and that attached to the roles played by the human person in his environment and community determine the human dignity for a people. However, a more detailed analysis of the linguistic usage of the concept of dignity among the Igbo (Africans) will be treated latter in chapter four.

2.6 Human Dignity as Philosophical History?

The conceptual problem of human dignity sets forth immediately, when one takes side in the question whether human dignity is conceived as a concrete reality in human beings, in other words, whether it is a given in human beings or achieved and realised through human reflections as a human good in the course of philosophical reflections.

According to Georg Mohr in his thesis on the historicity of the concept of human dignity, "Human dignity is nothing different from what in the course of philosophical history has come to be conceived as the human dignity".[106] Drawing his theses further, he proved that the whole edifice of the contemporary European concept of human dignity is based on the philosophies of Kant and Fichte.[107] Consequently, different reflections on the dignity of human person have created a kind of mosaic concepts of the same reality. In this sense, it will not be out of place to see the concept of human dignity as a dynamic concept, a principle that fashions the human image in cultures. Human image follows the interpretation of the principle of human dignity in a culture and there are so many human images as there are many cultures and peoples. However, there is at the basis of these differences a uniting factor of all namely, 'common humanity.' It is important to note that even the quarrelling and bickering among the different cultures on the human images, form a positive opportunity for a unified greatness.[108]

---

106 Georg Mohr, „Grundlagen der Menschenwürde bei Kant und Fichte" 14.
107 Mohr, „Grundlagen der Menschenwürde bei Kant und Fichte" 14.
108 Cf. Bernhard Vogel (Hg.), Im Zentrum: Menschenwürde. Politisches Handeln aus christlicher Verantwortung Christlicher Ethik als Orientierungshilfe. Germany 2006 13ff.

In the history of philosophy two main sources have played up as distinctive concepts of human dignity. Hans Jörg Sandkühler distinguished between what he terms: a metaphysical substance concept from an anthropological concept[109] (a pragmatic function of the concept of human dignity). The former refers to the fact that before all positive law human dignity as a value has been infused in the human being by God. Put in other words, it is based on the natural law theory, while the later lays stress on the functionality of the concept. In this last sense, dignity would be ascribed to someone by someone else and not necessarily because it is recognised as an innate or inborn value of a human person. Paul Tiedemann classified the interpretation of human dignity according to the above two major concepts namely, a) Heteronomy concepts (referring to those interpretations based on the understanding of human dignity as an innate value given to every human being from birth or from above); b) the autonomy concepts (referring to those interpretations based on the human functionality and reason).[110] The question borders on the source of the human dignity: whether human dignity is given by man or given to all human beings by God, in other words whether dignity is a human invention or discovery. The criteria for the grouping of the concepts of human dignity hover between the questions of the source of human dignity, the bearer of dignity, and who is recognised as the guarantor of dignity.[111] Each of the positions has ethical as well as theological implications in the interpretation of human dignity among the various peoples and cultures.

2.6.1 Metaphysical Concepts of Human Dignity

The theory of an indwelling dignity given to human beings, either by God or human nature has within it, the recognition of the role of substance in the understanding of dignity as an accompanying value of human person. In this sense the interpretation of human dignity as a sublime value refers

---

109 Cf. Hans Jörg Sandkühler, „Menschliche Würde: Transformation moralischer Rechte in positives Recht" 66.
110 Cf. Tiedemann, Was ist Menschen Würde? 51.
111 Cf. Hans Jörg Sandkühler, „Menschliche Würde: Transformation moralischer Rechte in positives Recht" 66.

to its substantial nature, which is founded on God or nature-given existence, of human beings. Human dignity as a principle is understood to have existed before every human or positive law, which the human reason can discover in the natural law. Meta-anthropologic concepts of human dignity sees the dignity of human person as founded in his ability to self determination, in so far as this ability is used for his agreement with the normative demands which are given from outside to the individual to articulate and to live out.[112] This is recognised as heteronomy. Representatives of this heteronymous concept include, a) Stoics, b) Christian Theology and c) Rationalised theory of Natural law.

2.6.1.1 Logos as Dignity by the Stoics

The Stoics played a very important role in the history and origin of human dignity. Western spiritual history reveals a very strong tie with the idea and concept of human dignity, which goes down to the Greek stoic school of philosophy.[113] This school was linked with Zenon of Kition (ca. 300 BC.), who was said to have taught in the coloured painted halls in the Acropolis of Athens. The Stoics view the cosmos (world) as a single organism that is ruled from one principle of world arrangement, which is known as *logós – (the Word or Reason)*. This *logós* was identified with God. The divine law gives the world a reasonable order. Every living being, as well as non-living nature, even the gods and human beings are subjects of the reasonable order in the cosmos. The human reason is a part of this divine reason, so that it must necessarily be the goal of every human being to know the reasonable world order in order afterwards, to live it out.[114] The human being must learn to control instincts and allow oneself to be led by reason.

One remarkable characteristic of the Stoic philosophy was its emphasis on ability to use language to communicate meaning. This according to the

---

112 Cf. Tiedemann, Was ist Menschenwürde? 39
113 Maximilian Forschner, „Marktpreis und Würde oder vom Adel der Menschlichen Natur", in: Henning Kössler (Hg.), Die Würde des Menschen. Erlangen 1997 35; cf. Forschner: „Die Würde des Menschen ist Unantastbar, ein Plädoyer für ein Verbot" 2.
114 Paul Tiedemann, Was ist Menschenwürde? 51.

stoics marks the human being out as a reasonable reflective being different from the animals or other creatures. Language is the hallmark of human transcendence. From this stand point, the stoics developed two philosophical terminologies namely; *axíoma* – translated as the received inner value and the *axía* – as every other value. The Roman politician Marcus Tullius Cicero (106-43 BC), in an erudite manner adopted the work of a famous Greek stoic author, Panaetion of Rhodes, who wrote his work about the "Duties" (*De Officiis*), which according to scholars came to light in 128 BC. Scholars are of the opinion that *"the Officiis"* of Cicero in 44 BC has at least the form of a Latin translation of the original work of Panaetion. Cicero translated the Greek word, *axíoma* to mean in Latin, *dignitas*. It was this dignitas that was translated into the English word, *dignity* as a form of a derivation from the French word, *dignité*.[115]

Cicero transfigured the concept of human dignity from a pure aristocratic limit concept of the term for a particular political group or class to all human beings irrespective of status or grade. Paul Tiedemann puts it this way: "What is applicable to the Roman aristocrats was ascribed to human beings by Cicero and linked with a rejection of a hedonistic or pleasure seeking way of life".[116] In his writing – *de Officiis*, for the first time, the concept of human dignity appeared where he wrote:

> When we want to think about it, how a surpassing position and dignity in our being lies, then we will realise, how destructive it is, to allow one self bask weakly in sinful pleasures and how honourable it is, on the other side, to live a reserved, self controlled, strict and modest way of life.[117]

In the above text the human person is called to a higher sense of morality. All those human beings, who are influenced by utility, profit, sensual pleasure, and opinions rather than virtue, are at most shrewd, but not good. Despite distinctions of race, religion, and opinion, individuals are bound together in unity through an understanding that "the principle of right living is what makes men better.[118] The notion that every thing is

---

115   See the earlier part of this Chapter2, Meaning of human dignity.
116   Cf, Paul Tiedemann, Was ist Menschenwürde? 52.
117   Cf. Cicero Marcus Tullius, De Officiis 1 105ff.
118   Cicero Marcus Tullius, *De Officiis* 1 105ff.

just by virtue of customs or the laws of nation is "a foolish idea." Cicero asked if that would be true, "even if these laws had been enacted by tyrants".[119] Cicero appealed to universal human rights laws that transcend customary and civil laws, and endorsed the idea of "a citizen of the whole universe, as if it were of a single city".[120] However, one reads from Cicero's statement a hasty generalisation and assumption that is typical of metaphysical theorists who base their claims on assumptions, which are difficult if not impossible to establish. Surely, Cicero could not have been opportune to experience the diversity of the world as we have it today. Perhaps, if he had, that could have mitigated his assumption on the notion of universality.

Coming back to the major tenets of the stoics, they emphasised the role of reason over and above instincts, which the animals and human beings share in common. The human being is to rise over and above his instincts and passions. Therefore, a mere control of the will towards the dictates of the law guiding the cosmos exemplifies the dignity of the human person. In comparison to the animals and plants, the stoics teach that they (animals and plants) are determined to act and react in specific ways that bespeak their nature. But human beings on the contrary have free will and freedom and run the risk, through their choices, of degenerating into the level of animals. As at the time of the stoic humanism, the human freedom of choice as a characteristic of a human being had not come into question. For them, the choice of the *"good"* in itself has a compelling consequence of the intention in the good. Sinful living is as a consequence of lack of good intention, while a reasonable life is as a consequence of a true intention, which is always the reserve of the wise.[121] This distinction of dignity as a moral value of the human person would have a lot of consequences for the future understanding and interpretation of human dignity. Human dignity has become a deep value of the human person and no more a reserve of the few aristocrats who attain dignity by title and political achievements in the society. Dignity becomes a universal quality of every morally sound human being.

---

119   Cicero Marcus Tullius, *De Officiis* 1 105ff.
120   Cf. Micheline R. Ishay (Ed.), The Human Rights Reader Major Political Writings, Essays, Speeches, and Documents from the Bible to the Present, New York 1997 xvii.
121   Cf Paul Tidemann, Was ist Menschenwürde? 53.

2.6.1.2 Early Christian View on Human Dignity

The early Church fathers were noted for their efforts in transforming the basic philosophical thoughts of the time into genuine Christian theology. The basis for their teachings was the teaching of the stoics on the natural law and on the Saint John's writing in his gospel: "In the beginning was the word (logos) ...." The old testament passage of God's creation of the human being in his image and likeness (Gen. 1, 26-27), and the teaching on the fall of man, through the original sin presented a great theological basis for the early Christian philosophers, who read in these texts the interpretation of human dignity.

The earliest of these teachings was found in the work of Theophilus of Antioch from the second half of the second century[122]. For Theophilus, the dignity of the human person lies in the fact of being created in the image of God. The whole creation is under the human being and serves his needs as the case may be. In this sense, dignity is not what one must or should earn, rather some thing that has been given to him from creation. Because one has not done much to merit this dignity, he can also loose it without much ado. This dignity is given to the human person for service and obedience to the commandments of God. It is for the good work of the creator, whose image man carries. This entails in no account, a licentious life of ones whims and caprices rather a life of imitation in that of God who is all-good and all knowing. The human person achieves his dignity through a rigorous fellowship in the footstep of his creator, who created him in his image. Such, were the teachings of the early fathers on the human dignity.

Augustine emphasised the role of the will while Thomas Aquinas extended this thought further by stressing the freedom in the human person as a capacity to decide for good or evil. This capacity belongs to every person, who can reason and has the control over his actions. In his work, Thomas Aquinas insisted that dignity implied responsibilities and duties. Unlike the Liberals of the modern era, who would stress the freedom alone, Aquinas insisted that all who are not just in their duties loose their

---

[122] Cf. Theophilus of Antioch, Ad Autolycum: http:/www.ccel.org/fathers2/ANF-02/anfo2-40.htm (07.05.2010) 150.

dignity[123]. In his answer to a question on the conditions under which a human being could be killed, Thomas Aquinas referred to human dignity as what could also be lost. Hence he opined:

> Through sin, the human person departs from the order of reason and by that falls short of the dignity of human person, as far as the human person is free and himself, and falls somehow short in the animalistic dependence, in so far as that has been confirmed he is now in the use of others ... as long as a human being damns his dignity to kill someone, it becomes also good to kill someone, who lives in sin simply as an animal; because the bad human being is worse than an animal and brings greater damages ....[124]

Human dignity as some thing that could be lost under sinful situations influenced the Christian vision of human dignity for a long time, especially among the Catholic philosophers and theologians. Robert Spaemann[125] sees the dignity of the human person in his or her capacity, to reflect and as well hold back oneself. On the grounds of this possibility, the human being becomes an absolute end, because as a moral being he or she represents the absolute. However the question remains, whether the human being can always recognise this capacity or ability in him in all circumstances. There could certainly be some debilitating factors, which can militate against the realisation of this ability in every person. For instance, a person can be incapacitated by the mere fact of sickness or physical imfavement. Furthermore, dignity is said to be present in the ability of one to control oneself and to view oneself in the eyes of others. It was on this note that Ernst-Wolfgang Böckenförde and Robert Spaemann opined that the people who take more responsibility for their fellow human beings are said to possess greater dignity than others who simply

---

123 Thomas Aquinas, Summa Theologica, Völls. Deutsch-Latin Ausgabe, Heinrich Maria Christmann (Hg.), Bd. 3 Salzburg 1939 1 question 29.
124 Thomas Aquinas, Summer Theologica, Question 64 Art 2, Response ad 3.
125 Robert Spaemann, „Über den begriff der Menschenwürde", in: Ernst-Wolfgang Böckenförde/ Robert Spaemann (Hg.), Menschenrechte und Menschenwürde: Historische Voraussetzungen – säkulare Gestalt – christliches Verständnis, Stuttgart 1987 303.

concentrate on themselves.[126] Therefore, inequality in the dignity arises from the levels of morality among the human beings and lies in the possibility of morality.

Morality of a person is always noticed in his conscience and free will. Conscience and free will are the decisive factors in the choice of an action, judged either to be good or bad. They are the basis of the dignity of human person. In the Christian humanism, one notices the emphasis on morality, which agrees with the paradigmatic change insinuated by Cicero's *'dignitas'*. Dignity is no more a function of political position alone as it was the case in the earlier Roman concept rather it has become a moral concept, a value that is attributed to all human beings in respect of their moral consciousness. The Christian interpretation of human dignity revolved around morality as a standard for human dignity.

The second Vatican council made two distinctions between two levels of human dignity. On the first level, the human dignity flows from the image of God, which was lost through original sin, but was given back to human beings through the redemptive act of Jesus Christ. This dignity cannot be violated and it cannot be taken away or estranged from the person. The Gospel of Christ nurtures and promotes this dignity and the commitment to this good news of Christ leads to the second level of human dignity. The human person qualifies for such a dignity when he frees himself from every imprisonment of passions, follows his end in free choice of the good and worries himself over the corresponding steadfastness.[127]

It is pertinent to point out that Martin Luther's Reformation teaching on the original sin and grace brought the dignity of the human person to a deeper dimension. Human dignity is said to be inviolable, no matter under any pretext because saved by grace the human person remains in tact with his dignity even if he falls short of his dignity due to sin. From this Reformation point of view, freedom from sin that is preserved by grace is not natural, but won by and through Christ. Human rights serve this pro-

---

126 Ernst-Wolfgang Böckenförde/Robert Speamann (Hg.), Menschenrechte und Menschenwürde: Historische Voraussetzungen – säkulare Gestalt – christliches Verständnis 303.
127 Cf. Gaudium et Spes, art. 17.

tection of freedom won by Christ for human beings. It is a kind of freedom put in the service of the love of neighbour.[128]

2.6.1.3 Rationalistic Natural Law as basis for Human Dignity

It is interesting to notice the movement of thought in the philosophical history of the concepts of human dignity. Each epoch has its significant change factors, which lead to the change in understanding. The Christian Theology reigned for a reasonable period, until the religious wars that ensued between the Protestants of Holland and the Spanish Catholics domination (1566-1572) broke the ginks. In Deutschland it was the 30 years religious war between the Catholics and the Protestants (1618-1648). In England it was the kingdoms populace against the absolutist Catholic King of England (1642-1649). In these cases, religion proved to be ambivalent, as the whole of Europe experienced as it where, the negative effects of religion and its attendant theology could no longer push through with the authorities it had before.

The theological interpretation of human dignity lost its aura and its position as soon as the rationalistic natural law theory of human dignity emerged. It was no longer God, who through his image in man fuses the dignity in human beings, rather the knowledge of natural law. Reason became the indices for such a wisdom that guarantees a human dignity. Thus, with reference to the stoic vision of logos and reason, a reflection on the natural law theories of human dignity sprang. Samuel Pufendorf – a state theorist and jurist, who influenced the 'Virginia Bill of Rights' of 1776 sees the dignity in the freedom of the human person, which he recognises through reason, to choose and to do; he associates dignity with the idea of equality of all human beings.[129] Pufendorf agrees with the stoics that the human person is created; this is his whole dignity and his lot. He shares position with Kant in his Metaphysics of morality, where

---

128 Cf. Huber, art. 1.5 "Menschenrechte/Menschenwürde" 581-582; cf. Trutz Rendtorff, "Menschenrechte als Bürgerrechte. Protestantische Aspekte ihrer Begründung", in: Ernst-Wolfgang Böckenförde, Robert Speamann (Hg.), Menschenrechte und Menschenwürde. Historische Voraussetzungen – Säkulare Gestalt – Christliches Verständnis, Stuttgart Klett-Cotta 1987 93-118.

129 Cf. Sandkühler, Menschliche Würde: Transformation moralischer Rechte in Positives Recht 65.

Kant refers to humanity itself as dignity because of the mere fact of the human person being an end and not a means. In line with Thomas Aquinas, Pufendorf distinguished between two meanings of human dignity. In the first place dignity is the ability of the human person through his free will power to decipher and to distance himself from his instincts. Secondly it is the ability to choose between options.[130] Pufendorf also identified another dignity that can be acquired and also that can be lost. For Thomas Aquinas, one looses this dignity when he digresses from the will of God and decides against the dictates of God. This is because for Thomas Aquinas all dignity is given to the human person by God the creator and it can also be lost if one proves unworthy of this gift. Against this position, Pufendorf argues that this dignity was not given to the human person by any act of God, rather from the rational capacity of the human person in its ability to be enlightened through the dictates of natural law. The human dignity in the teaching of natural law cannot be understood as infused into human beings as something that leads to the becoming of a human being, rather as something already in the reasonable nature of the human person.[131]

Furthermore, Pufendorf sees the role and importance of the community as constitutive in the dignity of the human person. The society or the community carry in themselves the enabling characters of duties and norms. Through the association in the society, the human person comes to learn the norms and duties of the society. He begins to appreciate the need to protect his personality as well as the social value he represents in the society.[132] With the combination of both the individual and the society in a symbiotic fusion, Pufendorf points to the situation in the African worldview, where the individual recognises the society as a determinant part of his existence. However, this attachment does not swallow or hinder the development of this individuality in the society.

In summary, for those who hold the rationalistic natural law as the basis of human dignity, the natural law takes over the concept of God as the sole giver of dignity, but do not deny the fact of dignity coming from

---

130 Cf. Horst Denzer, Moral philosophie und Naturrecht bei Samuel Pufendorf. Eine Geistes und wissenschaftsgeschichliche Untersuchung zur Geburt des Naturrechts aus der Praktischen Philosophie, München 1972 92.
131 Cf. Paul Tiedemann, Was ist Menschenwürde? 57.
132 Cf. Denzer, Moralphilosophie und Naturalrecht bei Samuel Pufendorf 94.

outside the human person. What it achieved was only to change the function of God with that of natural law. While in the Christian teaching the conscience of the human person is formed through his faith in God, now it has to be formed through the rational wisdom got from the natural law. Therefore, Tiedemann concludes that from this stand point, the authority of the priest for instance in the practice, has been replaced by the academic Jurists and philosophers as the promoters of natural Laws.[133]

It is pertinent to point out here without further explanations that the following development in the European intellectual history took up from this radical standpoint of the natural Law theory of human dignity, especially in the German idealism of such thinkers like Kant, Friedrich Hegel and the materialistic utopia of Karl Marx.

2.6.2 Autonomy Concepts of Human Dignity

In contrast to the above exposé of the metaphysical approach to the interpretation of the human dignity, we now encounter another set of interpretations that base their parameter on the autonomy of the human will. The autonomy conception of human dignity in this sense concentrates on the ability of the free will to form its judgements whether good or evil. The primary thing is the ability to decide, without much reference to the remote cause of the decisions. This paradigm shift, took place gradually in the cause of a century of philosophical dynamism.

2.6.2.1 Free Will as basis of Human Dignity in Augustine

In the western philosophical history, there emerged at the beginning of antiquity, the question of the human free will. It was Aurelius Augustine who impressed on the western thought with his writing on the free will. Even though this work was not directed on the then nascent humanism of the time, his insight was of great value in the philosophical discussions on the theme. For Augustine, his preoccupation in his work on the free will was the preservation of the Christian teachings on monotheism against the agnostic ideas of his time.[134] It was a great task to wrest the teaching

---

133 Cf. Paul Tiedemann, Was ist Menschenwürde? 58.
134 Cf. Paul Tiedemann, Was ist Menschenwürde? 58.

of good and evil from the hands of the agnostics and the Manicheans. How could it be explained that there is evil in a wonderfully created world? This was the standpoint of the debate. While the Manicheans posited the existence of two principles namely, evil and good, Augustine insisted on the origin of evil as a privation of the good. He set out in his work on the human will to discover in the human will the capacity to choose, both from good and evil. The emphasis here is not on whether one chooses evil or good, but on the fact that the human being has the capacity to choose. According to Augustine, God gave this capacity to choose from good and evil to show that He (God) created the human person as a moral being, and therefore, as a moral being has the capacity to choose against evil, at the same time the freedom to choose evil.[135] What is at stake in his argument is the presence of the free will in every human person, distinguishing him as a moral being. Herein, lies the basis of human dignity. In his work on the human free will he clarified:

> God has not withheld his goodness to any of his creatures, from whom he knew that he would be falling into sin through his choices and notwithstanding still called him into existence ... on the merits of the dignity of his being, the high position he occupies before other creatures in their type, so praise worthy is the creation which he misses in his self indulgence.[136]

Even though Augustine had linked the free will to the dignity of human person, he neither intended to convert them by any means into inalienable rights nor into the positions of rights. Just as Tiedemann puts it, Augustine did not want to make of it moral laws. His concern was mainly to show that the free will exists.[137]

---

135 Augustine Aurelius, De Libero arbitrio – Vom freien Willen. In: Theologische Frühschriften – Vom freiem Willen-Von der wahren Religion. Zürich und Stuttgart 1962 396 (Buch Kapital).
136 Cf. Augustinus, De Libero arbitrio III 15.
137 Paul Tiedemann, Was ist Menschenwürde? 59-60.

2.6.2.2 Creativity as Human Dignity by Pico Della Mirandola (1463-1494)

Pico Della Mirandola's oration on the dignity of man stands as the manifesto of Italian version of the European Enlightenment. In an erudite manner of reflection, Pico brought it to the sinews of his audience that the nature of the human person stands indeterminate.[138] God has created the human being with such a freedom of the will that even sin cannot mitigate. This emphasis on the ontological prerogative of the human person has very little to do with morality.

Augustine had reflected on the freedom of the will some one thousand years ago, but limiting the scope to that of the capacity to choose either good or evil. On a different note, Pico invented a new human image born out of an emphasis on the undeterminable nature of the human person, quite different from the usual understanding of human nature as determined by the divine will[139]. In a creative manner, Pico brought in an aspect of humanism to his contemporaries, which until then was overlooked with little or no interest namely, the creative ability of the human being. In the creation narrative, God created all things out of nothing. Likewise, the human being is called also to create his world around him out of nothing. This power has been given to man to look outside creation and to become what he will like to be.[140] *Creatio ex Nihilo*, according to Pico entails no determinism, rather an invitation to plan, shape and determine one's life. In one of his famous passages in the oration, Pico wrote:

> Finally, the Great Artisan mandated that this creature that would receive nothing proper to him should have joint possession of

---

138 Cf. Richard Hooker (Trans.), Pico Della Mirandola: *Oration on the Dignity of Man* http://www.wsu.edu:8080/~wldciv/world_civ_reader/world_civ_reader_1/pico.html 10.05.2010.
139 The Middle Ages theology favoured a descent methodology that preferred to think of God- man relationship only from the stand point of God as a mysterious substance. It had little consideration for the standpoint of the human being as a historical reality.
140 Cf. Richard Hooker, *Pico Della Mirandola: Oration on the Dignity of Man* (15th C. CE) http://www.wsu.edu:8080/~wldciv/world_civ_reader/world_civ_reader_1/pico.html.

whatever nature had been given to any other creature. He made man a creature of indeterminate and indifferent nature, and, placing him in the middle of the world, said to him Adam, we give you no fixed place to live, no form that is peculiar to you, nor any function that is yours alone. According to your desires and judgment, you will have and possess whatever place to live, whatever form, and whatever functions you yourself choose. All other things have a limited and fixed nature prescribed and bounded by our laws. You, with no limit or no bound, may choose for yourself the limits and bounds of your nature. We have placed you at the world's centre so that you may survey everything else in the world. We have made you neither of heavenly nor of earthly stuff, neither mortal nor immortal, so that with free choice and dignity, you may fashion yourself into whatever form you choose. To you are granted the power of degrading yourself into the lower forms of life, the beasts, and to you is granted the power, contained in your intellect and judgment, to be reborn into the higher forms, the divine.[141]

The emphasis on the individual to make up himself resounds in every facet of the oration. For Pico, the individual is not just free to choose from either good or bad, but the individual is also free to create his own environment, in which he finds suitable to live his life without any inhibitions of norms or prescribed moral laws. Instead human wrongs or sinful choices would reduce the dignity; rather it confirms the possibilities open to the human person to choose.[142] This kind of liberty could be likened to the modern liberalists' concepts of freedom and Democracy, where individual rights and privileges are emphasised over and above his duties.

With Pico, the theology of *"Imago Dei"* acquired a new understanding and meaning. The human person from the point of view of *Creatio ex Nihilo* now has the obligation to fashion his life as it suits him here on earth. Therefore, he should no longer be as he is, rather he should be what he would like to be.[143] By emphasising the position of the human person

---

141 Cf. Richard Hooker, Oration on the Dignity of Man http://www.wsu.edu: 8080/~wldciv/world_civ_reader/world_civ_reader_1/pico.html.
142 Richard Hooker, Oration on the Dignity of Man http://www.wsu.edu: 8080/~wldciv/world_civ_reader/world_civ_reader_1/pico.html.
143 Cf. Tiedemann, Was ist Menschenwürde? 61.

in God's creation plan, Pico enjoins human beings to ascend to the dignity given to them by God, to be closer to him and not even to allow the angels and principalities to suppress them, but to use wisdom and intelligence to achieve their dignity. Thus in Pico's understanding "The idea of Imago Dei linked with human dignity and at the same time with that of human development.[144]

Human dignity is nothing else outside that in the freedom of the will. This dignity cannot be estranged or lost in the human person even if she abuses it, so that she (the human being) can take cognisance of the possibilities, which has been given to her in the freedom of the will.

2.6.2.3 Kant's Moral Autonomy as Human Dignity

With the stage so well set through the "Enlightenment manifesto" of Pico, Immanuel Kant entered the stage with a new concept of ethics of the dignity of human person. Kant rather, went back to the stoics to seek a discussion on the nature of human beings as determined by the order in creation, which through the *logos* is accessible to the human reason. However, Kant departed from the stoics on the grounds of his insistence on the independence of the human person from all sorts of his propensities and proclivities.[145]

Further distinctions noticed in the teachings of Kant and that of the stoics stem from his new understanding of reason. Traditionally the stoics taught that the *logos,* is evident in the nature itself, and that the human reason had to struggle to align its tendencies and proclivities with the order in nature. Kant rejects this understanding of reason as correspondence to nature by insisting that this order is already entailed in the nature of human beings because they have already this part of reason in them as a categorical imperative. The morality of the human being exists only by the mere fact that he is an autonomous subject. According to Kant, "this

---

144 Cf. Pico della Mirandola: Oration on the Dignity of Man.
145 Cf. Immanuel Kant, „Die Religion innerhalb der Grenzen der bloßen Vernunft", in: ders. Werke in 10 Bänden, Wilhelm Weischedel (Hrsg), Bd.7, Darmstadt (2. Aufl.) 1983 (1794) 78.

autonomy is the reason of the dignity of the human person and every reasonable nature".[146]

Kant celebrated the autonomy of the human person as the basis for his dignity. But through this clarification on morality as an absolute value he wanted to show the difference between morality in itself and the insinuated acts of morality, which he named strategic moral actions. In his Maxims, Kant emphasised the need for identifying the end of every action to decipher whether that is moral or not. For him contingent ends cannot be recognised as moral actions as such because their motives are subjective and not objective.

Kant went further to specify how conditions for a "good" act could be delineated into substantial, independent and contingent, dependent situations, which makes a good act conditional or unconditional. Kant argues that if an act must be moral it must not only have subjective ends but objective ends which, through reason one can access. Kant calls this "categorical imperative".[147] He argues that it is through reason alone, that human beings can actually carry out a good moral action, which is not dependent on any contingent conditions.

Reason then, becomes an absolute interpreter of moral actions. But how did Kant link the absolute value of reason to the dignity of human person? He argues, because human beings share in this reason, they have also this absolute value, which is the absolute basis for human dignity. The categorical imperative, which is an absolute value of reason, can also be expressed in this sense: "Do handle humanity, also your person as in the person of any other, all the time at the same time as end, never as a means".[148]

Kant therefore, defines dignity as: "that, which has a price, on whose instance some other thing as equivalent can be replaced; but what in the contrary over and above all prices could be possessed, cannot be exchanged by any equivalent that has a dignity".[149] However, it might be pertinent to remark here that Kant did not make this categorical impera-

---

146 Cf. Immanuel Kant, „Grundlegung zur Metaphysik der Sitten", in: ders. Werke in 10 Bänden, Wllhem Weischedel (Hrsg), Bd. 6, Darmstadt 1983 (1786) 79.
147 Kant, Grundlegung zur Metaphysik der Sitten 79.
148 Kant, Grundlegung zur Metaphysik der Sitten 79.
149 Cf. Kant, Grundlegung zur Metaphysik der Sitten 79.

tive the basis of his philosophy of law. This has a remarkable implication for the contemporary human rights' discourse, as we shall see later.

2.6.2.4 Human Dignity as a dynamic Principle in Avishai Margalit

Avishai Margalit introduced an important aspect in the philosophical discussions on human dignity through his emphasis on the dynamic nature of the human person and the existence of other human values outside human dignity. While Pico Della Mirandola based his argument on the creative capacity of the human person and Kant on the autonomous moral subject, Margalit sees in the human person a future that is shaped always in his dynamism; an ability to transform and change his mistakes. Sin and mistakes are understood not from the point of view of regrets of the past or as debilitating powers but more, as a future opportunity to transform and change for the better.[150] Nevertheless, this optimism is limited in the presence of the difficulties involved when it has to do with minors or infants who may lack this capacity or powers due to the mere fact that they have not yet attained the age of reason; the disabled persons and the less-privileged, whose disabilities may lead to lack of required reason to change themselves by a corporate will power.

In his later writings Avishai Margalit became more conscious of the above-mentioned limitation and opted for a broader coverage of human dignity that will include the whole humanity. His universal concept of human dignity is based on the nature of the dignity itself as something indefinite and embracive. In every culture and race one finds human dignity without much ado about the definition and interpretation. Above all Margalit holds as important, first and foremost, that the respect of all human being corresponds with our human nature[151]. Margalit found in other ethical principles outside the autonomic argument, to disagree with the argument for the killing of the heavy disabled persons. Other ethical principles hold the extinction of human life as evil. Therefore, the dynamism of Margalit's concept of human dignity is based on his ability to

---

150 Cf. Avishai Margalit, Politik der Würde. Über Achtung und Verachtung. Frankfurt am Main 1999 92ff.
151 Cf. Margalit, Politik der Menschenwürde 106f.

inculcate in the autonomic understanding of human dignity the recognition of other ethical principles as constituents of the human dignity.

2.7 Dignity as Moral Value

The above schematic excursus of the interpretations of human dignity reveals a huge difference in the conception of human dignity. Nonetheless, one thing is clear and that is, all take dignity to be a human value and a human good that is indispensable in the human person. Suggestively the reason for these differences may also be found in that, which unites the whole concepts. I therefore find it necessary before proceeding further in this discussion to establish what value is in relation to the human dignity.

Dignity is a peculiar type of value attached to the state of being human. Values can be said to be what the human being hold as usefully important, meaningful and worthwhile. Dignity is a peculiar value of the human person because, while values could as well be attached to other objects of nature, human beings as values remain all the same invaluable. Therefore human dignity can only be referred as a value in a metaphorical sense[152]. Without prejudice to the current arguments on the dignity of animals and plants,[153] it is only the human being that has dignity. Here again mention can be made of Professor Peter Singer, a Swiss professor of ethics, who has become very popular for his arguments for the dignity of animals and plants in Swiss, which has led to a historical acceptance of the Bill on the protection of rights of the animals in the House of Parliament; and the subsequent passing of the Bill into law. However, valuation or evaluation refers principally to two different value systems, which are not the same, dignity and price. Valuation remains at the basis of the both values. One could still try to go further and find out what is valuation.

According to Paul Tiedemann in his meticulous explication of dignity as valuation, he pointed out that valuation itself as a process of attaching values to things is abstract.[154] It only becomes tangible when we begin to

---

152 Cf. Margalit, Politik der Menschenwürde 70.
153 For further readings see, Peter Singer, "Animal Rights: The Right to Protest", in: *The Independent,* January 21 2007
154 Tiedemann, Was ist Menschenwürde? 71.

attach values to an object. In the course of valuing we distinguish between items and objects as "good" or "bad", "fine or ugly" et cetera. Such a statement is referred always as value judgement. Value judgements of this kind can only be meaningful when one knows the standard by which such judgements are made. It is therefore necessary to set the standards of value judgement to reflect the factual need at the time of judgement. For instance, some one may require a house based on the size of the family. Based on the family size some one may value a house as good, bad, fine or ugly. Therefore, the standard for the value judgement remains indispensable if the valuation will remain understandable and meaningful.

In the case of human dignity as a human value, that means a value attached to human beings as being human, the standard of this valuation remains abstract. Acceding to the nature of human valuation as abstract Tiedemann observes, that the point of human dignity is always seen in its difference from those other individual standards found in human roles. For instance, someone can be valued as a good husband or as a good wife. Human dignity on the contrary is concerned with human being as human being; this is why to value a human being like other objects of human interest would likely have a very little chance.[155] If actually a human being is to be judged without reference to his roles and interests the standards of such a judgement would not be set on the basis of morality but on ontology. For instance, a person is good or bad based on the value of the choices he makes: the judgement, valuation and choices of his handlings are normally based on the principles of morality. But what chances human dignity as an absolute moral value has remains a question, which burgs the minds of scholars in modern contemporary times.

In his own opinion, Herbert Schnädelbach sees the chances of the ethic normative solutions to the problems of human dignity as the only possible chance. In his grammatical explication of the problem of "values and dignity" Schnädelbach mentioned three main approaches to the interpretative problem of human dignity namely, the ontological, anthropological and ethical normative approaches. Whether human dignity flows from the ontological or anthropological approaches depends on ones faith on the basal statement on the creation of the human person in the image

---

155 Tiedemann, Was ist Menschenwürde? 71.

of God[156]. The Christian interpretation, of course favours this view as the resounding basis of the human dignity. The 'Imago Dei' theology finds expressions both in the Catholic, Protestant and Lutheran Theologies. The difference in accentuation lies in the effect of the original sin. While the Catholics teach the continuity of the image of God even after the fall, the Protestants and the Lutherans see no connection between the redeemed man in Christ and the fallen man.

The ethical normative interpretative approach favours the Kantian idea of the human person as a moral subject. At the basis of this morality is the possession of reason. It is with this ability that the human person can ascribe value (dignity) to others and receive values from others; and also apportion prices to things. Kant distinguishes between dignity and price when he wrote: "In the kingdom of ends every thing has either a price or dignity. What ever has a price, can be exchanged with something else as an equivalent; what on the contrary that is above price, and cannot be replaced with any other, that has a dignity".[157] The concept of value is already contained in the above description in the mention of price and dignity. Price refers to the relative value while Dignity refers to the absolute value. Dignity as an absolute value refers only to those who have the enabling reason to ascribe and to be ascribed dignity. In other words, human dignity becomes only the sole prerogative of the reasonable. Kant interpreted dignity as a function of reason, but did not explain the fate of those who lack this reason due to sickness – the mentally sick or even those who in potency would come to reason – human foetus. Therefore basing the interpretation of human dignity alone on morality may be difficult to handle, especially in the face of the ongoing discussions on bio-ethics.

Ludger Honnefelder looked at the issue of values and human dignity from another perspective by positing dignity as the source of human values. His approach to the human dignity interpretation tends to the anthropological view. According to him, the ability of the human person to link up with human values in connection with that of dignity constitutes the

---

[156] Herbert Schnädelbach, „Werte und Würde", in: Christian Thies (Hg.), Der Wert der Menschenwürde, Paderborn 2009 21-32 here 31.
[157] Immanuel Kant, Grundlegung zur Metaphysik der Sitten, BA 77.

basis of human dignity.[158] His anthropological position rather than the normative position presents the human person as a being that can take a reflexive position and at the same time free in his actions and choices.

In line with Helmut Plessner, who referred to the human person as an eccentric being, who can take position outside self, Honnefelder understands the respect of human dignity at the same time, as the respect of human rights. Human rights are the results of human reflection on the protection of human dignity in different respects: Freedom of religion, freedom of opinion, equality, justice et cetera. The recognition of these values of human person according to Otfried Höffe remains, at least the beginning condition not the realisation conditions.[159] Honnefelder insists on a comprehensive interpretation of the human dignity principle, which is based on the integral meaning of life. A universal interpretation of the human dignity and rights that is not based on the life forms and integral meaning, he insists, looses not only its motivational deep grounds, but also the stimulating attractions of its spread and concretisation. Religion plays a very vital role in its character as a comprehensive organ of the good.[160] Values for the human person therefore present themselves as good. Human dignity presents itself as the absolute good of the human person and consequently as absolute good, remains in this sense the absolute value. It can only be realised in so far as human beings take advantage of the corresponding values, which includes: freedom, justice and equality.

2.8 Dignity as Principle, Concept and Norm of Rights

It is pertinent at this juncture, to flash back on Kantian categorical imperative of the autonomous subject as basis for the dignity of human person. This categorical imperative fundamental though could not be posited by Kant, as a basis for a sound philosophy of law. He purposely left this imperative at the level of morality and perhaps never intended to make

---

158 Ludger Honnefelder, „Würde und Werte", in: Christian Thies (Hg.), Der Werte der Menschenwürde, Paderborn 2009 33-43 here 33.
159 Cf. Thies, Der Werte der Menschenwürde 42.
160 Cf. Thies, Der Werte der Menschenwürde 42.

this the basis of his philosophy of law. It was only the originality of Fichte to have seen in the dynamics of interpersonal acknowledgement of one another as the primitive instance of right and law.[161] According to Fichte, the fact of interpersonal relationship presupposes some kind of regulation by means of laws and rights. The day-to-day conflicts of choices and interests buttress this assertion. If human beings in their nature can hope for peace, then a regulation in form of law would be inevitable.

In his insightful work: *"Human Dignity: Transformation of moral laws into positive laws"*, Hans Jörg Sandkühler saw in the inviolable nature of human dignity, a practical invitation for a legal protection of the human values to which the human dignity relates as "relative absolute".[162] Pointing out the effects of rhetoric of inviolability of human dignity as an effort in futility, and as such the cause for the myriad of conflicting interpretations in history Sandkühler affirms in his thesis: "Only the conception of human dignity as principle, concept and norm of law can lead to a substantive understanding of that, which should be protected through the guaranty of human dignity: Freedom and equality of all, who are human beings."[163]
In the first place, Sandkühler argues that all human beings exist as individuals. All existence statements, which operate with the verb "to be", are attached to the material world. There is neither the human being, nor the person, nor the subject, nor the society but there is the individual.[164] A human being has dignity and every human being has dignity. 'Dignity' is a conveyance and relative concept, in which an operational side-by-side acknowledgement of all is registered. It is always the individual whose dignity is violated and not the conceptual or theoretical idea of 'creation', or 'humanity'.[165] Consequently interpreting human dignity in such con-

---

161 Cf. Georg Mohr, „Grundlagen der Menschenwürde bei Kant und Fichte" 30.
162 Cf. Sandkühler, „Menschenwürde und die Transformation moralischer Rechte in positives Recht" 62.
163 Sandkühler, „Menschenwürde und die Transformation moralischer Rechte in positives Recht" 58.
164 Cf. Sandkühler, „Menschenwürde und die Transformation moralischer Rechte in positives Recht" 58.
165 Cf. Sandkühler, „Menschenwürde und die Transformation moralischer Rechte in positives Recht" 58.

ceptual and metaphysical manner makes a mockery of the term and what it stands for, because it is this individual who is the subject of the human dignity; this person, yesterday, today and tomorrow as long as the society does not defend his dignity with required strength and power.

Therefore, the principle of human dignity takes a normative position in the constitution of states especially in democratic states. It becomes the foundation of laws itself. The declaration of human rights in a formal legal pattern speaks of the recognition of this already given inborn value of the human person and sought to protect those functional values such as: Freedom, Justice and Equality. Sandkühler explains that the protection we accord our dignity, is the protection, which we ourselves created, the protection of laws, of the norms and of the sanctions.[166] Commenting on the very nature of dignity, he points out that dignity is not a legal terminology or legal concept, but a relative absolute concept in a non metaphysical sense that means: absolutely linked to the sphere of positive laws as relative absolute.

From the above exposé it is important to stress the need of seeing the value of human dignity as a relative absolute. That means, relative to individuals in their historical and cultural realities. Human dignity is a dynamic principle, a principle, which accommodates different interpretations. This dynamism, accounts for the variety of interpretations in the history of philosophy as presented earlier in this inquiry. It differentiates itself from a form of relativism, which seeks to make nonsense of morality in the world. On the contrary it refers to the task of philosophy to reflect on the dignity of human person, but most importantly that the dignity of human person cannot be realised or concretised as a metaphysical engagement. It is always practical and always attached to 'this individual' or 'this people'.

With the understanding of the practical need to protect the dignity of a concrete, historical individual or person, morality became the instance of law. Dignity becomes more realistic in the respect and protection of those values, which the human being cherishes. In the universal declaration of human rights (UDHR) person, dignity and respect built an indissoluble unity. Dignity is a situation of a human person, who in the insistence for

---

166 Cf. Sandkühler, „Menschenwürde und die Transformation moralischer Rechte in positives Recht" 58.

his rights is the master of himself, and the possibility of his autonomy in the society.[167]

2.9 Human Rights as Rights from Human dignity

A breathtaking question at this juncture is at what point, human dignity came to be recognised as rights. In the course of history the absolute value of human person came to be legalised and codified as rights. It later came to be known as human rights. Are these rights extracted from human dignity itself or rights of human dignity? The formulation of the human rights charter stressed that the human rights were not highlighted from positive laws rather from a principle, whose obligation strength does not base on mere human postulation. It comes from something unique and inherent in the human person, something given to all human beings from birth. The formulary makes it understandable that human dignity in itself is not a law as such, but a source of human rights. Dignity according to Sandkühler is no longer, just a constitutional law, but the foundation and reason for human rights.[168] Accordingly, the formulation of the human rights declaration speaks of a right from dignity, not right of dignity.[169] Pope Benedict XVI captured this connection succinctly in his address on the World Peace Day January 1 2007 with the title of his speech as: "Die Menschenwürde ist undiskutierbar".[170] On another occasion, during his Angelus the Pontiff clarifies:

> Today there are different speeches on human rights, but it is often forgotten that the rights need a stable, not relativistic, not negotiable foundation. And that can only be the dignity of the human per-

---

167 Cf. Sandkühler, „Menschenwürde und die Transformation moralischer Rechte in positives Recht" 71.
168 Sandkühler, „Menschenwürde und die Transformation moralischer Rechte in positives Recht" 74.
169 Sandkühler, „Menschenwürde und die Transformation moralischer Rechte in positives Recht" 23.
170 Benedikt XVI. Pope, „Der Mensch-Herz des Friedens. Botschaft zur Feier des Weltfriedenstages", in: Amtsblatt der Österreichischen Bischofskonferenz 43 2007 10-16.

son. The respect of this dignity begins with the recognition and the protection of ones rights to life and freely to profess ones personal religion.[171]

Based on the above clarification, scholars argue nowadays on the development of human rights as a tangible aspect of human dignity, and whether human rights can replace the concept of human dignity itself. Authors like Jack Donnelly in his work, *"Human rights and Human dignity: An analytic Critic of non-Western Conceptions of Human Rights"* argues that a replacement of human dignity with human rights would be a mistake because while human rights could be an aspect of human dignity developed by the West, it can not be taken to be the complete body of human dignity which exists from time in every culture. Thilo Rensmann agrees with this fact when he wrote:

> Während die Menschenwürde in der Philosophie auf eine mehr als 2000-jährige Genealogie zurückblicken kann, beginnt ihre Karriere als Rechtsbegriff erst 1945 mit der Vereinten Nationen, die das Bekenntnis zu "Würde und Wert der menschlichen Persönlichkeit" an die Spitze ihrer Präambel stellt.[172]

Therefore, Human rights as the ingenuity of the West remains a giant stride in the recognition and protection of human dignity but cannot be taken as human dignity in Toto, rather an aspect of it. There could be other possible discoverable aspects of the human dignity and better ways of protecting the human dignity in other cultures in the course of history.[173] The following subheadings, discuss in form of a brief survey, the various efforts at the protection of the human dignity in forms of rights in history.

---

171 Benedikt XVI. Pope, Angelus am 1. Januar 2007 am Petersplatz Rom cited in, Severin, J Lederhilger (Hg.), Gott verlassen Menschenwürde und Menschenbilder, Frankfurt am Main 2007 7.
172 Thilo Rensmann, „Die Menschenwürde als universaler Rechtsbegriff", in: Christian Thies (Hg.), Der Wert der Menschenwürde, Paderborn-München-Wien-Zürich 2009 75-92 here 75.
173 Jack Donnelly, "Human Rights and Human Dignity: An Analytic Critique of Non-Western Conceptions of Human Rights" 306; Cf. Konrad Hilpert, Die Menschenrechte in Theologie und Kirche 84-85.

2.9.1 The English Magna Carter, (15 June 1215)

The English Magna Carter as it is popularly known; the premier human right document serves as what one may describe as a landmark and as it were, the matrix of modern human rights' movements. It is the charter of rights and concessions which King John Lack land was obliged by the English feudal chiefs to grant to the English. After he lost the battle of Bovines in 1213 to Philip Augustus of France, his territorial integrity from within and without was shaken. The feudal lords could no longer contend with his arbitrary manipulation of laws and customs. His careless and arbitral regime culminated in a deviant tyranny that made the lords force him to sign into law the great Charter for the freedom and protection of the freemen in England.[174] Intending not to go into the details of this charter, since doing that will be drifting outside the interest of this inquiry, suffice it to say that the importance of this act lies in the fact of its attempt at guaranteeing what is very vital to the human person, namely freedom. Although it was limited in nature, that is, addressing a group of English feudal lords, its effect and import transcended its milieu to offer the subsequent human rights efforts form and basis. G. M. Trevelyan opined that: "The term was limited in 1215, but owing to the economic and legal evolution of the next three hundred years it came to embrace the descendants of every villain in the land, when all Englishmen became in the eyes of the law 'freemen".[175] Alluding to this insight Nwachukwuike S.S. Iwe concluded with the remark that, "The importance of the Charter, in the sphere of human rights and as it affected these rights lay in the future, when, the restricted pale of *'liber homo'*, under the impact and strain of socio-political evolution, would expand to embrace all English citizens."[176]

In several clauses of the charter the seed of freedom had been sown. It was left to time and history to make it grow and flower, and to future generations to reap it in human rights and liberties. Under the banner of this Great Charter the Englishmen would wage their constitutional con-

---

174 Nwachukwu S.S. Iwe, The History and Contents of Human Rights A Study of the History and Interpretation of Human Rights, Frankfurt am Main 1986 90.
175 G.M. Trevelyan, History of England, London 1960 91.
176 Nwachukwu S.S Iwe, The History and Contents of Human Rights 93.

flicts and battles in defence of rights and liberties. In this line of thought, James Williamson succinctly puts it thus: "The men of Runnymede had built more greatly than they knew and the gratitude of the people of England would always base on the fact that the practical expediency of one age became the consecrated legend of the next, fit to do even greater deeds in the days to come".[177] On the side of religion, Christianity acquires thereby a stronger foothold in England through a pioneering work of Bishop Stephen Langton,[178] who stood behind the Charter with a great effort of a genius. He showed among others ecclesiastical interest in the issues of human rights as a defender of the rights and liberties of man.[179]

2.9.2 The English Bill of Rights, (1225-16889)

The historical documents of human rights under review have their bases on the English Charter on human rights, which was confirmed by subsequent governments in England. The object of this confirmation and reconfirmation remains the Anglo-Saxon hatred of tyranny, especially when this is imposed. As a consequence, their sensitivity is always heightened whenever a government becomes tyrannical. Historically speaking there were not less than thirty-five formal confirmations of the Charter before the advent of the Tudor Sovereigns.[180] Apart from the Magna Charter the following bills speak for the freedom, liberty and fundamental rights of the individual. These include the petition of Rights, the Bill of Rights and the Act of Toleration.

A) The Petition of Rights, (1628)

On 7th June 1628, the English parliament reflected the spirit of the Magna Carter, when on this day it sought to protect the rights of the Englishman from the long hands of the Sovereign. Due to the financial crunch of the

---

177 J. Williamson, The Evolution of England², Oxford 1961 102.
178 Archbishop Stephen Langton was an influential personality behind the formulation of the Charter. He saw to it that the freedom of religion was guaranteed to the Church of England.
179 Nwachukwu S.S. Iwe, The History and Contents of Human Rights 94.
180 Iwe, The History and Contents of Human Rights 94.

time due to useless wary abroad, the crown resorted to incessant and unlawful taxation of the polity. This royal operation made the Hoses of the English parliament petitioned the crown for redress. Among others the Houses declared the quartering of soldiers among civilians unlawful taxation and the subjection of civilians to martial laws and arbitrary imprisonment as illegal. The Authority of the English constitution was tacitly restated in the petition of rights. King Charles accepted this petition at least legally.[181]

B) The Bill of Rights, (1689)

The petition of Rights protected the freedom of the masses against tyranny and oppression followed by the bill of rights of 1689. In a series of thirteen articles or clauses it declared, also in the manner of the Magna Carter, "the Rights and Liberties of the subject, and settling the succession of the Crown."[182] It condemned every autocratic and arbitrary exercise of power and affirmed that the king has no right to violate the fundamental laws of the kingdom. The bill of rights ascribed to parliament once more, its own freedoms. The provisions of the Bill remain still very fundamental to the Anglo-Saxon system of Government. The Bill stood in the modern age as the Magna Carter stood for the feudal middle Ages. It sought to assert the laws, rights and liberties of the English.[183]

C) Toleration Act by John Locke, (1689)

The intellectual basis for toleration in John Locke was laid by his famous essays – *"Essay Concerning human Understanding* and *Essay On Civil Government"*. In the essay concerning human understanding, John Locke emphasised the role of experience in our ways of understanding. As a

---

181 Iwe, The History and Contents of Human Rights 94.
182 The heading of the bill of Rights reads: "The Rights and Liberties of the subject, and settling the succession of the crown". The essential aim of the bill was to redress the popular grievances aroused in the reign of the Stuarts, to assert the laws and liberties as against absolutism and to settle the crown of England on Prince William of Orange and his consort, Princess Mary and to protect the interest of the Anglican Church.
183 Iwe, The History and Contents of Human Rights 97.

consequence Locke insisted on the variation of human understanding, and repudiated attempts at generalisations based only on innate ideas as held by Plato and Descartes. According to Locke human experience remains a reliable source of knowledge. This philosophical position merited him, in his time the first empiricist in England. In his two essays concerning the civil government Locke saw the protection of rights and the welfare of the people as the sole aim of civil government. Drawing from his description of the state of nature, where rights are natural to human beings, he sees the need for ordering and protection of this rights to avoid wars and anarchy, hence he advocated the civil government as an instrument of human rights. At the same time he advocated rebellion when the government becomes oppressive to the people. He referred to it as the end of civil government. Toleration was one of his pleas for recognition of the dignity of human person, and the mitigation of dogmatism in the Church. This Act of 1689 ended the series of persecutions and political disabilities, which the Protestant Non-conformists suffered at the hands of the established Anglican Church. It was a major breakthrough in the struggle for religious liberty.[184] G. Trevelyan remarked the toleration act of 1689 as one that has substantially freedom of religious worship, with certain exceptions, won the day.[185] However, the Toleration Act was a limited success, because the Roman Catholics were not emancipated from legal disabilities imposed on them until 1829, and the Jews could not yet sit in Parliament until 1858. The Church of England merely ceased officially to be a persecuting body, but remained throughout the coming era a body with exclusive political and educational privileges.[186] Principally, the Toleration of John Locke sought to protect the religious freedom and liberty of the human person. Thus in the English world, it could be rightly seen that rights came into being as a measure for protecting the rights of human beings from tyranny and operations. The interpretation of the human rights is based on the fact of equality, freedom and liberty. However, these human values are based on the fact of the human person having an inherent dignity, which these values portray and so in need of protection.

---

184 Iwe, The History and Contents of Human Rights 97.
185 Cf. G. Trevelyan, History of England 474.
186 Cf. Trevelyan, History of England 474.

2.9.3 The Peace of Augsburg and the Edict of Nantes (1555-1789)

The effect of the reformation in Europe was enormous. One of them was rivalry between kingdoms and empires. There were many wars among the various kingdoms for the protection of their religious territorial integrity. In the German front, under religious banners princes had begun to fight for their civic rights and economic and commercial liberties and had sought to gain and assert for themselves a measure of political independence against the emperor Charles V. Religious wars in Europe were complex, because they were compounded with several motives other than mere religious. There were economic and political motives hiding behind the upheavals, which lasted sometimes several years. However, some of the obvious reasons for these rivalries could be said to be freedom and liberty. The following peace treaties represent legal codifications of rights for the guarantee of freedom and peace.

A) The Peace of Augsburg, (1555)

The peace of Augsburg was born as a panacea to religious intolerance of the German princes at the time. The edict was based on the famous principle: *"Cujus regio ejus religio"* – the religion of the ruler is the religion of the ruled. This edict was not a true guarantee of religious freedom in the right sense of it, but only regional and limited freedom. Thus it read: "In order to bring peace into the Holy Empire of the German nation between the Roman Imperial Majesty and the Electors, Princes and Estates: let neither this Imperial Majesty and the Electors, Princes and Estates do any violence or harm to any Estate of the Empire on account of the Augsburg Confession, but let them enjoy their religious belief, liturgy, and ceremonies as well as their estates and other rights and privileges in peace"[187] From the above edict, it is clear that the freedom was only a politically and territorially motivated guarantee of religious freedom. Moreover, this freedom was only targeted at the Roman Catholics and the Lutherans alone for a peaceful coexistence and friction – free governance of the various political jurisdictions. The liberty guaranteed, did not seem

---

187 Peace of Augsburg-Clause 15, Cited in: Iwe, The History and Contents of Human Rights 98.

to have any intention to safeguard the human conscience as a respectable aspect of the human person in questions relating to religion. It was exclusive in character and nature as the Calvinists, for instance and other protestant confessions seemed not to have been included in the pact[188]. It was no affirmation of man's liberty in matters of religion, but the confirmation of two Christian groups each in the rectitude and intolerance of its own stand.

The consequence of this limitation was imminent. By the positive exclusion of other protestant bodies (such as the various forms of Calvinism) the parties of the Peace of Augsburg postponed the resolution of the issue of religious liberty and peace in Europe, and relegated it to the future. Unfortunately, this contributed as part of the reasons for the outbreak of the thirty-year War.[189]

B) The Peace of Westphalia, (1648)

At the end of the thirty-year War in Europe another peace accord was reached and signed. It was so much different from the motivating principles of the former treaties. What seemed to be different and new, was the inclusion of the Calvinists in the pact. The concept of religious liberty as the inalienable right of the human person to be left free and unmolested in his choice of belief and worship was foreign to this treaty. In principle, the peace of Westphalia pointed to the fact that Europe was religiously disintegrated.[190]

However other efforts in forms of Edict were made in the region even before the peace of Westphalia. For example, in the Edict of Nantes, the French Sovereign King Henry the IV freed his subjects from the burden of religious conscience by granting a tolerant religious atmosphere. The Edit of Nantes considered in the right understanding of religious liberty, was no more than a practical religious compromise. It merely confirmed Catholicism as the state religion and made practical concessions to the Huguenots (Calvinists) on matters of religious worship. It could be valued from its effective and practical guarantee of the Protestants liberty of conscience and in certain places and under certain conditions. They were

---

188 Cf. Iwe, The History and Contents of Human Rights 98.
189 Cf. Iwe, The History and Contents of Human Rights 100.
190 Iwe, The History and Contents of Human Rights 100.

allowed to regulate their own religious and educational system. In all, they enjoyed Liberty of worship. Nevertheless the Edict of Nantes remained a temporary practical compromise.[191] Religious liberty had to wait until the events of 1789 in France before the national atmosphere would be cleared of the miasma of religious intolerance. In the expression of Iwe, "it is a pity that man and his rights had to wait for so long".[192] But the import of this historical review of the efforts at guaranteeing the religious freedom and liberty through rights is to show the importance of a positive practical effort by human beings to legalise either through edicts, pacts and treaties the respect of the dignity of human person in form of rights.

2.9.4 The American Declaration of Independence and the Bills of Rights (1776)

The migration from Europe to the "new world" – America in the sixteenth and seventeenth century was caused mainly by religious intolerance, social disabilities and persecutions of the Anglo-Saxon world (English and Ireland).[193] It was the descendants of these early emigrants that fought and declared the American constitution in 1776. It was almost becoming unbearable from the English King George III led government in the collection of taxes and contribution abroad. The inhabitants of the new world –America, felt so much enslaved, exploited unjustly without their consent or being represented in the parliament that they began to seek for a way out of the English tyrannical regime. Just as Iwe puts it: "The declaration of independence is and will remain a symbol of the American repudiation of the English autocratic colonial system; an immortalised assertion of the liberty and autonomy of the American people".[194]

---

191 The Edict of Nantes was not based on the general principles of tolerance. It was just a practical concession to enable different confessions co-exist side by side. Its vulnerability was shown when the Edict, was repealed by King Louis XIV.
192 Cf. Iwe, The history and Contents of Human rights 101
193 Cf. F. Battaglia, Classici del Liberalismo e del Socialismo (Le Carte del Dirriti², G. C. Sansoni (ed.), Firenze 1947 40.
194 Iwe, The history and Contents of Human rights 102.

The American Constitution declares:

> We hold these truths to be self evident that all men are created equal, that they are endowed by their Creator with certain inalienable Rights, that among these are life, liberty and pursuit of happiness, that to secure these rights Government are instituted among Men deriving their just powers from the consent of the governed. That whenever any form of Government becomes destructive of these ends; it is the right of the people to alter or abolish it, and to institute new Government laying its foundation on such principles and organising its power in such form as to them shall seem most likely to effect safety and happiness.[195]

The consequence of this declaration was "to entrench the rule of law, a government of laws and not of men, a polity in which all decisions and statutes could be measured against the words of the written constitution – the rule of law".[196]

The basis of this constitution and bills of rights were the philosophies of Jean Jacques Rousseau and John Locke and meant to be universal and personal in character. These rights are solemnly declared to be natural to man, deriving from his being and therefore are inviolable and inalienable as well as repugnant to every form of despotic government. Nonetheless, just as Iwe pathetically puts it:

> Unfortunately the founding Fathers of America, who declared the innate equality of all men and the natural liberty of all, had many Black slaves in their plantations, plying an infra-human and squalid existence for the profit of their masters.[197]

However, what is of interest here is the fact that America was able to take a positive and practical step in the line of law to protect the moral value of human dignity through the declaration of rights and liberties.

---

195 The American Declaration of Independence July 4 1776, Preamble.
196 Simeon Onyewueke Eboh, Human Rights and Democratization in Africa: The Role of Christians, Enugu Nigeria 2003 84, 85.
197 Iwe, The History and Contents of Human Rights 105.

2.9.5 The French Declaration of the Rights of Man and the Citizen (1789)

The human condition in France worsened day by day, as Feudalism had its ploy on the poor masses. Coupled with the incompetence of the French King Louis XVI both in controlling the excesses of the feudal lords, the economy of the state went bankrupt. The people of France therefore, saw the King as an obstacle to their political and economic progress. Commenting on the weakness and absolutism of the French King on the eve of the famous Revolution, J. Thompson remarked that, "this mixture of arbitrariness and impotence was the tragedy of Louis XVI government".[198] He affirmed that the national bankruptcy ignited the practice of despotism, and oppression, which led to the famous Declaration of "The Right of Man and the Citizens".[199] The essential and prominent aspects of the Declaration emphasised the universal right of Man. Like the American Declaration, the French Declaration asserts the right to Liberty, equality, to private property, to freedom of thought and expression. The French declared these rights as universal, natural to Man (*'tuos les hommes'*), inalienable, imprescriptibly and inviolable.

Despite the extremes to which the French Revolution ran, the Italian scholar F. Battaglia concluded that it remains true that the Declaration of the rights of Man stands as one of the bright contributions of the Revolution to human progress and man's liberty and dignity.[200]

The American and French Declarations paved the way for the United Nations' Universal Declaration of the Fundamental Human Rights on June 26th, 1945. The two World Wars, the excesses of Fascism, Nazism and Socialism necessitated this Declaration.

---

198 J. Thompson, French Revolution Documents (1789-94), Blackwell Oxford 1948 319.
199 Thompson, French Revolution Documents (1789-94) 320.
200 Cf. F. Battaglia, Classici del Liberalismo e del Socialismo (Le Carte del Dirriti) 110-113.

2.9.6 The Universal Declaration of Human Rights UDHR (1948)

The stage was set in 1948 after the devastations of the World wars I and II for a new world order, in which the dignity of human person would be universally guaranteed; no longer as a mere moral obligation, but also as a legal obligation in form of rights and declaration. The opening statement of the Declaration reads:

> We the people of the United Nations, determined to save succeeding generations from the scourge of war, which twice in our lifetime has brought untold sorrow to mankind, and to reaffirm faith in fundamental human rights, in the dignity and worth of the human person, in equal rights of men and women and of nations large and small, and to promote social progress and better standard of life in larger freedom have resolved to combine our efforts to accomplish these aims.[201]

The Declaration recognizes the inherent dignity of the human person, the inalienable rights as the foundation of freedom, justice and peace in the world. It made the world conscious of the fact that the infringement of these fundamental rights leads to outrageous barbaric acts. The Declaration pledges to promote among others human rights and fundamental freedom for all irrespective of race, sex language or religion.[202]

After the declaration, which was presented in form of moral law and obligation, the subsequent human right conventions formulated them into laws and gave them the force of law. While the declaration was universally binding to every human person, the convention required a legal commitment on the side of the contracting nations. Meanwhile there were – three major U.N Organs on human rights namely: The Economic and Social Council. This council produced two finished legal covenants, which where ratified by the U.N General council in 1966 namely, 1."On Economic, Social and Cultural Rights" (ESCR); 2. "On Civil and Political Rights" (CPR). The International Labour Convention (ILO), produced five conventions namely, 1 The Freedom of Association and Protection of the Right to Organise Convention of 1948 (FAPROC); 2 The Employ-

---

201 Universal Declaration of Human Rights 1948: Preamble.
202 Cf. Eboh, Human Rights and Democratisation in Africa 86

ment Service Convention of 1948 (ESC); 3 The Right to Organise and Collective Bargaining Convention of 1949 (ROCBC), 4 The Equal Remuneration Convention of 1951 (ERC), 5 The Abolition of Forced Labour Convention of 1957 (AFLC). Others include: 1 Committee on the Elimination of Racial Discrimination (CERD); 2 Employment and Occupation Convention 1958 (EOC); 3 Committee on the Elimination of Discrimination against Women (CEDAW); 3 Committee against Torture (CAT); 4 Committee on the Rights of the Child (CRC); and 5 The Convention "On the Discrimination in Education" (UNESCO). Later, the United Nations High Commissioner for Human Rights (UNHCHR) was added to supervise and report annually to the UN General Assembly (UNGA) on the implementation of human Rights in the world. It has been replaced with the Human Rights Council 2006 – (HRC), followed by the Universal Periodic Review Working Group 2007 – (UPRWG) and The Human Rights Council Advisory Committee 2007 – (HRCAC). More recent ones includes; Committee on the Protection of the Rights of All Migrant Workers and Members of their Families (CPRMWMF), and Committee on the Rights of Persons with Disabilities (CRPD).

The above practical bodies and conventions struggle to legalize the moral standards and policies enunciated by the solemn declaration of the fundamental human rights based on the dignity of human person.

Finally, the world has been grouped into regions with the effect that each has developed its own adapted Human Rights Charter. First among them is the Pan-American World, comprising of the American States since the 14th of April 1890 (when the first International Conference of American States was held in Washington D. C). Second is the West-European World, which has given more effective measures to U.D.H.R of the 1948[203]. The third among them is the African Region, comprising of Africa and Madagascar which declared in 1978- The African Charter on Human and Peoples' Rights under the auspices of the then OAU (the Organisation of African Unity) now AU (African Union).

For the purpose of specification, in this review only the African Charter of Human and Peoples' Rights will be discussed.

---

203 Cf. Iwe, The History and Contents of Human Rights 133.

2.9.6.1 The African Charter of human and Peoples' Rights (1978)

With the Universal Declaration of Human Rights (U.D.H.R) and the resolve of the United Nations to universalize its concepts world wide, regions accepted the responsibility of bringing home the concept of human rights. Africa as a region came together under the then OAU (Organisation of African Unity), now known as AU (African Union) to articulate in positive terms the implications of the universally thought out concept of human dignity in legal binding terms for the African people.

Among other literatures on the analysis and understanding of the African Charter on Human and People's Rights the explicatory and systematic work of Professor Osita C. Eze is enriching. In his Theoretical Perspectives and objectives of the African Charter Eze explored the background facts of the Charter, stating the problem created by the influence of the two major Western ideologies in the choice of African political identity since the independence of African States. He affirms that: "Independent African States have been confronted with a choice between socialist and capitalist development. In most of these countries capitalist modes of production have been injected even though feudal socio-economical formations also subsist".[204] Liberalist view propagates capitalism, while the socialist view propagates communism. These two extreme ideologies struggled for supremacy for almost half a century in a cold war in the West. Unfortunately the fate of Africa in the events of colonisation and anti-colonisation processes inherited a kind of a mixture of the two ideologies, with the effect that this has caused more harm than good. It has been thought erroneously that Africa as a continent could develop in the line of capitalism and then settle later for socialism. However, it is also doubtful, if Africa will be capable enough to develop socialist economies.[205] This is to be understood in Africa's long history of struggle for survival and the emergence of a bunch of capitalist class in the system. On the contrary, Marxism was not even clear in its tenets on the possibility or the nature of such a transition from neo-colonial economies to socialism.

---

204 Osita C. Eze, Human Rights in Africa Some Selected Problems, Nigeria 1982 4.
205 Cf. Eze, Human Rights in Africa. Some Selected Problems 4.

Eze traced the historical and theoretical background of the Charter right from the pre-colonial, colonial and postcolonial eras. He argued that Africa had a concept of law and rights before the African encounter with the West in the 15th Century. Although scanty materials and information about the nature of rights existent in the pre-colonial era makes the study of rights in this era very difficult, there are also no evidences that rights as we conceive them today did not exist in the primitive African societies. He opined that colonialism, even though it established law courts and systems of rights, remains a basic contradiction of human rights. It suppressed the right of self-determination, which is a prerequisite for the maintenance and protection of human rights and by dominating and exploiting the natural and human resources denied the colonised people the material means to ensure effective promotion and protection of human rights.[206] The post colonial era has produced so many dictators under whose dictatorial regimes the realization of the human and people's right have remained a mirage. Halkima Abbas in his work: *Africa's Long Road to Rights* traced the account of how and why Africa has developed its own system for protecting human and peoples' rights. Among others, the problem of the achievement of the purpose and aim of the Charter has been lack of political will on the side of the various African governments to make the principles functional and viable.[207] He concluded by pointing out that,

> The success of the African Commission on Human and Peoples' Rights, in spite of the seeming lack of political will on the part of African states and governments to hold one another accountable for violations of fundamental freedoms, lies primarily in the distinctive engagement of civil society.[208]

In the same vein, Eze focusing on the issue of international interventions in cases of human suffering with regards to the danger of its instrumentation as a political measure blames the lack of promotion and protection of human rights on the African states when he wrote:

---

206 Eze, Human Rights in Africa 4.
207 Hakima Abbas, Africa's Long Road to Rights, Reflections on the 20th anniversary of the African Commission on Human and Peoples' Rights, Nairobi and Oxford 2007 1.
208 Abbas, Africa's Long Road to Rights 2.

Yet ironically it is because the agencies, policies and laws of a particular state have in many cases proved inadequate or because the state authority has abandoned its role as a defender or protector of human rights that the need for international protection arises.[209]

It is pertinent to note from the fore going that the human rights developed among the West as a body of rights for the protection of the dignity of human person are not to be confused with human dignity itself. Human right as a protection of the sublime worth and value of the human person are based on the dignity of human person. However, the human rights' idea that was inherited from the colonial powers by African states was a body of rights cultured and adopted by the Western civilization. The postcolonial adaptation of these rights from the African point of views has not even helped matters as the basic structures of the society still bear the traces of the colonial masters. As a result the African spirit wonders between the western individualistic human dignity interpretation and the African communal and person-oriented understanding.[210]

Human dignity, primarily as an ethical principle draws its content from the socio-cultural and anthropological realities. Values are formed at the long run from the experiences cultivated through the value judgement of a particular people and culture. Although every culture has a common characteristic that links it with others, cultures differ in their experiences and meanings, which the communities make out of them. That is to say the bedrock of cultures is normally founded on the historical narrative of a group, burn out of the total sum of their experiences. For this simple reason, the meaning of a term can only be discovered in the very use the people make of it.[211] This approach has always proved true in the course of history, because a term can loose the meaning it possessed at immergence in the course of time due to interpretations. This

---

209 Eze, Human Rights in Africa 5.
210 Cf Leonhard Harding, „Menschenbilder und Menschenrechte: Afrikanische Erfahrungen", in: Burghart Schmidt (Hg.), Menschenrechte und Menschenbilder von der Antike bis zur Gegenwart, Hamburg, 2006 277-305 here 302.
211 Cf. Victor C. Uchendu, The Igbo of Southeast Nigeria, New York 1965 11; cf. Emefie Ikenga Metuh, Comparative Studies of African Traditional Religions, Onitsha-Nigeria 1996 61.

difference in experience and meaning is of high significance in the integral development of a people. Africa in general and the Igbo in particular are victims of ideological captivity, because the frame work of the principle of human dignity imposed on them at the wake of the colonial era had little or nothing to do with their ethical system. According to Leonhard Harding, The western model was inherited and received in the independence constitution of many African states, which were foreign and with no cognisance of the African worldview and human image. In the Banjul charter there was a successful change and correction of the direction to the old African values and norms. But the newer drafts of the constitutions have once more gone back to a form of an individualistic thinking and this has led to a gross decadence in the states just like it had existed shortly in the decades after the independence.[212]

Unfortunately even after the post-colonial independence most African states have remained with a set of human rights' ideas fashioned from the colonial human dignity framework. Osita Eze points to the foreign model of the colonial hegemony that the independent African states have been confronted with a choice between socialist and capitalist development.[213] Historically the two ideologies have remained irreconcilable in the political stage. Unfortunately the frustration from the confusion has led to untold human hardship and civil unrest in the continent. To worsen the situation, political Wars and poverty; sickness and disease have made human promotion among Africans so difficult. The value of human life has so much depreciated as many selfish politicians in the name of democracy draw new understandings from the constitutions and legal systems, which are fraught with corruption, lacking in basic cultural foundation. In short these have ended up creating, despots, cabals and dictators.

For the Africans in general and the Igbo in particular life is the absolute value of a human being. Life is paramount – *"Ndu bu isi"*. Over and above this value attached to life, one notices in the Traditional African societies several atrocious ritual killings, the *osu* cast system, ostracism, killing of twins and so many other taboos against the dignity of human

---

212 Cf. Leonhard Harding, „Menschenbilder und Menschenrechte: Afrikanische Erfahrungen" 302.
213 Osita, C. Eze, Human Rights in Africa: Some Selected Problems, Lagos Macmillan Nigeria 1984 1.

person. Unfortunately, poverty,[214] diseases and sicknesses have become an African symbol and lately the HIV/AIDS, which has become the greatest human challenge so far threatening to decimate the entire African race. In the traditional Igbo African society human sacrifice was practiced, but nowadays, human life is been exchanged for a ransom by kidnappers. One can ask: where then is the famous African love and respect for human life? Nevertheless, of all one can lament, as human abuses in Africa, colonialism and the Trans-Atlantic slave trade remain the greatest against the African soul. The effects of the trauma have refused to be tranquilised by every available measure

Our interest here at this juncture is not to elaborate on the nature and details of the African Charter of human and peoples' rights; the effectiveness or causes of ineffectiveness of the implementation, but just to show that Africa received a concept of right, which leaves much to be desired due to internal and external factors. African human rights status owes its frustration partly, due to the fact that a regional institution for the promotion and protection of human rights and legal commissions to prosecute offenders are yet to be realized in the region.

2.10 Universal Human Rights?

Among scholars today, the discussions on the universal application of human rights have become popular. However, what is at stake here is the use of the human right idea as an instrument of influence internationally and not merely the fact of its presence in every culture as a universal concept. Consequently human rights as legislative codes for the protection of human dignity are not to be confused with human dignity, as we have explicated earlier in this inquiry. They are neither: the laws of nature (natural law), that means, neither 'immutable laws nor the laws *of* human dignity. Human rights are simply laws drawn *from* the dignity of human person.[215] Moreover, way of rights may not, as a matter of fact be the

---

214 Poverty is used here from every ramification of the word. Not just economic poverty but also socio-cultural and moral poverty.
215 Cf. Hans Jörg Sandkühler, „Menschenwürde und die Transformation moralischer Rechte in Positives Recht" 66.

only way of protecting the dignity of the human person, there could be other means and ways existing in other non-western cultures to protect the dignity of the human person.[216]

Hans Maier's work on *Die Menschenrechte als Weltrechte nach 1945: Universaler Anspruch und kulturelle Differenzierung (The Human Rights as World Rights after 1945: Universal Prerogative and cultural Differentiation)* traced the stages of the discussion on the Universal application of human rights. He pointed out the moments at which the human right idea faced factual realities and no more metaphysically presented as a protected idea. In the presence of the cold war between the communistic world and the liberal democratic world, it was a matter of systematic difference. In the first place, the socialist saw in the liberalists' generated idea of human dignity as lacking in social and communistic principle, but rich in individualism.[217] Unfortunately, the two ideologies have different understandings of freedom. Communistic understanding of freedom anchors on the absolute value of the state over and above that of the individual, while the liberal capitalist bases on the individual freedom as justice, as the sole point of reference against that of the state as a moral person. The situation in the East and West block was so intense until the debacle of the communistic block as from the 90s.

With the fall of communism and with the third world beginning to have seats in the United Nations General Assembly things started changing. Consequently, the third world delegates began to vote and agitate for a human right idea peculiar to their culture and moral views. This self-consciousness on the side of the third world members signalled, yet another epoch in the history of human dignity and rights. Interest on a new form of rights started winning new advocacy with strong intents and might. A new social, ethnic-national cultural way of interpreting the hu-

---

216 Cf. Jack Donnelly, "Human Rights and Human Dignity: An Analytic Critique of Non-Western Conceptions of Human Rights", in: *The American Political Science Review*, Vol. 76, No. 2 (Jun., 1982) 303-316 here 303; See also, Hilpert, "Die Menschenrechte in Theologie und Kirche" 84-85.
217 Cf. Hans Maier, „Die menschenrechte als Weltrechte nach 1945: Universaller Anspruch und Kulturelle Differenzierung", in: Michael Durst und Hans J. Münk (Hg.), Theologie und Menschenrechte, Freiburg-Schweiz 2008 50-64 here 55.

man rights known popularly as: "The third Generation Human Rights Catalogue" became important to the regions.[218] In the Asian and other non-Western fronts it was the demand of a human right that is purely culturally oriented, whose interpretation according to Maier was no more universalistic – on being human; and has no more reference on the metaphysics of human being as human being, rather pluralistic in understanding.[219] Human beings, in relation to their worldviews, where they belong and to specific cultures with their specific needs are now at the centre of the human rights discuss.

The conflict between the second-generation rights that means those rights referring to the socio-economic rights of the human person was orchestrated by the demand of the acknowledgement of the third generation rights as a *conditio sine qua non* for their universal acceptance. Still on the point, the birth of the African charter of Human and Peoples' Right in 1981 in Banjul brought with it a kind of indication towards a relativistic idea of human rights, which have sentiments for cultures and traditions of the African peoples. This is to be seen in the appended clause – 'Human and Peoples' rights', indicating already, a tendency towards a cultural specification.

As a consequence to a seemingly polarized idea of human right, a dialogue became inevitable for a viability of human rights framework capable of unifying the world in its diversities. This necessity of interaction among the different competing world views-North and South gave birth to the so-called "North-South Dialogue": Africa, Latin America and Asia versus North America and Europe.

Against the backdrop of this dialogue Bujo Bénézet argues for a more realistic idea of human right, which is linked with the cultural moral life of the people. Hence he insists that, the human rights are in the mouth of every person – they seem surely not realistic, if someone would want to make them into a collective ideal for the whole human race.[220] Hans Küng's idea of a *Projekt Weltethos* hopes for a unified body of ethical understanding that can guarantee a one world. Hence he asserts:

218　Cf. Maier, Die Menschenrechte als Weltrechte nach 1945 55.
219　Cf. Maier, Die Menschenrechte als Weltrechte nach 1945 55-56.
220　Cf. Bujo Bénézet, Die ethische Dimension der Gemeinschaften. Das afrikanische Modell im Nord-süd-Dialog, Freiburg 1993 134.

> Immer deutlicher wurde mir in den letzten Jahren, dass die eine Welt, in der wir leben, nur dann eine Chance zum Überleben hat, wenn in ihr nicht länger Räume unterschiedlicher, widersprüchlicher und gar sich bekämpfender Ethiken existieren, Diese eine Welt braucht dies eine Grundethos; diese eine Weltgesellschaft braucht gewiss keine Einheitsreligion und Einheitsideologie, wohl aber, einige verbindende und verbindliche Normen, Werte, Ideale und Ziele.[221]

Wolfgang Schild shared same opinion when he wrote:

> Die Bedeutung des Menschenrechtsdenkens liegt für die heutige Situation der Menschheitsgeschichte gerade darin, eine gemeinsame normative Grundlage für das Zusammenleben aller Menschen in Frieden und Gerechtigkeit unabhängig von einer möglichen religiösen bzw. weltanschaulichen Begründung in Sich zu bringen.[222]

In all Maier disagrees with any form of idea of a 'world ethos' that would tend to reduce the world into a phantom or utopia. Rather he advocates strongly for a cultural convergence in form of dialogue and understanding between cultures as the only chance for a universal idea of human rights.[223] It is a system where by the various cultural differences would be received as an option for a universal realisation of a viable idea of human rights.

Miao-ling Hasenkamp established in his work: Universalization of Human Rights? The Effectiveness of Western Human Rights Policies towards Developing Countries after the Cold War the intrigues involved in the facts of universalizing the human rights as a game of the stronger. The one who has more votes and more economic and capital whip dictates the pace of the human rights. Citing an example with the United Nations intervention during the decimation of the Jews in the National Socialist regime of Hitler in 1948, and juxtaposing that with the position

---

221 Hans Küng, Projekt Weltethos, München 1990 14.
222 Schild Wolfgang, „art. Menschenrechte", in: Ruh, U, Seeber, D, Walter, R (Hg.), Handwörterbuch religiöser Gegenwartsfragen (Sonderausgabe), Freiburg i. Br. ²1989 271.
223 Cf., Hans Maier, „Die menschenrechte als Weltrechte nach 1945: Universaler Anspruch und kulturelle Differenzierung" 64.

of the United States of America in the issue of the ongoing Iraq's invasion and the diplomatic reinterpretation of intervention in issues of human rights in international foreign policies he shows how precarious, the universal application of human rights could be.

Describing the nature of the western policies towards developing countries Hasenkamp opined:

> To be sure, Western human rights policies towards developing countries involve interactions between unequal actors with sharp disparities of capabilities, i.e. between rich and poor. They also involve the encounters among divergent or even conflicting normative paradigms, based on which the idea of human rights is conceived and the preferences of state actions come into shape.[224]

The United Nations Organisation as a 'guarantor' of equality among all nations of the world, even in the case of international human rights has been greatly influenced by some countries that finance her operations in the so called human interventions. As a consequence, it has become doubtful nowadays to speak of a trust worthy UNO capable of guaranteeing a fair and free operation in issues of human intervention in the case of human rights violation among the countries of the world.

Although the universality of the human right has been put into question due to the above-observed faults the idea of a human right that would guarantee brotherhood among peoples and nations will ever continue to be the desire of the world.

2.11 Summary

So far, we have tried in this first part of the inquiry, to introduce the major issues involved with dignity as an interpretative principle of the human person. The general introduction highlighted in the statement of problem, areas of inquiry on human dignity especially; the interpretation of the concept, which is the major preoccupation of this inquiry; the scope of

---

224 Mao-ling Hasenkamp, Universalization of Human Rights? The Effectiveness of Western Human Rights Policies towards Developing Countries after the Cold War. With Case Studies on China, Frankfurt am Main 2004 7.

human dignity, relative or universal; the applicability of human dignity in peculiar circumstances for instance, in the case of terror and the bio-ethical questions of our time, genetic manipulation, euthanasia cloning et cetera.

A theological framework was described in chapter one, pointing out the connections and basis that can enable a discussion on historical-anthropological questions in theological terms. Human dignity remains an anthropological key to the understanding of the ideal on the person. This framework is found in the Melchior Cano's epistemological principle, where he considered human questions as part of dogma- *'Loci Theologicus aliene'*. Consequently, this epistemological principle will enable a viable theological dialogue between the Western human dignity conceptions and that of the Igbo (African) culture of Nigeria.

Chapter two reviewed in a systematic historical manner meaning and etymology of human dignity from the stoics to the present. The variety of the concepts of human dignity discovered in the literature review reveals a necessity to clarify the concept as an interpretative open principle of the human ideals, with so many approaches. It's variability in approach and meaning testifies to the fact that norms of morality and rights are necessarily based on the culture of a particular people.

Above all human dignity reveals itself as an – 'interpretative open concept'. Two major currents of interpretations were discovered namely, the Metaphysical and the Autonomic. Human dignity as a moral value of the human person, which does not allow an interpretation in a single understanding shows that, the above interpretations, whether metaphysical or autonomic, existed in the history of philosophy as complete ideas. Any attempt to mix up the two currents would definitely not succeed.[225] The two currents hold universality of human dignity as possible and realisable. The developmental history of the concept shows the gradual change from norms to rights as a guarantee of human dignity. These human rights however, which have their origin from the ingenuity of the West and the North are just an aspect of human dignity and cannot replace human dignity itself. Universality as a topical issue of today speaks of an intercultural dialogue and convergence of ideas, not just a form of instrumentation.

---

225   Cf. Tiedemann, Was ist Menschenwürde? 67.

Part Two
Conceptual Analysis of Human Dignity among the Igbo (Africans)

Chapter Three: Social Anthropological Survey of Igbo World View

3.1 Introduction

Generally speaking, a concise articulation of human dignity as a subject of inquiry is no less a difficult venture. From the outset, Spielmann remarked that the word: "human dignity", even though found virtually in the mouth of every one, no one cares much to say exactly what it is.[226] The reason for this is obviously linked with the very fact that the concept is a collective heritage of humanity and as such interpretative open. Experience has shown that the whole of human development: moral and ethical norms depend inexonerably on the conceptuality of human dignity.[227]

Even though human dignity as an idea is contemporaneous with humanity and exists in every culture, well developed reflections on the subject are still scanty in some cultures. In the West where the concept has been transformed into moral rights one can boast of well reflected and referred materials, which have been systematically documented. On the contrary in Africa discussions on human dignity and rights are still in the collection stage. The reason could be the very little interest shown in the issues of human dignity and human rights. Moreover scholars prefer to concentrate more on the human rights issues, rather than fighting on grounds and interpretations of human dignity. Recently, there is a growing tendency to relegate these controversies to the background in the various cultures, religions and worldviews. Unfortunately this pretension has not solved any problem either rather it has exacerbated it. The modern naiveté towards the interpretation of human dignity is born out of the difficulties posed by the differences in worldviews, culture and religion. Nowadays multiculturalism has created a myriad of human images, so

---

226 Cf. Spielmann, „Welche Menschenwürde?" 9.
227 Cf. Thies, Der Wert der Menschenwürde 9.

that a single global human image has become very difficult to think about.

Against this backdrop, a systematic reflection on the Igbo concept of human dignity from the Igbo standpoint is not an easy task either. There are little or no specific Igbo authors or literatures dealing per se, with human dignity or the dignity of human person upon which this research can be based. All one can lay hands on are works on the general worldview of the Igbo (African), and those on ethnology mainly done by non-indigenes; or those touching on African socio-cultural anthropology. There are also researches on the idea of personhood while the most available materials are either reports on human rights violation, or western articulations of the human rights. This is to say, that already existing systematic works on human dignity per se among a cultural group such as the Igbo of Nigeria is not accessible to the researcher. Moreover a standard theological interpretation of human dignity in the Igbo culture is yet to be achieved. Perhaps it is not saying too much, if the present research is said to be in some sense one of the pioneer efforts in this field of research.

Therefore, as a dialogue this work struggles to combine every available material within reach to articulate as clear as possible the conception of human dignity traceable from the Igbo African worldview and as one can read from the socio-cultural anthropology of the Igbo. With a phenomenological approach the researcher tries to showcase the human image predominant in the Igbo socio-cultural setting as a sample for a moderate and prudent generalisation over the big continent of Africa. Within a framework of indigenous phenomenology; of an insider, the researcher maintains a first hand originality in thought and style, however not neglecting the relevant extant contributions of experts in their various fields. A combination of reports from oral interviews and discourses with Igbo indigenes adds a blend which makes this part of the research interdisciplinary in outlook, far reaching in scope and a first hand information this time, from an Igbo indigene. First, we shall now review the available extant writings and works on Igbo (African) socio-cultural anthropology and their worldview.

3.2 Extant Works on Igbo (African) Socio-Cultural Anthropology

Various Igbo (African) authors have written quite extensively on the above subject. However, with reference to the dignity of human person in the Igbo (African) perspective not much is available to the researcher. Therefore, the scanty availability of relevant literature on the theme of human dignity among the Igbo (Africans) makes it necessary that all available works dealing with Igbo worldviews in general, and also those dealing with the socio-cultural anthropology of the Igbo are considered to be veritable sources of information.

The traditional Igbo (African) societal or communal living was based on the moral norms and tradition of the people, other wise known as the *Omenala*,[228] which is believed to be the heritage left behind to posterity by the ancestors and ratified by the gods. For the Igbo (Africans), the community plays an outstanding role in the realisation of the individual's goals and aspirations through the observance of the omenala. It is in the community that one achieves and looses his dignity as well as personhood. The community approves and disapproves the individual according to the laws, customs and traditions of the land. The following literatures extant from the African scholarship are selected because of their relevance in this inquiry.

George T. Basden's books: *Among the Igbo of Nigeria and Niger Ibos* written while he was working as missionary at Awka in the southern part of Nigeria in 1920 and *1938* complement each other. Written by a missionary who 'knew the people of Igboland', they provide a general ethnographic picture of a part of Igbo Land, the Onitsha-Awka hinterland in the early twentieth century. These serve as an observers attempt at what looked like the entire life and culture of the Igbo. Basden's ethnographic documentary known as: "The Igbo as seen by the early white men" enjoys what one may also term a 'premiership' in the field of documented

---

228 *Omenala* is a compendium of the norms, culture and tradition of Igbo communities, which were articulated and handed down by the ancestors as the dos and don'ts of the community. The morals and the legal bindings of the traditional Igbo communities are founded on the *Omenala*.

research on the Igbo. It enjoyed as it were wide readership, quoted and referenced in many works on the Igbo, especially those written abroad; and has qualified to rank as a footnote to other further researches in Igbo ethnology.

The disturbing aspect of this work is that it remains a traveller's breakfast view of the rich Igbo culture, but always being quoted and taken very seriously as a matrix of the Igbo documented literatures. However, it is pertinent to note that Basden from the out set denied the responsibility for the appearance of his book, but acknowledged his motivation for engaging in this herculean task as a suggestion from a Magazine Article to write a report of the Igbo.[229] Without mincing words he pointed out his limitations of "not being qualified in carrying out such a work; and that he was neither a historian nor a literary scholar in that sense." Even though the work was based on experience, Basden expressed his convictions, but rightly too that "it is a practical impossibility for the European to comprehend fully the subtleties of the native character".[230] For him the substance of the Igbo world was not just easy to grapple with, and sometimes one would not know when one harped at the consciousness. He tried to palliate this shallowness with what he terms "strangeness of thought and logic in the life pattern of the natives".[231] Among others, Basden pointed out a deep-rooted fascination for community life by the natives as distinctive in his observations:

> The will of the tribe or family, expressed or implied, permeates his whole being, and is the deciding factor in every detail of his life. It is a sort of freemasonry; the essence of the primary instinct of the people ....[232]

Although his documentaries have been widely quoted and developed by future writers most of whom were indigenes of Igbo culture, Basden's ethnological study remains an observation of a foreigner with little or no insight into the ontology of the people who he preferably referred to, as 'natives'.

---

229 Cf. George T. Basden, Among the Ibos of Nigeria, Nigeria 1982 9.
230 Basden, Among the Ibos of Nigeria 9.
231 Basden, Among the Ibos of Nigeria 9.
232 Basden, Among the Ibos of Nigeria 9, 10.

Other observers among whose works will only be mentioned as belonging to the group include: Major Arthur Glyn Leonard, *The Lower Niger and its Tribes, London Macmillan and Company Ltd, 1906*; Margaret, M. Green, *Ibo Village Affairs, London 1947* and Amaury, P. Talbot, *The Peoples of Southern Nigeria, London 1926; Tribes of the Niger Delta, London 1932*.

Placide Tempels' *Bantu Philosophy* (*La Philosophie bantoue*) in French was written in 1945. It was through this land breaking work from a missionary in the then Belgian Congo, but now the Democratic Republic of Congo that the first hope of an African ontology materialised. Placide Tempels insisted on the need to look beyond ethnology into the philosophy of the Bantus, insisting thereby that the Africans (Bantu) as rational beings have a genuine ontology, which forms the bedrock of their behaviours, actions and beliefs. He argues that the people of Sub-Saharan Africa have a distinctive philosophy, and attempts to describe the underpinnings of that philosophy. In his book, Tempels argues that the African philosophical categories can be identified through the categories inherent in language. According to Tempels, the primary metaphysical category in the thought of Bantu-speaking societies is *Force*. That means, reality is dynamic, and *being* is *force* as he succinctly puts it:

> We can conceive the transcendental notion of *'being'* by separating it from its attribute, *'Force'*, but the Bantu cannot. *'Force'* in his thought is a necessary element in *'being'*, and the concept *'force'* is inseparable from the definition of *'being'*. There is no idea among Bantu of *'being'* divorced from the idea of *'force'*. Without the element *'force'*, *'being'* cannot be conceived.[233]

Tempels argues that there are three possible views of the relationship between being and force: 1) Being as distinct from force, that is, beings may have force or may not. 2) Force as part of being, that is, being is more than force, but dependent upon it. 3) Being is Force, that is, the two are one and the same. He argues that the Bantu hold the last view of force. Specifically:

---

[233] Placide Tempels, Bantu Philosophy 2nd ed., Trans. A Rubbens Paris 1959 34.

> *Force'* is not for Bantu a necessary, irreducible attribute of being: no, the notion of *'force'* takes for them the place of the notion *'being'* in our philosophy. Just as we have, so have they a transcendental, elemental, simple concept: with them *'force'* and with us *'being'*.[234]

Tempels argues that as a result of this fundamental difference in categories, the African life is structured around understanding and defining *Force*, which contrasts sharply with the Western enterprise of understanding and defining Being.

Even though Placide Tempels distinguished himself as a fore bearer in African ontology and enjoys thereby, a wide readership, his *Bantu Philosophy* has been criticized, primarily on the ground that his conclusions are gross generalizations, which seek to characterize the thought of an entire continent, with an imaginary construct called 'force'. Ideally one would have sympathised with Tempels if he did not go out of his 'great-lake' region environment to claim knowledge of other parts of Africa which he never set his foot into. His assumed basis for the difference between the Western and African ontology as a misplacement of 'being' for 'force', remains too shallow and artificial to be metaphysically acceptable.

Chinua Achebe is recognised in African literature for his pioneering works on the traditional Igbo society, before and after the colonial and missionary eras. In his books: *Things fall apart* and *Arrow of God* published in 1958 and 1964 respectively, Achebe presented the dignity of the Igbo person as what one achieves and looses in the community. The story of Onoka the father of Okonkwo in *Things Fall Apart* was that of a man who merited no dignity in the community because he was simply lazy. He would play his flute and drink his palm wine without earnings. By so doing Onoka became a known debtor in the community. He died a poor wretch and did not merit a dignified burial.[235] On the contrary, Okonkwo the son of Onoka who is also the chief character in the novel did not take after his father. Okonkwo resolutely struggled to earn his dignity and respect among his kinsmen, by so doing carried his destiny in his own

---

234 Placide Tempels, Bantu Philosophy 36.
235 For the Igbo a dignified burial marks a successful acceptance in the land of the dead by the ancestors and insured chance of reincarnation.

hands. He was a great wrestler; he defeated *Amalinze* nick-named *the cat*, because of his great wrestling records in the neighbourhood.[236] No one outside Okonkwo had ever defeated him in a wresting contest. Okonkwo married many wives as sign of affluence. Because of his bravery and honour the slave boy *Ikemefuna* was entrusted into his care. *Ikemefuna* fondly called him father like Okonkwo's blood son *Nwoye*.

For all these, his community accorded him great honour and guaranteed his dignity and respect. Later in the narrative Okonkwo did not mind the fact that *Ikemefuna* took him as a personal father and had a hand in his death. This led to his being despised by his kinsmen as one who has no feelings for life. The killing of the boy *Ikemefuna* by Okonkwo his foster father was an abomination in the eye of the community. As a sign of disapproval by the gods Okonkwo was caught by nemesis by shooting the son of Ogbuefi Ezeudu during his funeral. For that reason, Okonkwo was penalised and sent into exile. He lost his respect and dignity amongst his people.

On coming back from his exile he found out that all had virtually changed; the missionaries had started an aggressive evangelisation of a culture he so much cherished and respected; the white man had changed virtually the traditional thought of the people through a new religion which he could no longer stomach again. In his anger he killed a messenger of the white missionary, who was molesting the *"egwugwu"*- spirit masquerade of the land. Okonkwo had thought that his people as usual would hail him with accolade for such a 'brave act' but to his greatest dismay and disappointment they abandoned him to his personal fate, for the land was no more the same as it was before. In his greatest amazement and frustration he committed suicide.

In the above narrative the role of the community as the guarantor of dignity shines out clearly. Dignity was just a functional concept that is based on individual status and achievement of success in the society. It was acquired and guaranteed in the same society where one can also loose the acquired dignity. It is a social construct, which has nothing to do with individual as created in the image of God as in the Christian conception, but through attainment of some set status, expectations and achievements in the society.

---

236   Cf. Achebe, *Things Fall Apart*, Heinemann London 1958 11.

The fate of Okonkwo in *Things Fall Apart* shows that, in Igbo culture every one is bound by the *Omenala* and within the observance of this *Omenala* (moral norms and laws) every one's right is protected and recognised. Even in the case of the slave boy *Ikemefuna*, his dignity was protected because he had changed his status as slave or ransom for the killing of *Ogbuefi Ezeugo's* wife and had dynamically qualified in the Igbo sense of the word[237] through recognising Okonkwo as his personal father, even to the extent of calling him 'father'. In this sense Okonkwo was not supposed to have murdered his child. For this abomination *Ezeudu* remonstrated: "... that boy calls you father".[238] For this reason Okonkwo was destroyed by the gods, who led him during *Ezeudu's* funeral ceremony to shoot the second son and had to be penalised and dishonoured with exile. Okonkwo was not reasonable and dynamic enough to notice the change in the status of *Ikemefuna*, which the custom and tradition demanded. On coming back from exile again Okonkwo was not docile and dynamic as a true Igbo to notice the change in the life of his community as that already influenced by Christian evangelization.

The tragedy of the two great characters of Igbo fiction, created by our great writer Chinua Achebe, depends to a largest extent on the failure of adjustment and dynamism demanded at all time of an Igbo person. Okonkwo of *Things fall Apart* took the Igbo principle of manliness to its limit and neglected other societal requirements such as; always acting in concert with your people and remaining dynamic in the face of changing realities. More than other members of his community, he failed to adjust to the coming of the white man. In the end, he had to commit suicide. The

---

237 Professor Donatus Ibeakwadalam Nwoga was a professor of English and literary studies in University of Nigeria Nssuka. He pointed out in his work on, "Nka na Nzere", *Ahiajoku Lecture Series* (1984), Owerri Nigeria 1984, the Igbo dynamism as the ability of the Igbo person to be flexible both in thought and status. The Igbo know that their status can change from time to time. Uchendu agrees with this view when he commented on the Igbo as a title loving folk. Cf. Victor Chikezie Uchendu, The Igbo of Southeast Nigeria, New York 1965 16.
238 Vgl. Chinua Achebe, Okonkwo oder Das Alte Stürzt (Things Fall Apart), (Hg.) Dagmar Heusler, Evelin Petzold, Bd. 138, Frankfurt am Main 1983 137.

great thinker, *Ezeulu* of *Arrow of God*[239] adjusted to the coming of the white man. But he failed to adjust to the balance which the Igbo people consider absolutely essential between the demands of the deities for which they have established certain procedures, and the demands of the community which require certain processes to be concluded at established times. He became blind to the balance between materialism and religion and ended up in the lonely grandeur of a mad man.

In summary Achebe's works stress the dynamism inherent in the life of the Igbo person whose dignity is tied to the standards of the community. The place of the individual freedom and conscience seem to have been subsumed in the "We" consciousness of the community. Achebe's disavowal of philosophy and anthropology in his works did not hide his intention to create the Igbo world and the person as that quite different from the insurgent colonialists and missionaries who he saw no reason to reconcile with the Igbo in a single genius. It is doubtful whether this relativism could create the required modern picture of a human being in relation with a society, which is globalised, seeking interconnectivity among human beings in all spheres of human endeavours including the idea of human dignity.

Victor Chikezie Uchendu's works: *The Igbo of South East Nigeria* and *Ezi na Ulo: The Extended Family in Igbo Civilization* published in 1965 and 1995 respectively are scholarly contributions to the study of the Igbo cultural anthropology. Uchendu's privilege as a member of the Igbo community and culture gave his works a vivid blend and edge over other works from other ethnographers or cultural anthropologist such as G.T Basden and A. G. Leonard. In an erudite manner of descriptive narrative Uchendu brought to the sinews of his readers the sublime values embedded in the Igbo culture. The indigenous phenomenological approach to interpretation of the Igbo worldview was a landmark in the assessment of the Igbo person and his dignity. In the personal narrative of his childhood experience among his kitts and kin Uchendu presents the Igbo cultural heritage as one that is anthropologically constructed towards the dignity of the human person. Personhood in the Igbo worldview is a kind of process and the individual inheres in a kinship network emphasising thereby, the indispensable role of the community in the life of the indi-

---

239 Cf. Chinua Achebe, Arrow of God, Heinemann London 1964.

vidual. With the acquisition of titles and the motif behind it, the Igbo understand dignity as a personal achievement. Dignity is also understood as functional, which is helping the community stand up.[240] This sense of achievement pivoted the Igbo ever to strive for higher status.[241]

In his lecture on the *Ezi na Ulo: The Extended Family in Igbo Civilization* Uchendu presented the *Ezi na Ulo* – extended family from a socio-anthropological point of view[242] as the kern of the community and the basis for human dignity in Igbo culture. This extended family is social and not necessarily conjugal. It is the *Ezi,* which extends the individual right from the *Ulo* to the realization of personhood, dignity and civilization in the lager polity. With characteristic analytical dexterity, Uchendu expanded the horizon of Igbo World View by time-tested propositions. *Ezi na Ulo* is an elucidation of the central position accorded to the family in Igbo life and the role which the family plays in the success or failure of the individual as well as in the celebrated group achievement spirit for which the Igbo have become truly famous. However, to what extent the *Ezi na Ulo* as the matrix of Igbo human social civilization can lead to a recognition of human dignity that can transcend the strong hold of family ties to become sensitive to others outside the kinship level remains unclear. The notion of universality in the Igbo family system is very limited as to accommodate the universality demanded by the UHDR. Therefore, it is pertinent to stress that a description of the Igbo, whether socially or culturally conceived that aims at isolating the Igbo from a purely anthropological stand point would not be competent enough to fathom the rich value of human dignity.

John S Mbiti has contributed immensely to the African scholarship in general. His works vacillate between theology and comparative Religion. In his work: *African religions and philosophies,* published in 1969 Mbiti systematically exposed the attitude of mind and belief, which have evolved in the many societies of Africa. Among others he inquired into the religiosity of the Africans through their worldviews and cosmology. For the African, life is religion and religion is life.[243] God is the author of life; he created the human being and holds him in being. The individual is

---

240 Cf. Uchendu, The Igbo of Southeast Nigeria 34.
241 Uchendu, The Igbo of Southeast Nigeria 84.
242 Cf. Uchendu, „Ezi na Ulo", Ahiajoku Lecture Series, Owerri Nigeria 1985 2.
243 Cf. Mbiti, African religions and philosophy 1.

understood as a member of the society beginning with the family as an extended unit of the society down to the wider society. In Africa, the family includes the living, the departed and the unborn.[244] The individual does not and cannot exist alone except corporately in communal life. He owes his existence to other people, including those of past generations and his contemporaries. He is simply part of the whole. According to Mbiti, "physical birth is not enough: the child must go through rites of incorporation so that it becomes fully integrated into the entire society."[245] This reveals the process nature of a person which Menkiti echoes as the hallmark of African personhood.[246] Mbiti's Anthropology traces the human person from birth to death and he describes death as the final stage reached when a person dies and he is ritually incorporated into the wider family of both the dead and the living.

The interesting work of Mbiti on the African religions and philosophy belongs to one of those efforts by African authors challenged by Western misrepresentation of the authenticity of African world. In Mbiti's thought one could notice the sharp distinction made between the individual as a member of the society and the individual as one distinct from the society. Hence he wrote:

> Whatever happens to the individual happens to the whole group, and whatever happens to the whole group happens to the individual. The individual can only say: 'I am because we are; and since we are, therefore I am'. This is a cardinal point in the understanding of the African view of man.[247]

Further more, Mbiti affirms in his description of the link between the individual and the community thus: "Just as God made the first man, as God's man, so now man himself makes the individual who becomes the corporate or social man."[248] By this statement he tends to arrogate to the society the authority of 'creating' the person, through a weak analogy.

---

244 Cf. Mbiti, African religions and Philosophy 106, 107.
245 Mbiti, African religions and Philosophy 107.
246 Cf. Ifeanyi, A. Menkiti, "Person and Community in African Traditional Thought", in: African Philosophy, an Introduction², USA 1984 171-172 here 172.
247 Mbiti, African religions and Philosophy 108-109.
248 Mbiti, African religions and Philosophy 108.

Mbiti refers to this process as: "a deeply religious transaction.[249] Unfortunately, it is difficult to see how this shallow anthropocentricism of a deep religious transaction can explain the mystery of man's origin and individual interaction with his God. Taken from Mbiti's analogy, the society would be seen as a representative of a God, who after creating humanity leaves it only at the mercy of the society. In that sense man's direct link with his God would be vitiated, by projecting a representation of the society. Therefore, from this angle it would be very difficult, even to gleam the rich African anthropology from the Christian theological point of view of God as the sole and only creator of man. In this pretext, Mbiti jeopardised the African sense of individualism and communalism to the extent that it could be mistaken for social communism, with little or nothing to do with the Judeo Christian God. This form of romanticism, which is characteristic of the thoughts and works of fore bearers of African philosophy and theology create more epistemological problems than they set out to solve. It was in line with the above problem that Cyril Chukwunonyerem Okorocha, in his book: *The Meaning of Religious Conversion in Africa: The case of the Igbo of Nigeria, 1987* commented on the danger of romantic approach employed by authors like, Mbiti and Idowu in their thesis that,

> African life is inseparably bound up with their religion, to distort the African religion or deny them any true or valid religious experience is the same as to deny them existence or humanness. This protest portrays a feel of an inner compulsion as a result of their own Christian faith, to present Christianity to their fellow Africans in such a way that it may be received without bitterness, and with no 'river between' but on the other hand this has also posed a major obstacle in the way of an objective study of the African religious experience.[250]

The above-described danger is often associated with thinkers, who try to extol the African sense of the community and religion the outcome of which is unsatisfactorily romantic.

Donatus Ibeakwadalam Nwoga's *Nka na Nzere. The Focus of Igbo Worldview* published, by the Culture Division, Ministry of Information,

---

249 Mbiti, African religions and Philosophy 109.
250 Cyril, Chukwunonyerem Okorocha, The Meaning of Religious Conversion in Africa: The case of the Igbo of Nigeria, Aldershot, u.a. 1987 29.

Culture, Youth and Sports, Owerri, 1984 was a subsequent edition of the annual Ahiajoku Lecture series of the Igbo after Michael J. C. Echeruo had delivered the first edition of this lecture series captioned: *Aham Efula (A Matter of Identity),* in which he encouraged the Igbo to search diligently for their identity. In a great manner of reflection as a follow up, Nwoga made a philosophical Journey in the rich and complex worldview of the Igbo, bringing it to the sinews of his audience that *Nka na Nzere* (old age and virtuous life) are the hallmarks of an authentic dignifying life of the Igbo. He made his task clear from the outset:

> What I am about to share with you then is the picture which I have derived from experience, research and interpretation, of the Igbo understanding of the structure of reality in the world and how this affects the operations of man both in society and within the inner recess of the individual person. I hope the picture I present is such that gives rationality and consistency to the behaviour of the Igbo as a people.[251]

Among others, Nwoga made a very important clarification on the notion of reality in Igbo Ontology. Regarding the nature of reality he pointed out that the Igbo recognise the existence of three different entities which sum up to what they understand as real: "In order to understand the Igbo world, it is necessary to accept that the Igbo recognize three types of reality namely, the physical, the spiritual and the abstract".[252] With these three entities in the Igbo ontology meanings can only be realized through conceptualisation.[253] This accounts to a larger extent for the reason why the Igbo are flexible and dynamic in their mentality; and at the same time giving a veritable clue to the understanding of the dualism associated with Igbo meanings and reality.

Nwoga hoped in the end to have proposed a world view that gives coherent, consistent, and adequate explanation of the behaviour observable and predominant among the Igbo by exploring: *(a)* The Igbo perception of the nature of reality. *(b)* The ideas of Igbo social life; and *(c)* The Igbo

---

251 Donatus Ibeakwadalam Nwoga, „Nka na Nzere. The Focus of Igbo Worldview", Ahiajoku Lecture Series, Culture Division, Ministry of Information, Culture, Youth and Sports, Owerri, 1984 2.
252 Nwoga, Nka na Nzere 2.
253 Nwoga, Nka na Nzere 6.

Ideal of the good Life.[254] In this sense his work and effort can be likened to that of Placide Tempels work on the Bantu Ontology, even though he was not a philosopher gave a land breaking insight in the understanding of why the Bantu behaved and believed the way they did[255]. Nwoga never claimed to be a philosopher in the professional sense but produced and achieved far more than a mere philosopher.

In his soul searching work on: *The Supreme God as Stranger in Igbo Religious Thought* published in the same year 1984, Nwoga tackles boldly the presumption among scholars that every religion has a supreme deity, both in the case of civilized religions and traditional religions. He contends that the Igbo traditional thought had no supreme being as collective substance of all other deities. Nwoga argues that *Chukwu* as the resultant supreme creative God found recently in Igbo cosmology was historically derived from the *Aro* deity of the southern part of Igbo land, whose political influence got recognised at a point as *"Chukwu Aro"* – great god of the *Aro*. It was not originally conceived by the Igbo in their metaphysics of God as *'chi'* but with the coming of the missionaries, who were searching for a supreme deity among the Igbo. Finding one, almost parallel to that of the Judeo Christian God the creator *'Chukwu'* became the most appropriate for filling of this lacuna. Hence one could hear the statements from the Igbo: *"Chukwu onye okike"*[256] – God who creates. Echeruo was in agreement with this conclusion when he wrote:

> … Our god is not the ONE towards whom all creation aspires, to paraphrase Plotinus and St. Augustine. He has no heaven and no troop of angels and saints ministering to him. He has promulgated no Decalogue, and he has not appointed a day when he will judge the living and the dead ….[257]

---

254 Nwoga, Nka na Nzere 8.
255 Cf. Placide Tempels, Bantu Philosophy 16ff.
256 Donatus Ibe Nwoga, The Supreme God as Stranger in Igbo Religious Thought, Enugu Nigeria 1984 7.
257 Michael, J.C. Echeruo, "Matter of Identity: Aham Efula", Ahiajoku Lecture Series 1979, Culture Division, Ministry of Information, Culture, Youth and Sports, Owerri 1979 21.

Thus, Nwoga and Echeruo argue that the Igbo traditional thought has remained polytheistic and not monotheistic.

However, an objection was raised by one of the Igbo erudite scholars in the person of Professor Nwachukwu S.S Iwe who argues that the notion of *'Chukwu'* as the supreme God of the Igbo predated the coming of the missionaries, there by extolling the Igbo traditional thought as monotheistic. He cited a writing of a German missionary, whose writing on the Igbo in 1841, confessed that: 'the word *'Tshuku'* God, is continually heard. *Tshuku* is supposed to do everything. Their notions of some of the attributes of the Supreme Being are, in many respects, correct, and their manner of expressing them, striking. 'God made everything: He made both White and Black' is continually on their lips. Some of their parables are descriptive of the perfections of God'. It is evident from the above that the Igbo belief in one Supreme God predated Christianity. He concluded: "It is not a modern theological development arising out of the Christian faith and heritage, as some modern Igbo Scholars would want us to believe."[258]

At this juncture, it might be relevant to note that from the history of ancient religions, not even excluding the Jewish religion, religious concepts and beliefs have continuously evolved. In the Igbo case it may not have been different, without prejudice to historical dates and findings. A hermeneutic inquiry would also reveal that the Igbo religious thought may have evolved into recognising a synthesis in the substance of divinity in form of a supreme deity, with or without the influence of the missionary theologians.

Nwoga succeeded in presenting the Igbo worldview as an erudite indigenous scholar, his phenomenological approach as an indigene produced an emergent human image of the Igbo person whose dignity is not only based on the fact of being human, but most importantly on what one achieves in the course of living. Hence he stated:

> One has first to be a human being. And in the tradition of Igbo assignment of being to action, it is not everything that looks like a human being that is a human being. And so, the question, when somebody is seen to behave in a certain way: *Ihe ọ wụkwadị*

---

[258] Nwachukwu S.S. Iwe, "Igbo Deities", in: The Ahiajoku Lecture (Onugaotu) Colloquium 1988, Culture Division, Ministry of Information, Culture, Youth and Sports, Owerri 1988 23.

mmadụ; ka ọwụ anụ ọhịa? (Is this a human being or a beast?), has meaning in ontological terms, not just in the assessment of behaviour. And in a similar manner the expression *ezigbo mmadụ* (real human being) does not have moral implications only, but also ontological implications.²⁵⁹

Nwoga extolled the Igbo rationality which enable them to abstract reality and by so doing remain docile and dynamic in the face of their world. He emphasised the ontology, which recognises being only in the framework of doing: "with the concepts of mutability of reality and of proper states of being, just being alive is not enough. No condition is permanent and people are to be assessed within the framework of reality not being made of static characteristics but of what beings do".²⁶⁰

Here it is clear that from this Igbo worldview human dignity becomes a mere social construct. Nonetheless, without prejudice to the Igbo sense of dynamism, it will be very difficult to accept any ontology of the Igbo human person as balanced if it is based solely on functionalism and achievement. Consequently, dignity would only be accorded those with the ability to function and to achieve in accordance with a given societal standard.

Sylvanus S. Nwachukwu Iwe's History and Contents of Human Rights: A Study of the History and Interpretation of human Rights; and The Dignity of Man as Foundation of Human Rights: A Message for Nigerians published 1971 and 2000 respectively are among the efforts at interpreting the dignity and rights of the human person by an Igbo (African) indigene. He wrote his first work on the history of human rights shortly after the Nigeria-Biafra pogrom in the late sixties. This was motivated by the experience from a war-turn nation at the wake of reunification after the infrastructural and human devastation. Hence he wrote:

> It is against this sad background of man's inhumanity to his fellow man and of catastrophic violation of human rights that I thought it most topical and a relevant contribution to peace, to base my work on the study of human rights, in the light of the encyclical of Pope John XXIII – *'Pacem in Terris'*.²⁶¹

---

259 Nwoga, Nka na Nzere 17 (Bracket mine).
260 Nwoga, Nka na Nzere 17.
261 Iwe, The History and Contents of Human Rights 19.

Iwe felt the need to set the principle of human rights aright by basing it on the edifying work of the noble Pope John the XXIII, who also wrote after the World War II. Through a historical survey of human rights from the Ancient Greco-Roman world; and by linking them with that of the United Nations Declaration in 1948 Iwe inquired assiduously the nature, basis and content of human rights provisions in the *Pacem in Terris*. Being mainly a historical work *The History and Contents of Human Rights* reviewed the progress and level of reception of the human rights charter in the various regions of the world. In his evaluation of Africa, Iwe expressed an unequivocal disappointment over the region's human rights situation by describing her as: "this darkened part of the world",[262] because according to him Africa could do well if given the chance even if left alone, but the exploiting colonialists have painted the continent and left it in the dark.[263] One had really expected more to have been said over one's own continent but unfortunately it was not the case.

Some years after this publication, Iwe felt the need again to discuss the missing link in the first work, namely the Dignity of man as the foundation of human rights this time, directed as a message for Nigerians. In this work Iwe tried to establish how the basic rights of man derive from, and are directly attributable to, the fundamental characteristics of the human personality.[264] Iwe appealed to biblical sources and Greco-Roman philosophical anthropology to bring home his message that the human personality as the ontological and dynamic embodiment of human nature has intellect and will as its indispensable basis. Liberty remains the most eminent characteristic of the human personality.[265] Iwe concluded his message by asserting that the human personality is the foundation of human dignity and the subject of rights and responsibilities.[266]

---

262 Iwe, The History and Contents of Human Rights 134.
263 Iwe, The History and Contents of Human Rights 134.
264 Cf. Nwachukwuike, S.S. Iwe, The Dignity of Man As The Foundation of Human Rights A Message for Nigerians, Calabar Nigeria 2000 7.
265 Cf. Iwe, The Dignity of Man As The Foundation of Human Rights A Message for Nigerians 17.
266 Iwe, The Dignity of Man As The Foundation of Human Rights A Message for Nigerians 44.

With great erudition in philosophical anthropology Iwe inquired into the nature of human personality, but not focusing these great principles specifically on a people or culture like the Igbo or Africans. As a message directed to the Nigerians one had expected a thorough interpretation of this anthropological theses among the Africans at least. However because of its Greek orientation the basis of mans dignity, as that won from his nature and personal characteristics needs to be further broken down to the Igbo (African) anthropology.

3.3 The Igbo Worldview: A Social-Anthropological Perspective

A worldview or *Weltanschauung* is a stereotype about a people, developed in the course of time and transmitted from one generation to the next. Enthusiasm to present who the Africans are and how they go about their life have presented a variety of stereotypes which span from condemnable reports to glorifying reports of one and the same people. Stereotypes can be positive or negative; constructive or destructive. For instance, to describe Africans as deeply religious people is positive, while classifying them, as merely 'salvage' is negative. To affirm that the Igbo world is a spirit dwelt world would not be simple, but complex because the fundamental basis for such an assertion cannot be easily exhausted. It would surely require that one digs deeper into some sort of social-anthropological as well as religious analysis. Due to the fact that the Igbo and in fact, Africans in general are deeply metaphysical in thinking a face value conclusion might be deceptive.

In his analysis of the Igbo conceptions of reality Donatus I Nwoga[267] pointed out that the Igbo ontology embraces three forms of realities namely, the physical, the spiritual and the abstract or conceptual. The physical embraces what we perceive with our sensory organs; while the spiritual and the abstract or conceptual refer to metaphysics, especially in the conceptualization of their gods and linguistic designation of things such as;

---

267 Nwoga, in the introductory part of his lectures on "Nka na Nzere" exposed the subject: stereotype in the presentation and appreciation of Igbo Worldview.

proverbs and idiomatic constructs. Therefore talking about the worldview of the Igbo without cognisance of the above fact could be risky because the meaning of a thing or a reality can be presented in manifold senses. Consequently, to decipher that, which one might regard as the motivation for a people's actions or what they do in the community; in other words, how a people behave in the community might be misleading at times.[268]

The above-mentioned possibility of deception sets a limitation to the validity of a stereotype in a culture. This limitation will depend on what one seeks to achieve, either on the analytical or the effective aspects of the peoples life. Moreover, in presenting a people's worldview, issues such as language, distance of the communities from each other, and the differences in time of settlement by the various groups that make up a people will have to be put into consideration. The Igbo nation for instance, is a conglomerate of different communities with hazy facts about their origin and migration. Elizabeth Isichei's book, *A history of the Igbo People* was an attempt to answer this question on the Igbo origin. The response of one of her respondents, an elder of Mbaise, in 1972 is quite revealing: "We did not come from anywhere and anyone who tells you we came from anywhere is a liar. Write it down".[269] This blunt but affirmative response points to the fact that the Igbo might not have migrated from anywhere. Nevertheless, some authors dare to construct what might be termed 'outside origin Hypothesis' which contrasts with an 'Ancient Origin Hypothesis'.[270] While the former would locate the origin of the Igbo from the East, from Mecca, from Egypt and elsewhere but always from the East,[271] the later would locate the origin of the Igbo from the Stone Age. These include, Victor C. Uchendu who in his pioneer work in this field succinctly elucidated:

---

268 Cf. Nwoga, "Nka na Nzere", Ahiajoku Lectures 17.
269 Elisabeth Isichei, A History of the Igbo People, London 1976 3.
270 'Outside Origin Hypothesis and Ancient Origin Hypothesis' refer to those hypotheses about the origin and migration of the Igbo from outside the geographical confines of what is known today as Igbo Land. This hypothesis stemming from cultural anthropologists like, C.R. Niven, A Short History of Nigeria, London 1952, cited by S. N. Nwabara, Ibo land: Century of Contact with Britain 1860-1960, London 1977 17; Frank Hives, Jaja and Justice in Nigeria, London 1968 248-252; See also, Emmanuel M. Edeh, Towards an Igbo Metaphysics, Chicago 1985 11.
271 Cf. Niven, A Short History of Nigeria 23.

The belt formed by Owerri, Awka, Orlu and Okigwe divisions constitutes this nuclear area. Its people have no traditions of coming from any other place. We assume an early immigration from this area into Nsukka-Udi highlands in the North, and into Ikwerre, Etche, Asa and Ndoki in the South and the eastern Isuama claim to have come from this centre. Ngwa tradition points to their secondary immigration from Mbaise.[272]

M. C. English based his own argument for a possible Ancient Origin Hypothesis on the postulation that with the separation of the Sahara desert at the end of the Stone Age people moved from there to the north and south of Africa, but not to what is known today as Nigeria because, she was already inhabited.[273] In line with M. C. English, Edeh confirms that Stone Age implements have been found at different points in Nigeria.[274] This shows in the words of Isichei, that "men have been living in Igbo land for at least 5,000 years, since the dawn of human history ...."[275] From the above discrepant sources and assertions on the origin of the present Igbo settler Columbus Ogbujah made bold to conclude that the evidences of the two hypothesis; Outside Origin and Ancient Origin Hypothesis of the origin of the Igbo is not clear. Hence he asserts:

> The Igbo as thus delineated has been faced with controversies regarding their origin and specific location in history. Igbo ethnologists and historians have fashioned out two hypotheses, each of which, nevertheless, is fraught with incongruity and a replete of traditions that have no relation to each other.[276]

Therefore, the Igbo as a people are a nation and not just a village as some have mistakenly thought it to be. They are different peoples with varied origins. Consequently, to form a stereotype that would truly represent the entire Igbo reality one must acknowledge the limitations placed by the above historical and ethnological complications discussed above. It

---

272 Uchendu, The Igbo of Southeast Nigeria 3.
273 Cf. M. C. English, An Outline of Nigerian History, London 1959 6.
274 Edeh, Towards Igbo Metaphysics 13.
275 Isichei, A History of the Igbo People 3.
276 Columbus N. Ogbujah, The Idea of Personhood A study in Igbo (African) Philosophical Anthropology, Enugu 2006 85.

means also that any attempt at forming a new stereotype about the Igbo peoples can be challenging, because the experiences and historical factors that make up a worldview of a people continue to run in a great flux. Nevertheless, a valid stereotype remains inevitable in the life and history of a people. But most recapitulations in forms of synthesis are speculations, and no matter how poor they may seem, also contribute to the general discussion about a people's worldview. Since it is through a careful synthesis of the various narratives that a comprehensive narrative of a people can emerge, the relevance of creating stereotypes in the presentation of people's way of life remains a necessary risk.[277]

Still on the point, creating a viable stereotype about a people draws attention to the relevant operational concepts prevalent among them. The use, which a people make of the concepts in their daily experience, is a veritable key to understanding their worldview. In the day to day encounter with the realities around them, human beings develop a complex whole of their beliefs and attitudes concerning the origin, natures, organisation and interaction of beings in the universe with particular reference to man.[278] It is through reflecting on the conceptualities in a culture that one can gain assess to the meaning of a particular reality prevalent there. Consequently, the complex interaction of these conceptions forms the worldview of a people. On this note Uchendu, pointed to the need for understanding, in the first place the *'Sinn des Lebens'* and the consequent *'Weltanschauung'* there from. Hence he opined:

> To know how a people view the world around them is to understand how they evaluate life; and a people's evaluation of life, both temporal and non-temporal, provides them with a 'character' of action, a guide to behaviour. The Igbo world, in all its aspects-material, spiritual and socio-cultural is made intelligible to the Igbo by their cosmology, which explains how everything came into being.[279]

From the above it becomes clear that, in the search for a conception of human dignity among the Igbo, their cosmology should be the first port

---

277 Cf. Nwoga, Nka Na Nzere 3.
278 Cf. Emefie Ikenga Metuh, Comparative Studies of African Traditional Religions, Onitsha-Nigeria 1996 61.
279 Victor C. Uchendu, The Igbo of South East Nigeria 11.

of call. That means in effect that it is in their religious beliefs and socio anthropological realities we can glimpse their conceptualisation of human dignity. At this juncture, it is important first and foremost to enquire into the human image operative among the Igbo Africans, which is in turn informed by their cosmology.

3.3.1 The Igbo Cosmology

To conceive a genuine and well-constructed Igbo African cosmology is far fetched. Chinua Achebe sadly remarked that the cosmology of the Igbo is marked with so many metaphors, myths and even sometimes poetry simply because no one till date has been able to construct a standard and scientific thought that can explain systematically the whole dynamics of creation for instance and the relationships existing in the universe.[280] Therefore, he cautions:

> Since Igbo people did not construct a rigid and closely argued system of thought to explain the universe and the place of man in it, preferring the Metaphor of myth and poetry, anyone seeking an insight into their world must seek it along their own way. Some of these ways are folk tales, proverbs, proper names, rituals, and festivals. There is of course the 'scientific' way as well as the tape-recorded interview with old people. Unfortunately it is often more impressive than useful.[281]

The above citation suggests a peculiar difficulty in the discussion of the Igbo cosmology in particular and Africa in general. Recognising this fact, V.C. Uchendu in his treatment of Igbo cosmology distinguished three ways of approaching cosmology. These are: cosmology as theory of origin and character of the universe; cosmology as a system of prescriptive ethics; and cosmology as an action system.[282] Cosmology as theory of origin and character of the universe concerns itself with the stories and myths of creation. That means, the actual narratives of how things in the cosmos were created in succession. Here the concrete time, way and

---

280 Cf. Chinua Achebe, "Chi" in Igbo Cosmology 67.
281 Chinua Achebe, "Chi" in Igbo Cosmology 67.
282 Uchendu, The Igbo of South East Nigeria 11.

manner would be necessary for an acceptable creation narrative. The second dealing with cosmology as system of prescriptive ethics deals with the people themselves; what interpretations and imputes they make of the world around them. In other words, the experience they make in the course of time and the influence the environment impresses on their mentality. Finally, cosmology as an action system speaks of the phenomenal existence of the people, who as a result of their understanding of their world now act in specific manner, which distinguishes them as a unique culture among others.

However, our preoccupation in this cosmological inquiry is going to be limited to the last two of the above-mentioned three-dimensional systems of handling cosmology generally. We are going to be concerned mainly with Igbo cosmology as it relates to Igbo moral system i.e., of their dos and don'ts in the community. Also of great importance in this inquiry will be the action system, which refers to their lives as they live it in the community. But the first approach, which is the theory of origins and character of the Igbo will not bother us. The system narratives of the creation of the world and all that is in it as we have them in the Genesis the first book of the bible for instance; and a myriad of Igbo creation myths may not be important in the definition of our research objectives.

The choice of a system of cosmology, which is based on the morality and ethics of the Igbo, offers us the chance of accessing the metaphysics as well as the psychology of the people. Igbo worldview is founded on their metaphysics, which resonates always in their deep sense of religion. It will not be an exaggeration to point out that religion seems to override every aspect of the socio-cultural lives of the African in general and Igbo in particular, as Ikenna Nzimiro succinctly put it:

> Society and morality are bound together by their (the Igbo) cosmological concepts and the social organisation of their institutions is sustained by their metaphysical views about life and the universe. Their religious beliefs provide support for law and order, and in particular *"Ala"*, the deity of the land, is the supreme moral sanction.[283]

---

[283] Ikenna Nzimiro, Studies in Ibo Political Systems. Chieftaincy and Politics in Four Niger States, London 1972 3 [sic].

In the narrative of the Igbo worldview cosmogony plays a very vital role in interpreting and transmitting the Igbo ideologies, experiences and believes. Through folklores and myths, which are presented in forms of story tales, idiomatic expressions, proverbs and symbols the world of the Igbo is embellished so that it shines forth more perceptible.

3.3.1.1 The Igbo World as "Spirit-Dwelt"

Perhaps the first Igbo (African) stereotypes found in world narratives and literatures are those concerned with their religious and spiritual attitudes, which are engraved in the relationship between man and his world. The Africans in general perceived the world first and foremost, as a spirit-dwelt world. The Igbo world is made up of human beings and the spirits. It is a real world where the two spheres interact with each other in every respect. According to Elisabeth Isichei,

> The Igbo were nothing if not profoundly religious, and all account of their life reflects the fact ... To the Igbo, the secular and the sacred, the natural and the supernatural are a continuum. Supernatural forces continually impinge on life, and must be propitiated by appropriate prayers and sacrifices.[284]

Writing about the Igbo in the early 1900, Major A.G. Leonard in his book *The Lower Niger and Its Peoples* remarked that:

> They are in the strict and natural sense of the word a truly and a deeply religious people, of whom it can be said that they eat religiously, drink religiously, bathe religiously, dress religiously and sin religiously. In a few words, the religion of these as I have all along endeavoured to point out is their existence and their existence is their religion.[285]

This observation is not only true of the Igbo but also of other Africans. J.S. Mbiti more than fifty years later in the opening sentence of the very first chapter of his book, *African Religions and Philosophy* has re-echoed similar statement which summarized the traditional religious attitude of Africans when he said,

---

284 Isichei, A History of the Igbo People 24
285 A. G. Leonard, The Lower Niger and its Tribes, London 1956 185

Africans are notoriously religious, and each people have its own religious system with a set of beliefs and practices. Religion permeates into all the departments of life so fully that it is not easy or possible always to isolate it. A study of these religious systems is therefore, ultimately a study of the people themselves in all complexities of both traditional and modem life. Religion is the strongest element in traditional background, and exerts probably the greatest influence upon the thinking and living of the people concerned.[286]

Similarly, after observing how religion thoroughly permeated the life of every Igbo, Bishop Shanahan was cited by John P. Jordan (1971:115) as having come to the conclusion that:

The average native *(Igbo)*, was admirably suited by environment and training, for an explanation of life in terms of the spirit; rather than of the flesh. He was no materialist. Indeed nothing was farther from his mind than a materialist philosophy of existence. It made no appeal to him.[287]

It is very necessary here to stress the role of duality in the Igbo worldview. This duality, rather than being a sought of contrast in the Igbo cosmology as it is the case in the Western concept of "good and evil"[288] is complementary. This complementary character is often noticed in the Igbo linguistic usage, where two words meaning the same thing complement each other to create a stress of the situation. For instance *okwu na uka*-speech and talk mean almost the same thing but here the *okwu*-speech (positive gift) combines with *uka*-mere talk (a negative lazy man's habit of shattering) to describe a trouble situation. Hence *okwu na uka*

---

286 J. S. Mbiti, African religions and Philosophy, London-Ibadan-Nairobi 1969 1.
287 John P. Jordan, Bishop Shanahan of Southern Nigeria, Elo Press Dublin 1971 115.
288 The doctrine of the Manicheans on the good and evil presented always two sides of reality: Good and evil as two separate substantial principles in the world. According to this teaching, God is both the source of good and evil in the universe. Whereas for the Igbo, evil is not substantial but anthropologically generated in the human social relationships. Man is the source of evil-*Mmadu bu njo ala* as the Igbo would say.

means for the Igbo; trouble or a palaver situation[289]. In some cases two contrasting words, differing in meaning when considered in isolation come together to embrace each other in order to show that the Igbo metaphysics of reality is embracive not divisive or exclusive. For instance words like *oke na nne*-meaning male and female, *esekere na edima*-big and small combine two realities, which could be opposite when taken apart to form an embracive and holistic meaning.

The Igbo believe like the Platonists in a world that is separated from our present world of experiences. These physical and spiritual entities are but two dimensions of one and the same universe. These dimensions dovetail into each other so much so that at times and in some places one is apparently more real than, but not exclusive of the other. In the words of J. S. Mbiti: For Africans, this religious universe is not an intellectual preposition: it is an empirical experience, which reaches its height in acts of worship.[290] The Igbo proverb: *Ihe kwuru, Ihe akwudebe ya,* meaning when a thing stands, another stands by it, shows that nothing exists on its own. It must be connected necessarily with something outside. Just like Chinua Achebe puts it:

> The world in which we live has its double and counterpart in the realm of spirits. A man lives here and his *"Chi"* there. Indeed the human being is only one half (and the weaker half at that) of a person. There is a complementary spirit being, *'Chi'*.[291]

The picture we are trying to paint is that of the world of the Igbo man that is mixed up with the Spirits; a spirit dwelt world. It is a world, loosely separated into two namely, the *ala mmuo* – the spirit world and the *elu uwa* – the land of man. Such a vision of a world would definitely colour the explanation of realities and challenges facing man. The spirits would be seen as occupying the mysterious positions in the explanation of reali-

---

289 'Palaver' in African usage means; a local communal way of settling issues among the people. For the Igbo specifically, it means problem or trouble-*okwu na uka* (speeches and talks). For further readings in African Palaver, See Bénézet Bujo, Die ethische Dimension der Gemeinschaften. Das afrikanische Modell im Nord-süd-Dialog, Freiburg 1993.
290 J. S. Mbiti, African religions and Philosophy 1969 57.
291 Chinua Achebe, "Chi" in Igbo Cosmology, 67.

ties beyond the immediate knowledge of the Igbo people. This superiority exercised by the spirit world the *Ala mmuo* over the world of man – *Elu uwa* explains also the Igbo preference of heteronomy[292] in their interpretation of human dignity.

3.3.1.2 The Spirit World "Ala Mmuo"

This is the abode of *"Chi"* the creator, the deities, the disembodied and malignant spirits, and the ancestral spirits – *"ndi iche"*. Ala mmuo is the future settlement of the living after death. The interaction between the world of the living and the world of the dead makes it possible to conceive the Igbo lineage as an unbroken one. An Igbo sees himself as going to join his ancestors after his death and also coming back in the human world through the process of reincarnation.[293] Therefore, the world of the Igbo remains one full of activities, which continues even in the spirit world after the earthly life. In this sense, death is no longer an escape from earthly hardship and reality; not even an escape from punishment and reward rather a continuation in the next. Hence the Igbo would say: *"Onye m kariri na-mmadu, akariri m ya n'ala mmuo"*, (My inferior in life, remains so in the spirit-world, meaning in the next life). One can see in this proverb the concept of continuity and interaction in the two worlds.

The abode of *"Chi"* (god) is in heaven above while the abode of "the living dead" – the dead ancestors and other spirits is under the Earth. Some times confusions abound over the distinction of these two kingdoms, *'ala mmuo'* spirit land and the abode of *Chi 'eligwe'* above. Both parallel supernatural worlds can be confusing at times. In an early anthropological

---

292 Heteronomy refers to the system of interpretation, which considers God or a metaphysical entity as the source and basis of human dignity. It differentiates from the autonomy system, which emphasises the role of reason and human will. For further readings on heteronomy and autonomy see, Paul Tiedemann, *Was ist Menschenwürde? Eine Einführung*, Germany 2006 33-67.

293 Reincarnation – *"ilo uwa"* is the Igbo belief in the soul as being born again after death. The human being comes back after his death in the resemblance of the ancestors who are the dead members of the lineage. For further readings see, John Obilor, *The* Doctrine of the Resurrection of the Dead and the Igbo Belief in the Reincarnation. Frankfurt am Main 1994.

study of the Igbo, A. G. Leonard at the beginning of this century documented the following account from one of his Igbo narrators:

> We Igbo look forward to the next world as being much the same as this ... we picture life there to be exactly as it is in this world. The ground there is just the same as it is here, the earth is similar. There are forests and hills and valleys with rivers flowing and roads leading from one town to another .... People in spirit land have their ordinary occupation, the farmer his farm.[294]

This "spirit land" where dead ancestors recreate a life comparable to their earthly existence is not only parallel to the human world but is also similar and physically contiguous with it, for there is constant coming and going between them in the endless traffic of life, death, and reincarnation. The masked spirits, the *mmaw*-Masquerades who often grace human rituals and ceremonies with their presence are representative visitors from this underworld and are said to emerge from their subterranean home through the ant holes. At least that is the story as told to the uninitiated. To those who know, however, the masked "spirits" are only symbolic ancestors. But this knowledge does not in any way diminish their validity or the awesomeness of their presence.

3.3.1.3 The Land of the Living "Elu uwa"

The land of the living comprises all created things including human beings themselves, (not excluding the yet to be born); animals, plants, objects-animate and inanimate, rivers, streams, sees and oceans; the sky and the earth. Among all these beings, man understands himself as the crown of all creation. The human being positions himself at the centre of the cosmos so that he determines the meaning he makes of each and every one of them. The authority exercised over non human beings, however does not repudiate the respect the Igbo man has for his environment. Most often these non human beings are worshiped and respected because of the functions they perform in the service of man or what man has made out of them. Mbiti remarks on some animals and trees held sacred by the Africans. Such animals like, birds, tortoise, snakes and also trees are respected and

---

294 A. G. Leonard, The Lower Niger and its Tribes 185-186.

some times worshiped.[295] In the same vein, the sky *"Eligwe"* and the earth *"Ala"* are worshiped together with the rivers, mountains and hills because of their significance in the world of man through their awesomeness.

3.3.1.4 The Igbo World as Real and Dynamic

The Igbo world is dynamic and real. People not only seek for equality but also accept changes as they occur. The Igbo see the world as operating, with a system of intrinsic dualities such that good and evil can come from the same universe. Basically, the world confronts every Igbo person with both moral evil and moral good, with existential creativity as well as natural destructiveness.[296] It is through this maze of a world of dualities that the Igbo person has to move, with his wits around him, in the pursuit of the goals of life. An old Igbo sage once put it brilliantly: *ụwa wụ mgbanwe mgbanwe*. (The world is in a state of change).

The relationship in the community is reciprocal and it remains the basic organising principle of Igbo social relationship. Hence the Igbo used to say: *"Ugwu bu nkwanye nkwanye, nwanyi amuta ibe ya"* (Dignity is a side by side respect and recognition by both parties). Since the spiritual and social worlds are contractually related, there is always the fear that the terms of the contract might not be fully honoured by their parties: the spirits often change their mind as do men. This uncertainty does not perturb the Igbo especially because he knows that social relationships can be manipulated. Through mutual interdependence and his ability to manipulate his world, the Igbo individual tries to achieve equality or near equality in both the world of man and the world of the spirits.[297]

A painstaking glance at the Igbo society will reveal a prevalent tendency among the people towards status acquisition in life. There is this race after titles and positions in forms of *'chief, ezeji, nze* and *ozo'* titles. In a metaphorical sense, an Igbo man percieves the world as a market place where one comes and buys as much as he is capable of buying. These titles stand for the Igbo as status symbol by which he can be recognised in the society. A special class structure is formed in Igbo land

---

295 Cf. Mbiti, African religions and Philosophy 51.
296 Nwoga, "Nka na Nzere" 15.
297 Cf. Uchendu, The Igbo of South East Nigeria 15.

through attainment of specific social status. For instance, those who hold various *Ozo* titles in the society are given a special status symbol. In fact, individuals fear low status in the community because they believe that this status continue even after death in the reincarnation – *ilo uwa*.[298] According to Uchendu,

> ... The social importance of reincarnation is that it provides the 'idea system' that rationalizes, interprets, accommodates, or rejects changes and innovations as well as tolerates certain character traits. Furthermore, it is at reincarnation that the individual works out a proper role for himself through face-to-face interaction with the creator (his *chi*).[299]

In this bargain between man and his *'chi'*[300] he struggles to come to terms with his *chi* to bequeath him fortune and fame and these are made manifest in his earthly riches and wealth; titles accumulated, fame and dominance. When successful in the above-illustrated sense he is said to have chosen well with his *chi,* and when not then he has chosen very badly and would desire another chance in the next world to make amends. Our main interest in these illustrations is to point out the influence of the belief in reincarnation in the socio-anthropological reality of the Igbo. We do not wish to go into details of this Igbo belief on reincarnation, neither are we interested in the judgement of its religious tenability in Christian teachings.

A socialised person in the Igbo sense of the word is one who maintains an open relationship in the community. The social relationship in the community counts as prior to every other form of privacy one may presume to keep. It is a strong weapon against evil in the society especially against fellow human beings. Relationships are purely social and transparent. Still on the point, Uchendu concludes:

---

298 In the Reincarnation as we have explained before, the soul returns back to the earth through a process, which the Igbo call "ilọ ụwa". A soul of a particular ancestor can come back as many times as necessary.
299 Uchendu, The Igbo of South East Nigeria, 16.
300 'Chi' in Igbo cosmology may mean different things: Chi- god, (creator or personal God), guardian Angel, destiny (aka), providence and the day. Cf. Chinua Achebe, "Chi" in Igbo Cosmology, in Emmanuel, C. Eze, African Philosophy: Anthology, USA 1989 67-72. In this sense, we mean a bargain with one's guardian Angel.

The concept of the good life among the Igbo is so built on the transparency theme that the individual dreads any form of loss of face. The Major deterrent to crime is not guilt-feeling but feeling of shame.[301]

3.3.2 Morality in Igbo African Society: A Socio-anthropocentric Concept

The concepts of evil and good in the Igbo worldview present human beings at the centre of the entire moral framework. Hence the Igbo would say: *"Mmadu bu njo ala"* (the human being is the cause of evil in the community). Consequently the causes and the remedies would have to be sought among the human relationships in the community. This explains the reason why the whole meaning of existence or rather the essence of life for the Igbo is to maintain a cosmic balance and equilibrium in the cosmos, which as it were remains dynamic and never static. Constant effort in forms of morality and taboos are placed in order to hinder the distortion of the cosmic equilibrium. This can be caused by sin or wickedness of human beings in the community.

Whenever an imbalance occurs in the society, a counter action is made to counteract the effect on the living in the community. Sin is understood purely from its socio-anthropological conception because the Igbo believe strongly that every known violation of the natural order has a consequence on the community. For Sundermeier:

> What is not known has no impact, and so can be regarded as not having happened. But anything that challenges society must be put in order again, by society and not by the individual acting alone.

---

301 Uchendu, The Igbo of South East Nigeria, 17; Cf, John S. Mbiti, African religions and Philosophy 213: "it is not necessarily the act in itself which would be 'wrong' as such, but the relationships involved in the act: if relationships are not injured or hurt or even damaged, and if there is no discovery of breach of custom or regulation, then the act is not 'evil' or 'wicked' or 'bad'"; Cf. Theo Sundermeier, The Individual and Community in African Traditional Religions 191.

The problem of evil shows, that African ethics is fundamentally social ethics, and is understood as such.[302]

In almost every cases of death in the community, some individual's violation of customs and tradition in the society will be responsible. Death remains the greatest catastrophe and a calamity, because it takes away human life, which is the greatest gift of *Chi* to man. Consequently, to ascertain the causes of sickness, epidemics, catastrophe and ultimately death remains a great challenge in the community. The services of the diviners and the medicine men would always be needed in this regard and most often it is attributed to the anger of the gods because of some misbehaviour of some individuals in the society.

The Igbo believe that evil emanates essential from human activities. Sin is always viewed in the socio-anthropological terms. The human being has always been located at the centre of the dynamics of morality in the society. The Igbo would always emphasis that, *"mmadu bu njọ ala"* (man makes the country wicked) it is the human person who "spoils" the country and not the spirits. On this note, Theo Sundermeier vividly asserts: "Evil in the African philosophy and religions is an anthropological reality, no more and no less. Human beings experience evil and know that people can be evil."[303] Evil is experienced as the destruction of interpersonal relationships. It is not tied to an eternal or abstract law. Rather it is placed on a social relational system, which more or less functions as a social ethic. Sundermeier explains:

> In Africa there is no such law but only the living law of tradition, which determines the present. Common life makes human beings and anyone violating this prepares the ground for evil. Evil does not exist without people: evil-doers have to bear the consequence, as well as victims.[304]

---

302 Cf. Sundermeier, The Individual and Community in African Traditional Religions 192.
303 Sundermeier, The Individual and Community in African Traditional Religions 190.
304 Sundermeier, The Individual and Community in African Traditional Religions 191.

The above view presents a simple socio-anthropologicaly based moral system, which recognises the common life as the only yardstick or standard for measuring what is good and evil in any given African society.

3.3.3 The Sense of Struggle and Egalitarianism among the Igbo

The Igbo world is one in which change is expected. Change constitutes a permanent feature of the Igbo reality. This includes adjustment to status and role structure, as an adjustment to the world around them. An Igbo person struggles through life to improve his lot; he struggles to change his position and status in life believing that he chose his roles; the Igbo person is constrained to make a success of his social position or career. In effect, the Igbo stress on the success goal is ideologically rooted in the reincarnation.[305] The spirit of daring in gainful ventures accompanies the day-to-day story of the Igbo. In fact it is often said in one of the Igbo prodigious proverbs that, "one who is overcautious of his life is always killed by the fall of a dry leaf". For a typical Igbo life must be faced and its problems overcome as is epitomised in their philosophy of *"uwa bu ndoli ndoli"* meaning, life is full of struggles. A life of struggle is far much preferred than death, *"kama m ga anwu ka m doliwa, uwa bu ndoli ndoli"* meaning, instead of giving up to die, let me continue to struggle to make ends meet, because life is full of struggles. Consequently, suicide is considered an abomination among the Igbo. Who ever that takes his life or commits suicide will never receive honourable burial. This is because the ancestors would not receive such a coward, who could not face the challenges of his life while here on earth. It is believed that in the next world such a weakling would continue with such a vice. Therefore such a death is loathsome to the Igbo. This can account for the minimal rate of suicide cases among the Igbo and perhaps among many other African tribes despite the frustrations encountered by the people. When we compare the Igbo African experiences of suicide with those of the European experiences in this regard the difference will be clear. For the Africans life is dignity while for the Europeans and in fact for the entire northern hemisphere dignity is life. We shall come back to this fact latter in this inquiry. It is pertinent here to note that freedom of the individual engen-

---

305 Cf. Uchendu, The Igbo of South East Nigeria 19.

dered by the African culture supports this success drive in every healthy normal individual in the Igbo traditional society.

The Igbo worldview on human being is that every human being is equal in principle. This equalitarian principle however, leads to an obstacle to the development of a strong central authority. Hence the saying: *"Igbo enwe Eze"* meaning, the Igbo has no King. That not withstanding, sex distinctions especially in roles and statues abound in the traditional Igbo society like every other human society. What the Igbo mean by an equalitarian society is that which gives to all its citizens an equal opportunity to achieve success. Thus a child will qualify for higher position through hard work and exemplary life. This fosters in the traditional society a form of conciliar and democratic socio-political atmosphere.[306] On this note Cyril Agodi Onwumechili, in his *2000 Ahiajoku Lectures* concludes:

> Our conclusion is that the implications of *Igbo Enwe Eze* are democratic, Self-reliant, scientific, modern and in tune with the best traditions of human kind. Indeed, in modern times, nations that have kings have been divesting them of political and religious powers that used to be their royal prerogatives.[307]

In this sense the Igbo adage: "when a child washes his hand clean he eats with the elders" mirrors the kind of Igbo social structure, which even though so respectful of elders and positions still creates room for a competitive ascendance to honour and recognition. It implies a sense of moral and right pattern of integration and development. Among the Igbo the human person is understood as a bundle of possibilities. This is buttressed in their philosophical question: *"echi di ime onye ma ihe oga amu?"* (Tomorrow is pregnant; who knows what it will bear). Through concerted efforts, a no body can rise to become a leader or an *"Eze"* (the king of his community) tomorrow, for a leader normally emerges. Hence the Igbo would often ask: *a humara eze ama?* (No one has the monopoly or kingship, or set aside from birth as a monarch), that means it can be any body that qualifies for elevation into position or status.

---

306 Cf. Uchendu, The Igbo of South East Nigeria 21.
307 Cyril Agodi Onwumechili, "Igbo Enwe Eze: The Igbo Has no Kings", Ahiajoku Lecture Series 2000, Culture Division, Ministry of Information, Culture, Youth and Sports, Owerri 2000 16.

Acquisition of status leads to the conclusion, that one has to struggle for a better position while alive in order to continue in the next one (reincarnation). It is an equalitarian society in which the leader, even though he or she has the authority to lead his people receives just a little means but will be expected to be optimal in his functions.

3.3.4 Influences and Manipulation of Forces in Igbo Metaphysics

The world of the Igbo is that, influenced by both visible and invisible forces. It is a world comprising the living and the dead; not excluding those yet to be born. It remains a world of interaction between these forces and personalities. Their social life is guarded by an ontological conviction that: forces can be manipulated, either for one's own growth in the society or to the detriment of the whole social life. The ability, however to manipulate these forces above other members of the society is a sign of virility and achievement. Placid Tempels described a Bantu man as a living cause capable of live influences.[308] This anthropological or psychological view of man presents the individual as linked with others. Hence no one can stand on his own without the community. He is certain of the fact that he is vital force, who stays constantly in connection with the other vital forces. He knows that he can, at any giving opportunity practice this vital force on others and at the same time can receive such influences from others.[309] The Igbo like the Bantus place man at the centre of the universe with an interconnection that one cannot easily disentangle. This accounts for their (the Igbo) socio-anthropological dimension of worldview. Every power in the Igbo society can be successfully manipulated. Not only deities and spiritual forces are manipulated, but also witchcraft has the capacity to manipulate human beings and social relationships in the society. Therefore the individual in the community has to be protected both from within and from without by the various agnates[310] in

---

308 Cf. Placide Tempels, Bantu Philosophie Ontologie und Ethik, Heidelberg 1956 62.
309 Cf. Placide Tempels, Bantu Philosophie Ontologie und Ethik, Heidelberg 64.
310 Uchendu describes Agnates as referring to the 'patrilineal kinsfolk'. They are men and women to whom one is related through males only. In other

the society. For instance, the *"Umune/Ibenne" (Mother's agnates among whom the individual enjoys the "Okene" privileges)* stands as a defence against the injustice, which may surge against the individual in his or her father's agnate, the *"Umunna"*. We shall return to this theme later.

3.4 Life is Paramount "Ndu bu isi" in Igbo (African) Worldview

Another popular stereotype of the African worldview is that on their value for life. For the African the foundation of every human activity is existence. Africans understand life as the moving force behind every existence and human activities. This primary important act – *to be* is the *"ndu"*. Life as the basis of existence receives the highest position of value in the African scale of value. Hence, among the Igbo, life is paramount *"ndu bu isi"*, and greater than everything and every relationship. For the Igbo, life is greater than dignity, more valuable than wealth. It is the greatest gift of *"chi"* god to man. Life is strength, that strength that a corpse has totally lost.[311] Africans in general, believe that life remains the primary category for self-understanding, and provides that basic framework for any interpretation of the world, persons, nature or divinity. Thus the Igbo say: *"adi ndu achowa ihe aga eme n'uwa."* (If there is life, then one can propose what to do in the world). Thus life remains the conditio sine qua non of every human existence and activities. For this reason, Africans value life above every other thing. Charles Nyamiti, expressing the immensity of life in African thought remarks: "Life is essential power ... one can almost say that for an African life is another word for *Vital-Force*."[312]

In his investigations on the ontology of the Bantus, Placid Tempels described the strongest basis of the Bantu reality as their belief in the

---

    words, a descent link from a man to a child is called an agnatic link while a descent link from a woman to a child is called a 'uterine' link. A social group tracing descent through males only is an agnatic group.
311 Cf. Theophilus Okere, *Odenigbo-Chibundu*, Owerri 1997 66-67.
312 Charles Nyamiti, "The Incarnation Viewed from the African Understanding of Person", in: ACS 6 (1990) 1, 3-27, here 8; Placid Tempels, La philosophie bantoue, Belgian-Congo-Lovania 1945 32.

"Vital force". It is the source and origin of energy in every living thing. Every existing thing must possess this vital force for it to be. Vital force is possessed in grades and forms, each category of being according to its own capacity. The Human person *"Muntu"* possesses a greater share of this force and can also manipulate it. In short, the Bantu, perceive the human person – *the Muntu,* as a "force" itself. Consequently this ability and privilege of manipulation in the *"Muntu"* confers upon him a dignity over and above other created beings. The Igbo philosophy of *"ndu bu isi"* Life is supreme subordinates every form of materialism which ultimately leads to the destruction of the concept of human life in the culture of the people.[313] The Igbo believe in the saying that life is far greater than wealth, *"ndu ka aku"; ndu* is the most precious, holiest and greatest gift of nature. Man loves it and loves to have it long and abundantly. Edmond Ilogu acceding to this primacy of life affirmed that in the Igbo system of things, life, the good life, is the *summum bonum* or highest value in nature.[314] Mbiti remarks how the African peoples so confidently ask for life as if it is a tangible thing, especially in their prayers: "We have come, *Odo* (God), to ask for life, help us to cling to it. Hasten to help us cling to life".[315]

Another aphorism of the Igbo is: *Ndu dika aguu; ona agu onye, ona agu ibe ya* (Every human being has an innate desire to live just as he instinctively longs to eat).[316] The significant belief in the supremacy of life is portrayed in personal names like, *Ndu bu isi,* (life is supreme); *Osonduagwuike,* (One is never tired of the struggle for survival); *Chinwendu,* (life belongs to God); *Chibundu,* (God is Life).[317] Life *(ndu)* in the Igbo-

---

313 Cf. Oliver Onwubiko, African Thought, Religion and Culture, Enugu 1991 23.
314 Cf. Edmund Ilogu, Christianity and Igbo Culture, New York-Enugu 1974 124.
315 J. S. Mbiti, The Prayers of African Religion, London 1975 36, 44.
316 Cf. George Maduakolam Okorie, The Integral Salvation of the Human Person in Ecclesia in Africa A case study of the theological implications among the Igbo in Nigeria, Frankfurt am Main 2008 330.
317 Cf. Peter C. Uzor, The traditional African Concept of God and the Christian Concept of God Chukwu bu ndu-God is life (the Igbo Perspective). Frankfurt am Main – Berlin – Bern – Bruxelles – New York – Oxford – Wien 2004, 257.

African traditional set up is considered sacred. Life ought to be whole and honourable. It should be long (*ogologo ndu*) and peaceful[318]. The members of the Igbo-African community greet one another with a wish for long life and prosperity – *iga adi ndu ogologo* (May you live long!). Hence sudden and unprovided death remains a catastrophe to an Igbo person. He is afraid of death – *"Onwu dim egwu"* and implores death to stay far away from him and his loved ones: *"Onwubiko"* oh death! Please have mercy, spear me!

It is a taboo to shed blood in the traditional African communities. Taking of ones life or another's life is an evil; an abomination. Among the Igbo, no child should be described as unwanted no matter the circumstance of the birth, hence the Igbo say: *ebe nwa si, ya hiri* (Wherever a child comes from, let it be). Abortion of any kind remained abhorring to the traditional Igbo society. One can read in the Igbo names the value, respect and love the Igbo accord to life as supreme principle of human existence. Names like, *Ifeyinwa* – (Nothing can be compared to a child); *Nwadimkpa*, (A child is precious); *Nwadiuto*, (A child is sweet); *Nwaamaka*, (A child is good and beautiful); *Nwakaego*, (A child is precious than gold – money); *Nwabugwu*, (A child is dignity or honour); *Chinenyenwa*, (God is the giver of child); *Chinwenwa*, (God is the owner of child).

From the above analysis it is clear that life-*Ndu*, for the African, stands supreme above every other human value. It is the foundation for dignity in the traditional Igbo African communities.

3.4.1 "Chi bu Ndu" God is Life for the Igbo (African)

The concept of a being so fundamental to man's existence in the world reverberates in the African ontology. *Chi* the god of the Igbo is alive in Himself, *Chibundu*. The word *chi* presents an epistemological challenge because of its varied usage in Igbo metaphysics. God is the source of every thing that is in the world, He is the source of life. Some Igbo names represent the conceptual forms of God, *chi* among them. Names such as, *"Onyekachi?"* who is greater than God; *"Onyedikachi?"* who is like

---

318 Cf. Peter, k. Sarpong, "Growth or Decay: Can Christianity Dialogue with African Traditional Religion?" in: Bulletin 69 (1988) 189-206 here 201.

God? clarify the position of *chi* in the life of the Igbo (Africans on the whole). The various functions and usages of *chi* in the Igbo traditional religion[319] also account for the dualism predominant in Igbo metaphysics. In Igbo ontology the same reality can be represented in three dimensions namely, reality as physical entity, reality as spiritual entity and reality as conceptual entity.[320] When an Igbo conceptualise the word *chi* for instance, he makes it complex for a foreigner to understand. He may conceptualise God *chi* in a physical individual by affirming: *Mmadu bu chi ibe ya,* man can be a god to the other. That occurs when some one is dependent on another for survival. At another occasion *chi* can also be conceptualised as a spirit or ones guardian Angel. This occurs when one recognises *chi* as the unseen force and principle of one's existence. *Chi* can also be understood as a total sum of ones fortune, fate or lot. Simon Eboh observes:

> *Chi* is not omnipotent, for sometimes the Igbo man blames his 'chi' for being unable to win him fortune and bring him protection. *Chi* is a kind of fate or fortune personified and spiritualized.[321]

Further more, Chinua Achebe in the *Things Fall Apart* describes the misfortune of one of the characters when he wrote:

> Clearly his personal god or *chi* was not made for great things. A man could not rise beyond the destiny of his *chi:* the saying of the elders was not true – that if a man said yea his *chi* also affirmed. Here was a man whose *chi* said nay despite his own affirmation.[322]

The Igbo saying *"onye kwe chi ya ekwe"* – if one says yes his god also affirms, portrays the *chi* in this case, as a personal spiritual entity apart from man. *Chi* can also be conceptualised in form of spiritual deities such as, *Ala,* the earth goddess, *Igwe,* the sky goddess et cetera. It can also occur that the Igbo create a *juju or arusi* (*mmuo*) by themselves in order to implore the power of god for help and salvation. In this sense the Igbo invoke on this mechanism a spiritual power as *chi*, all conceptualised from the same concept of god as spirit, *mmuo*. Nwoga points out that:

---

319 Cf. Chinua Achebe, "Chi" in Igbo Cosmology 69.
320 Donatus I Nwoga, The Supreme God as Stranger in Igbo Religious Thought, Ahiazu Mbaise, Imo State Nigeria 1984 33-34.
321 Simon O. Eboh, *Ozo* Title Institution in Igbo land, Munich 1993 79.
322 Chinua Achebe, Things Fall Apart, London 1958 92.

"Given this interpretation of being, this structure of reality, within Igbo ontology not all spirits are gods. *Mmuo* is "spirit" and it is not automatic that every spirit is a god".[323] Therefore, it is by conceptualisation and activation that a god, *chi* is realised in Igbo ontology.[324] It is pertinent to note that this pattern of conceiving reality often leads to the confusion in many who misunderstand the Igbo belief system as animism, pantheism, fetish, superstitious et cetera.

Notice a conscious and careful choice of linguistic style in this presentation. In presenting names characters are chosen for the first letters. This is simply because the same word can stand for two different conceptual entities. For instance, the word *"ala"*, when written with a capital letter "A" will mean the earth goddess. But when written with a small letter "a", *ala* will mean in this case the physical earth upon which we stand. The same is also applicable to the word *chi* as god, guardian angel or fortune and when written in capital *Chi* as day in Igbo language. Furthermore, the word Igbo can mean two things namely, "Igbo" as referring to the people of a particular geographical location in the south east Nigeria and *"Igbo"* as the language spoken by the people.

Chukwu is another designation of God as the 'almighty' among the Igbo. *Chukwu* as the creator of all other deities and other natural beings has developed to be paramount among the Igbo people. The word *Chukwu* is made up of two words *chi* or *chu-god* as the prefix and *'ukwu'-great* as the suffix, meaning *Chukwu* – the great God. This God is symbolised among the Igbo with 'sun'. However, whether the traditional Igbo religion has a concept of a supreme deity above all others is still a challenge to religious scholarship. The name *chi* is the god, who the Igbo people hold tenaciously and speak about with great passion. It also refers to two other things at the same time namely, 'the day' and 'a personal god or destiny'.

In fact, the relationship between this *'chi'* of man and the great *'Chukwu'* is not clear. For instance whether the great *'Chukwu'* delegated *'chi'* to create man, as some other cultures purport or created man personally remains a hair-splitting question. For instance, among the Yoruba of western Nigeria, who are equally counted in size and shape among the

---

323 Nwoga, The Supreme God as Stranger in Igbo Religious Thought 34.
324 Nwoga, The Supreme God as Stranger in Igbo Religious Thought 34.

great peoples of Africa the Supreme God, *'Oludumare'* (one of whose titles is, incidentally, owner of the Sun), sent the god, *'Obalata'*, on a mission of creation to make man. Achebe insists that,

> The Igbo are not so specific about *Chukwu's* role in the creation of man but may be suggesting a similar delegation of power by the Supreme Overlord to a lesser divinity except that in this case every act of creation is the work of a separate and individual agent, *'chi'*, and a personified and unique manifestation of the creative essence.[325]

Whether *Chukwu* and *chi* have the same substance or are entirely of different substance is not clear. With reference to this seeming complication in the various Igbo names for God as *chi*; *Chukwu* and *Chineke* Michael J. C. Echeruo delineates:

> I will however want to assert that unless I am mistaken, there is no capital letter god among the Igbo outside *Ala*. God, among the Igbo, is certainly nothing like the God of the Christians. That is to say, as I tried to argue with members of the Faculty of Arts at the University of Nigeria Nsukka, some two years ago, our god is not the ONE towards whom all creation aspires, to paraphrase Plotinus and St. Augustine. He has no heaven and no troop of angels and saints ministering to him. He has promulgated no Decalogue, and he has not appointed a day when he will judge the living and the dead. In fact, the dead are not dead in the Christian sense, because among Igbo people, there is a continual coming and going from this life to the other and back. What we have is *CHI*, probably one of the most complex theological concepts ever devised to explain the Universe. It is a concept, which, both accounts for the Universe, explains Good and Evil, tragedy and good fortune, order and conflict, character and destiny, freewill and metaphysical order. There may be parallels in this idea with Christian thought.[326]

This goes to prove our earlier assertion that the Igbo cosmology is fraught with some obscurities. Each man in Igbo culture has a *'chi'* that accompanies him daily in the fulfilment of his destiny here on earth. It is this

---

325 Chinua Achebe, *"Chi"* in Igbo Cosmology 70.
326 Michael J. C. Echeruo, 'Matter of Identity' Aham Efula 21.

'chi' of the Igbo man that relates with him so intimately that he consults even in decision-making. He believes strongly in the adage, which says; "No matter how many divinities sit together to plot a man's ruin, it will come to nothing unless his *chi* is there among them.[327] Clearly *'chi'* has unprecedented veto power over a man's destiny. Achebe insists however that: "Power so complete, even in the hands of *chi* is abhorrent to the Igbo imagination. Therefore the makers of proverbs went to work again, as it were, to create others that would set a limit to its exercise. Hence, the well-known Igbo adage: *onye kwe chi ya ekwe*-If a man says yea his god affirms, points to the fact that the initiative or some of it at least, is returned to man."[328] This again explains the position which man ascribes to his self in the order of the universe. Man is not left out in the decisions of the *'chi'* rather he enjoys some sort of consultative privilege. He is the centre of the universe and possesses also some worth of authority and therefore can cause something to happen, but only in consultation with his 'chi'. To show this close affinity with his *chi*, man inserts as a prefix in so many Igbo names, the prefix *'chi'*. For instance, "*Chidiadi*" God exists; "*Chibundu*" God is life; '*Chibike*' – God is my strength; "*Chibuezem*" God is my king; '*Chijioke*' – God has all fortunes; '*Chijindu*' – God holds live in being, et cetera. However there are also other spiritual beings outside the *'chi'*. These are simply known as 'spirits'. They can be either good or evil. A detailed account or systematic discussion on the meaning of God as *chi* in Igbo metaphysics and religion thought, in view of its acceptance in the post Igbo Christian era as *Chineke* or *Chukwu* will obviously remain outside the competence of our present inquiry.[329] Nev-

---

327   Igbo Proverb.
328   Achebe, "Chi" in Igbo Cosmology 69.
329   For a detailed treatment of the question on *"Chukwu"* as the supreme God in Igbo religious thought read Donatus I. Nwoga, „*The Supreme God as Stranger in Igbo Religious Thought*". Nwoga argues that such an idea of a God, supreme and overwhelming, who created heaven and earth is a great ideological imposition on Igbo religious thought; See also, R. C. Arazu, „The Supreme God in Igbo Traditional Religion", Workshop paper for the Workshop on: *The State of Igbo Studies*, Nsukka, Institute of African Studies, June, 1982. Here the idea of a „Supreme God" in Igbo traditional religious thought is seen as a foreign imposition, and insists that different religions have different conceptual framework and as such to use the ready-

ertheless, one cannot conclude this section without pointing out the theological relevance of this discussion to our theme.

The ideas proffered by our authors creating the impression as if *'chi'* and *'Chukwu'* are different 'gods' in the Igbo cosmogony may be accepted according to specialization of their different authors but they are not theologically convincing. It is not theologically right to create the impression that the Igbo are polytheists, religiously complex but we are dealing with a people whose total life and world is impregnated with the divine. The appellation and use of *'chi'* goes deep into the spirituality of the Igbo. Without insinuating a pantheistic worldview, the Igbo believed in *Chi-ukwu*, God as the creator of the universe and all therein. In this sense, the distinction is made between the supreme God and the minor deities, who are more or less emissaries of *Chi-ukwu*. As a spirit-filled-world, the Igbo world is entirely a world encapsulated in the divine. *'onye na chi ya'*, (each with his/her god), *onye na chi ya so*, (each person is accompanied by his/her god) speaks of 'chi' as destiny, *'chi'* as personal god, and moreover God as an ever present presentness/reality. In other words, Igbo use of *'chi'* would insinuate the idea of a 'divine concursus' no less different from the Judeo-Christian idea of divine indwelling and accompaniment. Moreover the idea of divine indwelling does not imply a sort of pantheism but bespeaks of the immanence and transcendence of God, who is not distant from the world he created and at the same time transcends the world; guiding and accompanying creation. Sometimes one has the impression that practically everything has a different *'chi'* but not implying polytheistic worldview: everything has an imprint of the divine/spark of the divine. Hence the Igbo world in review pays total allegiance to God-*Chi-ukwu* the creator and his creatures, humans, animals and trees as symbols of divine revelation; and as such possess in themselves by this virtue, inviolability and inalienability in the dignity that is divinely bestowed on every creature.

---

made categories of one (in our case Christianity) to study another religion (Igbo traditional religion) can only lead to distortion. He also rejected the concept of „Chi-na-eke", as God who creates on the ground of its origin from western Christian concept. A God who created all out of nothing is foreign to Igbo. The word „*Okike*", in Igbo means simply to divide or to apportion and not to create, as in the sense of the biblical creation account.

3.4.2 "Ndu bu Ugwu" Life is Dignity for the Igbo

In the course of our analysis it has been significant that life for the Igbo is the supreme good and life is greater than wealth *"ndu ka aku"*: life *"ndu"* is invaluable. If dignity is a "relative absolute value" as opined by Georg Mohr's[330] analysis of normative and legislative capacity of moral values, then it is life for the Igbo. *Ndu bu ugwu* – life is dignity. On the contrary, if dignity is just a value among other kingdoms of human values, then Life, *ndu* for the Igbo is in fact greater than dignity. This position may run contrary to the western worldview, where the dignity of the individual stands before to make life meaningful. For the Africans, life is meaningful with or without dignity. Hence the Igbo would say: *"Ndu kariri ihe eji efe ya"* life is greater than its dignity; *"nnoro m ele uwa kariri onwu mma"* Just to be is far preferred than death. This difference in perception however, needs to be clarified further.

As we have indicated above the world of the Africans, particularly the Igbo is a spirit filled world, their understanding of life follows from a religious interpretation of reality which places the gods at the apex of their ontology. Donatus Nwoga made this point clear when he argued that,

> According to Igbo ontology, everything that exists has a *chi* – "a portioned-out-life-principle" given to it by the Supreme C*hukwu,* which is "Life" *per se*. Though this self-same "portioned-out-life-principle" is given to both man, animals, and plants, it differs, however, in degree. For just as *Chukwu* is higher than man, man is above the animals and distinguished from them by virtue of the fact that man gets higher degree of this divine life; and the animal is also above the vegetable. Similarly, the latter is distinguished from the inanimate.[331]

It is important to note that no strict ontological hierarchy exists instead one perceives a kind of dynamism between the different levels. Consequently, one notices a paradox in the Igbo African understanding and treatment of human life, which affects also their interpretation of the dignity of human person. *'Chukwu'* the almighty God as the source of life

---

330 Cf. Georg Mohr, „Grundlagen der Menschenwürde bei Kant und Fichte" 30.
331 Nwoga, "Nka Na Nzere: The Focus of Igbo Worldview" 15; Cf. Placid Tempels, *Bantu Philosophy* 67.

and life himself is the source and origin of dignity. This heteronomy[332] in the system of interpreting life and dignity among the Igbo Africans could be based on the following theses:

1) That the source of sacredness of life among the Igbo Africans stems from God *"chi-ukwu"* as the source of life- *"chi bu ndu"*, god is life; *"Ndu bu isi"*, Life is Supreme;
2) Even though they (gods) may possess life like the humans, this life is ontologically higher in hierarchy than that of human beings. Consequently, in hierarchy of possessing life force, the gods are ontologically greater than humans and the humans in turn are greater than animals and plants, while animals are greater than the plants and organic substances. Nwoga, in his work on Igbo worldview *Nka na Nzere* harped on a loosed form of hierarchy in the Igbo ontology.[333] According to this hierarchy however, lower life may be given back at the request or envy of a higher being. This life can be offered to a deity as a higher form of sacrifices or expiation. It is in this sense that one can understand the rational behind the condemnable practice of human sacrifices in the traditional African societies;
3) That the gods or deities *"chi"* as the case may be are feared beyond imagination by the Africans because the gods are no friends of man and are ever ready in their frenzy to punish men at the least provocation.

It is on this truism of the sacredness of life *ndu*[334] that one understands that this sacred gift has a link with God, with a religious overtone in-

---

332 Heteronomy refers to a system of interpreting the human dignity from the point of view of God being the source and origin of human dignity, while the Autonomy system emphasises the capacity of man to ascribe and receive dignity from one another.
333 The clause „loosed form of hierarchy" is used to distinguish it from a rigid or dogmatic one, which would complicate the recognition still accorded to lower being by man. For instance, among the Igbo some big old trees are not cut down without first reposing them elsewhere through a ritual of honour and respect. This fact purports at the same time, a kind of parallelism instead of absolutism in the Igbo ontological hierarchy.
334 Life *ndu* as sacred is one of the stereotypes associated with African literatures as pointed out earlier in this section. The Igbo African holds God as

spired by the fear of gods, *'chi'* source and origin of life *ndu*. From the ontological hierarchical point of view *chi-ukwu* as the owner of life endowed the deities with a greater portion of life and force than the humans. In Igbo religious thought deities and other spirits wield an incredible fear and respect among the people. Unfortunately, superstitious belief based on fear and respect for the gods among the traditional African communities; and some times, on the intention to increase ones force by extracting the life force of another led paradoxically to violation of the same life through ritual killings and human sacrifices. Cyril C. Okorocha, listed out in his work: *The meaning of Religious Conversion in Africa* a litany of taboo practices the traditional Igbo held as abnormal which include: giving birth to more than one baby at once (twins or triplets etc); a baby cutting an upper tooth first; et cetera as abnormal among the Igbo as a consequence of which the life of the poor victims would be sacrificed.[335] On the same note of Igbo religious Puritanism and extremism Isichei captured it succinctly:

> Their religion led the Igbo into oppression and injustice. Single births were regarded as typically human, multiple births as typical of the animal world. So twins were regarded as less than human, and put to death (as were animals produced at single births). The desire to offer the most precious possible sacrifice led to human sacrifice – for what is precious as a human life? The belief that the worlds of the dead mirror the world we know encouraged the sacrifice of slaves at funerals, to provide a retinue for the dead man in the life to come. The intention was good – to aid and honour, for instance, a beloved father. The result was an institution of great cruelty.[336]

The above narrative challenges the African claim to love and respect of life as sacred. First of all it would seem that this paradox could be explained by the ignorance in the primitive African societies and the fear of the gods as jealous entities, higher than human beings, who would look

---

the true source of life. *Chi* is indeed that life, *chi bu ndu*. Here lies the ground for its respect and dignity.

335 Cf, Okorocha, The Meaning of Religious Conversion in Africa, 105; G. T. Basden, Among the Ibos of Nigeria, Lagos 1983 57.
336 Isichei, A History of the Igbo People 26.

for the slightest violation to plunder them. Wole Soyinka[337] dramatised this paradox in his African drama, *"The gods are not to blame."* African respect for life is based theoretical on the fear of the anger of gods, the deities and *"chi"* as owner of life and as hierarchically greater than human beings, and not from a moral conviction of human being as an individual autonomous subject as it exists in western idealism. In the traditional Igbo society, a life of a person could be sacrificed at the prompt of the gods or deities for the fear of abomination on the part of the community. This accounted for the infant mortality rate in the traditional African societies and the killing of twins. For a woman to give birth to twins was an abomination, because the people believed that only animals could give birth to twins, triplets et cetera. It was seen as a degradation of human life by malignant spirit in women. Therefore, both the woman and the children should be made to suffer the curse and not the community. *"Ala"* the earth goddess was the most feared and must be appeased to avoid further calamities in the land.

In Igbo traditional society specific types of diseases were also viewed as curse and abomination in the land. The victims are most often helped to die fast and their unwholesome corpse thrown into the evil forest so as not to defile *"Ala"*. Depending on the need of the sacrifice or reparation; even for the sake of dignity of a king a human being can be offered. Moreover, an individual can be sacrificed if it is so pleasing to a deity or god. In his description of life in the Igbo society of the 18th century G.T Basden, a white missionary has this to say: "For the actual burial of a king or for the second burial of a chief it was customary to put to death one or more slaves *(ndi iji kwa ozu)* meaning those meant for burial sacrifice."[338] Human dignity among the Igbo can only be understood as a socio-anthropological construct as we are going to see later. Dignity for the Africans is more or less functional. It is based on the hierarchy of

---

337 Prof. Wole Soyinka a Nigerian Nobel prize-winner in literature wrote his drama book, *"The gods are not to blame"*, produced by Ola Rotimi, published by the University Press PLC. Nigeria 1971 and 1990, on the African destiny question. It questions the roles of the gods, the spirit world and the role of human beings in the present dispensation of the African destiny.
338 Basden, Among the Ibos of Nigeria, 122; See also Niger Ibos, London, Seeley Service.

human functionality and ability. It has little or nothing to do in this sense, with the individual as an autonomous subject as prescribed by Kant or with the biblical statement on man as, "created in the image and likeness of God" (Gen 1, 26). Dignity for the traditional Igbo Africans is purely functional, but at the same time seem to transcend this earthly existence in the sense of their belief in the other world. What a man gathers in his community in forms of titles and dignities leads him through the next world *ala mmuo,* the land of the ancestors – the living dead. Unfortunately, among his butties, with which he departs would include his slave. Therefore, the slave must have to suffer this fate.

Therefore, the discrepancies noticed in a culture that holds life in the highest esteem and at the same time looks away from the greatest violation of the same life could only be understood in the above pictured paradox where the whole respect and dignity are subordinated under a religious innocence and fear of their unforgiving gods before whom they must appease, even to the extent of laying down their live. Talking about dignity among the Igbo therefore refers only to their socio-anthropological construct, which bases solely on their understanding of the person in the community. This point has been the challenge faced by evangelisation since the 18th century in Igbo land. It is pertinent to mention, that with the influence and bull walk of Christian evangelisation, these ugly practices have been eradicated to a large extent.

Although comparison can be said to be odious, one with the religious beginnings of the Western cultures would reveal a breathtaking similarity. In the early history of Europe we read about a similar spirit-dwelt world during the time before the enlightenment witches and wizards were publicly executed ceremoniously and officially with a seal of religious authority. Religion therefore has been at the basis of human interpretation of experiences and environment, whether one considers it in the earliest times or in the modern dispensation. In the so called modern and contemporary times when religion is said to have been replaced by the state in history in the various state theories,[339] the idea of human sacrifices in the defence of the state is still being acknowledged as a mark of heroism.

---

339 Hegel opined in his philosophy of history, the 'absolute spirit', which engulfs all in the state so that religion may not be necessary again, but must have been understood as having played her role in history and now must

Consequently, the utopia of the state as the Leviathan – a Sea god[340] has replaced the gods of the ancient religions in the west. Imagine in this 21st century the American led war in Iraq and Afghanistan, which has claimed many innocent lives, that someone was bold enough to describe this senseless avoidable waste of human lives and resources as necessary; an absolute price/ sacrifice paid in defence of freedom and lives of citizens of American. Based on this anti-life ideology, fallen soldiers can be buried as gallant heroes with accolades and pride to pacify the bereaved families. I seek to be clarified the difference in this sense of sacrifice of human beings because of one's belief in the state the sea god-Leviathan and the sacrifice to the gods in defence and abeyance of the calamity that could befall a society as a consequence of violating the land.

This comparative analysis however, does not in any way justify the sacrifice of human beings, be it in the traditional African setting or in the western developed cultures. It is only a proof of the perennial and congenial nature of human ignorance and his limitation in understanding. It is also a proof of the congenial nature of evil in a world created by a good God. On the other hand, it is a pointer to the challenges facing theology in our search for the meaning of human dignity in our time. The problem of human dignity remains a perennial human question, which seeks constantly to be answered in time and space. That means a concept, which develops as human beings develop. Understood in this form, the question of human dignity becomes a matter for theological concern in the sense that the human being continues to look unto God for answers. Consequently, the whole analysis has a great implication for the current universal human rights discussion and the Christian theology, as we shall see in the later part of this enquiry. It is pertinent to note therefore, that the meaning and interpretation of human dignity, which we are presenting here, rely heavily on the religious and cultural sphere because of their relevance in human existence.

---

give way to the state. However, it is still questionable whether the Hegelian state has been achieved in history or yet to be achieved.

340 Hobbes theory of Civil Government talks of a strong entity in form of a Sea god- the leviathan that would have the capacity to guarantee a civil state and no more the gods of the ancient religions. This Utopia was replicated in different forms by other political theorists of his time, who have influenced our present day theories.

3.5 The Human Being in Igbo Anthropology

Every culture has its own definition of human being based on the outcome of their relationship with their environment. In the west we read about divergent notions of the same human being. The idealists' approach differs from that of the empiricists', which is also far different from that of the existentialist. For the idealist, reason stands as the distinguishing factor, while for the empiricist it remains sensation. The existentialist would see man from the phenomenological perspective. That means the human being is an existential reality, in time and space. On this parlance therefore, the Igbo culture differentiates its notion of man from all these through her belief and cosmological convictions that the human person is only someone identified as a being – with others. This communality in the Igbo African human image distinguishes this culture as one in its own genius, whose socio-cultural structures can only be studied and understood on its own epistemological terms.

However, psychologists have purported that these definitions or notions of man can be influenced at the level of hierarchy of needs, which a particular culture has attained. Maslow lined up in his theory a hierarchy of needs, which drive the human behaviour. At the base of this hierarchy of needs is that of food and shelter, while at the apex one finds the need for self-actualisation. The human being finds himself at one level of the needs or another at a given time in life and this, conditions the attitudes and behaviour of a human being. But to define the human being simply on the basis of needs would only be naïve. As Ogbujah argues; "Even though these appear to be general human needs, the means to satisfy them may differ from person to person, community to community and from time to time".[341] He concludes that these divergences are both valid and legitimate in so far as the notion of the person springs from the outcome of man's relationship with his environment, which definitely is never the same for all peoples and epochs, irrespective of Maslow's theory of hierarchy of needs.[342] Contextually speaking then what is the notion of human being in the Igbo African worldview?

---

341 Ogbujah, The Idea of Personhood 149.
342 Cf. Ogbujah, The Idea of Personhood 124.

3.5.1 Human Being as "Mmadu" the Beauty of Life

In Igbo thought, human being is translated with the word *Mmadu*. As a notion, *Mmadu* is viewed from the standpoint of his etymology and derivation; as a reality (being) he is ontologically traced from his origin to final destination, as well as from his ontological relationships.

From the point of view of *Mmadu* as a notion it can be etymologically derived from two Igbo words, *Mma* meaning beauty and *du or di* as the case may be, meaning "is" or "exists." *Mmadu or Mmadi* (as the centralised version)[343] translates: Beauty that is or exists. It can also be translated as: "there is beauty/ goodness"; "let goodness be" or "there is goodness".[344]

However, another tradition has it that man in the Igbo context is derived from two words, *Mma* meaning *beauty*, and *Ndu* meaning *life*. *Mma-ndu* then would mean the beauty of life. In order to form the current short form of it, the letter 'n' in *ndu* is removed and the resultant *du* is then suffixed to *mma* to get *mma-du* meaning the beauty of life; the synthesis of all that is good is creation.[345] This linkage of the good that is, with the ultimate source of being *chi* has its root in the Judeo Christian faith in Yahweh the creator of heaven and earth who after creating all things crowned it with man, who he created in His own image and likeness (Gen.1.27). He saw that all was good. The scholastics affirmed that *agere sequitur esse,* action follows a being and as a being is so does it act. Therefore, fashioned in the image of God, the human being is good. For this reason the scholastics also proclaimed: *"Esse est Pulchrum"* – being is beautiful. God is the Supreme Being. He is beauty in himself.

The Igbo understand man therefore, as a child of God *Nwachukwu* or *Nwachi*. He is recognised and named as: creature of God, *Okechi* or *Okechukwu*. Since all men share in the goodness of God, they have a common nature, which creates an intimate bond of solidarity among mankind.[346] Viewed from the standpoint of his origin and final destiny, man is

---

343 Cf. Edeh, Towards an Igbo Metaphysics 100.
344 Michael I. Mozia, Solidarity in the Church and Solidarity among the Igbo of Nigeria, Rome 1982 184.
345 Ogbujah, The Idea of Personhood 125.
346 Mozia argues that it is this traditional insight that enhances the communitarian spirit of the Igbo, although the bond of union is more intimately expressed among themselves than it is outside their circle.

best understood in relationship with his *chi* and the ancestral spirits – *ndi iche* the living dead. Man gets his divine spark directly from his *chi* the creator god who inflames the vital force in every being. Ontologically considered the human person is understood as a vital force among other vital forces. According to Tempels, the *"Muntu"* meaning human being occupies a central position in the cosmos.[347] He however pointed out that the *Muntu* does not exist by itself as an individual without the link with others. John Mbiti concurs with this ontology when he wrote: "Man is at the very centre of existence and African peoples see everything else in its relation to this central position of man. God is the explanation of man's origin and sustenance. It is as if God exists for the sake of man".[348] The former Tanzanian president Julius Nyerere in one of his political ideas presented man as: "the purpose of all social activity. The service of man, the furtherance of his development, is in fact the purpose of society itself. There is no other purpose above this; no glorification of 'nations', no increase in production – nothing is more central to society than an acceptance that man is its justification for existence".[349]

Igbo ontology revolves in a triadic form namely, God, Man and Nature. Man is at the centre of this triadic relationship. How man understands his relationship with God, fellow human beings and other created beings determines the position and respect he accords to each. In his relationship with his *"chi"* – God his creator man sees himself as having a definite mission from his *'chi'* and believes he will eventually go back to his *chi*. Man is a force, because he embodies a universal vital force.[350] He manipulates the world around him through which he acquires more force or looses force as the case may be. Socially the Igbo doctrine of man strikes a balance between his personal identity as a unique individual person and his collective identity as a member of his society.[351] He is all the time interacting with other beings in the universe with whom he is

---

347 Cf. Placide Tempels, Bantu Philosophie Ontologie und Ethik 64-65.
348 John S. Mbiti, African Religions and Philosophy, London 1990 90.
349 Julius Nyerere, Freedom and Socialism, London 1968 4.
350 Cf. Placide Tempels, Bantu Philosophie 65.
351 Cf. Emefie Ikenga Metuh, African Religions in Western Conceptual Schemes: The Problem of Interpretation, Jos 1991 109.

linked-up in a network of relationship.³⁵² Consequently, man is a being-with, if he must maintain his ontological balance. Hence Metuh affirms:

> Man ontologically is best viewed as a 'living force' in active communion with other living forces in the world. Each person is a nexus of interacting elements of the self and of the world, which determines and is determined by his behaviour.³⁵³

It is within the framework of this balance between the individual and his society that his dignity is located and guaranteed.

3.5.1.1 The Constitutive Elements of "Mmadu-Ahu na Nkpuruobi" (Body and Soul).

Igbo anthropology conceives the human being *mmadu* as integrally composed of a material element *ahu* (the body) and an immaterial element *obi, mmuo* (the soul, spirit) and *nkpuruobi* (the heart) and *mmuo* the soul. *nkpuruobi* or *mmuo* according to the Igbo belief is the centre of human activities. Accordingly, the Igbo believe that the source and origin of this *nkpuruobi* or *mmuo* is God Himself. Man participates in the divine life and shares in union of God more than any other created being, due to the spiritual aspect in him, which is *mmuo*.³⁵⁴ The unity between the various elements of the same man presents a very impressive difference between the ancient Greek dualism that sees the body and soul as separate entities. The Greek anthropology conceived the soul as imprisoned in the body, whereas for the African the separation of the body and soul as entities does not apply. Even though each could be seen in its function as performing differently, they are unified by one principle the soul-*mmuo*. The soul is not encapsulated and imprisoned in the body rather they both function together in constituting the principles that make up a human being. This relationship is "… often pictured as separate entities rather loosely held together, each having a different source and a different func-

---

352 Cf. Emefie Ikenga Metuh, Comparative Studies of African Traditional Religions², Enugu 1999 171.
353 Emefie Ikenga Metuh, O. Ojoade, et al., Nigerian Cultural Heritage, Jos Nigeria 1990 165.
354 Cf. Ferdinand. Nwaigbo, Church as a Communion: African Christian Perspective, Frankfurt am Main 1996 213.

tion".[355] The entities or principles with different capacities include: The body, *ahu*; the breath (the soul) *obi-nkpuruobi, mmuo*; the destiny spirit, *chi;* the personality, *eke;* and the shadow, *onyinyo*. The following report recorded by Arthur Glyn Leonard, a British Igbo researcher throws more light on the Igbo perception of the unity of body and soul:

> We Igbo, living in this part all believe that inside the body of every man is soul, which we call *"nkpuruobi"* and that without this soul a man cannot see or touch, but a thing which they can feel. It is without form, or substance such as man or animal has and we believe that, all soul are of one kind, and that each person has not more than one soul. This, our forefathers and the priests have told us, does not die, and it seems to us to resemble something, like shadow or the wind, or perhaps the breath. What we speak of, as *ndu* or life implies everything connected with our being in a state of existence, such for example, as growing, moving, seeing, touching and speaking. In the same way or sense, the soul, we think is the fruit of the body or of that organ which is said or thought to feed or supply the body, while the spirit is the living or vital energy of a person. The reason that the soul does not perish with the body is because it is the only thing, which the Great Spirit wants from each person individually, so that as soon as the body dies the soul naturally goes back to *Chukwu*, except in certain cases, where it is claimed by evil spirit. We too believe that all souls survive after death, and that none perishes, and that when the soul leaves the body and goes to its destination in the spirit land, it becomes a spirit. As to there being any difference between the soul and spirit, we do not know of any except that (which) speak of the former as soul when it is confined to the body of a man or animal or transferred to a plant or object and the latter as spirit when it is not so confined.[356]

The above narrative from a traditional Igbo, I believe, represents a doctrine of body and soul consistent with the spirituality of the people. An authentic human being is therefore defined in terms of some one having body and soul in an inextricable unity. The rites of final passage, burial

---

355 Metuh and O, Ojoade et al., Nigerian Cultural Heritage 165.
356 Arthur Glyn Leonard, The Lower Niger and Its Tribes, London 1968 140-141

and the way a dead human body is treated with respect and dignity makes the point, that although a person may be dead, death robs no person of this dignity and respect. Moreover the dead person is not regarded as dead but referred to as the "living-dead" because for the African, the dead are never dead but stands in daily communication with those still on earth, the living. This intermingling between the living and the dead bespeaks of the corporate nature of life among the Igbo. There is no lone individual but each person is defined within the context of a web of relationships: the family, the kindred, clan, the ancestors and the wider society. A person is, because we are: you are, because I am. The African person contrasts sharply with the lonely individual of the West.

3.5.2 The Individual "Otu Onye" in Igbo African Society

The individual *"otu onye"* in the Igbo African society is understood as a member of a given community, not in terms of the current Western ideological mindset of the person as an autonomous individual in the society standing alone against the state for his rights. In most Western societies, especially in America success drives are based on the fact of the society being individualistic in character.[357] An ideology of the individual as one distinct from the society in his rights (individualism), which may be translated in Igbo language as *"onwe m"* is loathsome to the traditional Igbo African society. Rather, in the Igbo African society the individual is perceived as part and parcel of the community. According to Cardinal Francis Arinze, "for the Igbo, as for many Africans to exist is to live in the group. Life is not an individual venture each one for himself".[358]

Critics of African Communalism and Communitarians hinge their arguments on the assumption that these political ideologies stifle to a large extent, the freedom of the individual members of the community. They maintain that although the individual person has a social nature destined to live – in communion with other persons, his identity as a unique individual should not be suppressed. In view of the customs and traditions, the group

---

357 Cf. Janet T. Spencer, "Achievement American Style: The Rewards and Costs of Individualism", in: American Psychologist, Vol. 40 (12) Dec. 1985 1285-1295 here 1289.
358 Francis A. Arinze, Sacrifice in Igbo Religion, Ibadan-Nigeria 1970 4.

solidarity suppresses the freedom of the individual to act on his own. The resultant system emerges as communalism there from, which creates a danger of authoritarian imposition. On the contrary, in Igbo African communities the freedom of the individual is guaranteed but not in the sense of the "cogito ergo sum" of Descartes,[359] rather it is an individualism that is rooted in a group consciousness. Buttressing the difference between the western and the African understanding of the individual, Leopold Senghor[360] on his African socialism explains:

> The individual is, in Europe, the man who distinguishes himself from the others and claims his autonomy to affirm himself from the others and claims his autonomy to affirm himself in his basic originality. The member of the community also claims his autonomy to affirm himself as a being. But he feels, he thinks that he can develop this potential, his originality, only in and by society, in union with all other men.[361]

From the above statement it is clear that the Igbo individualism: *otu onye* (one among many) is not 'rugged individualism', but it is individualism guaranteed by group solidarity. The Igbo believe strongly that community living is strength. Hence they say: *igwe bu ike,* (Group living is strength). There is a great emphasis on communal co-operation and achievement as we have earlier seen in the Igbo world.[362] The Igbo understand the "I" as distinct from the "we", which goes beyond the limits of rationality, and reaches into the supernatural sphere where he visualizes the "I" as bound together into a united whole with the "other."[363] There could exist sometimes of what one may

---

359 Rene Descartes formulated his philosophical idealism at the wake of the modern era in his famous 'Cogito ergo sum' I think therefore I exist. This thinking self becomes the basis of existence, which stands also as the basis for his metaphysics. This idealism is based on individualism. It is different from the ideological concept of the Igbo African mentality of the 'we' consciousness. Hence the Africans would say: "We are, therefore I exist. The 'I' exists because of the 'We'".
360 Leopold Seder Senghor was the first president of Senegal and wrote his political ideology in his book: 'On African Socialism'.
361 Leopold S. Senghor, On African Socialism, New York 1964 49.
362 Cf. Uchendu, The Igbo of Southeast Nigeria 103.
363 Cf. Okorie, The Integral Salvation of the Human Person in Ecclesia in Africa 322.

term as healthy tension or rivalry between the 'individual' and the 'community', which is accordingly taken care of by the claims the individual makes of the group and that which the group makes of the individual. To explain this further, we can visualize a traditional African political society where individual families gather together under a regent who offers the group protection with his might and connection, while the subjects on their own side bring to him their allegiance and respect.[364] In his effort to describe the individual in his community, Leonhard Harding has this to say.

> The individual is attached to the community for the sake of survival. It is only in the community he finds the possibilities of his development and expansion, which are understood as the development of the personal abilities that would enable him to serve the commonwealth. Individual rights above and against the community in this constellation had no place. The community must have to, on her own side build up for all the members a survival strategy, which means protection. She remains the same for the individual; protection and duties.[365]

Against this backdrop that the individual realises in the community both his protection and survival strategies he remains loyal to it. Ham pâté Bâ

---

364 Cf. Leonhard Harding, „Menschenbilder und Menschenrechte: Afrikanische Erfahrungen", 284 behauptet; "Schließlich war das politische Denken und Handeln in vielen afrikanischen Gesellschaften überlebensorientiert. Weil und solange die Gesellschaften klein waren und in einer vergleichsweise feindlichen Umwelt lebten, mussten sie alle Kräfte mobilisieren und zur Sicherung des Überlebens der Gruppe einsetzen. Diese Ausrichtung wurde noch dadurch gefördert, dass soziale Hierarchien sich nicht nach dem materiellen Besitz richten und materielle Ausbeutungsstrukturen, auch Formen der zentralisierenden Fremdherrschaft, sich nicht bilden konnten. Das Denken war stärker am Menschen als Teil der Gruppe orientiert. Die Folge war, dass der Einzelne für das Überleben der Gemeinschaft wichtig war, dass die Gemeinschaft auf seinen Beitrag angewiesen blieb. Sie gewährte ihm deshalb auch ihren Schutz, unterwarf allerdings auch seine Rechte den Bedürfnissen der Gemeinschaft".

365 Harding, „Menschenbilder und Menschenrechte: Afrikanische Erfahrungen" 286.
This dualism leads to the confusion in many who misunderstand the Igbo belief system as animism, pantheism, fetish, superstitious et cetera.

confirmed: "The individual does not count over and above the community. The family, then the kindred or the village present oneness, whose interests or fate stands first before that of the individuals".[366]

3.6 The Igbo sense of Community-African Communalism

The human being by nature is a gregarious being. An individual who is thrown into a world of needs and wants will definitely need others for the fulfilment of some of these needs. For example, the need to communicate can only be satisfied by the availability of the second partner. Further more, the need to procreate will also need the opposite sex to achieve this. Community therefore is native to the human being in several respects. For the Igbo, the community is strength, *"umunna bu Ike."* Thinking about the Igbo African sense of community would presuppose the existence of other forms or senses of community. For instance, the Western form stands out in its rights as an individualistic society.

In individualistic communities, individuals are thought to form communities with other individuals while in the African notion of community, it is the community that moulds and creates the individual; without his community the human being is nothing, he is equivalent to the dead, or inanimate objects.[367] In the words of Nwoga:

> Within this contest, there is a balance between the claims of community and the claims of individualism. The individual is a member of the community that sets the goals that have acceptability 'within that' community. It is the community that sets up reward and punishment systems. To a large extent, the individual in Igbo land is subsumed within the requirements of the community.[368]

For the above reason, the dignity of human person is based on the socio-anthropological construct of the Igbo community as we are going to see

---

366 Amadou Ham pâté Bâ, Aspects de la civilisation africaine, Paris 1972 136f.
367 Cf. Z. Nthamburi, "Making the Gospel Relevant within the African Context", in: *AFER 25* (1983) 3, 162-171 here 163.
368 Nwoga, "Nka na Nzere"1984 44.

later. In the communal structures; in the agnatic functional processes we discover an interpretation of the individual dignity in terms of functions fulfilled or allotted to an individual in a particular community and the corresponding claims there from. Recent ethnological studies on the Western and the African communities establish the difference between the two conceptualities. In the case of the European, being a person means being the centre of one's own activities, especially thinking; being the centre of one's activities, in turn is largely defined by incommunicability. The distinctive mark of the western and African sense of community resides in the fact that, the central question for a European is how to be an individual – a valuable person. Even the case of more communal lines of thinking, for instance, before there can be *'we'*; there must be *'I'* and *'thou'*. In African conceptions however, there is first the 'we' before 'I' can exist. E. Mveng argues that the crucial question is not the individuality of a person, but rather his communality without which he cannot be a person.[369] Guided by a set of morality based on strong religious fears the Africans live in a kind of responsible freedom. The individual takes decisions based on the agreed norms and face consequences when the laws of the land are defiled. There were taboos guiding the human behaviours. Every one watched over the observance of the laws of the land. It was every ones business to see to it that the community survived. Julius Nyerere of Tanzania once stated: "We were individuals within the community. We took care of the community and the community took care of us".[370] Community sharing affords one the opportunity of contributing his own quota to the growth of the community that has nursed him into existence. Commenting on the Igbo community spirit Uchendu has this to say:

---

369 Cf. E. Mveng, L'art d'Afrique noire: Liturgie cosmique et Langage religieux, in: K Appiah-Kubi et al., Libération au adaptation? La théologie africaine s'interroge: Le Colleque d'Accra-Paris 1979 167-173 here 169, 170; see also: M. N. Nkemnkia. II pensare africano come "vitalogia", Rome 1995 146-147; K. Kaunda "Spirituality and world Community", in: A Shorter (Ed.), African Christian Spirituality, Maryknoll-New York 1980 117-121 here 120.
370 Julius Nyerere, Ujamaa: Essays on Socialism, London-New York 1971 6-7.

Community spirit is very strong among the Igbo. Amongst the first, the individual is aware of his dependence on his kin-group and his community. He also realizes the necessity of making his own contributions to the group to which he owes much.[371]

This ideology – communalism deviates to a large extent from the communist agenda as we have them in history. In communism, the freedom of the individual is subsumed and compelled by the absolute will of the social state.

3.6.1 Conflicting Issues in Igbo African Communalism

It is not as if the Igbo African sense of community-communalism escapes the ambivalence associated with other social ideologies. On the contrary, the Igbo social system cannot be said to be perfect. It has got its pitfalls. For instance the Igbo communalism is also partly dominated by the lords, who are luckier with acquisition of wealth and might. In the African traditional society there was almost little or no guarantee of respect for the weak, children, the disabled less privileged, the mentally sick and the poor. To say the least, human rights were not defined as we have them in the west. It will not be an over statement to observe that many leaders of African clans were simply dictators and wielded power so that borrowing the words of Shorter, one can also talk of infantilism.[372] The traditional African communities were limited in size and scope; and had the capacity only for parochial and local ventures. The individual is limited within his particular community so much that in the face of globalisation a little chance of survival existed.[373] The tribal and ethnic conflicts in the African

---

371 Uchendu, The Igbo of Southeast Nigeria 23.
372 A. Shorter, African Christian Spirituality, London 1978, 204, 205 talks about infantilism as a risk of a superior father-figure or mother-figure, who takes decisions for the children and who sees the superior's task as testing the subject obedience and imposing pattern of life on them.
373 Metuh made reference to Horton's argument from the limited survival possibility of the African communities as the motif for conversion in Africa as a false one. For Metuh the motif for African conversion was religious. However, Horton insists that conversion among the Africans was elicited through the urgent and dare need of facing the emerging global and robust

continent are partly consequences of a globalising experiment of these different peoples, brought under a quasi unity. Unfortunately, the colonial government for the sake of what has been termed an act of, 'administrative conveniences' amalgamated many peoples and cultures that never belonged together. Therefore, as the emergent African social system that was neither indigenous in the sense of being autochthonous or migrant in the sense of being foreign could not satisfy the holistic vision of a community for the people, therefore, some elements, though dangerous had to be introduced. Ethnicity was politicised in the quasi-African nationalism to create a monster in a form of tribalism.[374] In the nation states, tribes were once more recognised as basic political units in the different sections of the country. These units in turn see themselves as political rivals who understand coming together in the centre as a ground for fighting for sectional tribal rights, which never was the case in the traditional African commonwealth. In the traditional African communities the commitment to the common wealth was total. It was not pretentious and selfish, rather every one sought after the good of the whole.[375] Traditionally, the African communities were not massive and imperialistic in nature and the idea of nationalism or a national state was foreign to the African communities. After the colonial invasion, the subsistence and survival of the real traditional African communities have been very minimal. They have experienced a gradual disappearance due to internal and external disorientation. Presently communities exist as quasi societies that can be best described with every sense of responsibility as more or less a hybrid society[376].

---

    society, which the small African communities would not achieve left alone. Cf. Emefie Ikenga Metuh, "The Shattered Microcosm: A Critical Survey of Explanations of Conversion in Africa", in: Peterson, K. H (Ed.), Religion, Development and African Identity, Uppsala 1987 11-27 here 13.

374 Cf. Eghosa E. Osaghae, "The Passage from the Past to the Present in African Political Thought: The Question of Relevance" in: Zaccheus Sunday Ali et al. (Eds.), African Traditional Political Thought and Institutions, Centre for Black and African Arts and Civilisation national Theatre, Lagos Nigeria 1989 53-75 here 66.

375 Osaghae, "The Passage from the Past to the Present in African Political Thought: The Question of Relevance", 68.

376 Chinua Achebe in his book *Things Fall Apart* describes the Whiteman as very claver. "He came quietly and peacefully with his religion. We were

Emefie Ikenga Metuh described it as the "shattered microcosm".[377] The absence of traditional African spirit and sense of community has always been mirrored as the cause of moral and socio-political intransigence in the society. Civil responsibility to a massive society with no ancestral connection became too lofty an idea to conceive. With different religious beliefs and moral diversities most African states have been turned into perpetual battlegrounds. Furthermore, the elite of the society; the statesmen try their best to assert once more the so called "traditional African community spirit" which has been wiped off by the imperial structures of the colonial masters, but these efforts have been seen as a purely selfish desire by the statesmen or politicians, who would want to abuse the submissive allegiance of the people, who are already used to submitting to the simple organic African communities, where conformity and unbridled loyalty to community marked the coexistence of the leader and the led. There was in fact total allegiance to religion and morality in the traditional African communities by all, which is not the case in the today African democratic states.[378] This new found communalism as an African political ideology has succeeded in creating dictators and despots who would not leave the office until death or until they are toppled by military coupe. Unfortunately, this effort to return to the traditional African spirit of community continues to fuel tribalism and ethnicity.

3.6.2 The Structure of the Traditional Igbo African Community

A typical traditional Igbo African community is structured around the socio-cultural realities of the human person. The human person is both historically and communally structured with so many relationship ties, which actually installs him as a member of a community. Since the dignity of human person among the Igbo Africans revolves around this

---

amused at what seemed to be his foolishness and allowed him to stay. Now he has won our brothers and our clan can no longer act like one. He has put a knife on the things that held us together, and we have fallen apart" 124-125.

377 Metuh, "The Shattered Microcosm: A Critical Survey of Explanations of Conversion in Africa" 11.

378 Cf, Osaghae, The Passage from the Past to the Present in African Political Thought: Question of Relevance. 67-70.

socio-anthropological structure and a network of relationships it is pertinent to consider this network, at least in a summary form.

3.6.2.1 The Igbo African Family-Ezi Na Ulo

The family as the basic social unit of the Igbo community embraces two basic structures. The first is the *Ulo*-household, a nuclear family, which may be either monogamous or polygamous. It is usually established through the union of a man and his wife or wives as the case may be. A typical example of a traditional polygamous Igbo family will be that described by Chinua Achebe in his book *Things Fall Apart* where he described the household of Okonkwo the chief character of his literature as having several wives with their different kitchens known as the *Onu usekwu*. Every woman catered for her own children in her personal *Onu usekwu* –kitchen and contributed in turn to the feeding and care of their husband as the head and regent of the family.[379]

The second is the extended family known as the *"Ezi na Ulo"* meaning an exogamous household made up of different nuclear families from the same ancestry living together as *Umunna*-literarily translated as children of the same father or related through the father. At the helm of affairs of such an extended household is the eldest male of the family, a *"Pate familia" – (opara nwe ezi)* who is morally and socially responsible for the well being of the larger family, the *Ezi Na Ulo*.

The forefathers are at the basis of every lineage. They are the founders of the lineage and remain in an unbreakable link with the living members of the lineage. Ancestors or the living dead as they are often called keep on regenerating the lineage through the process of reincarnation, *ilouwa*.[380] It is partly for the prolongation of the family and kindred ancestral lineage; and the economic production that the children are very much cherished in Igbo African communities. The *Ezi Na Ulo* is the basic complex unit of socialisation in the life of every Igbo African child. It distinguishes itself further

---

379 Chinua Achebe, Things Fall Apart 37-38.
380 *Ilo uwa* – reincarnation is a strong belief among the Igbo, which holds, that when some one dies, the soul does not die but rather joins the family and lineage ancestors who are the founders of the lineage. These souls reincarnate through the birth of new members of the family and lineage.

from *Ama* village or clan as a wider and lager form of relation as we shall see later. A child at birth and early childhood stages is integrated into the family before he is exposed to the wider community *Ama-village*. Commenting further on the nature and genius of the Igbo family; and the level of complexity involved with the concept of *ezi na ulo* Uchendu clarifies:

> *Ezi n' ulo* is more than a homestead. It is a cultural phenomenon of great complexity. A basic spacial unit in Igbo social organization, analytically *ezi* precedes *ulo* in structural time, but *ezi* loses its functional integrity once *ulo* disintegrates. It is the peace of *ezi* that brings prosperity to *ezi n'ulo* and poverty that leads to its fusion. *Ezi n'ulo* should not be confused with *ezi na ulo*. Although in structural time, *ezi* precedes *ulo*, both protect *ezi n'ulo*. In cultural terms *ezi na ulo* constitute a unity. You cannot meaningfully think of the one without thinking of the other. In structural analysis *ezi na ulo* are polar concepts but they are also complementary. Their complementarity lies in the fact that it is the social life in the *ulo* that activates the cultural life of the *ezi*, the achievements of the *ulo* that are celebrated in *ezi* and vice-versa.[381]

Igbo family household, the *ezi na ulo* are usually big and extended. For this reason it has been difficult for foreigners to understand the dynamics of the social relationships involved. The idea of Western nuclear family is transcended by an embracive one, which is extended in Igbo family system. The emphasis in the extended family is not necessarily conjugal but rather social. Granted a child is normally born by a man and a woman through conjugal act, but related to others by a strong social tie achieved through a descent from common ancestry.[382] No one person owns a child in the Igbo African community so that some times this extended family may include people who have little or no blood relationship just as S. N. C. Obi explained:

> Extended family as a social institution, consists of the persons who are descended, through the same line ... from common ancestor,

---

381 V. C. Uchendu, "*Ezi Na Ulo*: The extended Family in Igbo Civilization", 1995 Ahiajoku Lecture, Owerri: Culture Division of Ministry of Information, Culture youth and Sports 1995.
382 Cf. Cletus, C. Osuji, The Concept of Salvation in Igbo Traditional Religion, Rome 1977 18.

and who still owe allegiance to or recognize the overall authority of one of the members as the head and legal successor of the said ancestral founder, together with any persons who, though not blood descendants of the founder, are for some reason attached to the household of the person so descended, have otherwise been absorbed into the lineage as a whole.[383]

The Igbo extended family system confers a moral authority and responsibility on the *opara* (First male borne of the family) who is usually the eldest son of the entire homestead, especially in the case of exogamous and polygamous families. Uchendu summarized the elements, which characterize the extended family in Igbo community as follows:

1. In an extended family, relatives other than husband, wife and unmarried children share residence or live adjacent to the nuclear family.
2. There is a pooling or sharing or joint ownership of resources, which is usually formalized or legally recognized and these resources normally include symbolic estates, that is, the inheritance of rights in relatives.
3. Recognition of kin relations either of a lineal or of a collateral character but usually of both.
4. Recognition of common responsibilities.
5. Allegiance to a common ancestor and pts worship.
6. Reciprocal assistance pattern.
7. Joint economic activities either on production or consumption or both.
8. Maintenance of expressive relations among extended family members through visits and support at crisis periods.
9. The use of the extended family as a reference group in decision-making.
10. Authoritarian control over relationships and decision-making by the elder who has command over the corporate resources and his house, the centre for all formal activities, both ritual and social.[384]

---

383 S. N. C. Obi, Law in Africa: Modern Family in South Nigeria, London 1966 9.
384 For further reading on the Igbo family, see V. C. Uchendu, "Ezi Na Ulo: The extended Family in Igbo Civilization", Ahiajoku Lecture Series 1995.

We shall next examine briefly the social relationships existing within the kinship network, in other words the agnates in the extended family system.

3.6.2.2 The Kindred – "Umunna" (Children of the Father)

The Igbo community is mostly patrilineal in formation. It is customary for the process of inheritance to be apportioned through the patrilineal order. That means every child born into an ancestral home – the kindred automatically acquires the membership of *Umunna*. This ancestral link to the lineage of the father of a newborn to a family guarantees it the rights in the community. These include social, political and economic rights but not without the corollary duties of uplifting the kindred. The members of this lineage are his *Umunna*[385]-literarily meaning, children of the father. There are also other agnatic groups in the community as we go further in our analysis. In Igbo communalism, the agnates are the strength of the individual in all the human ramifications hence the Igbo adage: *Umunna bu Ike* (the community is the strength of the individual). The Individual resides in the midst of his *Umunna,* which is made up of the different families of the same ancestral lineage. It is thus among them, the *Umunna* that his rights are protected, and his life is secured. In the midst of the *Umunna,* the individual develops, matures and becomes a "person". It is in this agnatic group – the *Umunna* (kindred) that he acquires and looses his dignity accordingly.

3.6.2.3 The Umuada/Umuokpu Agnate (Daughters)

Because the *Umunna* seem to suggest only male membership, the *Umuada* or *Umuokpu* agnate – meaning daughters complement their male counterpart. These are the females of an ancestral lineage not yet marry or not married and those giving out in marriage. In the case of the married ones, even though they have their rights in their husband homes as married women they still play influential roles in their ancestral and natal homes. They are often involved or invited home especially, in the occasions of disputes, community celebrations and burials in the lineage. Even though the *Umuada* role as interventional is respected, the authority

---

385 Cf. Uchendu, The Igbo of Southeast Nigeria 64.

of the lineage kindred resides in the hands of the *Umunna* who possess as it were the *ofo*[386] of the land. The *Umuada* have little or no inheritance through their fathers and *Umunna*, but were most often brought home at death and buried in their fathers compound, amongst the Umunna.

The individual would always prefer to die and be buried amongst his *Umunna* and join his ancestors as a mark of honour and respect. Nevertheless, this sense of security and guarantee in one's agnate – the *Umunna* does not relegate the fact that one's *Umunna* can also be vindictive. It can most often than not come to injustice and suppression of the individual's right in the community. For this reason, a person is also protected by other parallel agnates such as the *Umuada/ Umuokpu* and the others as we are going to see. The *Umuada* has proved to be a strong and respectable agnate among the Igbo communities in the restoration of peace, law and order amongst warring and rivalling parties in the *Umunna* kindred. Their authority is based on the love the *Ala* the earth goddess has for them as her daughters. No one dares to thwart decisions of the *Umuada* on settlement of stubborn disputes in the land.

3.6.2.4 Mother's Agnates-Umunne/Umune or Ibenne

The uterine agnates, otherwise called the *Umunne*-literally meaning children of the mother plays another important role in the guarantee of one's dignity in the Igbo community. Relationship with one's *Umunne*-mother's lineage underscores a contrast to the patrilineal agnate the *Umunna*. In his mothers agnate a person is honoured and also pampered as the case may

---

386   *Ofo* is a sacred wooden symbol carved from a specific tree known as the *Osisi ofo* – the *ofo* tree. It is a sacred staff of authority held by the eldest of the family among the *Umunna*. *Ofo* is a symbol of truth and innocence in the land. Whenever it is brought out it means that the truth must prevail, no more no less. The desecration of *ofo* or disobedience of its binding injunctions could be deadly and the consequences are dreaded in the community. Sacrifices of life chickens are made to the *ofo* routinely. At times of decision-taking in the community or at times when certain behaviours and moral practices are to be bound in the community the *ofo* stick will be hit three times on the ground with a unanimous voice, *ise ooo*. Meaning "Amen" or May it be so. For further readings see, Christopher I. Ejizu, *Ofo: Igbo Ritual Symbol,* Ibadan Nigeria 1986.

be. It is punctuated with so much love and security that whenever one looses the confidence of his *Umunna*, the next place of shelter would be the *Umune* or *Ibenne*-maternal home. In times of banishment or exile one finds a safe haven by his mother's lineage the *Umune*. However, one enjoys only honorary privilege by his maternal agnate, but has no right of heredity. The *okele*-meaning our daughters child can take what he wants from his maternal home without express permission of any body. These are usually foodstuffs and some times articles of clothing. He is always welcome and respected as member of the lineage from the maternal side. On no account should his blood be spilt or be wounded in his maternal home. The earth goddess the *Ala* does not look kindly on the offenders of this taboo. All his mother's children and the mother's brother's and sister's children are his *Umunne*-mothers children. The uncles and aunties, are all *Nna ochie* and *Nne ochie* respectively – my mother's brothers and sisters. The father of his mother he calls, *Nna nna*-father of my mother and the mother's mother as, *Nne nne*-mother of my mother. The same is applicable if the parents of his father were to be alive. He calls them *Nna nna* and *Nne nne* respectively as well. The affinity and love that pervades at the *Umunne* level are so cordial that it cannot be compared with that of the father's lineage the *Umunna*.

3.6.2.5 The Remote Kinsmen

The father's mother's and the mother's mother's lineages constitute a person's remote kinsmen. They are nevertheless important in the life of a successful Igbo. The relations with one's mother's mother's agnates are more solid than those with one's father's mother's agnates. In none of these social groups however do the Igbo command any general defined privileges[387]. He makes use of these connections mostly during ceremonies such as burial ceremonies, chieftaincy titles et cetera. There are no extra rights or dignity accruable from these relationships except that they are always there for him. He is forbidden to take a wife or husband from these lineages.

---

387 Cf, Uchendu, The Igbo of Southeast Nigeria 67.

3.6.2.6 The Igbo Village-Ama or Ogbe

The Igbo village-*Ama or Ogbe* comprises of different agnates the *Umunna* with different ancestors and lineages. This union popularly referred to, as the *amala* constitutes a formal relationship of the different agnates in the community. It is characterized by a political undertone that differentiates it from the *Umunna* ties which is stronger and closer. Due to the heterogeneous nature of ancestry, the individual considers the relationship at *amala* level as simply far. A regent who, by virtue of his economic strength and ability, enjoys the respect and dignity of a village chief often heads the *ama* or *ogbe*. Basden commented on the traditional role of a village chief thus: "Each village or ward has its own chief who enjoys the dignity and right of a patriarch. He takes the lead in all public affairs, religious, social and political. He settles disputes, and presides at the trials of criminal offenders. He also officiates at the sacrifices appointed for certain delinquencies, such as infidelity[388].

Every village has its own market place, shrines and public meeting ground. The markets are called by the names of the day on which they are held viz, *Eke, Orie, Afor, and Nkwo*, these corresponding to the four days of the Igbo week.

3.6.2.7 The Igbo Town-Obodo

When villages come together they form a town-O*bodo,* which is a broader and wider community. At the level of the town one finds a more political representation among the constituting villages. Again this relationship is represented for instance, in Eziudo town through the various chiefs and elders from the villages in a collegiality known as the *Orieukwu*-central council. The name was derived from the day normally chosen for meetings which falls on every other Igbo week-the *Orie- ukwu*, the big *Orie*. The phenomenon of recognising and appointing a king-*Eze* by the government over the town is recent to the Igbo communities except in those areas where the monarchical institution was in place. For instance, towns in the Onitsha areas are known for their long existing dynasties. The *Eze* rules in council with his cabinet, but still the idea of having an

---

388 Basden, Among the Ibos of Nigeria 47-48.

Eze in most Igbo communities still remains an experiment because of the political involvement in both the selection of candidates to the throne and the activities of the thrown. In short, the statement that the Igbo have no king, *Igbo enwee Eze* portrays both the veracity of the above assertions and the democratic nature of the Igbo society.

3.7 Summary

In this chapter on the Igbo worldview, we reviewed extant works on the Igbo socio cultural anthropology. Through a journey in the Igbo world view the cosmology and the picture of who the Igbo Africans are emerged through their environment, experiences and actions. The Igbo world is deeply religious, a spirit dwelt world separated albeit, into two- the *ala mmuo* and the *elu uwa*, which dovetail into one another. Life *ndu* is paramount for the Igbo (*ndu bu isi*). It is a special gift of God to man. For the Igbo, God- *chi* is this life, *chi bu ndu*. Thus the African respect for life stems from the conviction that all lives come from God. It is therefore, sacred. Consequently, life is greater than dignity- n*du kariri ihe eji efe ya.*

However, the Igbo ontology apportions much regard and respect to their gods whom they must appease always at all cost even through sacrificing human life. Their sense of religion and sense of innocence before the world around them leads them to some violation of the same life they cherish so much.

The human being as the creature of God remains an aggregate of body and soul, in an indivisible unity. Among the Igbo, the individual is alone when he is not related to the community. This is what a true Igbo abhors. The Igbo individualism is not a rugged ideology, but an individualism that has the community at its basis. Consequently, the 'I' needs the 'We' to function and not vice versa. The community is the life of the individual, structured from the anthropological patterns, in an inclusive relationship, from the Family to the town, which is a wider level of the Igbo community.

Having situated the Igbo human person in his world, we have also been able to glimpse his dignity, which is tied to his socio-anthropological reality. Therefore, the next enquiry will examine human dignity as a socio- anthropological construct among the Igbo.

Chapter Four: Human Dignity: A Socio-Anthropological Construct among the Igbo

4.1 The Linguistic Analysis of Ugwu na-Nsọpụrụ (Dignity and Respect)

In the second chapter of this inquiry we started a linguistic analysis of the twin words *ugwu na – nsọpụrụ* – dignity and respect. These words belong to the group of words often used together in the Igbo linguistic tradition to depict almost the same meaning, in this case dignity. The word dignity confers a sense of value and worth, while respect is the actual acknowledgement of dignity possessed by a thing or person. To have dignity, is to be in a state of honour, worthiness, usefulness, importance; to be appreciated, reserved, protected, admired, desired, acknowledged; to be pleasant, good, beautiful, awful, feared, elevated et cetera. However, it is pertinent to point out quickly that, these are only descriptive attempts by way of synonyms, which can only point to the sublime meaning of dignity, because the actual meaning and full description of dignity is difficult, if not elusive to achieve. The Igbo ascribe dignity not only to humans but also things, but life as a value; human life as the greatest gift and value is incontestable. Even though the Igbo use dignity and respect, one for the other with a subtle sense of presumption there is always a marked difference. A further analysis of each will make this difference clearer.

4.1.1 Ugwu (Dignity)

One of the linguistic problems encountered by the non-native speakers, which applies to the case of *'ugwu'* as human dignity is the flexible use of words among the Igbo. In Igbo language, a word may mean several things at the same time depending on the context. At the first sight scholars have hastily concluded that this was as a result of lack of enough vocabularies in Igbo language, but on the contrary, research has shown that it is far from being the case.

For example, early Igbo ethnologists like Major Arthur Glyn Leonard, in the "Section III: The Dualism of the Natives" of his insightful work, *The Lower Niger and its Tribes* have commented on the Igbo cosmological perspective of reality as dualistic. Achebe in turn in his essay on *Chi in Igbo Cosmology* described it with famous Igbo adage of *"ife kwulu ife akwudebe ya"*- wherever something stands, something stands beside it. However, it was the genius of Nwoga, in his Ahiajoku lectures, *Nka na Nzere* (1994) to have in an erudite manner of reflection attributed the reason for this dualism to the Igbo metaphysics of reality, which is dynamic. According to him, the Igbo ontological framework has been responsible for this duality, because the duality of a given object is realised from a combination of elements from the three forms of entities recognised in Igbo Thought: the physical, the spiritual and the conceptual.[389] Nwoga concluded that: "It was within this Igbo ontological framework of three types of entities that some of the statements made by some ethnographers and philosophers of the Igbo scene acquire more satisfying meaning".[390] For instance the word *ala* means earth or land but when written in capital, *Ala* means the earth goddess, while lightening-*Amuma* when written in small letter as *amuma* means the god of thunder – *amadioha* – (deity). *Amuma* can also mean *prophecy*. The word *Igwe* – means the sky or the community regent but when written *igwe* it means the sky deity.[391] As a result, in other to make the sense intended in a particular context easier for the reader to understand the Igbo language experts created what we now know as tone-marking.[392]

---

389 Cf. Nwoga, The Supreme God as Stranger in Igbo Religious Thought 33-34.
390 Nwoga, The Supreme God as Stranger in Igbo Religious Thought 33-34.
391 Cf. Nwoga, The Supreme God as Stranger in Igbo Religious Thought 33-34.
392 The rising and falling of sounds in word pronouciation in Igbo language is referred to as *'tone-marking'*. This process helps to distinguish meanings of the same word from each other through sounds carefully signified by marks on the particular stress points of the word.

The Igbo word *'Ugwu'* embodies a shed of meanings:

1. *Ugwú* – means, mountains or hills, while 2. *Ùgwù* means circumcision- *ibi nwata ùgwù* (to circumcise a child). 3. *Ùgwù* means also to reduce something in quantity for instance, the act of drinking a glass of wine or water into a half – *iñu mmanya/mmiri ùgwù*. 4. There is also another one that means hatred or enmity – *ụgwụ*. 5. The one that refers to honour and dignity reads *ugwu*. *Ugwu* – dignity in Igbo worldview means a state of being respected and honoured for developing those remarkable qualities and abilities received at birth from *chi*- the personal provident god. The Igbo use the *ugwu*- dignity for every thing done well, rightly and correctly. *Ugwu si na chi* (dignity is from God), lays stress on the personality traits received from *chi* as a benevolent god, who has done every thing well in all wisdom; and has given man the ability to develop them according to the societal norms and customs. Therefore, a person for the Igbo is not just a human being, but one who has all necessary characteristics, potentialities and the ability to realise them. Life is the greatest gift of God to man – *ndu bu isi* (life is paramount); and is greater than dignity – *ndu kariri ihe eji efe ya*, but at the same time it is only a meaningful life that merits the title – *onye* – human person who is the human being – *mmadu* in the right sense of being human. When the Igbo say that *'mmadu bu ugwu'* – a human being is dignity they actually mean person- *onye*. This is because in Igbo worldview, not every living individual is a human being – *mmadu* or a person – *onye*

To elucidate this further, as mentioned shortly it is a common knowledge among the Igbo that every human being receives some distinctive characteristics and abilities from his *chi* the personal god of the Igbo person, the god of destiny also recognised as one's *eke* – god of good luck and success. *Ikenga* is a personal *chi* responsible for man's strength, wisdom and ability to bring into fulfilment all these endowments. *Mbata aku* is the personal *chi* responsible for riches and wealth. Nevertheless, the gift of life is not restricted only to the humans but also to animals and plants. All must show and convince the Igbo of their relevance and function in the Igbo anthropocentricism before their dignity will be acknowledged in a form of respect. A thing, animal or plant has to be functionally useful for it to be accorded respect as recognition of dignity.

Therefore, human dignity for the Igbo lies in the ability of an individual within boundaries and limits of the community; within the *Omenala-*

meaning the norms, customs, culture and tradition of the land to achieve his or her personhood. When one receives certain staling qualities and abilities from his *chi* to become a full grown member of the community, and through personal efforts, and in the process of Personhood[393] makes good use of these gifts from *chi*, the Igbo would say: *"chi ya keziri ya ekezi"* meaning, his god created him very well, his *chi* adorned him with honour. On the contrary, when one is unable to develop these gifts from *chi*, the Igbo would say, *"chi ya kegburu ya ekegbu"* meaning, his god did not create him well.[394] Even the ability to bargain well with one's *chi* in his first life[395], is been regarded as a sign of dignity and favour. Hence the adage: *"Onye kwe chi ya ekwela!"* when one says yeah his chi would concur. Most often the Igbo do not excuse any one for being lazy or even for being less privileged. Some times weakness and disabilities are interpreted as ones carelessness, irresponsibility and love for leaving a foul life, which the Igbo dynamism abhors; or even as punishment from the gods. In this sense the penalized deserves no understanding or mercy. This is because for every thing that happens, someone or something must be held responsible for that. However, because the Igbo wisdom cannot explain every mystery surrounding human destiny, they acknowledge and concede innocence to some one at some cases and situations. One such cases, is when one has made every effort but due to no fault of his, remains unlucky. In this case the effort made must be visible and concerted. Then only then the Igbo would say: *"Omewere ma chi ekweghi, onye uta atala ya"* meaning, once one has done his best but his *chi* says no, let no one blame him.

From the above analyses the concept of human dignity can be understood as an anthropological construct, having its source from God, but interpreted in the community as a functional concept embedded in ones

---

393 Personhood in Igbo culture as process of maturity and attainment of required statutes in the community, so that the Igbo would say: "*Ọ ghọla Mmadu"* (he has become a human being – person) is a very important theme which we will dedicate attention in this inquiry hereafter. For the Igbo the real human being is the person.
394 Achebe, "Chi" in Igbo Cosmology 70; Cf. Nwoga, "Nka na Nzere", 25; Uchendu, *The Igbo of Southeast Nigeria*, 17.
395 Cf. The doctrine of *ilọ ụwa*-Reincarnation in the previous chapter.

ability to achieve a set of societal goals and expectations. Thus one's dignity is only respected and acknowledged in the community for being first and foremost, a human being but not just because he is a human being[396] created in the image and likeness of God as we read in the Judeo Christian conceptions (Gen. 1.26-27); or redeemed by grace in Christ; rather only through attracting respect engendered by concerted effort and achievement; by becoming a person in the community through the process of personhood; by the acquisition of riches, wealth and titles and by meriting a befitting burial rite.

4.1.2 Nsọpụrụ- (Respect)

Nsọpụrụ – is a performative word used in Igbo language to depict an attitude of respect to some one or oneself. It is in fact, an actual recognition of dignity accorded to persons or things for achieving certain position in the society. *Nsọpụrụ* is a word coined from a root word, *nsọ* meaning holy. While the suffix *sọpụrụ*, as a verb means to revere, to keep off, to avoid, to set apart, to be afraid of, to be conscious of; not to be tampered with as in the case of something or someone sacred, holy or a taboo. It is a conscious and wilful act to acknowledge one's dignity in form of respect. *Nsọpụrụ* in the Igbo context refers to an act of sacral attitude to a person or thing; an ascription of honour or a guarantee of a measurable level of recognition of one's own dignity or someone's dignity in the society as the case may be.

That every human being, who qualify in Igbo terms as 'a person'[397] is endowed with dignity – *mmadu bu ugwu* is not arguable in the Igbo thought and culture. In the first instance *mmadu* – human being is one, who possesses life *ndu,* which is a sacred gift from God. Life – *ndu,* which comes from the Supreme Being, God confers on every human being dignity, which should be respected as sacred – *nso.* Therefore, life

---

396 Cf. Nwoga, „Nka na Nzere" 17.
397 'Person' is highlighted to point to the fact that, the Igbo believe that not every human being is a person. It is only character, qualities, functions and roles of a human being, which qualifies one in the strictest sense of the word as a person. Personhood in Igbo (African) view will be treated latter in details.

for the Igbo is respected, beginning from the individual; for instance, he should not take his life for whatsoever reason. It is a taboo among the Igbo either to take one's life or another person's life just at will. However, it is pertinent to note that although every human being by virtue of this precious gift of life is predisposed to dignity, it is only in a functional sense, a matter of respect, which is often based on the achievements and actualization of the God- given potential that one is said to possess dignity.

The more one grows in personhood the more respect he acquires among his kin. More acquisition of traditional titles and wealth means more respect and so dignity. For this reason the whole concept of dignity is subsumed in the conceptuality of dignity as respect. In this sense dignity becomes a matter of respect based on the ability of individuals to actualise their God- given potentials. Thus understood, dignity looses its depths to mere functionalism and existentialism. The English saying: "respect is reciprocal" translated into Igbo world view as *"ugwu bu nkwanye nkwanye, nwanyi amuta ibe ya"* (Dignity is reciprocal so that a woman gives birth to her kind), refers to dignity as the standard for human and societal development. The philosophy of *"egbe bere ugo bere, nke si ibe ya ebela nku kwaa ya"* (let the kite perch let the Adler perch and who ever that denies the other a place to perch let his wings brake), expresses the mutual acknowledgement of respect and dignity which should prevail as a matter of moral principle of communal coexistence among the members of the community. This understanding of respect as dignity which one accords the other person in the expectation that one will receive back the same respect, in other words, this reciprocity, is not only restricted to human beings but even extends to the relationship with their gods.[398] The Igbo world as we have seen before now lays much emphasis on communal living, the basis of which is mutual trust, respect and personhood. That means every one worthy of dignity and respect in a community must be qualified according to the standard of being a person

---

398 Uchendu remarked that reciprocity is the organizing principle of the Igbo social relationship near equality is their ideal. All spirits and deities whose help is invoked during a period of crisis and who stand firm throughout would be rewarded with appropriate sacrifice. Cf., Uchendu, *The Igbo of Southeast Nigeria* 14-15.

for the Igbo, by going through a stipulated recognised processes of attaining personhood in that community.

Nsọpụrụ – respect is a true mark of Igbo communalism. In the Igbo communities as well as in all African communities respect is based on the hierarchical order. The young respects the old, but whether the old reciprocates is arguable. In most cases the elder would be expected to reciprocate with a gesture of favour or protection. For instance, it is typical for the Mbaise in the southern part of Igbo land for the younger ones to call the elders by names such as; *"dede, dada or daa nne"* (*dede* for males and *dada* or *daa nne* for females) as a prefix of respect before the actual name. The elderly actually reciprocates with *nta m (*my younger one). It is pertinent to stress here, that the younger person may forfeit a right from the elder for not recognising and designating him or her in the appropriate respectable stipulated names. The same is applicable to the *ozo*[399] title holders of Onitsha, where cases are raised for a wilful neglect of ones title in ceremonies. There are also some other names set apart as forms of respect among the various clans in their respective dialects. The Igbo would say: *"Nwata sọpụrụ okenye, okenye eru ya aka"* – (If a child respects the elders he reaches old age as a reward) meaning that old age as favour from God will come to those who respect their seniors and elders. Many titled men and women would take it very seriously when their titles are not put before their names. The same can be said of the elder if the junior refuses or forgets to add the prefix, *dede* or *dada* as the case may be.

Another long disturbing issue in the Igbo (African) human dignity profile is the sort of dignity and respect, which they claimed to accord women. It is that based on the functionality and use of women as marriageable and children bearing mate of man. African cultures have always placed the person of a woman under that of a man. Hence most societies in Africa with only a few exceptions are patriarchal in structure. Male chauvinism is the characteristics of such societies. Dignity as an ontological possession of every human person is often reduced to mere func-

---

[399] Ozo title is an achieved position of respect through affluence and acquisition in the society.

tionalism dictated in most cases by the males. In Africa, an unconditional equal respect for women is yet to be achieved.[400]

On another note, deities, spiritual beings, important places, animals and trees such as *Osisi Ofo*[401] (*Ofo* tree) are also respected due to the functions they perform in the socio- cultural life of the people. In other words, their function and utility guarantee their dignity, hence the respect accorded to them. In some Igbo communities certain animals due to religious reasons are respected, for instance, python, particular birds et cetera are not tampered with.[402] Some important places such as shrines and places of gathering due to their religious significance are respected. For the traditional Igbo African women the period of menstrual circle is a period of *nso* – respect and taboo against sexual intercourse. There are several other taboos in the Igbo culture as mark of respect. The same respect- *nso* goes also for the dead, especially those who led a noble life while alive and in some cases a taboo debarring young women from going near the corpse of a woman made barren by nature; and people from going near the corpse of one who died from a disease as a result of curse from the gods.[403]

Ugwu na-Nsopuru – dignity and respect are attributed to a fully inducted adult person, who is useful in the community. It is not only restricted to human but extends to things physical, spiritual and abstract. For instance: deities, birds and trees. The question of the dignity and rights of children, and that of the invalids in the Igbo culture remains a disturbing scandal in the African societies. The imbalanced assessment between women and men in Africa remains a matter of great concern. It would not be exaggerating the fact, to say that some African children have been and are still used as means of affluence and cheap labour. It is doubtful also, whether the Igbo have regard as such, for those at the margin of the society; the mentally sick and some form of disabilities, espe-

---

400 For the reason of scope and competence the researcher wishes, only to mention this aspect as a special area challenging human dignity and rights in Africa and not to delve into it in details.
401 Cf. Christopher I. Ejizu, *Ofo*: Igbo Ritual Symbol, Ibadan Nigeria 1986 37.
402 Cf. Mbiti, African religions and Philosophy 51.
403 Cf. Mbiti, African religions and Philosophy 154.

cially those they regard as incurred from the gods as punishment or as a curse; and those whose personhood are wilfully denied in the community.

4.2 Human Dignity and Personhood in Igbo (African) Social Anthropology

In Igbo (African) social anthropology, not every human being is a person. When the Igbo affirm: *"Mmadu bu Ugwu"* it ordinarily translates as 'a human being is dignity' and it means in fact, 'it is dignity that makes a person'. This subtle but interesting distinction between manhood and personhood cannot be simply understood phenomenally. Rather a possible key to the understanding of a *person* in the Igbo social anthropology is dignity, which could only be understood through their ontology.

Being in the Igbo ontology is associated with its acts or roles. This capacity of association should not be mistaken with Placide Tempels opinion in his Bantu philosophy that, *force* is to the Bantus what *being* is for the West.[404] On the contrary, the Igbo recognises the separation existing between this being and his action- force, and can only recognise a being as a person through his acts.[405]

The English word person was translated from the Latin one, *"persona"*, which referred to the mask worn by the actors on stages and theatres to depict different roles played by actors. For the very fact that they could wear these masks and remove them after the play, the scholastics distinguished between the role and the person playing the role. Standing on the Aristotelian tradition, the scholastics found clarification for their distinction of *'Potency and act'*, *'substance and accident'* with the Aristotelian principle of act and potency where the human person is not a product of his act but existed prior to his acts. Thus the scholastic-Aristotelian tradition stands in direct opposition to the Igbo concept of person. Hence M. Nodencelle opined: "To assume a role is to be captured by the role. We end by becoming what we meant only to appear to be. Function cre-

---

404 Cf. Placide Tempels, Bantu Philosophy 35.
405 This is one of the critics against Tempels Bantu Philosophy. A case of generalisation one notices in the work of Tempels on Bantu Ontology.

ates the man; in a large measure, the personage makes the person".[406] Roles here are constitutive parts of the person not just as a part played by the individual person portraying his personhood. In this way, the role and the person are bound together.

The Igbo identify the person with what roles he performs, so much that they hardly talk of a person in isolation, without reference to his community and his position in the world. This distinction based on role and functions mark out the Igbo personhood as a communally structured reality. Personhood is something, which has to be achieved in the community. When asked what the Igbo understand by personhood, Ogbujah's respondents were all agreed that a person in the Igbo understanding is,

> ... A grown up man or woman ... some one who comes from a family a community ... you have to marry, build a house of your own, and have wealth to take care of your household before you can be said to be a person ... That is, apart from the fact that God created everybody, it is not all that qualify to be addressed as persons in the Igbo version.[407]

The dead who attained personhood on earth are not lost forever, they are known as the *living dead*, the ancestors who are helped by the living to facilitate their possible reincarnation (*ilọ ụwa*).[408]

Sequel to the above distinction between persons and human beings there is always a hierarchy of personhood based on gender and achievement. Ogbujah's respondents made further distinctions between persons hierarchically. For instance, asked whether children qualify as persons in Igbo Land, they answered: "Children are not yet taken as persons because they have not achieved any thing. They have nothing to be known for".[409] Another respondent emphasised: "Yes there is a difference. It is true that they are all human beings, but there is a difference: an old man shares more fully in personhood than a child".[410] Among the Igbo a man shares more fully in personhood than a woman, while uninitiated children in contradistinction to initiated adults are not even regarded as 'persons' in the

---

406 M. Nodencelle, Love and Person, Shed and Ward, New York 1966 145.
407 Ogbujah, The Idea of Personhood 32, 42, 45.
408 Cf. the meaning of the concept ilọ ụwa among the Igbo above.
409 Ogbujah, The Idea of Personhood 42.
410 Ogbujah, The Idea of Personhood 47.

strict sense.[411] Further more, it is doubtful whether the mentally retarded sick persons, outcasts and foul members of the society merit personality among the Igbo. Nwoga clarifies this among the Igbo when he affirmed that: "One has first to be a human being. And in the tradition of Igbo assignment of being to action, it is not everything that looks like a human being that is a human being ...."[412]

Therefore it is easy to misconstrue the concept of manhood with that of personhood among the Igbo, especially when it is considered from the scholastic viewpoint.[413] Manhood in Igbo Anthropology is derived from nature, while personality or personhood is a sociological concept grounded in nature.[414] From a phenomenal perspective, role or personality portrays personhood. They are bound in one unity man. Ogbujah affirms: "Function creates the man. In a way, the personage makes the person. Phenomenally, without the role, there is no person".[415] It is under this framework that one can understand the Igbo conceptualisation of dignity. Suffice it to say that, to talk of a dignity so universal based on equality and from the fact of being human is foreign to the Igbo traditional society. Dignity for the Igbo is socially and anthropologically constructed. It inheres in the person through the roles he or she plays; roles and achievements recognised; valued and approved by the society.

4.2.1 Human Person: 'Onye' as Communally Structured

The word person meaning *onye* or *onye a* (someone or somebody), explains the origin of human society. It is a relational term, which empha-

---

411 Cf. Ogbujah, The Idea of Personhood 49.
412 Nwoga, "Nka na Nzere" 17.
413 The scholastic view of the person as conceived in the Aristotelian framework of 'potency and act', 'substance and accident' made a difference between the human being and the roles he plays, thereby placing the individual as a permanent substratum, while his personality is the accident. Such an estrangement of personality from the so called substratum was turned over by the modern thinkers like Descartes, Hume, and Locke et cetera, who identified the person with his roles.
414 Cf. Ogbujah, The Idea of Personhood 77.
415 Ogbujah, The Idea of Personhood 77.

sises the human extensions in forms of relationships. In his Article: *"The structure of the Self in Igbo Thought"*, Theophilus Okere stresses this relatedness of a person or self to his or her community through the family when he affirmed: "Every one has a source, a link, belongingness, the parents being the source of their children. Every one comes into the world belonging and relating."[416] The person is part of the community, and the community a constituting part of the person. He is a congenitally communitarian self, incapable of being, existing and really unthinkable – except in the complex of relations of the community.[417] Thus one can say with Leonhard Harding without any fear of contradiction that the African society is a "person oriented society".[418]

Ogbujah's grammatical analysis of the meaning of the word *'onye'* – person reveals two senses: *'onye'* as a noun and *'onye'* as an adjective.[419] As a noun, it can be used for interrogation in which case, it can always stand alone as in the *"onye?"* Who?, or be used to introduce interrogative statements as in *"onye no ebe a?"* Who is here? On the other hand, *'Onye'* can be used as the self or subject. In this sense, its nearest but not exact English equivalent is person.[420] In this last sense, it can be used to refer to both human and supra human realities.

A peculiar feature of the term *onye* is that even when it is used as a noun, it must be prefixed as an adjective to another noun. For instance: *onye oru* – a worker; *onye ocha* – a white man; *onye Fada* – a priest, et cetera. In this wise the word *'onye'* as a noun is not used in isolation.

When used in interrogative forms the word *onye* elicits not just a simply answer for example, *onye ka ibu?* Who are you, will require more than a first name for an answer in the Igbo understanding. It will be expected that one should mention the lineage or the family where he comes from. A normal and acceptable response would be *"a bu m nwa ...."* (I am the child of ....). It would be necessary, in this case to give the family name

---

416 Theophilus Okere "The Structure of the Self in Igbo Thought," in: Theophilus Okere (ed.) Identity and Change, Washington D.C 1996 159.
417 Cf. Okere, Identity and Change 160.
418 Cf. Harding, Menschenbilder und Menschenrechte: Afrikanische Erfahrungen 238.
419 Ogbujah, The Idea of Personhood 138.
420 Cf. Edeh, Towards an Igbo Metaphysics 94.

because it counts more than the individual first name. The term *onye* is thus used to situate an individual within a cultural group.[421] Notice the emphasis on the group consciousness, which pervades the whole Igbo African personhood. It has a serious implication for the understanding of human dignity among the Igbo who have been described by scholars as person oriented people, in contrast to the western individualism.

The structure of the human person in Igbo society is fashioned from the appreciation of the being of man in Igbo social anthropology. The human person in Igbo anthropology embodies the relational capacity needed to live a genuine community life. A person is defined in Igbo African society in terms and categories of his community. That means his family, ancestral lineage, and the agnatic organisation. Thus Edeh argues:

> Whereas most western views of the human person are a result of the abstraction of some physical or psychological qualities of the lone individual, Igbo views of a person are abstracted with special reference to the environing community: the community of male and female, of man and animal, of sentient and insentient beings, of sensible and supra-sensible realities, and of the living and the dead ....[422]

This relational capacity as a defining mark of personhood is much stressed by John Zizioulas and the Orthodox Eastern theological tradition.[423] Influenced by Zizioulas, Elizabeth Johnson[424] and Catherine Lacugna[425] have shown in their different works how communion among persons forms the basis of Trinitarian community. From the above analysis it becomes clear in what conceptual categories the Igbo situate a person. The person is not understood from the individual subjective standpoint but from the communal and relational stand points. This again has a marked implication in

---

421 Cf. Ogbujah, The Idea of Personhood 138-139.
422 Edeh, Towards An Igbo Metaphysics 94.
423 See John Zizioulas, Being as Communion: Studies in Personhood and the Church, St. Vladimir Seminary, New York 1997.
424 See Patricia Fox (ed.), God as Communion: John Zizioulas, Elizabeth Johnson, and the Retrieval of the Symbol of the Triune God, Liturgical Press: New York 2001.
425 See Catherine Lacugna, God for Us: The Trinity and the Christian Life, Harper One publishers, New York 1993.

our understanding of the concept of human dignity operating in the Igbo African societies, which is purely functional and socio-anthropological.

4.2.2 Personhood as Process among the Igbo (Africans)

Personhood among the Igbo (African) is something one attains through a process. A process stipulated by the community in accordance with her worldview. The community grooms and prunes the individual through a process to full personhood. This process runs right from the time of birth to death and burial of the individual. Ifeanyi Menkiti observes to that effect that,

> Persons become persons only after a process of incorporation. Without incorporation into this or that community, individuals, are considered to be mere danglers to whom the description 'person' does not fully apply.[426]

Although Menkiti did not pin point the particular ritual, after which one becomes fully incorporated for instance, the *ịma ọgwụ* ceremony which normally takes place within or after puberty among the Mbaise Igbo he succeeded in bringing out a very important aspect of the Igbo African procedural nature of person in the Igbo thought-pattern. The individual must be seen as going through a long process of social and ritual transformation until he or she attains a status truly definitive of a person.[427] Personhood has to be achieved not by mere inheritance or by the very fact of being born of human seed. Menkiti insists that the notion of person has to be normative, that means recognition of personhood based on the principles of the cultural norms operating among a people.[428]

---

426 Ifeanyi, A. Menkiti, "Person and Community in African Traditional Thought", in: R. A. Wright (ed.), African Philosophy: An Introduction³, U.S.A. 1984 171-181 here172.
427 Cf. Ifeanyi, A. Menkiti, "Person and Community in African Traditional Thought" 172.
428 Cf. Ifeanyi A. Menkiti, "On the Normative Conception of a Person", in: Kwasi Wiredu (ed.), A Companion to African Philosophy, Oxford, 2005 324-331; see also, Didler Njiramanda Kaphagawani, "African Conception of a

4.2.2.1 The Person at Birth and Initiation

Every one comes into the world belonging and relating[429]. Here, the importance of the parents, the family and the community are been stressed. The child at birth is received into the human family with specific rituals differing from one community to the next. In the main, among the southeast Igbo, it is native to bury the umbilical cord of the baby, popularly known as the *"alọ nwa"* beside a palm tree. This act alone claims the palm oil tree automatically for the child as *alọ nkwụ*. After eight days the child will be ceremoniously circumcised and a family and personal name given to the child. All these however, do not qualify the child to personhood as such. Prior to the rituals of puberty, one enjoys manhood or womanhood as the case may be, but not personhood. Rather, the ladders of personhood begin with the rigorous and manly ritual of initiation into personhood as Ogbujah remarked:

> In traditional Igbo societies, when one passes through puberty rites (whether physiological or social puberty), one is then admitted, strictly speaking, into personhood. A person thus, is a human being who has consciously realized himself / herself through social roles and functions in the society.[430]

Panteleon Iroegbu refers to an Igbo person as the: "Communally and self-embodied being that is in search of transcendence".[431] This transcendence however, can only be realised in the community.

The ritual ceremony known as *ịma ọgwụ* or (introduction to the secrets of personhood) among the Mbaise people of southeast part of Igbo land introduces a young man into personhood after his puberty. Within this ritual, which lasts at least, four weeks the young man is tested to endure hardship, fear, and pain; to survive different human challenging situations. At the end of this rigorous mystagogy the young initiate comes out with the firm readiness to face the ups and downs of life. Later in life,

---

Person: A critical Survey", in: Kwasi Wiredu (ed.), A Companion to African Philosophy, Oxford, 2005 332-342.
429 Cf. Okere, Identity and Change 159.
430 Ogbujah, The Idea of Personhood 148.
431 Panteleon Iroegbu, Kpim of Personality: Treatise on the Human Person, Owerri 2000 107.

the individual proceeds to the next stage of the initiation known as the *itu anya* or *iwa anya,* (manliness, endurance and bravery) which will enable him to discuss with spirits of the land, the ancestors. The last stage will be the *itu ebi or ịgwọ aja* (becoming a master in spiritual mysteries) with this; one can become a medicine man – *dibia* or a seer – *ọhụ-ụzọ* as the case may be. He can now own a personal shrine.

While in some other part of Igbo land, for instance among the northern part of the Igbo, the *Mmaw* masquerade society popularly known as the spirits of the land embodies at times the ritual which introduces the individual to personhood.[432] The young initiate is introduced to certain secrets of life concerning some puzzles that stand enigmatically before the individual. Only those initiated have access to these mysteries and their meanings. Those not initiated remain outsiders and may not be regarded in the long run as personalities. Rituals reveal values established by the group/ community, according to which individuals must act for a harmonious living; they are a key to an understanding of the essential constitution of human societies.[433] Therefore, the rite of initiation in the Igbo culture is specifically structured to integrate the individual properly into personhood. For the validity of these rituals, the community specifies and guarantees the whole processes.

4.2.2.2 The Age Grade System

Age serves as a denominator of groups among the Igbo. Young people, mostly the males group themselves according to their age grades. In some areas the grading system is based on three-year basis, while some maintain a loose system of grouping system, which does not necessarily depend of the above-mentioned basis of three years. The age grade system serves as one of the significant stages in the process of personhood in Igbo Land.

In the southeast part of Igbo among the Mbano, Obowo and some parts of Ekwerazu Mbaise in Imo State Nigeria, there exists a popular ceremony called the *'iwa akwa'* or *'mwam akwa'* (wearing of cloth) ceremony performed on a particular age group who have attained a recognised age of personhood. A ripe adult appears in public dressed in a garment of re-

---

432 Cf. Basden, Among the Ibos of Nigeria 117.
433 Cf. V. Turner, The Ritual Process, Chicago 1969 6.

sponsibility, officially pointing to the fact that he is no more a child. In some other areas of Igbo Land the same ceremony is known as *'ifuta ebiri'*, which means the presentation of age grade. The young adults would parade themselves before the community as a set ripe and mature; as people who have attained personhood and now ready to undertake responsibilities in the community. This passage from young to adulthood is remarkable in the processes of personhood in the community. It is expected that at this point, the individual should have got married and established his own family. After this ceremony, the person qualifies to engage and contribute positively in the development of the community. It is a very sad thing both for the individual and the relatives to be left out of this prodigious ceremony under any pretext what so ever.

4.2.2.3 Marriage and Family Life

Marriage as a process through which young adult girl and boy come together with the sole intention of forming a family has remained a societal affair both in the traditional and modern Igbo (African) communities. Marriage is the most important event, which the Igbo look forward to experiencing in the life; upon which a very high value is set upon.[434] Igbo marriages can be classified as traditional marriage; church marriage, and civil marriage. All these marriage forms are validated by the payment of bride wealth. The two innovations in present-day Igbo marriages – Church marriage and civil – have their foundation on the traditional form. Whether the final rituals of marriage are performed in the church or in the court registrar's office, the marriage must begin with families- the family of the bride and that of the bridegroom.[435] Leonhard Harding attests to this traditional fact when he wrote:

> Elders have a very important consultative weight in the founding of new families; Marriage does not stand from the personal decisions of the young couples alone; it is often understood as a contract between two families, who should see to it that the whole group survives.[436]

---

434 Cf. Basden, Among the Ibos of Nigeria 68.
435 Cf. Uchendu, The Igbo of Southeast Nigeria 87.
436 Harding, Menschenbilder und Menschenrechte: Afrikanische Erfahrungen 308.

Marriage confers a status on the individual thereby enhancing his or her personality as J. Marquette observes:

> To be an adult is above all to be a mother or a father. If bachelors exist in (Igbo) African societies, their situation is not a normal expected social role.[437]

A married person is taken more seriously in the community than an unmarried person. However, it is pertinent to note that the traditional Igbo society suffers from a deplorable caste system known as the *osu na diala*[438] caste system. On no account should a *diala* marry an *osu* in the Igbo cultural set up. Although this unreasonable position is controversial today both by Christianity and civilisation any one who ventures intermarriage between the two risks a kind of a diminished personhood. Marriage confers a sense of responsibility on the couple to make sure that the care of children is guaranteed. They are to be seen as mature personalities who should also help the community to get up.

Having children remains the primary purpose of marriage among the Igbo. Every human being is expected to propagate his or her specie. A marriage without children is said to be a failure among the Igbo. The reason for this conclusion is partly due to the high premium placed on immortality through reincarnation; and partly due to the social security which children guarantee their parent, especially at old age. Uchendu notes:

> Children are a great social insurance agency, a protection against dependence in old age. To have a child is to strengthen both the social and the economic status for it is the male child who inherits the father's property.[439]

---

[437] J. Marquette, Africanity: The Cultural Unity of Black Africa, Oxford 1972 67.

[438] Osu na Diala phenomenon is an ugly cultural stigma which demarcated between a person said to have been dedicated to a deity – the osu and an indigene – the diala of a particular community. As such the osu receives a respect in form of a taboo; an untouchable status from the normal members of the society – the diala. This theme will be handled in detail in the following part.

[439] Uchendu, The Igbo of Southeast Nigeria 57.

Children enhance personhood in the Igbo (African) culture. This is replete in the name given to children at birth: *Oche eze*, meaning my throne, *Amaechi, Ahamefule, Amaefule*, et cetera (May our name, family or ancestral lineage not lost); *Nwabugwu* (a child is one's pride and dignity). More children are regarded as affluence in the Igbo economic terms, because children in the traditional African communities contributed immensely towards the up keep of the family. Today however, this practice of involving children in the economic process has been condemned as 'child's labour'. In the traditional marriage, polyandry is never tolerated; polygamy that is often occasioned by bareness is also seen as a sign of affluence since having a large family is a noble achievement and a boost to one's personality in the society.

Celibacy in the traditional Igbo (African) societies is said to be unthinkable. An unmarried young man or woman is seen as a failure or sign of irresponsibility. Basden described it in these terms: "Celibacy is an impossible prospect. Unmarried persons of either sex, except in special cases, are objects of derision, and to be childless is the greatest calamity that can befall a woman. Hence a very high value is set upon marriage".[440] In the same vein, Uchendu remarks: "Igbo is a society which has no concept of celibacy but tolerates celibates as victims of economic forces".[441] Unmarried bachelors are not taken seriously in the society. They are seen as irresponsible people and merit insignificant personality.

4.2.2.4 Death and Traditional Burial as Symbols of Personhood

Death is a necessary end of biological life. It is understood in Igbo Land as transition to the world of the dead, *ala mmuo*. As we have discussed earlier the Igbo belief in two worlds: the world of the living and the world of the dead. These two worlds are peopled by persons, who have qualified as such through the evaluative functions performed in the community of the living. Uchendu captures the interaction between these two worlds thus:

> In the Igbo conception, the world of the 'dead' is a world full of activities: its inhabitants, manifest in their behaviour and thought processes that they are "living" ... In the Igbo view, there is a constant

---

440 Basden, Among the Ibos of Nigeria 68.
441 Uchendu, The Igbo of Southeast Nigeria 86.

interaction between the dead and the living: the dead are reincarnated, the death making the transition from the corporeal to the incorporeal life of the ancestors possible.[442]

Nevertheless, death remains a calamity for the Igbo; it disturbs the existing social and ritual relationships and demands a new mode of adjustment for the bereaved family. The status goal of the one who dies young seems frustrated, and creates a vacuum in his family in its role structure through the loss of a member. The uncertainty about the cause of such death is a source of concern for all. Most often, divination would settle this uncertainty through a thorough search for the cause of death and thereby recommending ritual remedies. The cause of death will always be blamed on the sins committed during the previous life- time.[443] A ripe old age is seen as a blessing, honour and respect among the Igbo (Africans). The death of an elderly is often celebrated thus, ushering him into the world of the ancestors, the living dead, who continue to sustain the lineage in an unbreakable coming and going through *ịlọ ụwa*-reincarnation.

A ground burial[444] of a well-deserved elder in the community is always a cause of hope for the perpetuation of the lineage, because by a worthy death the dead acquires another remarkable stage of personhood, namely *ndi iche* status (ancestors – the living dead). Ancestors, other wise known as the living dead are the ancestors who have died within the last five generations. Their memories are still with the living in one-way or the other. During prayers the oldest men of the various communities remember them in a special way by pouring libations. They are the closest link that men have with the spirit world. Some of the things known about the Spirits apply also to the living- dead. Mbiti describes them thus:

---

442   Uchendu, The Igbo of Southeast Nigeria 12.
443   Uchendu, The Igbo of Southeast Nigeria 13.
444   Ground burial among the traditional Igbo society was reserved only to a death member of the community, who died with dignity without incurring the rat of the gods through abominable life style, which was often denoted by the way and manner of death. For instance, deaths due to severe and shameful sicknesses such as stroke, *mba- mmuo* as it is called in Igbo; Haemorrhage in the case of a woman and some other horrible stomach related diseases attracted abnormal treatment as the dead are not buried normally in the ground but simply thrown away in the *ajo ohia* – evil forest.

These are still part of their human families, and people have personal memories of them. ...The living-dead are still 'people', and have not yet become 'things', 'spirits', or 'its'. They return to their human families from time to time, and share meals with them, however symbolically. They know and have interest in what is going on in the family. When they appear, which is generally to the oldest members of the household, they are recognised by name as 'so and so'; they enquire about family affairs, and may even warn of impending danger or rebuke those who have failed to follow their special instructions.[445]

Suffice it to say that the living-dead, the ancestors are recognised as moral and ethical guardians of the society and occupy a very high position among the Igbo. It is only those who lived a meritorious life that are respected and honoured as the ancestors. On the contrary, those who did not merit the status of ancestors because of dishonourable life on earth are forgotten in the land of the living and as Okot p'Bitek observes "they may be malevolent and can be also hostile and cause sickness and other misfortunes to an individual."[446]

To qualify for a befitting burial among the Igbo is glorious, thus accounting for the detailed and prolonged period of mourning and burial rites. Basden tries to show case the immensity of this practise even though in the Christian mind, so barbaric at some points, especially when it involves a burial of a king with human beings.[447] Regrettable though, as crass ignorance, the practise mirrored the respect and level of personhood achieved by the dead person among the Igbo. The respondents of Ogbujah were unequivocal in their responses about the reality and meaning of death; and the significance of burial rites and ceremonies among the Igbo. In their responses they made it clear that when a person dies, he goes to join his kinsmen in the spirit world and will only be remembered if the dead had a male child and or children.[448] Befitting burial rites are performed

---

445 Mbiti, African religions and Philosophy 83.
446 Okot p'Bitek, "The Concept of Jok among Acholi and Lango", in: The Uganda Journal, 27, 1 (March 1963) 15-29 here 25.
447 Cf. Basden, Among the Ibos of Nigeria 112-126.
448 Cf. Ogbujah, The Idea of Personhood 48.

to make it easier for the ancestors to receive the departed as a worthy member of the lineage and to facilitate a speedy reincarnation.

4.3 Dignity as Function among the Igbo

That the Igbo (Africans) conceptualise dignity from the existential and purely functional view can be seen in their attitude toward the acquisition of status, titles and wealth. The Igbo has a saying which summarises their understanding of existence in the world: *"Uwa bu ahia, onye zuru nke ya y' alaa"* (Life is like buying and selling, when one finishes his transaction he leaves), all referring to living as an activity. Life for the Igbo (Africans) is dynamic and can change. The Ability to change with the changing world is always in line with the peoples' philosophy of life. No condition is permanent. The Igbo believe that their situation can change; and that forces can be manipulated including factors and forces of change. This existential view of life permeates every aspect of the life of the Igbo (African), through associating *force, activity* with *being*. A human being is recognised and dignified by his or her functions, achievement and the roles he performs in the society.

4.3.1 Dignity and Status Placement among the Igbo

Most ethnological observations on the Igbo reveal her as an egalitarian society, in which almost everybody is equal. However, this generalisation beclouds at times the various status maintained within the social and individual profiles. There exist differences and levels of social relationships in the communities. In spite of these differences, all Igbo share the same equalitarian ideology: the right of the individual to climb to the top, and faith in his ability to do so because for the Igbo, *uwa na eme ntughari* – (the world changes) reality is never static but dynamic.[449]

The Igbo conceptualise status placement in two categories namely, common basis and hierarchical order.[450] The common basis refers to the kinship system, the *Umunna* agnate where every member enjoys a com-

---

449 Cf. Uchendu, The Igbo of Southeast Nigeria 54.
450 Cf. Uchendu, The Igbo of Southeast Nigeria 84.

mon status of *Nwanna* that means belonging to one ancestral father; and changes which could occur to one leading to diminishment of the status or loss of it, just as in the case of *Osu, Ohu* and *Pawn*.[451] While the hierarchical order refers to the different statuses attained by virtue of age stratifications, which are based on seniority- juniority profile; leadership and the association status attainable by the individual with or without personal efforts. The first-born son of every family and kindred – the *Umunna* is the most senior and by that fact occupies the *"Opara"* position. By virtue of his natal position as the first- born son, the *"Opara"* becomes the harbinger of political and moral authority; a custodian of justice and order; the *pate familia* in all matters, especially the in the performance of rituals in the family and kindred. His authority is symbolised by a possession of the family or kindred *Ofo,* which is the symbol of authority and justice in the family and community, which is handed down from one generation to the next. While the first born daughter of the family, the *Ada ezi* in her own rank retains a special right among her siblings in the family even when she latter marries outside the kindred. For many Igbo communities, special names are reserved for special status. For instance, in Mbaise in the southeast part of Igbo land, *dede* or *dada*, are designated as status name for senior brother or senior sister respectively. Status names, like *ọpara* and *ada* refers to the first-born son and first daughter of the family respectively. Other status names such as *ụlụ, ịbari*, meaning the second born and the rest respectively and *ọdụnwa* the last child are all names derived from the positions in the family, which carry with them respects and dignity.

Therefore, age status seen from the point of view of *juniority-seniority* remains a very important parameter for attributing respect and dignity in the Igbo society. An elderly person acquires automatically a greater recognition than a younger one, not just for any other reason but due, to the mere fact of age. Age plays a significant role in attributing dignity and respect to individuals. Furthermore, Leadership status and associational status determines to a large extent how a person is honoured and respected in his community.

Another status worthy of mention is that of women in the Igbo society. The women members of an Igbo village are of two categories: the

---

451 Status among the Igbo replete the *non-diala* status, which in contrast to the *diala* status is dehumanizing.

umuokpu or *umuada* as they are called in some areas who may be unmarried, married divorced or widowed women who belong to the village by descent, and the *ndom alu alu* meaning simply, married women who belong to it by marriage. The rule that women should always be married gives marriage the precedence over descent[452]. However, the *umuokpu* or *umuada* performs some institutionalized authority over the married women of the kindred – *ndom alu alu,* especially during the mourning rites marking the latter's widowhood.[453]

The last but not the least to be mentioned is the *diala and non- diala Status*. Besides the differences in the masculine and feminine status placement discussed above, the most important distinction the Igbo make in their stratification system is that between the *diala* and *non-diala*. The *diala* is a freeborn, whose navel cord is buried preferably at the foot of palm oil tree. To be a *diala* is to have the doors of title societies and other institutions open to one. The *diala* is accorded a high social and ritual status, regardless of his age, sex or wealth[454]. In contrast to the *diala,* the *non-diala* is a subordinate of the *diala*. Uchendu distinguishes types of *non-diala* status, the *ohu* – slave, the *Pawn* – debtor and the *osu* – outcast.[455] Except the status of diala, which has respect and dignity attached to it, the non- *diala* status bespeaks of human degradation.

4.3.2 Acquisition of Wealth and Titles as Dignity

The assessment of the Igbo world as that, which offers the individual the opportunity of striving for wealth and seeking titles – *ozo* is a fair one.

---

452 Cf. Uchendu, The Igbo of Southeast Nigeria 86, 87.
453 Widowhood is a state of mourning a departed husband or wife. In Igbo Land the period of widowhood in the Igbo culture plays an important role in the maintenance of respect and order during the lifetime of the couple, especially on the side of the woman against her husband. The *umuokpu* as members of the community by descent play a protective role for their brothers against some unhealthy and unbecoming treatments in the hands of the wives. The time of Widowhood is a veritable time for reckoning.
454 Cf. Uchendu, The Igbo of Southeast Nigeria 88.
455 The issue of *non-diala* status as degradation of human dignity among the Igbo will be treated elaborately in the following part.

The Igbo are basically status seekers. Metaphorically speaking, they believe that the world is a marketplace where status symbols can be bought. For the Igbo, the whole lifetime is a struggle for achieving status and personhood, which culminates in the achievement of ancestral honour in the world of the dead.

There is a society known as the *'ozo-title'* society among the Igbo. In this society, ranks and achievements are tied together. One can only qualify through fulfilling the necessary conditions. These conditions are talents and hard work most often translated in monetary and wealth. For instance, the *ozo-title* society in the West north part of Igbo land, the Awka and in some Onitsha areas present such societies where the acquisition of titles are very ostentatious. While the *ezeji* title (Yam chiefs) remains a show of affluence and hard work for the South Eastern part, the Ngwa, Mbaise and Umuahia areas. There are numerous other titles existing in other parts of Igbo land, which we may not mention here, but suffice it to say that the motivating factors are just the same: The more one is able to gather these title while alive the better, because what ever one gathers here follows one to the next world; and one's reception among the ancestors depends also to a large extent on how many one was able to buy this titles here while alive.

The Igbo model for viewing their social stratification is based on wealth. It does not matter what occupation a person engages in, in order to provide for his old age. In this line of thought the Igbo distinguish between the *ogbenye or mbi* – the poor from *dimpka* – the moderately prosperous and the latter from *nnukwu mmadu or ogaranya* – the rich. This classification still ignores the widespread practice of occupational combination, the *diala-osu* caste dichotomy, the chief sources of wealth-whether from farming, trading, or medicine as well as other kinship variables which affect status placement. According to Uchendu, "Its chief utility lies in the fact that it commands general consensus and provides a normative frame which guides behaviour".[456] The wealth-prestige model appears to be the only status model that is coextensive with the Igbo society. The Igbo make clear distinctions between wealth (*aku, uba*), status position (*okwa*), and prestige (*ude*). Some one may be wealthy and at the same time positioned but has no prestige. Uchendu points out that:

---

456 Uchendu, The Igbo of Southeast Nigeria 92.

The Igbo "big" man, whether a politician, a college professor, a chief, a merchant, or a company director may be wealthy, but his prestige depends on how he "converts" his wealth into prestigious acts: taking a title, owning a country house, providing his relations with a college education and donating generously to his town's scholarship or to the development fund are the modern ways of converting wealth into prestige[457].

The above description of wealth, title and their use in uplifting the Igbo community, through philanthropic gestures portray the sources of human valuation and dignity prevalent in Igbo thought and culture. Dignity is more or less a social construct among the Igbo. It can be acquired and can be lost as well.

4.4 Loss of Human Dignity and Rights in the Igbo Traditional Society

Dignity as a social construct among the Igbo can be acquired and can as well, be lost. In such a socio- anthropological setting where the society has an upper hand in the making of the individual; and the socio-religious norms, customs and tradition play major roles scholars argue on whether there were human rights among the traditional African societies and if there were, what types of rights these could have been?

Some scholars like Joy Mukubwa Hendrickson, in her work: *Rights in Traditional African Societies*, argues that the question whether the African traditional societies had human rights came from a bias that the idea of human rights came solely from the west. The idea of rights in the west stemmed from the experience of the individual fighting for his rights from the state or feuds as the case may be. Even though the African chiefs existed and still exist, rights standing in contra distinction with the community or the chiefs were not known. What one could trace could be sanctions limiting the excesses of the chiefs, but these are not rights. African societies as rational people have cultures, laws, customs and tradition, which were got-

---

457 Uchendu, The Igbo of Southeast Nigeria 92.

ten from moral norms. She argues however, that right, as a moral practice and as an idea can be conceptualised in the different cultures.[458]

According to Hendrickson it is therefore, "not to seek to define the idea of human rights in terms of what it should mean, but she is interested in what it has meant to Africans".[459] While humans universally oppose injustice, specific interpretations of the concept of human rights have varied across time and place. Hendrickson affirms that, "a truly universal concept of human rights encompasses all shades of meaning and includes an African perspective"[460]. Since an idea begins with time and alters with time, an idea of rights in African traditional societies should have begun with the pre-colonial time, but should have also continued with a process of evolution in the colonial and post- colonial time.

For Paulin J. Hountondji, rights or dignity are not just mere metaphysical and moral principles, rather they have some ethnographical and geographical implications namely; referring to this particular people and time.[461]. African societies, the Igbo inclusive had rights which where ethnically limited. An idea of human rights, universal as the declaration of Human Rights Charter claims, was not in the perspective of the African societies. Hendrickson summarised this point succinctly:

> Although rights understood as claims of a legitimate nature based on a general theory to be treated in a particular manner existed in traditional African societies, these rights cannot be seen as human rights. Examples have shown that the general theory, which legitimizes these claims as rights, is not one, which argues that we are all members of one human race and as such deserve equal treatment from all other human beings. Instead the general theory operating in traditional societies to legitimize claims as rights, is one which

---

458 Cf. Joy Mukubwa Hendrickson, "Rights in Traditional African Societies", in: John, A.A. et al., *African Traditional Political Thought and Institutions*, Lagos 1989 19-39 here 19.
459 Joy Mukubwa Hendrickson, "Rights in Traditional African Societies", in: John, A.A. et al., *African Traditional Political Thought and Institutions* 19-39.
460 Hendrickson: Joy Mukubwa Hendrickson, "Rights in Traditional African Societies", in: John, A.A. et al., *African Traditional Political Thought and Institutions* 20.
461 Cf. Paulin J. Hountondji, African Philosophy, London 1983 177.

societies from each other and recognised rights as belonging only to particular categories of people and not all peoples at all times. These traditional ideas of rights can only be seen as examples of precursors to the modern idea of human rights.[462]

The above citation on the African traditional 'particular human rights' as a precursor of modern rights brings to focus the *Magna carter* known today as the mother of all human rights in the west. Even though the Magna carter outlined some basic principles of human rights as we have them today, it was aimed at protecting the rights of a few namely, the feudal lords and the merchants. The serfs were all the same excluded from these rights.[463]

Therefore, some works on the Igbo (African) socio-cultural anthropology reveal a peculiar scenario of the Igbo systems of dignity and rights, where dignity and rights as realities are acquired and also lost among the Igbo. Chinua Achebe's writings, *Things Fall Apart* written as an Igbo precolonial and colonial experiences; and *Arrow of God* as the Igbo post colonial experiences portrays the Igbo world view and their life. These works, already reviewed in the previous chapter three present the system of rights from the Igbo conception of human dignity in different circumstances. Achebe, through his fictions in Things Fall Apart presented Onoka, the father of his chief character Okonkwo, as one lacking in personhood and therefore lost all his dignity and respect, even to the extent of not meriting a befitting human burial. On the contrary Okonkwo his son, merited several titles and respect but also lost all for not acting in line with the community norms and customs.[464] For instance, *Ikemefula's* death in the hands of a man Okonkwo who he called 'father' was uncustomary. As a consequence the gods avenged the dead boy's course by leading Okonkwo into an unintentional shooting of one of *Ezeudu's son*, during the funeral ceremony of their father *Ezeudu*. It will be recalled also that it was this same Ezeudu, who came to Okonkwo while he was alive on the issue of *Ikemefule* the village slave victim to remonstrate him: that boy called you father, have no hand in his death. Therefore, this mishap for the Igbo was not just a mistake or

---

462 Hendrickson: Joy Mukubwa Hendrickson, "Rights in Traditional African Societies", in: John, A.A. et al., *African Traditional Political Thought and Institutions* 35.
463 Cf. Iwe, The History and Contents of Human Rights 93.
464 Achebe, Things Fall Apart 13ff.

chance, but a calculated vengeance from the gods. As if that was not enough, the god's in order to show how much Okonkwo has lost his dignity among his kin, led him to kill a white man and thereafter commit suicide a dishonoured and undignified death in the Igbo culture and tradition. By so doing he merited no right to a befitting burial as a suicide victim. Uzowulu as the chief character in the *Arrow of God* thought he could escape the wrath of the gods when he violated the communal norms of his community by following the white collar job of the white man as it was called. His paranoid behaviours as a latter consequence proved that no one could escape the wrath of the communal gods.

In these fictions, Achebe brings it to his readers the prescriptive and normative position of the Igbo (African) sense and respect of the community, which are now been jeopardised by the colonial invasion. He makes the distinction so clear that no matter what havoc the European invasion of the Igbo culture must have caused; the community spirit remains unique for the Igbo (Africans). Above all, Achebe in an erudite manner of a literary genius combined both orality and literacy to show case the Igbo (African) community as that capable of guaranteeing and protecting the dignity and rights of the individual. However, he makes the customs and tradition stand out as the legislative hammer of the gods.

Some ugly practices in the traditional societies, which may have lasted till date, may have been as a result of loosing ones dignity and rights in the society. Issues like, the *osu* caste system, widowhood and communal ostracism belong to these issues. The process and details of this loss and consequences will be discussed latter as special issues.

4.5 Summary

The linguistic analysis of *ugwu* na *nsopuru* (dignity and respect) reveals a subtle difference, which creates a serious import to the understanding of dignity in the Igbo ideogram. The Igbo refer more to respect for life and what one can achieve with this life when they talk in practical terms about dignity, because ontologically every being has force. Contrary to the opinion of Tempels, Africans know the difference between being and force. They know that they are different from their acts. What one achieves determines his or her dignity, which can either be positively influenced or diminished. The society is the measure of human dignity, which can only be understood as a social construct.

The idea of Personhood among the Igbo is that conceived to lie at the basis of dignity. It follows a set process from birth to death. The Igbo make distinction between human beings as such and persons, only those who qualify are persons and worthy of dignity and respect. Not every human being is a person in the Igbo anthropology. To qualify one has to belong first of all to the community because the person (*onye*) is communally structured, hence *"mmadu anaghi agba ka ugba"* (the person does not just explode and fall from no where like an oil bean seed). A person has to achieve personhood through efforts and achievements in the community. The amount of titles, wealth and achievement gathered here on earth; and how one transforms these in helping the society grow up determines ones level of dignity and respect, since these would boost ones personhood. The relevance of life as a market place where one transacts and departs is often emphasised through this proverb: *uwa bu ahia, onye zuru nke ya y' alaa* (Life is a market place, after the transactions, one carries his or her goods home). Above all, marriage is very much respected among the Igbo, since through marriages offspring – children are guaranteed. Status structure in the Igbo community is such that certain personalities are respected and honoured or despised because of their status. For instance, the *opara* is respected for his status and the same is applicable to all *diala,* while the *osu* is despised because of no status. Death is a stage of personhood, even though seen as a calamity, especially in the case of the death of young people the death of a ripe old person is celebrated as a meritorious passage to the ancestral status, from where one can replenish the lineage through a process of reincarnation, *ilo uwa.*

The role of the community as the guarantor and protector of dignity is paramount. Igbo communities are ruled and organised by norms and traditions promulgated by the ancestors and ratified by the earth goddess *Ala.* Dignity as a social construct therefore, means that one can acquire dignity in the society where one can loose the same dignity. According to the worldview of the Igbo, reality is mutable and not permanent. The Igbo world is basically dynamic, *"uwa na eme ntughari"* (life situation is in a constant flux).

Part Three
Theology of Human Dignity

Chapter Five: The Judeo-Christian Perspective on Human Dignity

5.1 Introduction

Different concepts of human dignity operating among European and African cultures have been identified in the preceding parts of this inquiry. The European concept dove-tailed into two distinct categories namely, heteronomy and autonomy. Heteronomy refers to an understanding of human dignity from the point of view of a transcendental being outside and above man as one responsible and source of human dignity. While on the contrary, autonomy lays more credence to the human being as the source. Interestingly the both concepts lay claim to a universal prerogative. Among Africans, particularly the Igbo of Nigeria human dignity is purely conceived as a social construct: dignity even though, ultimately bestowed by God it is the community that determines in practice who gets the dignity through its institutions. Generally, in the two distinct cultures of Europe and Africa the idea of human dignity reveals itself in each case as an interpretative principle of the person.

Historically speaking, human dignity has been approached and understood from different points of emphasis, namely as moral norms as in the case of various religions and cultures and also as rights as in the case of UDHR and state constitutions. Consequently what played off in the history of rights in Europe and America culminating in the human rights declaration of 1948; in fact that which has come to be known today as an European idea of human dignity; and its formulation into laws of rights in the state constitutions of European and American states can be said to have been derived from the Christian anthropology, which in turn was informed by the biblical assertion that the human being is created in the image and likeness of God (*Imago Dei*) (Gen.1, 26-27).

In the light of the above therefore, it can be asserted without fear of contradictions that without prejudice to its Greco-Roman history, what came to sediment as the final product of the Western conception of human dignity have been influenced by the Christian view of the human being as created in the image and likeness of God.[465]

Theology of human dignity tries at the first instance to excavate the Judeo-Christian origins of the concept. First of all, Christian understanding of dignity can be distinguished or summarised in three major categories, 1. Ontological or Innate dignity. This refers to the worth or dignity possessed by human beings by virtue of their created nature, a dignity which is inherent in that nature, and which as such belongs to all human beings; 2. Existential or acquired dignity is that which belongs to those human beings who live out their lives well in accordance with the end or purpose that God has for them; 3. Definitive dignity belongs to the perfection of human life in the exemplary life of the saints who are enjoying the beatific vision in heaven.[466] In addition to the history of the development of human dignity as Imago Dei was the subsequent development of the concept of 'person' in Christian anthropology as a subsistent individual of an intellectual and rational nature, which is precisely what gives him his dignity.[467] However this definition later broadened to emphasis the person

---

465 Cf. Hilpert, Die Idee der Menschenwürde aus der Sicht christlicher Theologie, 47.
466 Cf. L. Gormally, Human Dignity: The Christian View and the Secularist View, Pontificia Academia Pro Vita, http://www.academiavita.org/template.jsp 11/09/2008 1-10 here 1.
467 Thomas Aquinas insistence on the link between the idea of dignity and that of person, stem from the significance of the mask worn by actors in stages in the ancient Greek theatres. Actors wore masks to represent people holding high offices (dignitaries) or distinguished positions in their societies. Remarkably it was the Augustinian treatise on the Trinity, which first changed the notion of mask to emphasise the hypostatic union of the Godhead in the three persons of the blessed Trinity as analogical to soul and the body constituting the unity in the human person. It was a reflection that transposed the Greek mask from its phenomenal relevance to a genuine philosophy of person. See also Thomas Aquinas, The Summa Theologiae 1 q. 29, a.3, ad 2.

as a subject, not just with intellectual and rational capabilities but also with his experience among others; with a "we" consciousness.

5.1.1 Historical Development of Human Dignity as Imago Dei

The Judeo-Christian perspective on human dignity as *Imago Dei* has continued to develop in the course of history after the early Christian and scholastic eras through inter- confessional interests and interpretations. The stage is set between the Catholic Church, the Reformed Churches and the Protestant Churches. While the Reformed Churches hold that the *image of God* in human beings was completely destroyed by the original sin, The Catholic Church hold that it was not completely destroyed but has been once more redeemed through Christ.[468]

It is however pertinent to note the immense contributions of the Reformed Churches in the discussions towards the current understanding of religious freedom as basic foundation of human dignity. The Lutherans base their point of reference on Luther's teaching on Grace, remaining vehement on their insistence on religious freedom based on the gratuitous nature of faith. Against this backdrop, Luther taught that the respect of civil authority does not warrant the intrusion of ones religious freedom and conscience.[469]

With the modern era *Imago Dei* theology faced continued challenges in a world that suddenly became multi religious and at the same time secular. There was this so-called *"anthropological turn"* in the intellectual history, which affected the whole human fabric and the society. During this period John Locke and other political minded scholars like Hobbes, Rousseau et cetera added their own interpretation to the dignity of human person as one in constant opposition to the political state and order.[470] Consequently some scholars continue to insist that *Imago Dei* conceived, as the only secure protective sphere of the dignity of human person has not succeeded as the enthusiast may have claimed. There was need to ask

---

468 Cf. Huber, „Menschenrechte/Menschenwürde" Art. 5.2, 592; Gaudium et Spes Ch. 1. Art. 22.
469 Cf. Huber, „Menschenrechte/ Menschenwürde" Art. 1.3, 580.
470 Huber, „Menschenrechte/ Menschenwürde" Art. 1.3, 580.

the anthropological question afresh: "what is man?" Anthropology became very relevant to the study of theology and all its enterprises. This will not be surprising, bearing in mind the era of enlightenment with its devastating questions on virtually every aspect of life.

Moreover, the contemporary world pursues assiduously a one-world government structure and consequently by so doing heightens the sensitivity to imperialism and dictation among cultures and religions. It is also true that these cultures and religions, even though accepting globalising influences would also want to maintain a peculiar originality. This situation has worked unfortunately, to the detriment of Imago Dei not being accepted on the grounds of suspicion as an imposed foreign lofty idea. On the other hand, the defence of human individuality and freedom among the Christian West have forced the modern- contemporary scholars to neglect the importance of Christian interpretation of human dignity because that could lead to the refusal of its universal acceptance on grounds of being simply misconstrued as a Western religious discovery.[471]

With the emergence of the secularist view of human dignity during the enlightenment era the theme of *Imago Dei* acquired a more responsive dimension through being sensitive to the contentions and the objections posed by emergent radical religious extremism. Moreover, the effect of the nascent modern rationalism based on the Cartesian *cogito*[472] and Kantians metaphysics of morality was enormous: the autonomy of the moral subject became the matrix of human dignity.[473] The predominant characteristic of this age was one in which God became estranged from his world.

---

471 Cf. Huber, „Menschenrechte/Menschenwürde" Art. 1.3, 581 und 591.
472 The Cogito of Rene Descartes puts premium on reason as the only faculty that guarantees human existence, and by inference also that which could guarantee human dignity. "I think therefore I exist" was to be maximised by the subsequent philosophers like Kant, who now made a home for this idea in the German idealism and his famous moral philosophy, the 'autonomous subject.'
473 Cf. The Manifesto of Pico della Mirandola (On the Dignity of Man) and latter Kant's moral automous subject, positioned the human person as a dynamic creative self.

5.1.2 Towards a Theological Interpretation of Human Dignity?

Efforts to establish a genuine theology of human dignity have presented some sort of mosaic. As there are many confessions with different orientations to the debate there are also varied points on some salient delineators in the debate. For instance there are obvious variance on major issues like grace, original sin and freedom among confessions. Nonetheless, a sense of convergence can also be noticed, especially when it comes to the major points of theological reference in the debate namely, creation and redemption. Although Christology has been the major source of variance among the Christian confessions it has also played an important role in the whole understanding of human dignity. Among others, it has contributed immensely in the fortification of the anthropological arguments found otherwise outside the theological circles.

The so-called *"anthropological turn"* in the intellectual history was like a wild wind that blew across the Northern hemisphere, with little or no regard for the already existing divine truths such as the trinity and the angels. We refer here to the modern and enlightenment eras with all their paraphernalia and versatility in secularism. As a result, some subsequent developments around the theme of *'Imago Dei'* have systematically drifted from the lofty Christian basis of the idea of human dignity. For instance, such scholars like George Mohr in his work: *"Ein Wert der Keinen Preis hat" Philosophiegeschichtliche Grundlagen der Menschenwürde bei Kant und Fichte* presented two theses supporting the above assertion: 1. Human dignity is nothing more than that conceived in the course of philosophical history as human dignity; 2. That our current understanding of human dignity has its basic perceptivity in the philosophies of Kant and Fichte.[474] Considering the above assertions on their merits one may fairly grant credence to Mohr, because secularisation tended to ignore all its patrimonies in the pretence of creating new ideas in the intellectual history. Such an attitude revealed in history does not and cannot preclude the fact that all human enlightenment function as a web, that means: they must be historically founded.

Therefore when one takes into cognisance the scholastic understanding of philosophy as *"ancilla theologiae"*, that is, philosophy as handmaid of

---

474 Cf. Mohr, "Ein Wert der keinen Preis hat" 14.

theology there would not be this problem of dichotomy such as that created by Mohr's thesis. Except for the sake of distinction and argumentation Christian theology right from time has not been divorced from philosophy. There has been a responsible level of agreement and compatibility between the two. Furthermore, a discussion of cultures in the light of Christian theology will be of advantage, based on the fact that Christian theology does not necessarily present unwholesome obstacles in understanding and representing revelations found in other cultural milieus and religious traditions. On the contrary it enhances naturally the ability for such a dialogue at all levels.[475] Therefore, the history of philosophy cannot be divorced from the history of theology. In my opinion, the contributions of Kant and Fitche in the history of philosophy and particularly in the history of human dignity and rights can not be taken singularly as *'sui generis'* but as part or continuation of the fecundation of human knowledge, which embodies both the religious and the spiritual. One would rather subscribe to a form of relatedness than opposition. Granted the influence of philosophy in the history of thought we still acknowledge the Christian thought as a veritable source of lasting legacy.

Without prejudice to the above assertion there is still a kind of internal sensitivity associated with a theology of human dignity and rights based on the Judeo Christian revelation. On the main, such a theological perspective runs the risk of being misconstrued or even seen to be championing a course of a particular religion, in this case the Christian faith.[476] However, it is pertinent to point out that this risk and tendency of deviation notwithstanding, theological interpretation should not be misunderstood as a simple religious imposition, but rather as a theological effort from the Christian perspective, which does not exclude other possible interpretations or perspectives. Hence the importance of emphasizing once more that the idea and

---

475 Cf. Wolfhart Pannenberg, Anthropology in Theological Perspektive 15; Cf. Konrad Hilpert, „Die Idee der Menschenwürde aus Sicht christlicher Theologie", in: Hans Jörg Sandkühler (Hg.), Menschenwürde. Philosophische, theologische und juristische Analysen, Frankfurt am Main 2007 41-55 here 50.
476 Cf. John C. Dwyer, "Person, Dignity of", in: Judith A Dwyer and Elizabeth L. Montgomery eds., The New Dictionary of Catholic Social Thought, Collegeville Minnesota 1994 724-737 here 735.

concept of human dignity itself is "interpretation open".[477] It is against this backdrop that we shall first of all, focus among others, on the foundations of the Christian perspective on human dignity.

5.2 The Special Position of Human Being in the Creative Plan of God

The Christian view on the dignity of human person has its foundation on the biblical anthropology handed down in the creation narrative. The Hagiographers carefully singled man out from all other creatures and accorded him a special position in the creative plan of God. Even though interpreted according to the proclivity of the various Christian confessions, the human person as created by God is accepted by all confessions. In the first creation account of the book of Genesis, God is presented by the priestly tradition as a creator, who single handed created heaven and earth with his word: "In the beginning God created heaven and earth. Now the earth was a formless void there was darkness over the deep with a divine wind sweeping over the waters" (Gen. 1. ff) On the creation of man, the priestly account brought in a very radical dimension to the dignity and respect of man among other creatures: "Then God said: let us make man in our image, and likeness. They should rule over the fishes of the sea, over the birds of the air, over the beasts of the field, over the whole land and over all creeping animals of the earth" (Gen. 1, 26ff). Going further we read: "God created man in his image, as God's image he created him. As man and woman he created them" (Gen. 1, 28). The priestly account presents a meticulous account of creation, which took seven days for a perfect completion.

In the second creation account the Jahwistic tradition presented a simple and uncomplicated account of the creation of man by God in the universe in these words: "God formed man from soil of the earth and breathed into his nostrils the breath of life. Man became a living being" (Gen. 2, 7). In their explanation of the differences between man and woman they presented it simply this way: God said: it is not good that the man stays

---

477 Cf. Hilpert, „Die Idee der Menschenwürde aus der Sicht christlicher Theologie" 49.

alone. I will make for him a help mate fit for him ...." (Gen. 2, 18-24) The rest of the verse narrates the dramatic reaction of Adam as he woke from his sleep. However, a more concise but detailed account could be found in the narrative presented by the Priestly tradition, whose insight was a more intellectual and detailed way of presenting a step-by-step account of creation.

Generally the Judeo Christian account sees in the world: a creative plan of God. The world and all its features are not a product of chance but creative will of God, who out of love for man has a special place for him in the whole structure. Hence man sees himself as a privileged creature of God over and above other creatures. The Catechisms of the Catholic Church (C.C.C.), by citing the Document of the Church on the Modern World, captures the dignity of man in these words:

> The dignity of man rests above all on the fact that he is called to communion with God .... For if man exists it is because God has created him through love, and through love continues to hold him in existence. He cannot live fully according to truth unless he freely acknowledges that love and entrusts himself to his creator (G.S art. 19 §1).[478]

In the same vein also the German Catholic Catechism for Adults articulates the fundamental biblical answer on the age long question: "what is man?" in the following words: "The human being is creature of God; he owes his being and existence to God. He is willed and sustained through God; he is because God has called him by name: I want you to be. The basic reason for his existence is this Thanksgiving and Trust".[479]

Nevertheless, contrary to the Judeo Christian view on creation some contentions exist against the idea of God's creation of man in his dignity or both the world and man as mere products of chance. There is this theory, propounded by scientist known as the Big Bang theory of evolution.[480]

---

478 The Catechism of the Catholic Church, St Paul's Press Nairobi-Ibadan Nigeria 1994 40.
479 Cf. Deutsche Bischofskonferenz, „Das Glaubensbekenntnis der Kirche", Band 1, *Katholischer Erwachsenenkatechismus*, Freiburg 2006. Ch. 1.
480 Big Bang theory of evolution came up as a scientific attempt to explain the evolution of beings in the universe. It was fashioned to be an antithesis to the famous Biblical creation narrative, which stood as it were as the unsha-

Some time in the last two centuries natural scientists tried to put across their findings as credible stories such as: the world as we know it came to be through a Big bang mechanics theory of evolution; living organisms and beings come to be through a very long process of mutation; and that the human being evolved from the apes and not just created by God. However after series of studies and investigations a number of the findings in the area of natural sciences were integrated in the Churches theology of creation. At this juncture it will be pertinent to present at least in a summary form the theses on evolution and creation, and the stand of catholic theology on the integration of evolution theories in the theology of creation.

5.2.1 The Summary of the Theological Statement on Evolution and Creation

The last two centuries have experienced a great influence in the field of natural sciences. On the side of theology it refers to the challenges purported by the evolutionary theories of Charles Darwin and that of Teilhard de Chardin. The 19th and 20th century's ingress in the discovery of evolution tended to tear apart the solemn faith in the one creator God, who in his infinite love and wisdom created the world and every thing out of nothing. After a long history of rejection and reviews, the Pastoral constitution on the modern world, Gaudium et spes clarifies that evolution theories together with their interpretation of the world can be understood from the point of view of theology of creation and can even be integrated into the theological corpus.[481] It is pertinent to note that Evolution and Creation however, distinguish themselves methodologically thus; evolution belongs to the category of natural science while creation belongs to that of theology. Both answer different questions. The teaching on evolution explains the material processes of existence and changes among the different life forms, in line with the laws of mutation and selection. However it does not answer the question regarding: 1 the origin and meaning

---

keable religious truth of all times. However proponents and representatives of this theory could not convincingly prove their thesis to a logical end. The question of the first principle and matter continue to rear their heads in an inexonerable enigma.

481 Cf. Gaudium et Spes, art. 5, n. 3.

of life; 2 the questions on the existence and that of the spiritual realities; and 3 the where about of the self-transcendence of complex system of evolution.[482] Naturally these questions belong to theology of creation.

Charles Darwin's theory of evolution presented scientifically the coming into existence of human life as a chance and through a process of natural selection. Such a quasi explanation cannot be accepted because of its inability to address some important questions on the transcendental aspect of the human person. The biological theory of evolution should be followed to its logical conclusions and complemented through the principles of information and cooperation, as is the case in the field of inorganic matter where Manfred Eigen presented the cosmological expansive theory of evolution.[483] To be rejected is also the Social Darwinism, which tries to translate the biological and evolutionary processes and laws in the human being and his activities in the society.

The traditional theological challenge against the theory of evolution became more critical in the 19th and 20th century through belief in the historicity of the creation narrative of Genesis and a static – timeless understanding of being of the neo-scholastic metaphysics. Pope Pius X condemned the evolution theory as a modern falsehood in his encyclical *"Pascendi"* of 1907. Shortly after this encyclical, the papal bible commission defended the historicity of the creation narrative of the book of Genesis in 1909. The encyclical *"Humani Generis"* 1950 of Pius XII concentrated on the tenacity of the teaching on *monogenism*.[484] After some years of arguments, the Vatican II acknowledged the different ingress made in the different fields of evolution as compatible and integrative with the theology of creation.[485] According to the position of Pope John Paul II before the papal academy of scientist on 22nd October 1996, the Charles Darwin's theory of evolution and other theories of evolution,

---

482 Cf. Alexandre Ganoczy, Schöpfungslehre, Düsseldorf 1983 156.
483 See Manfred Eigen, Stufen zum Leben. Die frühe Evolution im Visier der Molekularbiologie, München 1987.
484 Monogenism refers to the church's teaching on the first human parents-Adam and Eve, who committed the original sin that was transmitted to the on coming generations. This teaching stands as the ground for the teaching on the sinful nature of man.
485 Cf. Gs, art. 5, 34, 44, 54, 66.

which have been thoroughly studied and complemented can now be integrated in a modern theology of creation, but only as "hypotheses".

Theologically understood, God creates every being as a dynamic and lively reality. Consequently it implies an evolutionary power or potential to unfold in itself, and also the capacity to cause its development in the course of time. God is the creator in his own law and order; hence the organisation and evolution of the world are in his hands as we read in the book of Genesis, chapters 1 and 2. Christian faith on God's creation holds that there is a starting point of God's creation. God enhances all creative, and above all, human competence. God shows his complete creative power through the allowance of his creatures to be personally causes in themselves, and gives each and every one the possibility of being effective.[486]

In summary therefore, the world as God's creation remains connected with the reality of God's existence. From the side of creation itself, God created out of nothing: created being only exists through linking up with God the source and origin, the determinant and the meaning.[487] The theological position of some who acclaim *"creationism"*, *"ontogenesis"* or even *"Generationism"*[488] cannot mitigate the teaching and belief in a world and creatures, who become through evolution and history that, which they are expected to be through the creative will of God. Conclusively, the long and short of it is that God remains the creator of all that exist.

---

486 Cf. Ganoczy, Schöpfungslehre 158.
487 Cf. Leo Scheffczyk, Einführung in die Schöpfungslehre 3, Darmstadt 1987 51.
488 Creationism is a teaching by minority theologians that creatures prepare themselves for the new creation, which would be operated in turn by the creator; they prepare the material upon which the creative force will fall in. In the same vein Ontogenesis hold that the body and also some part of the psyche of the child come from the parents, while the soul or at least his individuality and personality come directly from God. Generationism holds that the child receives every thing from the parents, soul, body and spirit even his individuality and personality. For further readings, See Leo Scheffczyk, Einführung in die Schöpfungslehre II, Darmstadt 1975 62ff; Alexander Ganoczy, Schöpfungslehre, Düsseldorf 1983 156, 157.

5.2.2 Human Being, Every Human Being is created by God

The second creation narrative by the Jahwistic tradition presented God as the creator of the world and all that is in it. The human being was created with the dust of the earth and God breathed life into it and it became life (Gen. 2, 7). However, the full understanding of *"creatio ex nihilo"* and the direct link between God and human being was expressed through the systematic presentation of the first account, the priestly creation narrative, which gave the creation of the human being a radical turn namely: "Let us make man in our image and likeness" (Gen. 1, 26 and 27). The two-creation accounts draw attention to the fact that God creates every human being personally and directly.

The priestly creation narrative reveals the fact that creation was arranged in a purposeful and hierarchical order, and that all aspects of creation were not standing in equal relation to God.[489] The Hagiographers presented the chaos or void as the farthest in relation to God the creator through presenting it as the first instance of creation; the plants for instance were presented as being directly related to the earth, but the birds of the air and animals relate more closely to man. Specifically it is only the human being that was linked directly with God. Against this background of the direct link in relationship with his creator, the human being enjoys a special place among all other creatures. Therefore Leo Scheffczyk opines that: "It is no more enough just to say, the world is placed on the human being. It is much more to add: the world is placed on the human being as a mandate but in direct link with God."[490] Consequently it is no more theologically possible to think of another creature that is greater in grade or relation to God than the human being; or to think of one in the future who will be greater than the human being. The direct link between the human being and his God the creator, who created out of nothing, does no longer accommodate any thinking in this direction. The utopia of some prognoses that the human being through some worth of human engineering would be completed in the future has no place any more, because what ever difference or improvement that would come in the future can only be based finally on the one and only creation

---

489 Cf. Scheffezk, Einführung in die Schöpfungslehre 109.
490 Cf. Scheffezk, Einführung in die Schöpfungslehre 104.

by God who has already created the human being out of nothing.[491] Even if one takes up the parents of a child in the creation of a newborn baby, the same argument meets a dead lock when presented with the transcendental aspects of the human person, which can never be provided by the agency of the parents. Furthermore, the Greek Demiurge[492] of the old world cosmogony, which was placed as the creative link between gods and man would not even supply as a creator who created out of nothing.

It is really surprising and will continue to challenge the thinking minds over the radicalism of the Jewish understanding of the human being. However it will be recalled that the Israelites took a lot of influence from the ancient near east religions, especially among the Persians who recognised their King as the only person created in the image of god. Ancient Near East kings stood as it were, as the only representatives of the image of gods on earth. The theological implication of such assertion was an indirect relationship between the gods and human beings through the king. This human image created a despotic image of the king in the Ancient Near East, which has lasted even up till date. Therefore, it was the ingenuity, a special reserve and originality of the Jewish theologians to have radically deviated from this popular conception of kingship as at the time but presented and preserved a direct relationship between God and every human being in their people's faith. This faith in a God who was the only king, in whose image every human being is created was in turn orchestrated in the Old Testament theological motif of the (*Imago Dei*), created in the image and likeness of God.

---

491 Cf. Scheffezk, Einführung in die Schöpfungslehre 104.
492 Demiurge is the ancient Greek word, which means 'craftsman' or 'artisan'. Plato, in the *Timaeus*, uses the word for the maker of the universe. Plato says of this maker that he is unreservedly good and so desired that the world should be as good as possible. The reason why the world is not better than it is at the present is that the demiurge had to work on pre-existing chaotic matter. Thus the demiurge is not an omnipotent creator. Early Christian Philosophers were quick to claim that the demiurge represented pagan Philosophy's anticipation of the God of revealed religion. For further readings see, F. M. Cornford, Plato's Cosmology: *The Timaeus of Plato*, tr. with running Commentary, London 1937.

5.2.3 Every Human Being Partakes in the Image and Likeness of God

Biblical faith proclaims that every human being is created in the image and likeness of God (*Imago Dei*). Even though understood differently today among the various Christian confessions it remains the bedrock motif for Christian understanding of human dignity (Gen. 1, 26-27; 5, 1; 9, 6-7). Created in the image and likeness of God serves as a theologomenon for the elevated nature of man by God his creator; and extends in the course of time through the redemptive work of Christ (Gal. 3, 28; 1Cor. 11, 7; Eph. 4, 24; Col. 3, 10). This biblical statement, as it were, remains the origin and basis of Christian Anthropology; it forms the theological foundation of human dignity. The human being created in the image and likeness of God as a theological theme has been developed from three historical epochs namely, biblical, patristic and medieval.

There exists a general consensus in the understanding of the biblical-Christian belief on God's creation of the world to the consequence that one can see among human cultures the same quality of faith in a God who created heaven and earth. Genesis 1, 26-27; 5, 1 teaches that human beings were created in the image (*tselem*) and after the likeness (*demuth*) of God[493]. In the course of time interpretations have varied as to the exact meaning of the statement. For a proper understanding and systematic analysis the twin words have been divided into two namely, *image* and *likeness*.

The image of God taken singly was associated with dominion over the brute creation. Catholic theologians especially, right from the patristic times taught that the image endures after the original sin because man being in God's image is the reason for the prohibition of murder (Gen. 9:6).[494] It is argued that the human nature upon which the moral legislations are meant to curb belong to the natural faculties of the human person. If his human nature were totally vitiated after the fall then the instruction against murder would have been needless and meaningless. However the two terms: image and likeness of God became a systematic theme for theologians, who tried to distinguish the two. Scheffczyk captures the subtlety this way:

---

493 Cf. Gormally, Human Dignity: The Christian View and the Secularist View 2.
494 Cf. Gormally, Human Dignity: The Christian View and the Secularist View 2.

Both terms are essentially in the biblical text presented as synonymous, even if resemblance can also be understood in the weak sense of the word. "Imago" would mean concretely and realistically the likeness of a sculpt and painted picture, "likeness" would mean just a resemblance of a general and abstract art, where by it would seem to mean, that the human being stays close to God, but certainly not to equate with him.[495]

Christ is the concrete visible "image of the unseen God" (Col.1, 15). The Fathers of the Church interpreted this statement in two different ways. The first group was those who understood Christ's human nature to be, the visible image of divine reality. For instance Irenaeus of Lyon separated the biblical term *"imago-similitudo"* and linked up the natural and the supernatural image of God.[496] The image is the nature, while likeness is the supernatural. Consequently, human beings having their origin from Adam are in the image of God, which has much to do with raw nature, while Christ the new Adam is the likeness of God that has to do with grace. In Christ is found grace, the supernatural gift of God to human beings. Therefore by separating the two spheres, nature and grace Irenaeus was able to favour the modern theological arguments on *Imago Dei*, which saw the two concepts *image and likeness* only as a two separate spheres. He described nature and grace as appearing only to be connected.[497] Some other Fathers in line with Irenaeus include, Tertullian and Marius Victorinus. However, this separation led to a negative consequence especially in the teachings of the scholastic theology on the achievement of the *"likeness"* of God (Grace or supernatural) through pure reason.[498] Consequently the image of God theology has been diverted and neutralized to represent only the potentiality in human being to be actualized and achieved in the future by human reason. With this line of thought, the Imago Dei theology became neutralized. The second group were those who argued that Imago Dei could only be the divinity of Christ that stands as "the invisible image of the invisible God." His human nature had nothing to do with the image of God. The basis for

---

495 Scheffczyk, Einführung in die Schöpfungslehre 106.
496 Cf. Scheffczyk, Einführung in die Schöpfungslehre 108.
497 Cf. Gormally, Human Dignity: The Christian View and the Secularist View 2.
498 Cf. Gormally, Human Dignity: The Christian View and the Secularist View 2.

their position is no other but that God being incorporeal cannot have a corporeal image.[499] Origen was the chief proponent of this idea of the invisible image of God theology.

On the question of man as the image of God, arguments and opinions were also divided. While some argued that the human being resembles God only in his soul or body alone, others argued for a holistic resemblance of God in soul and body. There emerged among the early Christian fathers a distinction between: 'in the image' understood as constituted by what man is in the order of nature, and 'in the likeness' understood as constituted in the order of grace.[500] St. Augustine distinguished the human being as *capax Dei* in virtue of reason, immortality and the natural knowledge of God, and man as *particeps Dei* through the supernatural gifts.[501] The heavy leaning on the platonic and neo-platonic philosophy could explain much emphasis on the soul as the source of human dignity, which in turn resonated in the early Church fathers choice of reason and spirit as avenues of grace.

In the medieval era, prior to Thomas Aquinas the influence of the platonic view of the soul was still heavily felt. Therefore the dignity of the human person based on the Imago Dei, had little or no place for the body as sharing in that dignity as the human soul did. For Thomas Aquinas an image is an expressive likeness.[502] There is in man a likeness to God, but not a perfect likeness. He explains further by stating that, a likeness is an expressive likeness only if it includes what is distinctive of what it represents. It is therefore, only intellectual creatures who posses the 'image of God'.[503]

Thomas gave reasons for the possibility of perfecting the imperfect image of God in man namely, possession of intellect, grace, likeness of glory. He added that the human dignity depends on the degree of the above capacities in a particular human being. The dignity that belongs to the human nature is never lost (ontological dignity); the Just are always in a state of dignity (existential dignity) and the beatified are also in perpetual dignity (eternal and definitive dignity).

---

499 Cf. Gormally, Human Dignity: The Christian View and the Secularist View 2.
500 Cf. Gormally, Human Dignity: The Christian View and the Secularist View 2
501 Cf. Gormally, Human Dignity: The Christian View and the Secularist View 2.
502 Thomas Aquinas, Summa Theologiae 1 q. 93.
503 Cf. Thomas Aquinas, Summa Theologiae 1 q. 93.

On the issue of the loss of dignity after the fall, arguments rage between the Reformation theologians and the Catholics. The Reformation view of the image of God regards it, not as the foundation of a distinct, actual communication with God namely, the divinely given justice of the first human being (iustitia originalis) but as identical with this actual relation to God.[504] The Reformers hold that the fall or the original sin not only vitiated the likeness of God in man but also the image of God. Man can only become the image and likeness of God through grace.[505] The doctrine of the reformed Churches on the dignity as *Imago Dei* is also located at the centre of their teaching on 'salvation through grace'. While Catholic medieval theology held that the original sin dealt a blow on the image of God in man, but did not destroy it completely, the reformed Churches hold on the contrary a complete destruction of the image. As a result human person can only hope for the image of God in the future through grace. Pannenberg presents it thus:

> The difference between the Reformed and the medieval Catholic views in the question of whether human nature itself was corrupted by the fall is therefore to be explained by different views on the relation between *iustitia originalis* and *Imago Dei*.[506]

For medieval Catholics evidence of the remnant of some natural attributes in human beings after the fall attests to the fact that the human nature (*Imago Dei*) was not totally vitiated by the original sin. Example of such natural attributes includes; reason, will and love.[507] Unfortunately this position as we have pointed before, further gave birth to a neutralized

---

504 Reformation theology holds that the image and likeness of God consists in the true rule and perfect knowledge of God, supreme and delight in God, eternal life, eternal righteousness, and eternal freedom from care. A parallel of the above idea of image and likeness could also be attributed to Calvinist theology.
505 Cf. Pannenberg, Anthropology in Theological Perspective 49.
506 Pannenberg, Anthropology in Theological Perspective 49.
507 The arguments between the 21st century theologians Karl Barth representing the Reformation theologians and Brunner as representing orthodoxy try to show to what extent the image of God in human nature was vitiated. Evidences show that the image of God was not completely vitiated in human being, but was dealt a blow, which only the Grace of God can remedy.

idea of image of God theology, which based its argument on the sole ability of the above remnant of human capabilities to attain to God only with the gift of spiritual powers in man and his reason. However modern theology has rightly criticized this position on the ground of unreliability of these powers in the human being. Rather they developed a relational-dynamic understanding of Imago Dei in human beings. In this relational-dynamism the human being retains a direct link with God in his whole structure as a human being, and not necessarily because he has spirit or reason. The human being is directly in correspondence with God. He stays directly before God face to face.[508] Furthermore, it is important to bear in mind that the human being was through the word of God created, and he remains open to God's communication.

The word of God in history can not only be understood as a complex communication requiring a complex intellectual understanding of the message content but more as a personal address. In this personal address lies the empowerment and enhancement, but includes within it also the demand to respond. Therefore, the actual correspondence to the image of God would rather be the ability of man to respond positively to this address from his God the creator. It does not matter where this response takes place. It could be either in that place where the human being understands God as the absolute in revelation or not.[509] Consequently, this personal dialogue between man and his creator transcends all human reason and capacities, but involves the whole human structure in its nature as a correspondent being with the absolute "Thou" God.[510] It is in this responsorial conception of the fallen man that the image of God remains even after the original sin; not because of his spirit or reason, but because of his nature and structure as answerable to the word of God. The implication of such understanding is that the sinner remains an image of God in a sense in which Leo Scheffczyk describes as follows:

> The sinner remains continuously in his structure as *'imago' Dei*, but freely an unaccomplished, empty, dark, *'imago.'* The content accomplishment of this response is first of all, through the affirmative yes-answer to God. The "Grace" of God comes as a loving re-

---

508 Cf. Scheffczyk, Einführung in die Schöpfungslehre 109.
509 Cf. Scheffczyk, Einführung in die Schöpfungslehre 109.
510 Cf. Scheffczyk, Einführung in die Schöpfungslehre 110.

sponse to the loving God. In this way the grace filled *Imago-Dei* becomes the accomplishment of the structure, natural image, towards which this accomplishment is always channelled.[511]

From the above arguments it becomes clear that the role of the spirit and the intellect was never relegated rather positioned rightly as the basis and *conditio sine qua non* for the relativity and responsiveness to God the creator. Therefore spiritual nature in man as entity is never the correspondence and responsorial act in itself but enabling conditions.

The theological implication of Imago Dei is that every human being created by God in his own image and likeness qualifies as a partaker in the dignity of all God's children. Discriminations on grounds of sex, colour, race, qualities, abilities and position in life; status, personality and talent can no longer be accepted as reasons for exclusion from the dignity of all human beings in respect of Imago Dei. The whole Human race partakes in this dignity of Imago Dei both individually and collectively.

5.2.4 Gender Equality: "Man and Woman He Created Them"

The first creation account reads: "God created man in his image; in the image of God he created him. As man and woman he created them" (Gen. 1, 27). The above citation representing the priestly creation account of the human race posited in the first instance a couple, which as it were formed the origin and source of the forthcoming human beings. In the first place it presents a theological motif for the equality of sexes, male and female. In the second place it shows that all human beings as having the same source of existence take part equally in the same humanity. In another style of presentation, the second creation account from the Jahwistic tradition reads: "God formed man from the soil of the earth and breathed into his nostrils the breath of life. By so doing the man became a living being" (Gen. 2, 7), and to explain the difference in gender; to show how man and woman came to be the Jahwistic tradition continued their narrative this way:

---

511 Cf. Scheffczyk, Einführung in die Schöpfungslehre 109.

The Lord God said: It is not good that man stays alone. I will make him a helpmate fit for him … Therefore the Lord God made man fall into a deep sleep, so that he took one of man's ribs and closed it up again with flesh. The Lord God formed out of the rib, which he has taken from man a woman and brought her to man. And the man said: At last this is the bone of my bone and flesh of my flesh. She should be called woman, because she is taken from man. This is why the man will leave his father and mother and cling to his wife and they will become one flesh.[512]

At the first glance the above second creation narrative would seem to suggest theological motif for a form of superiority or subjugation of women by men. However on the contrary it is pertinent to note that Jewish understanding of the use of man's rib to form woman refers only to their equality not man's superiority over woman. We also read in the letter to the Galatians (Gal. 3, 28), that man and woman stand in the same level with one another before God. They are to grow together in love, freedom and responsibility; they are to become one flesh. Nevertheless, some passages in the writings of Paul and Peter seem to go against women in the issue of equality; and seem to encourage human slavery. For instance in his letter to the Ephesians, 5, 22-25 Paul wrote: "Wives should be subject to their husbands as to the lord, since, as Christ is head of the Church and saves the whole body, so is a husband the head of his wife; and as the Church is subject to Christ, so should wives, be to their husbands in every thing". Paul used this analogy of Christ and his Church in the spirit of his Jewish culture at the time, which in the current dispensation can also be understood only as one of those mentalities of the ages past. Above all Paul calls for respect and love on the side of the Husband towards his wife (Eph. 5, 25-33). Contextually speaking Paul's concern just like that of Peter was to ensure peace and serenity in the Christian Family, and the principle for this peace is love and respect. Again in 1 Cor. 11, 7ff, Paul wrote:

> But for a man it is not right to have his head covered, since he is the image of God and reflects God's glory; but woman is the reflection of man's glory. For man did not come from woman; no,

---

512 Gen. 2, 18-28.

woman came from man; nor was man created for the sake of woman, but woman for the sake of man: and this why it is right for a woman to wear on her head a sign of authority over her, because of the angels. However, in the Lord, though woman is nothing without man, man is nothing without woman; and though woman came from man, so does every man come from a woman, and everything comes from God.[513]

It is interesting to see how Paul justifies his regulation for women to wear headscarf from the image of God theology. Here the *image of God* theology seems to have become a rational for segregating between women and men. Nonetheless, towards the end of his thought Paul tries to balance the difference he had created by again placing both man and woman at the same pedestal before God. Unfortunately such manipulative subtlety as we have it in the above passage, even though accepted by the early Christians may be very difficult to be interpreted and accepted in the current emancipated world of women. The same ideas are also found in (Col. 3, 18; 1 Peter, 3, 1-6; 1, 22-23; Col, 11, 3).

In Ephesians 6, 5ff, Paul calls for obedience on the side of the slaves to their masters. 1 Peter 2, 18 also encourages slaves to be obedient to their masters, since there will be reward for suffering at the end of it all. One would have expected the apostles to condemn slavery out rightly after they must have experienced the suffering and death of their master who now reigns as the victor. However, it does seem that their theological understanding of Christ's liberation was not just physical but more of spiritual liberation. Jesus said: "My Kingdom is not of this world" (Jn. 18, 36). He went on to draw a great contrast between the world and the disciples, "if the word hates you, you must realise that it hated me before it hated you ...." (Jn. 15,18ff) This apathy to the world could be the reason why the early Christians were not much perturbed by the physical order of their society. They saw the world order as that passing away and being replaced by grace. Unfortunately these seemingly contradicting double standards in understanding equality as the benchmark of human dignity in Christ led to the compromising of the principle in different societies, not exempting the Christian communities. However the apathy towards the inequalities

---

513 1Corinthians, 11, 7ff.

existing in the world order seemed to have been addressed convincingly and realistically with the passage of time in various Papal social encyclicals and the Vat. II council. In this council the full implications of the whole life, death and resurrection of Christ challenged Christians to see the world as needing deliverance from the hands of evil doers; to participate in building a just human society[514]. It was no more the attitude of theological indifference to the world or that of spiteful and hateful attitude of the Church during the Vat. 1 era but a more welcoming attitude and challenge to be part of the world. The Vat. II in the pastoral constitution on the modern world art 1 no.1 declared:

> The Joy and hope, the grief and anguish of the men of our time, especially of those who are poor or afflicted in any way, are the joy and hope, the grief and anguish of the followers of Christ as well.[515]

From the above declaration it becomes clear that the Church acknowledges the world as a place of responsibility and challenge to contribute to the betterment of mankind. In the new dispensation, the person is called to creative engagement and shared responsibility in the world, with and on behalf of other human beings. The person is called to participate in shaping the society in such a way as to promote the well being of its members, and it is in this act of participation that the essential dignity of the person is both achieved and revealed.

Even in the ancient Greek myths of origin, the equality of man and woman in dignity and rights were emphasised:

> First, you all will learn about the nature of humanity and its experiences. For long ago its nature was not as it is now – one became the other. For at first there were three species [or sexes] of humans, not two, just as now: male and female, as well as another third one [androgyny], sharing things in common with both of these (of which its name remains although it has disappeared). For the androgyny back then was distinct in shape and name, out of having in common both male and female, but now its name survives only in reproach.

---

514 Cf. GS, art. 75.
515 Cf. GS, art. 1.

Second, each human was in the shape of a rounded whole, its back and sides making a circle having four hands, and legs the same number as hands, and two faces upon a circular neck (identical in all ways), and a head for the faces (each one facing the opposite way), and four ears, and two genitals, and everything else likewise. They stood upright (just as now) whichever of the two ways they walked. But when they started to run quickly, the eight limbs would revolve in a circular handcart, just like tumblers, fixing the limbs to complete the circle and return upright. I have said there are three species and such things because the male was originally a descendant of the Sun, and the female of the Earth, and the species sharing both is of the Moon, because the Moon shares both [the Sun and the Earth]. Both their [planetary] roundness and their revolving were passed on to their offspring [making them do circular handcarts when moving rapidly].

After that, with their natures hewn in two, each one missed the union with its other half. They threw their arms about each other and were woven together with one another, desiring to grow together, so that they died off from hunger and laziness, for they were willing to do nothing apart from the other. And when one half died, and one was left, the one left would seek out and weave together with another, either from half of a female whole (who is now called a woman), or a man. And they went on dying. Then Zeus pitied them and provided another way, and moved their genitals to the front. For hitherto they were in back and thus they had procreated and given birth, not one with another in sex, but just as cicadas. By moving them up front, He made them procreate with each other, through males being in females. If men and women interwove at the same time, then they procreated and the race continued; or if men [interwove] with men at the same time, then they satiated desire for intercourse, and they ceased [desire for intercourse] and turned their energies to work and took care of the other things of life ..."[516]

---

516 "Hen Ek Duoin": One out of Two, Aristophanes Speech from Plato's Symposium as translated Connell O'Donovan, see Plato's Symposium (ed. Kenneth Dover), Cambridge 1980 189C-193E. (Http//www.connelodonovan.com/hen.htm 22.10.2011).

The over-emphasis on sexual difference is not actually the direct consequence of creation. God created one humanity, comprising of male and female and both share equally in the divine image, the dignity that all share in common. Surprisingly enough the erotic feelings of one sex for the other explain the yearning for completeness in man and woman. Each compliments the other in the attainment of full humanity. The dignity of man and woman lies in the realization of the need each has for the other.

In a very sharp argument Louis Bouyer in his *Woman in the Church* appeals to what could be referred to as the transcendence of man and woman beyond sexism. For him womanhood is a mystery that surpasses the argument of sexism. As he puts it;

> The mystery of woman, precisely because it is the mystery of creation redeemed, completed and espoused by God himself, presupposes the mystery of God and cannot be understood without reference to him. However, the mystery of God is not at all, for all that, simply the reverse side of the mystery of humanity. To put it better, it encompasses the mystery of man (*homo*, man and woman) as well as of *vir* (the male), but it surpasses it and in such a way that the mystery of woman in particular finds its source there, a source wherein one might say it is reflected, but, as in every reflection, reversed. We must begin by sorting out, as much as possible, this paradox to which we are driven by the properly Biblical knowledge of God, in order to see the mystery of woman in proper perspective. Thus the ministries of man and of woman both will be seen in their proper places. It is sometimes said, and it is true in a sense, but only in a sense, that God, the God who has spoken to us through Biblical tradition (as opposed to the ancient Near Eastern divinities who were so heavily sexualized), appeared to transcend the division of the sexes. It is suggested, too, that he unites in himself the most exalted characteristics of both woman and man. This is not without some justification, but nevertheless it cannot be admitted as a truly satisfying expression of his revelation.[517]

This already is tantamount to saying that that which is most truly divine in God, if we may put it this way, is expressed in man (*homo*) by the po-

---

517 See Louis Bouyer, Woman in the Church, Ignatius Publishers, New York 1979.

larity between man (vir) and woman, yet nevertheless surpasses and transcends man just as much as woman, to the point that man (*vir*) as such seems incapable of becoming complete in himself. This is, in fact, true in two senses. On the one hand, the fatherhood of man cannot be realized without woman, not to say in woman. But on the other hand, he is not distinguished from her or opposed to her in the relation by which they complete one another. Except by this representation of one greater than he; he is himself nothing more than a touchstone and he will never do better than to evoke, without ever truly assimilating, the fatherhood which is only properly realized in God. For fatherhood, in its whole and true sense, can be nothing other than divine, since it is the quality of being a source-the source of all beings as of one's own being-and therefore of pure being, always in act. Even masculine spouse hood itself, we shall see, as it derives from the association of creature to creator which is brought about by the divine Word alone, is only fully and primarily realized in his incarnate person. More simply and profoundly, as St. Gregory of Nyssa saw so clearly, the divine fatherhood, the only true fatherhood worthy of the name, is essentially virginal. In other words, far from presupposing complementarities that is, the joining of man and woman – God's fatherhood is anterior to this distinction. But, it must be added, if there is nevertheless some analogue to this fullness, expressed in the distinction of the sexes and surpassing them, we do not find it in man (*vir*). Just as with fatherhood, so virginity in man can only be predicated in an approximate, imperfect sense. On the natural, created plane, it is only woman who can claim true virginity. The unmarried woman, in fact, contains, in herself, at least potentially, all future humanity, both masculine and feminine, for it will never come to being if not by an interior development in the feminine being which the male does nothing but set into motion, playing, again, only a representative role, at most as a transmitter of the creative initiative which remains purely divine. Even if this initiative happens to pass through him, one can never say it belongs to him, whereas in woman, on the contrary, the creativity received from on high is carried, and at the same time is exercised within her and remains with her. It follows that in Woman physical integrity has a completely different meaning and a different reality than in man. What one might improperly call virginity in man is only a matter of not exercising a potential fatherhood, which, even when he is called to exercise it, still does not truly belong to him, for it is in him always a matter of a single instant in which he still does not become the source, but rather a momentary channel of fatherly creativity. In woman, on the other hand, this integrity is the unmitigated fullness wherein exist all the possibilities of human developments *in potentia*, since they will simply be developments of her being.

So far one can see from the foregoing that theologically both creation narratives and the Greek myths of origin make it clear that man and woman are equal in dignity. For this reason the church has maintained the equality of both sexes in dignity in the Church's social teachings. There is neither a privilege position nor a prerogative given to men over women in terms of subjugation except the unfortunate abuses as we still have them in various cultures today. Most condemnations received for such maltreatment of women or the weak strengthens the Church's believe in the equality of the sexes based primarily on the dignity of human person. The descent from *one parent motif* of the whole human race latter provided the theological basis for the idea of one brotherhood of the entire human race.

5.2.5 Universal Brotherhood: The Goal of Justice and Human Socialization

A central theological implication of the creation of the first parents of the whole human race Adam and Eve points to the fact of the brotherhood of the entire human family. This motif put forward in the book of Genesis, if not for the accuracy but for the fact that the whole humanity is from one stock namely Adam and Eve. From the creation narrative we learn that the human being is a relational being. He is not meant to be alone, but fashioned towards living in the society with others; and because he is relational he is also a person among others. In his ontological nature and in this relational capacity he is truly a person who can relate to other persons including God at the first instance in whose image and likeness he was fashioned. By his death and resurrection Christ restored the fallen human race to its original dignity that was lost by sin. He became for all a brother and a new Adam (Phil. 3, 10; Col. 3, 10ff) who relates us once more to God and our fellow human beings. Through Christ the divided world has become once more a universal brotherhood. Jesus defined relationship with God in terms of our relationship with other human beings.

He never called for structural changes in society, and many are troubled today by that fact, but the liberty that Jesus brought empowers the engagement of the Christian in political and social concerns both at the national and universal levels.[518]

The word brotherhood has become a biblical and theological concept in both the early church and in the subsequent times. The benchmark of this brotherhood is justice. Justice in the society stands out as the basis of every human society especially in the sharing of the earth's goods in which every one by virtue of universal brotherhood is a partaker. A just consideration for the weak, the poor and the less privilege will be a sign of the reality of that universal brotherhood. In the New Testament Jesus spoke out in strong terms against the societal rank order of his time. He preached for a change in the gap between the poor and the rich; Jesus deplored the mentality of the time regarding the status of servants and the served; the segregating tendencies and hate existing between peoples and cultures. There was little or no attention to the weak, the humble, children, women and the abandoned of the society. People sought for ranks and places of honour at occasions, struggling as it were for political recognitions and positions. To illustrate the value of humility and innocence he told many parables and at one occasion presented a child before his disciples and said "for it is to such as these that the kingdom of God belongs" (Matt. 18, 16).

Paul in his writings reflecting theologically on the dignity of human person, who is now restored in the person of Christ wrote: "there is no more Jew and gentile, no more slave and freeman, no more man and woman; you all are one in Christ Jesus" (Gal. 3, 28). The Letter of James makes it however clear that every human being, without fear or favour would be brought to the judgement seat of God at the end of time to answer for one's actions towards the other (2 James 1, 9; Cf. Mk.12, 14).

Finally this conviction has led to a constant social action against the various social inequalities existing here and there in the history of humanity. Humanitarian support and encouragement for care of the needy; sensitivity and friendship towards the less privileged have been a central part of the Christian moral teachings.

---

518 Cf. John Dwyer, Person, Dignity of 728.

5.2.6 The Human Being as created in Responsible Freedom

Freedom as a central theme in the interpretation of human dignity has its basis on the *Imago Dei* theology. The Christian understanding of freedom refers to that one given to man by God in responsibility (Gal. 4, 7); that which frees from slavery of sin. It is a kind of freedom that sets free for the loving call of God (Gal. 5, 1ff). As long as this freedom is linked up with God it is relative and limited but not absolute[519]. God in his loving kindness created the human being in freedom, because he wanted through freedom to guarantee the existence of individuals in their different worldviews. Therefore it has become the basis for the side-by-side acceptance of the various humanistic worldviews today. Christian theology has taken up the task of interpreting and explaining fully the implications of freedom among all the peoples of the world. Unfortunately the word freedom has not been easily understood in history. Some negative philosophies abound; for instance the ideas of Jean Paul Sartre, who presented human freedom as negative. Such nihilists' ideas would not be theologically acceptable. Sartre writing after the devastating experience of the World Wars could not reconcile freedom as destructive (human aberration) and freedom as ontological (freedom meant to be for the good of man). Just as Karl Rahner explains in his writing on freedom, that freedom as an existential quality of the human person runs the risk of being misunderstood.[520] According to Rahner freedom as 'choice' is possible only where a spiritual person is transcendentally open to the infinite God. Freedom is in itself a product of the person as a limited material before the infinite God. As a result, freedom is an issue for theology and theological anthropology because without it the human being could not act, be held responsible, correspond in dialogue and stand in partnership before God; he could not be a subject of sin before God, subject of giving and taking of

---

519 Cf. Scheffczyk, Einführung in die Schöpfungslehre 111.
520 Cf. Karl Rahner, Würde und Freiheit des Menschen, in: Schriften zur Theologie Bd. IV 247-277 here 259.
Rahner saw the risk of freedom being misunderstood by the modern interpretations, especially in its absolute claim on freedom; he therefore set himself to explain the term in details.

salvation and receiver of grace.[521] It was in this sense of the responsibility of the subject in his acts that Karol Wojtyla (Pope John Paul II) clarified in his work: *The Person: Subject and Community* opined:

> The self constitutes itself precisely through the acts proper to man as a person. It also constitutes itself through the totality of psychosomatic dynamics or acts, which only "occurs" in the subject, but nonetheless in some fashion forms the subjectivity of the individual … Man is a person "by nature", by means he is entitled to the subjectivity proper to a person.[522]

John Paul II was very faithful to his phenomenological approach to the human person as a moral subject. Freedom stands out as the benchmark of morality since according to him the act, which was defined traditionally as human act (*actus humanus*), should be called "act of the person" (*actus personae*) because the causality on which it is based is precisely that of the person[523]. In his work on: *The Acting Person*, John Paul II explained a person's action as having in it the capacity to reveal him as either good or bad. It is an act related to the freedom of the subject as a responsible doer. Hence he asserts:

> Action makes man good or bad. It is mans actions, his conscious acting, that make of him *'what'* and *'who'* he actually is …. It is morality that is the fruit, the homogenetic effect of the causation of the personal ego, but morality conceived not in the abstract but as a strictly existential reality pertaining to the person who is its own proper subject. It is man's actions, the way he consciously acts that make of him a good or a bad man- good or bad in the moral sense …. Freedom is the root of man's goodness or badness.[524]

---

521 Cf. Rahner, Würde und Freiheit des Menschen 559-260.
522 Karol Wojtyla (John Paul II, Pope), "The Person: Subject and Community", in: The Review of Metaphysics. A Philosophical Quarterly, Vol. XXXIII, No. 1 Issue no. 129, Sept. 1979 273-308 here 277.
523 Karol Wojtyla, The Person: Subject and Community 280.
524 Karol Wojtyla (John Paul II, Pope), The Acting Person, Vol. 10 Analecta Husserliana, ed. Anna-Teresa Tymieniecka. The Yearbook of Phenomenological Research, Dordrecht Holland 1979 98-99.

The understanding of freedom in the modern age is one that places little or no premium on the morality of the subject as the performer of his action. Such an ideological depravity conceives morality metaphysically but not existentially. In this case, it deceives itself by hiding under the shadow of the autonomy as a product of idealism in the age of enlightenment. In his *Metaphysics of Morals* Kant insisted on the categorical imperative as the autonomy of the subject. This autonomy spoken of in his metaphysics of moral is merely autonomy qua autonomy no more no less. It has little or nothing to do with the existential reality of morality which John Paul II addressed in his phenomenological anthropology. Consequently the automous subject problematic has led to a state of morality which seems to place little or no limit to human liberty and freedom, which in turn reflects in the different facets of the society. Regarding freedom as a constitutive element of human dignity, it is pertinent to underscore here that God made man in responsible freedom, which includes among others, the responsibility of taking care of other created species and side by side acknowledgement of fellow human beings in intersubjectivism. The modern freedom seems not to have truth and value as basis upon which reference could be made for such excessive desires only that it stems from the human whims and caprices. Freedom for the modern mind has become just the ability to throw ones weight on whatever one could; an infinite capacity to do and carry out whatever that is possible. The philosopher Sartre also knew quite well that such a freedom was no gift from God at all, but only a self-destruction. As a result he spoke of human beings as people being condemned to be free.[525]

For the purpose of illustration, the liberal democratic notion of freedom is problematic because although it insists on the removal of external coercive factors, it shows little interest in the value of the act or choice in itself, usually on the grounds that it has no non-coercive way of determining which actions are valuable in themselves apart from the consensus of society, and on the grounds that no individual or group can safely be given the authority to determine which ones are valuable and which are not.[526] This view, to say the least is inadequate in the contemporary

---

525 Cf. Scheffczyk, Einführung in die Schöpfungslehre, 110; See also H. Kuhn, Die Kirche im Zeitalter der Kulturrevolution, Graz 1985 90ff.
526 Cf. Dwyer, Person, Dignity of 730.

Catholic social thought. Human dignity is a transcendent value, not created by human choice, and that liberal democracy, in the absence of some way of identifying and committing itself to objective value, constantly runs the risk of becoming the tyranny of the majority. Dwyer insist that the understanding of the defence of human freedom must be based on the biblical concept of freedom and its role in human dignity. He however lamented that it is surprising and unfortunate that Western thought has drawn so little on those biblical sources that stand at the origins of so much Western culture- namely, the OT and NT.[527]

From the above illustration of the liberal democratic understanding of freedom as absolute we learn even from history how enslaving and destructive such a conception of freedom has been. It is quite different from the Christian conception of freedom, which flows from the image of God in man that has responsibility attached with it. Absolute freedom presents a philosophical meaning but politically it produces slavery and destruction. The freedom of the people of God spoken about in the Gospels and made clearer by Pauline letters is the one that sets free from bondage of law and slavery (Rom. 8,2; 21, 2Cor. 3, 17; Jn. 8, 32). It is that freedom which leads to the truth, to goodness and finally to God. Christians are reminded in1Peter not to abuse the freedom given to them by God: "You are slaves of no one except God, so behave like free people, and never use your freedom as a cover for wickedness" (1Peter. 2, 16). In the Gospel Jesus emphasised the power of the son of man to set one free: "So if the son sets you free, you will indeed be free" (Jn. 8, 32). Peter Hünermann calls this freedom: *"die erlöste Freiheit"* – redeemed freedom, that means, an understanding of freedom which neither undermines the place of God as the giver of freedom in His son Jesus Christ our redeemer from slavery of sin; nor the human reason having a role to play in freedom as autonomous subject.[528] This freedom in the words of Leo Scheffczyk is: "a kind of freedom in responsibility and not in indulgence or self aggrandisement."[529] Every human being is responsible for his actions in freedom

---

527 Cf. Dwyer, Person, Dignity of 730.
528 Peter Hünermann, „Erlöste Freiheit, Dogmatische Reflexionen im Ausgang von den Menschenrechten", in: Zeitschrifteninhaltsdienst Theologie Ausgaben 1-6, Universität Türbingen 1985 1-14 here 13.
529 Cf. Scheffczyk, Einführung in die Schöpfungslehre 111.

because God has endowed man with reason. Consequently he will give account before the judgements seat of God at the end how he has put his freedom into use. Those who lived a life of license will be condemned while those who lived in responsible freedom will rejoice in God's kingdom (Matt. 25, 31-46). Dwyer understands freedom in the context of the human dynamism when he wrote:

> Freedom is not the absence of limiting and constraining factors in our lives; it is the ability and the power to make use of them. The very factors commonly regarded as limiting freedom are nothing other than the raw material we are summoned to use in becoming free. Our freedom is not an abstract quality; it is accepted and exercised in the presence of every concrete limitation in life.[530]

However the concept of freedom for the Christians has remained in the words of Karl Rahner: *"Stichwort und Schlachtruf"* of the most different religious and spiritual movements of the West.[531] On one of the occasions (Der österreichischen Katholikentag) Rahner was invited for paper presentation on *"Würde und Freiheit des Menschen"* and he introduced his presentation this way:

> Die Bedeutung und Situationsgemäßheit dieses Themas ist uns ohne weiteres verständlich. Aber auch seine Dunkelheit. Man braucht nur daran zu denken, dass vor allem das Wort Freiheit Stichwort und Schlachtruf der verschiedensten geistigen und religiösen Bewegungen des Abendlandes war: des Paulus gegen den jüdischen Legalismus, der Französischen Revolution und des Liberalismus im Kampf gegen die Staats- und Gesellschaftsordnung des christlich- abendländischen Mittelalters und gegen die Kirche .... Und es ist seltsam: vor 100 Jahren war unter Pius IX „Freiheit" der Gegenstand der Kritik und Vorbehalte der Kirche, heute unter Pius XII. ist das Wort das Stichwort eines Katholikentages.[532]

The above statement from Rahner helps to summarize the history of the interpretation of the word freedom. It has never been easy to understand,

---

530 Dwyer, Person, Dignity of 731, See also Karol Wojtyla (John Paul II, Pope), The Acting Person 98-99.
531 Cf. Rahner, Würde und Freiheit des Menschen 247.
532 Rahner, Würde und Freiheit des Menschen 247.

even when it seemed to have been understood there was not enough strong will on the people to put it into practice. It is therefore heart warming to note that in our age the Vat. II gave a great resonance to human freedom in her document on religious freedom, *Dignitatis Humane*. It was an attempt to deconstruct the Hellenistic and scholastics constructions on the nature and mystery of free choice; and a fair critique on the liberalist construct of non-interference in the Western democracies. According to Dwyer,

> The return to biblical concept is closely connected with an important shift in Catholic social thought since the Second Vatican Council. Since freedom is the power to create the selves that we are called to be, and since we are called to a life in community with others, freedom is by definition the power to act in concert with others in order to achieve the common good. In other words, it is the power to participate in shaping the political, social, and economic order in a way that is appropriate to those who have been called to transcendence while in the world, and called to express this transcendence by transforming the world and creating a more human society.[533]

It is really a paradigm shift from an austere abstraction and extremism to an existential notion of freedom that is transcendentally open to others in love.[534] We shall treat the document on religious freedom because of its importance later in this section.

5.3 The Person of Jesus as the True Image and Likeness of God

In the economy of salvation we are called to see the whole human history as a single story. This economy presents the Love of God the Father who in his infinite goodness created Adam and Eve in his own image and

---

[533] Dwyer, Person, Dignity of 732.
[534] Karl Rahner and Bernard Lonergan developed the transcendental aspect of knowledge, which opens up the love of God in freedom. Their teaching was in line with Thomas Aquinas on the human intelligence as simply *Capax entis,* meaning simply: open to being as such.

likeness; placed them in the Garden. Unfortunately the first world order got destroyed by sin, the fall. After the flood, in the new world order God resettled human beings with the injunction: "He who sheds the blood of man by man shall his blood be shed, for in the image of God was man created. Be fruitful and multiply, teem over the earth and subdue it" (Gen. 9, 5ff). With Abraham the father of faith, hope was beginning to gleam but for the killing of Abel by his brother Cain out of jealousy and envy humanity was no more to be stopped in her evil ways.

The Exodus event (the Pass over and the crossing of the red sea) stands as the hob of both the Old and New Testament theologies. It is evident that the whole redemption wrought by Christ has theological base from the Jewish paschal mystery. In a sense, but rightly too the incarnation of Christ could be taken as the replica of the creation in the book of Genesis. While the Book of Genesis presented Adam, who was created by God as the first human being, Jesus is being presented in the New Testament as the new Adam. In his letters Paul proclaimed Jesus as the image of the unseen God, the first born of all creation, for in him were created all things in heaven and on earth (Col. 1, 15; Rom. 8, 29; Heb. 1, 3; Eph. 1, 10). The theological basis for this motif can be linked with the salvation economy, which sees a direct link between Adam, the first man in the Old Testament with that of Jesus as the new Adam in the New Testament.

Hilpert captures the implication of incarnation in the whole salvation economy when he opined that the Person, but also the Good news and the fate of Jesus of Nazareth is in the eyes of the early Christian theologians and authors like Paul, the place of accepting the human existence through God (Incarnation) and the restoration and in this wise the particular image of God. In this sense the hope is based and hidden, that death is not the end point, which means the last say and also never the final answer to the struggle, formation as well as shattering and misconstruction. The human being- the hope, which was witnessed to by Paul is much more an invitation to take part in a new creation in which there will be nothing more that oppresses, endangers or destroys.[535] Consequently the human being redeemed in the person of Christ the true image and likeness of God became the theological standpoint in the Christian anthropology and human

---

535 Cf. Hilpert, Die Idee der Menschenwürde aus der Sicht christlicher Theologie 50.

dignity. The concept of 'person' among the early Christians and more especially, in the medieval anthropology, applies only to a distinct subsistent individual of an intellectual and rational nature, which is precisely what gives him his dignity.[536] It might be pertinent at this juncture to enquire briefly about the development of the term *'person'* in its Grecoroman origin; its reception in the early Christian theology of Incarnation and Trinity; in medieval, modern and contemporary Christian theology; and the implications for our enquiry on the dignity of human person.

5.3.1 Human Being as Person in Christian Anthropology

The age long question of who the human being is has produced a mosaic of theories of human person in the history of philosophy. This question, which was raised by the Psalmist: Lord what is man? and further asked by renowned thinkers from Antiquity to the declaration of human rights has revealed the human being from the beginning of his life till death as a person[537]. However it is very pertinent to assert from the outset, that the Christian understanding of person did not stem from a philosophical speculation, it is founded in the gratuitous revelation of God himself to man.[538] The concept of person became thematic in the Christian philosophy through the process of understanding the mystery of the Trinity and Incarnation. Ontologically the early Christians taught the singularity of the person, unique and unrepeatable, and as a matter of fact, the substantial equality in the dignity of every human being.[539] It was the Incarnation of Christ and his position in the salvific economy the Trinity (God head) that gave rise to the reflections on the personhood of God. Among others the Christian ontological concept of Personhood profoundly transformed pa-

---

536 Thomas Aquinas, Summa Theologiae 1 q. 29, a.3, ad 2.
537 Cf. Regine Kather, Person. Die Begründung menschlicher Identität, Darmstadt 2007 7.
538 Cf. Richard Heinzmann, „Der Mensch als Person-Verständnis des Menschen aus jüdisch-Christlichem Ursprung", in: Richard Heinzmann, DER., (Hg.), Menschenwürde, Grundlagen in Christentum und Islam, Stuttgart 2007, 45-56 here 53.
539 Cf. Battista Mondin, Philosophical Anthropology, Rome 1985 244.

ganism, gave birth to medieval and modern cultures and set the footstool for the emancipation of contemporary times from reckless materialism.[540]

The origin of the word itself as (*Prosepon*) προσεπον meaning simply mask worn by actors in stage in the Greek amphitheatres came to be used in the Roman world as *persona*.[541] However with the early Christian philosophy and the subsequent development *persona* became the matrix of Christian anthropology, where the human being in his soul and body can only be properly understood as a *'person'*.

The remote sources of the historical development of the Christian concept of person is further traceable to the early Fathers of the Church, who found in the theology of Christ, the son of God, the real image and likeness of God a great spiritual and theological force to confront the Gnostic Pagan philosophy of the Greco roman world. Their first task was to re-theologize the Greek λόγος- (divine wisdom of the gods) into a vibrant Christology. Christ as the only Son of God became as it were the "word of God" for humanity.

5.3.2 The Early Christian Thinkers-From Mask to Person

5.3.2.1 Origen (ca 185-254 A.D)

Origen was among the first Christian thinkers who could qualify both as philosopher and theologian of the early Christian era. Even though along the line his thoughts became suspects of unorthodoxy his views were revered among his contemporaries, especially his reflections on the nature of Godhead as both independent and indivisible unity with relational capabilities. Origen succeeded to a great extent in transposing the then intellectual edifice of the Gnostic Philosophy and the great stoic philosophies into a strong Christian ontology of the divinity as a particular not just a universal substance[542]. Origen guarded the notion of 'particular'

---

540 Ogbujah, The Idea of Personhood 7.
541 Cf. Georg Mohr, Einleitung: Der Personenbegriff in der Geschichte der Philosophie, www.mentis.de/download.php?media_id=00000252 28.06.2012 26.
542 Cf. Edward Moore, *Origin of Alexandria* (185-254 AD), in: Internet Encyclopedia of Philosophy 02.05.2005

against the 'universal' and insisted on the uniqueness and unrepeatable self-subsistence nature and personhood, which provided as it were, the basis for a genuine Trinitarian theology. His emphasis on relation rather than substance; particular rather than universal paved the way for genuine Trinitarian theology capable of standing ontologically without necessarily seeking support on the Aristotelian substance metaphysics.[543] Persons as persons relate to one another without losing their personality as Godhead. Thus relation forms the ontological string between the Father the Son and the Holy Spirit with each maintaining his individuality, but meaningless without the relationship binding the three. Edward Moore wrote of Origen thus:

> He was an inspiration to the Renaissance Humanists and, more recently to certain existentialist Christian theologians, notably Nicolas Berdyaev (1874-1948) whose insistence on the absolute autonomy and nobility of the person in the face of all objectifying reality is an echo across the ages of the humanism of Origen.[544]

Gregory of Nyssa (ca. 386 AD) adopted and developed in his writings the Origen ideas on *apokatastasis* or restoration of all things[545]. Nonetheless scholars claim that outside Augustine Origen has remained an influential thinker in the philosophy and theology of persons and the Trinity. The lofty edifice of the oriental Trinitarian theology is linked with Origen. For instance future oriental theologians like John Zizioulas would insist on the ontological priority of relation over the substance, thereby decon-

---

543 Cf. Edward Moore, Origen of Alexandria (185-254 AD), in: Internet Encyclopedia of Philosophy 02.05.2005.
544 Edward Moore, Origen of Alexandria (185-254 AD), in: Internet Encyclopaedia of Philosophy 02.05.2005.
545 Origen taught in his famous work: Treatise on First Principle that the soul is constantly in motion towards the process of purification. Every thing will belong to God at the end through Christ- apokatastasis. Basing his argument on the Pauline writing, 1 Cor. 15, 25-28 especially 28, "when all things shall be subdued unto him ... that God may be all in all". All will be all in Christ here means no one would be lost in Hell even the Satan called the devil will be changed into meriting heaven. The souls will be redeemed in Christ at the end of it all. Origen resisted the dualism of his time and this got him into serious problems with the orthodoxy of the Church's faith.

structing the Hellenism or Greek substance philosophy (οὐσία) and replacing it with (ὑπόστασις) hypostasis.[546]

5.3.2.2 Augustine (354-430 AD)

With the Christian reflections on the incarnation of Christ and his position in the divine economy (God head) as both man and God, the western view of the human person as both body and soul developed.[547] Augustinian insight based on the Ancient Greek conception of impersonal creator God who stood at the beginning as perfection in every thing but a person. Plato wrote of him in his *Timaeus* as a creator god who created every thing in perfection so that it could only reflect his perfection. There was nothing known in the ancient Greek world about a god revealing himself to man or making himself known to human mind as a person.[548] He was always conceived as the absolute, ápathea, the great in every sense of it, and creates humans, as he will. The philosopher Plotinus, in 300 AD said of this god as: the only one who is the centre of his own being and at the same time that of the universe[549]. It was therefore the originality of the early Christian philosopher and theologian Augustine to have emphasised the concept of person in the economy of salvation- the Godhead. Consequently this presented a new problematic which embellished the anthropology that would remain a point of reference for the whole western world and above. Through his emphasis on the hypostatic concept of person rather than substance Augustine was able to ensure the individuality of the three persons in one God at the same time preserving their unity. Augustine emphasised not only the uniqueness of the three persons but also their relational capacity, which links them to what they share together – the substance.

Although hypostasis does not define precisely the ontological concept of person, it succeeded in bringing in a new element in the Christian un-

---

546 Alan Brown, "On the Criticism of Being as Communion in Anglophone Orthodox Theology", in: Douglas H. Knight, The Theology of John Zizioulas England 2007, 35-78 here 53.
547 Cf. Regine Kather, *Person*, 20.
548 Cf. Regine Kather, *Person*, 20.
549 Regine Kather, *Person*, 20.

derstanding of man: the human being as a composite of body and soul and the relationship existing within them as a hypostatic union. The body and soul as composites was extrapolated from the Trinitarian model, that is, in the relations of the Godhead as a hypostatic union. Accordingly it is the Greek *Prosepon* meaning mask that has lead to a philosophy and theology of person. This motif of the Greek mask engendered a genuine anthropology of person in a Trinitarian dimension. Consequently for the early Christian thinkers, the human body became the mask from which the soul expressed itself, and this influence was felt in the intellectual history, even in the medieval- scholastic era. Even though the soul and the body are not conceived singularly as person, they can be conceived differently on their personal merits. However, neither the soul nor the body taking singularly can be persons but only put together. Thus, with such a congealed manner of reflection Augustine succeeded in transposing the Greek *Prosepon*-mask into a viable theology and philosophy of *persona*. The individuality and singularity mark out a person[550] but this was to be made clearer in the philosophy of Boethius, scholastic, neo scholastic, modern and contemporary thinkers.

5.3.2.3 Boethius (480-524 AD)

Boethius in his *Contra Eutichen et Nestorium*, made the first systematic attempt at the ontological definition of person as: *"persona es naturae individua substantia"*-person is an individual substance of a rational nature.[551] Here Boethius used substance to exclude accidents, which in themselves are metaphysically imperfect and as such could not constitute a person. Authors argue that Boethius could have applied substance in two distinct senses namely, first and second instances. The first referring to the concrete substance as existing in the individual, while the second referred to the substance conceived abstractly as existing in the genius and the species.[552]

---

550 Augustine, *De Trinitate* (On the Trinity) XV, 6, 11 *"singulis quisque homo (...) una persona est* (every single man is a person).
551 Boethius, Contra Eutichen et Nestorium (Against Eutychen and Nestorium), C, 4, cited in Battista Mondin, *Philosophical Anthropology*, Rome 1985 7.
552 Cf. L. W. Geddes and W. A. Wallace, Person (In Philosophy), New Catholic Encyclopaedia Vol. XI, New York 1967 166-168 here 166.

Boethius did not make clear the particular sense he meant for the person but instead multiplied the multiplicand by using almost another similar word in meaning – the qualifier "individual" to make his meaning similar to the first substance. Thus the singularity of the word individual fascinated him only, such that the undivided nature of the person makes him all the more ontologically unique. This leads to the result that person is not any other than the individuality of any spiritual nature. That means: For Boethius the individuality as such is the specific constituting factor of the person.[553] In other words: For him the individualized spiritual substance as such and not a personal specific act of being (substantia, existential) constitutes the being of the person. Geddes and Wallace conclude that: "The sense of Boethius's definition is that a person is a particular type of supposit, namely one with a rational nature".[554] However Walter Kasper points out a weakness embedded in the Boethian understanding of person. The Boethian definition seems to have understood individuality and personality to be identical concepts. Hence he opined: „Individuality is (...) a *what*-determinant and still not *who*-determinant; it is a natural conditioner of a person, not the self itself".[555] Therefore, relation has no part to play in the Boethian understanding. That means that, the relation from person

---

553 This "Individual" is for him different from that of the Neo-Platonist, not conditioned through accidental differentiation of the being. "Persona accidentibus non posse constitui": Cf. Contra Eutychen II, 15.18, but different from the Aristotelian thought the principium individuationis of the person does not reside in the materia quantitatae signita, but person is an irreducible personal substance, which is above the general form – 'humanitas' from the outset – distinguished through every individual form, so that the spiritual individual remains the personal substance. Therefore the person for Boethius is distinguished through 'independence, yes through 'the absolute being-for-self' of this independence. (Cf. J. Auer, *Person*, Regensburg 1979 30) For Boethius Person is understood „from societal self understanding of the Roman regent, who himself in his independence and monarchical structure surely knows (individua substantia). (Cf. John, D. Zizioulas, *Being as Communion* 34).
554 Geddes and Wallace, *Person* 166.
555 Walter Kasper, *Der Gott Jesu Christi*, Matthias Grunewald Verlag, Mainz 1982 194 opined, "Individuality, however, defines *a what* and not *a who*; it describes the person's nature, not the person as such".

to person has no place in the definition of a particular being. Thus „the content of Boethius 'individuality' is incommunicability, an immediacy based on an ultimate indivisibility and unity".[556]

5.3.3 The Medieval Era-Ontological Perspective

5.3.3.1 Thomas Aquinas (1225-1274 AD)

Accepting the definition of Boethius however, Thomas Aquinas improved its depths by making the individual substance become "a substance that is complete, subsists by itself, and is separated from others."[557] When one considers the definition or rather the contribution of Aquinas to that of Boethius's complementary elements emerge: (a) Substance; (b) Complete nature; (c) Subsistence by itself; (d) Separate from others and (e) Of rational nature, this does exclude all other *supposits* that lack rationality. A person is an individual substance of a rational nature. Human beings are constituted as individual substances of rational nature by virtue of having rational souls. The rational soul is the form and life- long actuality,[558] which gives dynamic unity to the complex material organisms we are and to the expression of our various powers (vegetative, animal and intellectual) in multifarious activities. Aquinas points out that: "From the essence of the soul flow powers which are essentially different ... but which are all united in the soul's essence as in a root".[559]

Each individual receives from the beginning this capacity and power of the soul, as wholly undeveloped, radical capacities. This forms as it were, the basis of the natural dignity, which belongs to every human being. An important contribution or implication of the Thomistic insight in the issue of personhood is the emphasis on the unity of the substantial form. One implication of this teaching is that the human body shares in the dignity

---

556 Walter Kasper, *The God of Jesus Christ*, 281; See also, *Thomas Aquinas*, Summa Theologica 1, 28, 2.
557 Thomas Aquinas, *The Summa Theologica*, 3a, 16.12 ad 2.
558 Cf. Thomas Aquinas, The Summa Theologica, 3a, 16.12 ad 2.
559 Thomas Aquinas, II Sent., d.26, q.1 a.4c.

of our rational nature in the sense that, as long as we are living human bodies, our corporealness is intrinsic to what gives natural dignity.[560]

Later scholastics applying negative theology emphasised the incommunicability of the individual intellectual nature, as the foundation of personality. **Don Scotus** (1266-1308), was known for this negative theology when he held that any thing that is non-communicable is a person, while all other communicable beings are not persons. It is pertinent however, to point out that Negation as the point of departure in Don Scotus theology deviates from the Thomistic thought. On the contrary, later scholastics like **Tommaso de Vio Cajetan** (1464-1534 A.D) in his traditional views held that the personality must be based on a positive determination, which he preferred to describe as the mode of subsistence.[561] Therefore a Person is self- subsistent that carries with it the reason and reality of its own existence.

5.3.3.2 Francis Suarez (1548-1617 A.D.)

Francis Suarez also insists that the ultimate foundation of personality cannot be a mere negation as opined by Don Scotus but must be a positive perfection. For him there is no real distinction between nature (essence) and existence, and does not regard personality as something that prepares the nature to receive its own proper existence. Thus personality for Suarez: "is the final term or complement not of a substantial essence but of existence itself"[562]. Person remains incommunicable, separate, complete and determined.

The ontological concept of Person placed a greater premium on reason. As a consequence, since some higher animal outside man possess some worth of rationality; such as Chimpanzees personality could also be accorded to them. On this note the ontological view leaves some obvious open questions.

---

560 Cf. L. Gormally, Human Dignity: The Christian View and the Secularist View 3
561 Mode of subsistence is a natural predisposition towards the reception of the positive determination, which in turn functions as the presupposed first instance necessary for the communication of esse or existence.
562 Geddes and Wallace, Person (In Philosophy) 167.

5.3.4 The Modern Era-Psychological Perspective

Another stage in the discussions on person was the modern age with its controversial turn. It emphasised more on the human psychology and anthropology as the only indices for measuring the human person. Philosophers such as Descartes, Hume, Locke, Freud, Nietzsche, Jean Paul Sartre et cetera were prominent in this age. Without much ado over their views, one could see the pitfall already in the effort to submit the entire human reality to psychology. Such shallow considerations of the human person seem to be unacceptable when one thinks of the great work attained already by the ontological view for instance.

5.3.5 The Contemporary Era-Dialogical-Existential Perspective

The Dialogical approach to the question of person yielded rather more dividend in the sense that emphasis on the existential approach to human issue seemed to be more acceptable in an age recovering from the shock of the World wars. Experiments in the social and psychological concepts have yielded monster in the society that the atomisation of the human person had no more place. In the light of the hefty criticism and rejection of the existing theories of person, the contemporary era reflected a new, the person, and this time playing up the dialogical (inter-subjective) perspective rather than the ontological or the psychological. In the list are prominent existentialists like, Jacque Maritain, Gabriel Marcel, Martin Buber and Karol Wojtyla.

5.3.5.1 Jacque Maritain

Jacque Maritain had a holistic approach to the concept of person. He saw in human person the totality of his capacities and independence, and never servile. In his use of the words 'person' and 'personality' he used them interchangeably showing a shift from the usual static notions found in the ontological sphere. The distinction between Person as the individual and the personality as the characteristics or the distinguishing marks of a person meant nothing, when considered holistically. Hence he wrote:

However dependent it may be on the slightest accidents, of matter, the human 'person' exists by virtue of the existence of its soul, which dominates time and death. It is the spirit, which is the root of 'personality'.[563]

5.3.5.2 Gabriel Marcel

Gabriel Marcel was famous for his idea of the 'I thou' relationship. Communication for him remains the basis for personhood. The recognition of inter-subjectivity in every relationship marks the beginning of an interpersonal recognition of the 'thou'. Marcel held that the more the 'I' recognises the 'thou' the more the 'I' enhances its own personality and vice versa. This existential point of view creates a community of persons, where objectification of individuals should does not thrive. The Christian community is based on such values.

5.3.5.3 Martin Buber

Martin Buber extended the discussion on human person to the various relationships that could possibly exist between persons. He sees a genuine relation as only that which can generate encounter. Encounter becomes the basis of all human inter-subjectivity. The opus magnum of Buber was his work on *Ich und Du*. In this work Buber, presented two basic forms of relationship, the *'Ich-Es'*, that is *'I-it'* and the *'Ich-Du'*, that is, *'I-thou'* that characterize human life. The 'ich-es' assumes the character of possession, utilization and monopoly, while the Ich-Du has that of presence, encounter and dialogue. There are conditioning situations namely- Relation and non-relation. Relation creates an encounter, while non-relationship engenders objectification. For Buber encounter has a great meaning over and above co- presence and growth of the individual. He searched for wisdom in which the people can engage themselves in order to encounter themselves. The basic fact of human existence was not the individual person or a collective as such but 'human being'. Just as Aubery Hodes writes:

---

563 Jacque Maritain, Christianity and Democracy and the Rights of Man and Natural Law, New York 1942 89

> Wenn ein menschliches Wesen sich an andere als andere wendet, als eine bestimmte und spezifische zu wendende Person und versucht, sich mit ihm durch Sprache zu verständigen, oder Schweigen, findet etwas zwischen ihnen statt, welche anderswohin nicht in der Natur gefunden wird. Buber bezeichnet diese Treffen zwischen Menschen als Bereich des Zwischen.[564]

Encounter is a case or a situation, in which relationship emerges. According to Buber we can only grow and develop, at the instance we learn to live in the relationship of the other, and to acknowledge the space between us. Someone experiences the completion of his person in the mutuality with one another, which he encounters. In this Sense Martin Buber has this to say:

> Alles wirkliche Leben ist Begegnung" zu verstehen. Anders ausgedrückt „Wirkliches Miteinanderleben von Menschen zu Menschen kann nur da gedeihen, wo die Menschen die wirklichen Dinge ihres gemeinsamen Lebens miteinander erfahren, beraten, verwalten (...).[565]

It is only in this relationship that the human being can become a person. The basic means to this relationship and encounter is nothing but dialogue and the reality of this space between persons is the focus of Martin Buber's philosophy.[566] Worthy of note in this philosophy is the idea that self-actualisation is only possible within the relationship with the other. Relationship exists in form of dialogue. Nonetheless self-knowledge is only possible when the relation between human beings and creatures are understood as dialogical relationship. Buber shows against this backdrop that dialogue incorporates all other types of relations: to oneself, to others and to the whole creation.[567] Therefore Martin Buber tried to answer the age

---

564 Aubrey Hodes, Encounter with Martin Buber, Allen Lane/Penguin Press London 1972 72.
565 Stefan Liesenfeld (Hg.), Alles wirkliche Leben ist Begegnung: Hundert Worte von Martin Buber, Verlag Neue Stadt, 2. Auflage München-Wien 1999 37.
566 The reality of "space" that is in-between Persons is the focus of Buber's philosophy." Dan Avnon, Martin Buber: The hidden Dialogue, Rowman and Littlefield Publications, London 1998 5.
567 Cf. Dan. Avnon, Martin Buber 6.

long question of Kant „was ist der Mensch?" (What is man?), with a critical inquiry in the history of philosophical anthropology of different philosophers, not just from the stand point of human person as such but also from the consideration of the whole person in his existential reality as a 'being-with'. First of all the human being, who realises himself in the possible relationships with his whole being in his life truly helps us to recognise the human being. Hence according to Martin Buber the human being is "... the creature capable of entering into living relations with the world and things, with a man both as individuals and as the many and with the mystery of being which dimly apparent through all this but infinitely transcends it"[568]. Judging from what the human being is Martin Buber understands the human being as partaker in different relationship networks, which defines him and designs his whole being. The human being is not a material element; instead he is a spiritual being. For this reason, "the concept of personhood stands out in the declaration of the being of God ... and it is acceptable to say, that God is also a person."[569] God is the absolute being, in whose person the human person comes to be understood ontologically. Even though as an absolute he exists without man but the human person relates to him as a person. Between man and God, the human person encounters God and thereby encounters himself and his fellow humans as persons. The human person has dignity only in this ability to encounter others and be encountered by others in the society. Hence Buber asserts:

> Human persons are essentially directed towards each other. To be man is to be fellow man: man becomes only in contact with those who have already become, only in relation with the 'thou' can man become an 'I'.[570]

Human existence for Buber remains a presence in communion, encounter and dialogue with the fellow human beings. This encounter guarantees the personhood and the personhood guarantees the dignity of human person.

---

568 Martin Buber, Between Man and Man, (trans.) R. G. Smith, Routledge Classic, London 2002 77.
569 Martin Buber, Das dialogische Prinzip, Gütersloher Verlagshaus, Gütersloh 1986 134.
570 Martin Buber, I and thou (trans.) by Clark, Edinburgh 1937 28.

5.3.5.4 Karol Wojtyla (Pope John Paul II)

Karol Wojtyla (Pope John Paul II) deep insight in the phenomenology of person is impressive and at the same time influential in the understanding of person in Christian philosophy and theology. Wojtyla could still achieve originality and uniqueness even by remaining faithful to the ideas of person developed in the history of philosophy and theology before him. Most especially, he appropriated the insights of Thomas Aquinas on the individual as self-subsistent; he acknowledged the inter subjectivity of Gabriel Marcel and the encounter of Martin Buber. However over and above his predecessors he introduced the phenomenology of man as a subject in the context of his experience. Wojtyla's focus and concentration on the "I" as a subject in the midst of "others" brings to bear the whole reality of the subject. Faithful to a strict phenomenology of person irrespective of the distractive tendencies bedevilling[571] such a subject-search he resolutely concentrated on discovering the subject as the acting person in all his transcendence as well as his psychosomatic dimensions as a concrete self.[572] His phenomenology illuminated among others, certain ethical facts that are indispensable for aiming at a more comprehensive idea of the human person, for instance freedom and responsibility.[573] It is an existential concern and no more a mere metaphysical speculation of the self on the side of consciousness but also the individual subject in his experience. This holistic approach to the discussion on person made a significant import in the Christian understanding of person as both conscious and existential subject.

Wojtyla's reflections on the human person are found in his two related works: *The Acting Person*, a work he dedicated purely to phenomenology, and *The Person: Subject and Community*, an essay dealing with the connection between the subjectivity of man as a person and the structure of the human community. These two essays complement each other. In *The Acting Person* Wojtyla gave a full phenomenology of the person in

---

571 There was always this tendency in the earlier enquiries to subsume the self in pure consciousness or the other extreme of modelling the whole reality of the self in experience. This was the weakness of the modern idealism and empiricism in their definition of man.
572 Cf. Wojtyla, The Person: Subject and Community 273.
573 Cf. Wojtyla, The Acting Person 98.

his different dimensions, exposing his nature as the author of his acts, with a transcendental quality. *The Person: Subject and Society* sought to clarify some issues of the person. It explores the subjectivity of the human person, based on his whole experience. He asserts: "His subjectivity belongs to the essence of experience, which is always an experience of "something" or "someone".[574] This subjectivity is not merely a metaphysical subject but an existential subject. Notice his emphasis on the phrase, "the experience of man" which portrays man both as the subject and the object of experience. This holistic approach to anthropology marked out his phenomenology as practically based on experience and existence. In experience man is given to us as he who exists and acts. All men and "I" among them participate in the experience of existing and acting; at the same time all the "other", along with myself are the object of the experience[575]. In this wise the inter-subjectivity shines out clearly. The human person therefore, is a subject, an "I" among "others". He discovers the ontological relation with the "you". It is the "I" and "you" that form the "we". This "we" does not in any way minimize the "I". Wojtyla further clarifies: "If in fact that does take place, as noted in *The Acting Person*, the reason should be sought within the relation to the common good".[576] Consequently the person is ontologically ordered to the society. This vocation however places on him some moral responsibilities. Because the individual is not just the individual alone, but with others Wojtyla links the morality of the person with his acts which he performs as a subject of his acts and responsible for his acts. Hence he points out: "It is man's actions, his conscious acting, that make of him 'what' and 'who' he actually is".[577] Linking the human person properly with his acts presents an existential reality of freedom, which carries with it responsibility. The act makes the person, designates the person as good or bad. On this note Dwyer concurs: "Our decisions are not merely choices of how to act; they are choices of who to be. The person is not a changeless being who makes decisions about objects or things; rather, we

---

574 Wojtyla, The Acting Person 98.
575 Cf. Wojtyla, The Acting Person 98.
576 Wojtyla, The Person: Subject and Community 299.
577 Wojtyla, The Acting Person 98.

ourselves change profoundly in the decisions we make".[578] Consequently, the person remains dynamic before his or her existential reality.

Wojtyla and Dwyer's notion of the person in relation to his acts; and his relationship with the community reflects the dynamism in Igbo notion of personhood where a person is known through what he does – his achievements in the community. Igbo anthropology understands personhood as a dynamic process generated through the acts of the individual; acts that qualify the individual to attain a certain level of maturity in the society as a person. This status is not just distinguished by ontological reasons but more by the experience in the community. Of course in the Igbo understanding not all human beings are persons. However, these acts that constitute the person in Wojtyla's phenomenology of the person have no time reference but spans from the beginning of life to the end. While for the Igbo personhood it has a time of inception; a time frame and point of maturity in the life of every Igbo person when the personhood actually sets in, namely at the point of initiation or at a stage of certain amount of achievement in the society.

For Wojtyla the dignity of human person resides in the fact that he acts as a subject of responsibility, bearing in mind that "he is the creature on earth that God has wanted for his own sake".[579] In line with Wojtyla Dwyer agrees that this human dignity is not abstract from concrete existing human being, which means, the human being can not be reduced to any single dimension such as race, colour, nationality, sex et cetera as basis for discrimination.[580]

In Summary, the implication of the discovery of the person in the study of human dignity is that, human dignity is inseparable from the person, and it does not depend for its reality on being acknowledged by others, whether by individuals or by the state; rather, it demands such recognition and acknowledgement. Human dignity only becomes meaningful, borrowing the words of Dwyer "when the existence of an individual man or woman is viewed from a certain perspective, as constituting a

---

578 Cf. Dwyer, Person, Dignity of 731.
579 Karol Wojtyla, Crossing the Threshold of Hope, V. Messori (ed.), London 1994 202.
580 Cf. Dwyer, Person, Dignity of 729.

task and a challenge for the existing person and as imposing certain obligations on other individuals and communities".[581]

5.4 Historical Documents of the Church on Human Dignity

The Christian belief in the doctrine of human dignity is one thing, while the factual recognition of this dignity is another. Right from the time of the early Church fathers the doctrine on the *Imago Dei* has served as the only motif for the dignity of man as the highest created being outside the angels and divinities. Although, based on the churches theologominon-*Imago Dei* the factual proclamation and recognition of the dignity of human person was severely hindered by her understanding of the basic constituent of human dignity namely, freedom. Historically speaking, the word: 'freedom' or 'liberty' has remained in the words of Karl Rahner: *"Stichwort und Schlachtruf der verschiedensten geistigen und religiösen Bewegungen des Abendlandes"*.[582]

The history of Christian dogma did not help matters either. Dogmas were positioned to stifle every thing considered worldly in the biblical point of view. The doctrine of the soul as superior to the flesh or body led to the disregarding of any thing that had to do with the flesh. These dichotomized and stringent teachings, made the doctrines instead of expediting the acceptance of the consequence of Imago Dei theology, it rather drifted from it. Consequently freedom as the most acclaimed implication and consequence of the Imago Dei was very minimally emphasised. Moreover, the early Christian interpretation of the Pauline teachings on freedom was restricted only to the freedom from sin. There were little or no intentions of its extension to human or political freedom from slavery.

---

581 Cf. Dwyer, Person, Dignity of 729.
582 Cf. Rahner, Würde und Freiheit des Menschen 247. Rahner points to the historical difficulties encountered in the West with the recognition of human freedom by the religious and spiritual movements.

Augustine writing in the 4th century made a great distinction between the city of God and earthly city, bedevilled by sin and imperfections.[583]

Although the teachings of the early fathers influenced the scholastic era, the content of their teachings were however severely coloured by the scholastic metaphysics and theology in the medieval era. This influence found its expression in the whole history of dogma for a long while. The implication was a theology that was purely stunted by Hellenistic rediscovery; and a dogma that has little or no regard for history, world or man himself. It was a theological framework totally intellectualistic in orientation; based only on natural law and relevant only from up to down methodology. This refers to the so-called scholastic inductive method. God dictated every thing to man and he in respect must accept all as *'de fide'*. There were many bottlenecks here and there, as can be attested to historically.

Scholars have described the events of the encounter between the Church and the rights of man before the 19th century, as *'eine langwieriger und schmerzlicher Lernprozess'* – (a protracted and painful learning process).'[584] Karl Rahner referred to this fact in his lectures during the catholic day celebration in Austria on the 1st of May 1952 as both "an object of critique and reserve of the church; and at same time a stitch word of a public discussion",[585] while Arnold Angenendt called this process, *"ein Wahnsinn"*.[586] However, it is not the intention of this inquiry to delve into this thematic simply because that would mean straying away from our limited scope. Suffice it just to mention in passing that the period before the 19th century was marked by a difficult appreciation of the human dignity because of the Churches dogmatic structure and its historical framework.

It was only recently that the Church took the bull by the horn and declared with the whole human race the facticity of the dignity of human person based on freedom, justice and equity. In the declaration of the human rights, after the sorry event of the World War II, the international

---

583 Cf. Saint Augustine, The City of God, (trans.) Marcus Dods, New York 1993 306ff.
584 Cf. Hilpert, Die Menschenrechte in Theologie und Kirche 71.
585 Cf. Rahner, Würde und Freiheit des Menschen 247.
586 Arnold Angenendt, Toleranz und Gewalt: Das Christentum zwischen Bibel und Schwert, Münster 2008 136.

community boldly legalized the moral norms of human dignity, so as to protect the dignity of human person. With reference to our findings in the early part of our inquiry there have existed before the UHRD some influential declarations both in Europe and America, which served as forerunners to it. For instance: the Magna Carter; the American Bill of rights and the French Declaration of the rights of Man. As a matter of fact, the documents of the Church on human dignity became more expressively historical in the event of the human rights declaration. Based on the universal declaration of human rights, the Church was inspired to bring out the full implications of the Christian doctrines on the human person as created in the image and likeness of God both from the Christological and anthropological points of view.

Papal documents on the dignity of human person were based on the Churches teachings on the natural law. It was a law that guaranteed the human being as being endowed with human reason and intelligence to discover the ordinances of God in his creation. Among others the church took up the concept of freedom once more in a new light but still under the basis of natural law and the theology of *Imago Dei*. We shall review some of these papal documents in order to appreciate their rich theological basis.

5.4.1 Selected Papal Documents

5.4.1.1 Libertas Praestantissimum of Pope Leo XIII (1888)

Pope Leo XIII wrote in his encyclical of 1884- *"Humanum Genus"* the basis for human equality as that flowing from the single fact of being human. According to him this equality is founded on the principles of justice and charity, and taking into account the differences among men.[587] On the basis of this human equality Pope Leo XIII set rolling the workers associations for the welfare of the workers and encouraged all authorities to support the idea. Sequel to *Humanum Genus* was a very serious one on the liberty, *Libertas Praestantissimum* in which Pope Leo XIII described liberty as:

---

587 Cf. A. S. S. XVI, 1884 431.

The highest of natural endowment, being the portion only of intellectual or rational natures, confers on man his dignity- that he is in the hand of his counsel and has power over his actions.[588]

This encyclical explored the right understanding of liberty different from the then liberalism of the time, especially in America. Among others it sought to assert the liberty of thought, teaching, of conscience and of worship without the state interference or other obstacles. All these liberties are to be exercised within the limits of morality and the common good, based on the equality of all human beings in their dignity.[589]

The encyclical *"Rerum Novarum"* came also on the 16th of May 1891 as the most important documentation on the subject of human rights, based on the dignity of human person in the works of Pope Leo XIII. It explored among others the conditions and rights of workers of the time of industrial revolution. The Pope defended the right to private property; elevated the rights and prerogatives of the domestic society and called upon the civil society to protect them. The pope defended the spiritual and natural rights of the human person to labour and at same time right to his just wages.[590] In order to ensure a just distribution of the common good, the Pope based his theologomenon on the early Christian teaching on justice, partaking and brotherhood of the children of God who enjoy the image and likeness of God. Consequently he did not forget the poor and the less privileged, who he said have genuine claim on the Church and the state.[591]

5.4.1.2 Pope Pius XI: Quadragesimo Anno

Traditionally, the encyclical of popes addresses particular situations in the Church and the society and or continues in the footsteps of their predecessors. In the case of the *Quadragesimo Anno* Pope Pius XI on the 15th of May 1931 affirms the teaching of *Rerum novarum* on the relative rights and mutual duties of the rich and the poor, and of the capital and

---

588 Pope Leo XIII, Human Liberty, Paulist Press Version, 5, par. 1.
589 Cf. Pope Leo XIII, Encyclical Libertas Praestantissimum, A.S.S. XX pp. 605, 606 and 608.
590 Cf. Pope Leo XIII, Rerum Novarum, A.A.S, XXIII, 1891 640.
591 Pope Leo XIII, Rerum Novarum, A.A.S, XXIII, 1891 640.

labour.⁵⁹² *Quadragesimo anno* asserted the right of man to private property with accent on its personal and social character as a person among others, having share in the common good as a 'being- with' as well as the duties inherent in proprietary rights.⁵⁹³After examining the indispensability of both capital and labour the Pope called for just wages and the amelioration of the conditions of the Labour conditions hence:

> Every effort ... must be made that at least in future a just share only of the fruits of production be permitted to accumulate in the hands of the wealthy and that an ample sufficiency be supplied to the workers.⁵⁹⁴

5.4.1.3 Pope Pius XII: Christmas Message Dec. 1942

Pope Pius XII was faced with the atrocities of the World War II, and the challenges of mending an already war torn world. In his Christmas message of 24th December 1942 the supreme pontiff substantially made a moving and animatedly appealing declaration: of the dignity and rights of man, of the family, of the dignity and privilege of labour, and of a regenerated juridical system. The importance of this Christmas message lies in the fact of its details and consistency with the Catholic social teachings. On the dignity and rights of the human person the Pontiff enjoins,

> He who would have the star of peace to shine permanently over society must do all in his power to restore to the human person the dignity with which God conferred upon him from the beginning; he must resist the excessive herding together of human beings as though they were a soulless mass; he must set his face against their disintegration in economic, social, political, intellectual and moral life; against their lack of solid principles and firm convictions; against their excessive reliance upon instinct and emotion, and against their fickleness of mood; he must favour, by all legitimate

---

592 Cf. Okorie, The Integral Salvation of the Human Person in Ecclesia in Africa 221.
593 Cf. Pope Pius XI, Encyclical Quadragesimo Anno, A.A.S, XXIII, 1931 177.
594 Cf. Pope Pius XI, Encyclical Quadragesimo Anno, A.A.S, XXIII, 1931 177.

means and in every sphere of life, social forms which render possible and guarantee full personal responsibility in regard to things both temporal and spiritual ....[595]

On the protection of social unity and especially of the family, he admonishes leaders not to handle the human society as formless mass, lacking organic unity and cohesion; as a raw material for domination to be misused and arbitrarily treated. Above all the dignity and the right of the individual must be respected. Among other things the Pontiff detailed the problems of the family; especially he harped on economic security of every human family and the moral responsibility of the head of the family in bringing up his family in love and dignity.

Regarding the dignity and prerogatives of labour he wrote: "He who would have the star of peace to shine permanently over society must give labour the place assigned to it by God from the beginning".[596] The Pope recognising the inalienable dignity from human labour directs that man's labour must be linked with his dignity and human development. However basing on the doctrine of original sin he enjoins that the burden of human labour must be endured in obedient submission to the will of God.[597]

Political theory and practise should be based upon rational discipline, noble humanity, and a responsible Christian spirit. The pope insists that the ultimate moral basis and the universal legitimacy of the right to govern, lies in the duty to serve.[598]

5.4.1.4 Pacem in Terris of Pope John XXIII

The encyclical, Pacem in Terris of Pope John XXIII given on the 11th of April 1963 can be said to be the most important and relevant document on the dignity and rights of the human person before the Vatican II. Nwachukwu S.S Iwe a professor of history remarks:

> In Pacem in Terris we see a programmatic and substantially exhaustive promulgation of all essential points of human rights as

---

595 CF. Pope Pius XII, Nuntius Radiophonicus, "Il Santo Natale e la Umanità Dolorante", A.A.S XXXV, 1943 19-24.
596 Pope Pius XII, Nuntius Radiophonicus 19-24.
597 Cf. Pope Pius XII, Nuntius Radiophonicus 19-24.
598 Cf. Pope Pius XII, Nuntius Radiophonicus 19-24.

enunciated and ratified in the recent encyclicals and teachings of the popes. With Pacem in Terris the teachings of Christianity on human rights came to its apex and culminating point.[599]

This encyclical was directed towards restoring peace in a conflict-wearied world; among all peoples of our earth in truth, justice, love and freedom. Pope John XIII wrote this encyclical shortly after the Cuba crises, which nearly turned the world into an unprecedented nuclear warfare. This was the first time a Pope wrote not only to the Catholics or Bishops but to the whole human race, just as the title of the encyclical reveal- 'to all men of good will'.[600] The Pope acknowledged among others, but most importantly the establishment of the international community, the UNO and its efforts in the proclamation of human rights as "a sign of the time."[601]

It will be recalled that before this encyclical, Pope John XXIII in 1961 wrote his *"Mater et Magistra"* in which he concentrated once more on social reforms in line with his predecessors. It was written in commemoration of the *Rerum Novarum* of Leo the XIII. However in Pacem in Terris the supreme Pontiff made it clear that "The dignity of human man is the key factor in the conception of man's rights and duties."[602] He went further and outlined the logic of the basis for human rights as that established by natural law asserting: "In the whole universe there reigns order (which the author of the universe has established).[603] The supreme pontiff therefore, saw in the human rights charter of 1948 a step forward in the establishment of law and order among peoples of the world. According to him, "through these articulations of the charter on human rights the dignity of human person for every human being would be happily accepted and recognised, and every human being will have the right to seek for the truth, to follow ethical norms, to practice out ones duties and obligations of justice and to lead a human dignified life[604]. In his understanding it is the function of this new found body the UNO to seek ways and avenues to protect the rights of the human person, which would in turn protect the

---

599 Iwe, The History and Contents of Human Rights 153.
600 Cf. Hilpert, Die Menschenrechte in Theologie und Kirche 69.
601 Pope John XIII, Encyclical Pacem in Terris no. 142.
602 Pacem in Terris Par. 44-48.
603 Pope John XIII, Encyclical Pacem in Terris AAS LV, 1963, 258.
604 Pope John XIII, Encyclical Pacem in Terris no. 144.

dignity of human person. Pacem in Terris went all out to present in details the different rights of the human person, agreeing in most parts with that of the already proclaimed rights of the human person in the UNO Charter on human rights.

Apart from the historical relevance of this encyclical, one can see a convergence of the teachings of the Church on social matters before the Second Vatican Council and the vision ahead for a Church that wishes to renew herself in a form of an *"aggiornamento."*[605] *Pacem in Terris* remains as it were, the precursor document to the land braking council of all times.

5.4.2 The Declaration of Vatican II on Religious Freedom, Dignitatis Humanae

One of the greatest achievements of the Church in the modern times is the declaration of religious freedom as a sign of human dignity. This declaration made in the full assembly of the Vatican II Councils in 1965 presented the greatness of a Church that has opened herself to the promptings of the Holy Spirit and the spirit of the time. Pope John XIII called this spirit, the 'sign of the time'. This word borrowed from the gospel of John summarised the theological foundation of the teaching Church faithful to her master's teachings and that of the apostles in an unbreakable long history of dogma.

The present state of the matter before the council was such that the religious freedom and conscience were only the reserve of the Church to avoid the possibility of the individual falling into mistake or error, which can lead to damnation. This sensitivity was heightened after the French revolution as a defensive reaction which the Church had to make as a protective measure against the anti-Christian, anti- religious, anti- clerical, rationalist and indifferentist spirit of the movement which produced the Charter of 1789. The Church's initial response to the French Revolution and the resultant Declaration of the Rights of Man and of the Citizen

---

605 *'Aggiornamento'* is an Italian word used by Pope John XIII to describe the task of his short pontificate. It was the founding word for the convocation of the second Vatican Council.

was complete rejection. This reaction was essentially made in defence of error of conscience, just as Pope Gregory XVI wrote in his encyclical *"Mirari Vos"* of 1832:

> We are coming now to another consequential source of evil, from which the church, to our worry is going to be visited namely: the indifferentism, that is, every form of careless opinion ... that a human being can save his soul through any form of confession of faith if he models his life on the norms of law and ethical goods...and out of this highest destructive sources of indifferentism flows every confusing and deviant ideas and more over, madness that there must be a guarantee and security of freedom of conscience to someone ....[606]

The above statement from Pope Gregory XVI throws light on the state of the Churches attitude towards freedom and her suspicion of religious freedom as a source of destruction to the faith. Thinking of separating the Church from the state was simply 'crazed absurdity'.

Furthermore, this sentiment received acknowledgement during the pontificate of Pope Pius IX, in his encyclical, *Quanta Cura and the Syllabus of Errors* of 1864 where he carefully outlined the known and hidden errors. The basic idea was that error has no rights.

However with the subsequent pontificates in the following hundred years this harsh stand of the Church on human liberty started waning gradually. Pope Leo XIII in his encyclical *"Libertas Praestantissimum" of 1888* recognised human dignity as the root of natural, universal and inviolable rights.[607] This positive development was not only noticeable in the Encyclicals of Pope Leo XIII but could also be found in the famous toleration plea of Pope Pius XII on the 6th of December 1953. Nonetheless, the force of the principle of dividing believers according to the religion of the ruler was still felt right before the pontificate of Johannes XXIII. This position was all the time justified by the Augustinian teaching: The State must protect the truth (the Catholic faith) and is allowed to tolerate the mistakes and wrong teachings of other religious bodies and unbelievers put never to guarantee them state protective rights.

---

606 Cf. Henrici Denzinger, Kompendium der Glaubensbekenntnisse und kirchlichen Lehrentscheidungen no. 2730-2732.
607 Cf. Pope Leo XIII, Human Liberty, Paulist Press Version (P.P.V) Par. 1.

It was only with the pontificate of Pope John XXIII in his encyclical *"Pacem in Terris"* that the language became clearer in support of human freedom and rights. Against the backdrop of the *Pacem in Terris* and other social teachings of the Church, Council fathers had to take a stand that would be likened to a *"Copernican turn."* This simply means that, the human person becomes now the subject of rights and no more the abstract concepts and truth.[608] Therefore it is now the right of the person to make mistake in freedom and no more that of the abstract truth (eternal life, the Church et cetera).[609] During the various sessions of the committee on religious freedom some American Bishops, namely Cardinal Ritter and Meyer who were members of this particular commission insisted on this freedom of conscience on issues of religion. Following in this line of thought also were several other members of the council, who concurred to this truth from different perspectives. For instance, the French argued from the point of view of philosophical anthropology, while the Eastern Block argued from the point of view of a lived experience of suppression and victimization in their countries.

Consequently, declaration on religious freedom came out in clear terms in its first article thus:

> Contemporary man is becoming increasingly conscious of the dignity of human person; more and more people are demanding that men should exercise fully their own judgement and responsible freedom in their actions and should not be subjected to the pressure of coercion but be inspired by a sense of duty. At the same time they are demanding constitutional limitation of the power of government to prevent excessive restriction of the rightful freedom of individuals and associations ....[610]

This freedom has to be properly defined and interpreted as one based on the light of the divine revelation:

> The declaration of this Vatican Council on man's right to religious freedom is based on the dignity of the person, the demands of which have become more fully known to human reason through

---

608 Cf. Dignitatis Humanae art. 2.
609 Dignitatis Humanae art. 2.
610 Dignitatis Humanae art I.

centuries of experience. Further more, this doctrine of freedom is rooted in divine revelation and for this reason Christians are bound to respect it in all the more conscientiously.[611]

The council recognised religious freedom or liberty as being one of the key truths in Catholic teaching, a truth that is contained in the word of God and constantly preached by the early Christian fathers that man's response to God must be free without coercion. The act of faith is of its very nature a free act. In this sense, freedom of religion was once linked to the being and essence of the Church. By locating the freedom of religion in the ambient of the dignity of human person, the council universalised the value of the Gospel in the minds of all mankind thus giving it the prerogative to search the hearts of men both Christians and non-Christians alike. Therefore, the council saw any attempt of attack on this liberty as an attack on the will of God:

> This is a sacred liberty with which the only begotten Son of God endowed the Church, which he purchased with his blood. Indeed it belongs to humanity to the Church that to attack it is to oppose the will of God. The freedom of the Church is the fundamental principle governing relations between the Church and public authorities and the whole civil order.[612]

Basing on the freedom of the children of God in Paul's letter to the Romans 8, 21 the council concluded with the hope of making this value of human freedom, which has surged and continue to surge among the people the basis of true religion and every genuine human society.

> Consequently, to establish and strengthen peaceful relations and harmony in the human race, religious freedom must be given effective constitutional protection every where and that highest of man's rights and duties- to lead a religious life with freedom in society- must be respected.[613]

Nonetheless, it will be necessary to underscore the fact that the declaration of religious freedom even though very generous in granting liberty to all

---

611 Dignitatis Humanae, Chapter II art. 9.
612 Dignitatis Humanae, Ch. II art.13.
613 Dignitatis Humanae, Ch. II art.15.

human beings sets at the same time its own limits. These limits are born due to the nature of human existence as a 'being with', which in turn sets the rational for duties and responsibilities of the individual in the society.

5.4.3 Gaudium et Spes (The Church in the Modern World)

The document on the Church in the modern world has been described as one of the high points of the entire Council. Its sensitivity lies in the fact that before this council, the relationship existing between the Church and the world was that of a sharp distinction. Right from the beginning of the Church, the Gospel has always made a distinction between the Christian and the world. In the gospel of St. John, Jesus reminded his disciples: "If the world hates you, you must realise that it hated me before it hated you. If you belonged to the world the world would love you as its own; but because you do not belong to the world, because my choice of you has drawn you out of the world, that is why the world hates you" (Jn. 15, 18-19). Going further in chapter 16 we read: "In all truth I tell you, you will be weeping and wailing while the world will rejoice; you will be sorrowful, but your sorrow will turn to joy" (Jn. 16, 20-21). Referring to the presidential prayer of Jesus in his famous farewell speech to his disciples in John, 17, ff Jesus presented the world as that clearly distinct from the children of God: "I am not praying for the world but for those you have given me…I am not asking you to remove them from the world, but to protect them from the Evil One" (Jn. 17ff).

This sharp distinction between the world and the Christian, coupled with the persecution experiences of the early Christians lead to a long lasting hate and suspicion towards any thing worldly. Christians have always seen themselves as in the world but not of the world. It has had many implications in the life and teachings of the Church. This hateful attitude to any thing worldly found expression in the body and soul distinction in the Christian anthropology, where the soul is recognised as the spirit and ruler of the entire self and detaches from the body at death as the principle of corruption and decay. Therefore the body needs to be chastised so that it will not corrupt the soul, which should be liberated in order that the body should not hinder it from entering into heaven. In the pontificates of the various Popes with name Pius the Church was solidified internally, while the world was recognised as a great opposing figure. The Council of Trent and Vatican I also left a very remarkable influence in this direction. On the contrary the statement of Pope John XXIII presented the Church as one having an important service in and for the world.

After a long period of hateful relationship, which reflected also in the history of dogma a dogmatic constitution on the world in the modern time seemed very impossible. It was not going to be easy to achieve such a rethink. According to Paul Wehrle, "that which was contradictorily spectacular in the *Gaudium et spes*, is that which gives the same word 'World' in John's gospel a complete different overtone and makes it a concept of godlessness and something to be conquered".[614] The history of Christian dogma reflected a mentality odious to the demands of the modern world already captivated in the spirit and thoughts of the *anthropological turn*. Human mind could no longer settle with a metaphysical presentation of the human person alone. The body and soul will have to be considered as equal parts of the same reality, the human person. Consequently a new theology of the person and his relationship to the world would have to be reformulated to enable the Church have a voice in the modern world. This was the background of the Pastoral constitution of the Church in the modern world.

Gaudium et Spes is divided into two large parts. Part 1 deals with the Church and Man's Vocation while part 2 addressed Some More Urgent Problems. Our concern on the dignity and rights of the human person is treated in the first part. Chapter I deals with the dignity of the human person, tracing his dignity ultimately from the biblical perspective of man as the image of God[615]. It went on to explain the implications of the *Imago Dei* namely, equality, freedom, moral responsibility et cetera. The constitution amassed a great ingenuity in its Christological discuss on Jesus Christ as the New Man. Basing on the theology of incarnation the council fathers presented Christ as the new Adam who by the revelation of the mystery of the Father and his love, fully reveals man to himself and brings to light his most high calling. It is no wonder, then, that all the truths mentioned so far should find in him their source and their most

---

614 Cf. Paul Wehrle, „In der Welt von Heute", Konradsblatts Nr. 50, 2005.
615 Cf. Gaudium et Spes, Ch.1 art. 12.

perfect embodiment.[616] He is the image and likeness of the invisible God (Col. 1, 15). Jesus Christ as the new Adam united himself with the very first creation in order to redeem the fallen nature of man. He was like us in every thing except sin (cf. 1 pet. 2, 20; Mt. 16, 24; Luke. 14-27).

The Council went further to discuss the communitarian nature of man's vocation as a design of God. It based its argument on the fact that God desired that all men should form one family and deal with each other in a spirit of brotherhood, since He "made from one every nation of men who live on all the face of the earth" (Acts. 17, 26). Furthermore, the council stresses that every one, every human being is both a subject and person having the responsibility of love towards his neighbours. Hence the scripture says: "you shall love your neighbour as yourself...therefore love is the fulfilling of the law" (Rom. 13, 9-10; cf., 1 Jn. 4, 20). The council calls for interdependency among peoples, in equal respect for the human person in all cultures. Social justice was singled out as the essential equality of all men. Among others it decried all forms of discrimination on the basis of colour, sex or race.[617]

The Pastoral constitution on the Church in the modern world succeeded in addressing the human person in his totality, bearing in mind the importance of his experiences and psychosomatic realities, which contribute to form his dignity as a human person.

5.4.4 "De Iustitia in Mundo" of 1971

Justice in the World, *"De iustitia in Mundo"* is a synod document issued by the world synod of Bishops in Rome from 30th of September to 6th of November 1971. The theme of this synod was: *"The Priestly Service and Justice in the world"* while the second document discussed the priestly office with the title: *"Ultimi temporis".* De iustitia Mundo was a post-Conciliar document on the social teaching of the Church, which was built upon the encyclical *"Populorum Progressio* of Pope Paul XI in 1967; and also proclaims the basic teachings of the Pastoral Constitution on the Church in the modern world, Gaudium et Spes of the second Vatican Coun-

---

616 Gaudium et Spes, Ch. 1 art. 22.
617 Cf. Gaudium et Spes, Ch. 2 art. 29.

cil 1965. Moreover, this document considered to a large extent the communiqué of the General Conference of the Bishops of Latin America in 1968.

The document: Justice in the world centred mainly on the importance of social justice in the life and ministry of the Church:

> While we hear the cry of those, who suffer from violence and are being marched under feet through unjust systems and mechanisms, while we hear the world's protest, which contradicts the plan of the creator through her depravity we are together conscious of the calling of the Church, in which she, in the middle of the world preach the good new of Christ to the poor, to the oppressed liberty and to the less privileged happiness. The Hope and motivation, which moves the world deeply, are not foreign to the dynamism of the Gospel, which liberates the human person from his personal sins and its effects for the social life.
>
> The lack of historical conscience and the collective human efforts born in pains on the way to the top leads us to the history of redemption. In it God has revealed himself to us and has made clear his plan of salvation and redemption to us, as it has been gradually realised and once and for all fulfilled in the paschal mystery of Christ. The engagement for justice and the participation in the restructuring of the world seem to us as an essential part of the spreading of evangelisation and the mission of the Church towards the salvation of the human person and towards the liberation of all kinds of oppression.[618]

In the above line of thought, the Bishops identified the various aspects of the society where Justice is urgently needed. These include: areas such as the socio-economical imbalance in the world; the neo colonial dangers posed by the developed nation to the developing one; and the right to development in all ramifications among the poor nations. The synod fathers identified the fact that the realisation of a social just order in the world lies in the hand of the Church as part of her vocation. Therefore they called for a conscientious training in the precepts of justice that starts, right from the

---

[618] Cf. „De Iustitia in Mundo" Deutsche Bischofskonferenz: „Römische Bischofssynode 1971. Der Priesterliche Dienst. Gerechtigkeit in der Welt." Trier: Paulinus-Verlag. 1972 1-2.

family, schools and spreading to all activities of the citizens.[619] The right to freedom of the married people was specifically underscored basing on the insight already laid down in the *Populorum Progressio*.

However, the Church tries to enunciate these principles of justice but the practical realisation of this justice in the world does not directly lie in her hands but in the hands of the world governments. Hence the Bishops clarify:

> It is not the concern of the Church, as a religious and hierarchical community to give concrete solutions for justice in the social, economic and political fields. Her mission includes much more the defence and support of the human dignity and the constitutional rights of the human person.[620]

In pursuance of this objective, the Bishops acknowledged the relevance of a world formed united body the UNO. The Bishops enjoined that the rights and dignity of all human persons in the world must be recognised as a matter of necessity. The newfound approach to this recognition of the human dignity through the declaration of the human rights as international law should be accepted by all and sundry. Hence the Bishops directed:

> It must be recognised, that the international order is founded on the inalienable rights and in the non-surrendering dignity of the human person. The declaration of the human rights of the UNO should, be ratified by all government who have not yet entered into this agreement and should be respected by all without any exception.[621]

Furthermore the synod reiterating the social teachings of the Church since the *Rerum Novarum*, *Octogesima Adveniens* and then to the *Gaudium et Spes* the fundamental natural rights of the human person have been gleamed. However the hallmark of these efforts on the line of justice and human rights was reached in the encyclicals *Pacem in Terris*, which dealt in the main, with the foundations of Christian human rights idea. While the encyclical *Populorum Progressio* dealt with justice in the form of rights to development among the peoples of the world, especially the

---

619 Cf. De Iustitia in Mundo 9.
620 Cf. De Iustitia in Mundo 7
621 Cf. Iustitia in Mundo 11.

poor nations. The encyclical *"Octogesima Adveniens"* in turn was meant to be the matrix and basis of political actions.[622]

Having touched on the various aspects of justice, its problems and possible solutions the synod suggested dialogue, not just a quasi one but one with every responsibility of justice in mind. It must be a dialogue in which the right to a spiritual and cultural development of the poor countries will be respected as a part of their dignity and rights as human beings. With a final word of hope for the poor and the oppressed the synod enjoined all members of the Church to work with God in the liberation from sin and the building up of a world, in which the meaning of creation would only radiate if she remains the work of humans for humans.

5.4.5 Working Paper of the Papal Commission Iustitia et Pax 1974

The *"Instrumentum Laboris"* as it is technically described refers to the working instruments used to arrive at the objective of the Papal commission on justice and peace. Through this formula the whole Church was involved by questionnaire, interviews and personal inputs from within and from without. It guarantees a reasonable objective assessment of the issue in question. Justice as the basis for a lasting peace remains the foundation of the recognition of human dignity and rights. The importance of this working paper on Iustitia et Pax lies in the fact that it followed consistently the principles of human dignity and rights founded already in the earlier Church's teaching, especially in the Dignitatis Humanae and Gaudium et Spes. To work for justice and peace in the world became the call and mission of the Church. It is might just be relevant to mention this working paper as being part of the efforts in promoting the Church's teachings on human dignity and rights.

5.4.6 Pope John Paul II Redemptor Hominis 1979 and Laborem Exercens 1981

The Pontificate of Pope John Paul II was marked with many encyclicals and addresses. The above encyclicals have much relevance with our

---

622   De Iustitia in Mundo 10.

theme of research. *Redemptor Hominis* as the first encyclical of Pope John Paul II presents Jesus Christ as the true and only redeemer of man, who is also the centre of the universe and of history.[623] The theme of human dignity and rights was handled in the number 17 of this encyclical. It reviewed the human rights already declared in the UDHR and the *Dignitatis Humanae* of the Vatican II to ascertain if they are just "letters" or spirits". According to him the century in spite of these lofty declarations still produced many injustices and sufferings.[624] Events in recent history still revealed signs of injustices and suppression of human rights even from the authorities that were supposed to protect these rights. For instance, reference could be made to the communist governments in the Eastern part of Europe and other ideological institutions in the world that stand against the dignity and rights of the human person. Acclaiming the efforts of the UNO so far, he called for a more concerted effort in the issues of human dignity and rights. In the following encyclical of his Pontificate in 1981, the *Laborem Exercens* on human work Pope John Paul II reflected on the theology of human work and Christ the Worker. Here the Pope elevates human labour to the dignity attached to it. The mere fact that it is done by the human person for his daily bread and development of the society makes it ennobling and dignifying. It was written to mark the ninetieth anniversary of the encyclical *"Rerum Novarum"* of Pope Leo XIII, which earlier addressed social questions in the Church and world. Among others this encyclical addressed the rights of labourers to a just wage and right to form association of workers. Pope John Paul II continued in this tradition pointing out the importance of the labour issue as one of the perennial matters of social importance of the Church due to its peculiar nature. It is the process through which capital emanate and distributed. Consequently labour and capital have remained the key factors in the socio economic life of the world and therefore have remained sensitive issues that have to be returned to from time to time. He defines work as:

> ... Any activity by man, whether manual or intellectual, whatever its nature or circumstances; it means any human activity that can and must be recognised as work, in the midst of all the many ac-

---

623 Cf. Pope John Paul II, *Redemptor Hominis* art. 1.
624 Pope John Paul II, *Redemptor Hominis* art. 17.

tivities of which man is capable and to which he is predisposed by his very natures, by virtue of humanity itself.[625]

Work bears the particular mark of man and humanity, the mark of a person operating within a community of persons. And this mark decides its interior characteristics; in a sense it constitutes its very nature. The Pope linked work and man through the book of genesis account where God enjoined man: "Be Fruitful and multiply, and fill the earth and subdue it" (Gen. 9, 7). However, the Pope distinguished between work in the objective sense and work in the subjective sense (man as the subject of Work). Work in an objective sense refers to the various technological epochs of culture and civilization, while the subjective sense points to the fact that man, as a person is the subject of work. He should not be treated as an instrument of production or even used as means to ends. Since man is to dominate his world the earth, the aspect of dominion from man himself must be taking into cognisance in all policies of labour both nationally and internationally.[626] Labour and Capital are linked together, because the work done should be commensurate with the wages. Hence a labourer deserves his just wages.

The relevance and greatness of these two encyclicals, *Redemptor Hominis* and *Laborem Exercens* lies in the fact that they were based first and foremost, on the phenomenology of the person, who is the subject of dignity and rights in the community.[627] The human person remains the focus in the theological discuss not just on the abstract truth.[628] While Redemptor Hominis emphasised the dignity of human person based on the Imago Dei and the anthropological lift given to him in the incarnation, Laborem Exercens singles out this specific aspect of the person; man and his work as source of his dignity and rights. These encyclicals will continue to form the basis of the Churches social teachings in the ages to come.

---

625 Pope John Paul II, *Laborem Exercens*, 14th September 1981 no. 1.
626 Pope John Paul II, *Laborem Exercens*, no. 7.
627 Cf. Pope John Paul II, Person: Subject and Community 1; The Acting Person 3.
628 Dignitatis Humanae, was like the 'Copernican turn' that shifted the emphasis from the abstract truth (church) to the concrete individual person in his freedom and liberty; Cf. Pope John Paul II, Laborem Exercens, introduction: "man is the way of the Church, and so we shall continue to return to this way".

5.5 Summary

In this chapter on the theology of human dignity, the Christian view of human dignity based on the theology of *Imago Dei* has been fairly presented. Even though understood differently among the various confessions, the theology of creation of man by a loving God runs parallel in all. The human being occupies a unique position in the creative plan of God. It is true to assert that the whole corpus of the western understanding of human dignity and rights has the Christian view as a footnote.

The person of Jesus in his incarnation and Trinitarian mysteries helped to intensify the debate on personhood in Christian Philosophy and theology. Early Church fathers and the medieval thinkers established a strong ontological base of the concept of person that served as a foot hold for the existential thinkers who struggled to divulge the concept of all sterile metaphysical obscurities. The influence of their great works found expression in the social teachings of the Church and the Vatican II council.

Although the process which brought the Church to its present appreciation of the dignity and rights of the human person has been labelled a "long painful process" the truth remains that she is faithful to her mission as the guarantor and co-operator in the issues of human dignity in the world and struggles assiduously to realise the respect and protection of the rights and dignity of the human person in the whole world.

Chapter Six: Dignity of Human Person: A Shared Heritage

6.1 Hermeneutical Approach to Differences in Cultures

Recent discussions on the idea of human dignity and rights vacillate between two extremes namely, imperialistic universalism and exclusive relativism. On the one side an autochthonous claim to a peculiar form of humanism projects a sense of cultural relativism, while on the other side theories that try to extol the universal idea of dignity and rights only from a single or some historical events of a particular culture tend to propagate a system that claims imperialistic imposition of its conceptual ideas on others. For instance, the African claim to a third generation of human rights bespeaks of a relativistic tendency through emphasis on the group rather than the individual as bearer of rights. Unfortunately the West would view this stand of the Africans as retrogressive and detracts from the essence of the human rights as a universal instrument. A hermeneutical approach to the development of the problematic will reveal the relevant moments of the development of human rights, founded on the belief on human dignity.

From the outset of the famous *Magna Carter* 1215 to the much celebrated UDHR of 1948 the West has articulated some relative bodies of rights which were established towards the protection of the dignity of the human person. From every indication, these rights reflect the embodiment of people's experiences and history in their individualistic mentality, which should not as such be taken as a prototype for every other people. For instance, Western human rights profiles are based on the individual as the sole subject of right, while for most African cultures; the community comes first before the individual, who eventually is nothing without the community. In the spate of this difference, the UDHR is seen and believed in many non Western cultures as simply limited in scope, addressing only the West as Jack Donnelly testifies: "As a matter of historical fact, the concept of human rights is an artefact of modern Western civilization".[629]

While many non-Western cultures maintain the above view of Donnelly, the West struggles to enforce a universal acceptance of the UDHR, and this has lead to a further suspicion of another systematized form of Western imperialism.[630] It has been remarked, that Western struggle for rights, which has always resulted in declarations of human rights seem to give the West the impetus to claim a prerogative of human rights authorship and sole power of interpretation, as M. Bimbo Ogunbanjo and Banwo Irewunmi asserts:

> These Documents reflect the relative consensus on human rights among Western states; typically these states have claimed a share of authorship and frequently consider themselves the authoritative interpreter of human rights.[631]

The above fictitious claim by Western states can not hold against the following assertion that: European societies seen in history as one full of struggle for rights of the human person can not in any away suggest a non existence of the idea of struggle for rights in other cultures such as the pre-colonial Igbo African culture.

In the pre-colonial Igbo African culture there were concrete sacred norms in the *omenala*[632] of the various Igbo communities, which have also lasted till date. Among the Igbo, rights which protected the individual's rights to live as a normal human being in the community carried with them duties and responsibilities to the community. The violation of rights of the individual and also the negligence of duties and responsibilities to

---

629 Donnelly, "Human rights and Human Dignity: An Analytic Critique of non-Western Conceptions of Human Rights" 303.
630 Cf. Hasenkamp, Universalization of Human Rights? 8.
631 M. Bimbo Ogunbanjo and Banwo Irewunmi, Human Rights and Culture in Human Rights Community: Beyond the Perspectives of Universality and Relativism, Department of Political Science and Sociology, Babcock University, Ilisan-Remo, Ogun State Nigeria 2003 1.
632 *Omenala* here refers to the sacred customs and traditions of a traditional Igbo (African) community.

one's community attracted severe punishments.[633] Furthermore, misunderstandings that eventually lead to inter village wars necessitated treaties and peace accords that lasted till date. At the wake of the colonial times, the historic fight for rights by the Igbo women in 1929 popularly called, *"the Aba women riot (war) 1929"*[634] remains in its own terms as proof of the existence of rights struggles among the Igbo. It is pertinent to note here that the UDHR as at this time in history had not seen the light of the day. However, it must be credited to the West that although the same struggle for rights existed in non Western societies, it was their genius to have articulated in legal terms these struggles for rights based on their own experiences, which provide important theoretical and symbolic settings for the global human rights struggle both in the past and present.[635]

Based on the above clarifications, the argument that human rights did not exist in the non-Western cultures such as the Igbo Africans can be contested. It is true that human rights as an idea of protecting the life and dignity of the person existed among all cultures but it depends on the conceptualization. From the arguments of shared human situations as described above the need for human rights existed and efforts were also made to address them in the different cultures, but in different conceptual schemes. For instance, for the West, it was the individual as the human index who carries rights to be protected from the taunts of the state. While in the case of the Igbo Africans, human being is only human through the community. Therefore when we talk about *humanness* as the

---

633 Achebe in his novel, "Things fall Apart" severally cited in this work describes these rights and obligations in the traditional Igbo community. For further reading on human rights in the African contest, see, Francis M. Deng, "Human Rights in the African Context", in Kwasi Wiredu (ed.), A Companion to African Philosophy, Oxford 2005 499-508.
634 The cause of this agitation by the women in Igbo land was the inhuman taxation of the women and their husbands by the colonial masters. For further readings see, Jude Uzochukwu Njoku, "The eastern Nigerian Women War of 1929 as a Model for the role of Women in the African Church", in: Journal of Inculturation Theology, Faculty of Theology, Catholic Institute of West Africa (CIWA) Portharcourt Nigeria, Vol. 7 No. 2 October 2005 118-135.
635 Cf. Ogunbanjo and Irewunmi, Human Rights and Culture in Human Rights Community: Beyond the Perspectives of Universality and Relativism 1

denominator in human rights' discusses it should be born in mind that the concept of *'humanness'* is the same while the conceptuality differs.[636]

Against this backdrop, human rights formulations cannot be static, because giving its generic nature attention should be paid to the various cultural contexts and experiences regarding their different struggles. For some it has been 'independence from colonial powers' as it was the case in the colonial Africa, popularly known as the 'second generation rights' or the right to equitable share of the earth goods known as the 'third generation rights'. The refusal by the UN to ratify the demand of these sets of third generation rights from the third world based on their historical experience in the hand of the West has resulted to an unfortunate situation that most African states possibly perceive the human rights criticisms often levelled against them as simply political, invasive of sovereignty; as a result of imbalances of power and ethnocentric. For instance, in the presence of the current criticisms against suppression of minorities and women among the third world countries, and the insistence on the need to apply human rights in their favour, the outcome seem to suggest a borrowing of human rights concept from Western societies, or the evolution of totally novel human rights ideas.

On the contrary, the idea of rights has been contemporaneous with humanity itself. That means wherever human beings are found, in all cultures human dignity and right have always played major roles in shaping the societal interpersonal dynamics. Whatever controversies and fears may be the idea of struggle for those ideals that distinguish the rights of the human person remains a shared human heritage. Bertrand G. Ramcha-

---

636 Ronald Dworkin makes a distinction between 'concept' and 'conception'. While concept represents an idea of what something means, conception refers to a particular and a more concrete specification of the concept. In the case of human rights, one can say that at the level of the concept, human rights are rights one enjoys because one is a human being (person); or as the Covenant refers to them as rights that "derive from the inherent dignity of the human person" However, what conceptualizing would mean will be the interpretation of what the different cultures understand rights, person and human dignity practically to be. Cf. Ronald Dworkin, *Taking Rights Seriously*. Cambridge: Harvard University Press, 1978 134-6, 226, Quoted in Donnelly, "Human Rights and Human Dignity" 304

ran, acceding to the fact that respect for a shared humanity existed in the major religious and philosophical traditions opined:

> Although emphasis on the language of rights was part of the Western tradition, ideas akin to rights may be found in many religions going back centuries before the first great Western human rights statement, the Magna Carta of 1215 ... The religious and cultural traditions of the five major religions uphold in common certain basic moral and ethical values for the promotion of which man must be enabled to exercise his rights and perform his duties in mutuality of relationships. Among these values held in common are human dignity and worth, equality, freedom, love and compassion, truth, justice, brotherhood and charity.[637]

In the above citation, it is clear that law, justice, freedom, love, compassion, truth, brotherhood, equity and equality remain the common heritage of humanity. In the traditional Igbo African society, these formed the constitutive elements of morality among peoples and groups especially in the norms, laws and customs – the *Omenala*. There is no gain saying that the concept of human dignity revealed itself in history as the veritable key to the understanding of the ideals of the person in every generation and culture. An idea of a universal declaration of human rights and dignity should therefore portray the truth that there are basic constituents of human dignity and rights in every society, such as law, justice, equity and equality.

In the light of the above analysis, a hermeneutical approach to culture difference reveals the idea of person, his dignity and rights as a shared heritage of humanity. It takes into account the different languages as well as the different uses made of the concept of dignity and rights at different times and places. Hermeneutics reveals the idea of human dignity both as a key concept and a limit concept of the person. The relevance of understanding the actual function and use made of the terms: Person and human dignity in history and in the particular cultures is that it would help one not to remain at the level of ideology; and also to avoid being esoteric in the expression of the concepts, but to be concrete in handling them.

For the sake of illustration human dignity has always been expressed in different languages and cultures. The Latin use of the word *dignitas,* translated into English as *dignity* and in French as *dignité; Würde* in

---

637 Ramcharan, Contemporary Human Rights Ideas 13-14.

German is also the same in meaning with the Igbo word *úgwu*. Interestingly the idea has been variedly conceptualised but the meaning remains the same: the inexhaustible value of the human person. Therefore, what we have tried to do here is to take a historical-analytical approach in trying to understand what constitutes the dignity of a person in his historical cultural embodiments. It is believed that it is only through this way that a viable theological dialogue between religions and cultures can ensue. Here we are concerned specifically with the West and the Igbo (Africa) in their rich socio-cultural and religious inheritance.

6.1.1 Human Dignity as a Limit Concept among Cultures

The idea of human dignity has been conceptualised differently among cultures in history. Consequently, the limitation of an idea lies in its conceptuality. Conceptualizing processes have always followed the axis of intellectual history. The spiritual world of the antiquity refers mainly to both the Jewish and Greek civilizations, which amassed a great measure of influence on the intellectual history of the West. Two currents were prominent: Religion and philosophy. In the Western Hemisphere, among the Europeans, the origin of the idea of human dignity has been traced to two main sources namely, the religious and philosophical. Religious source refers to the Judeo Christian identification of the human being as being "created in the image and likeness of God" (Gen. 1, 26/27). This radical understanding of man as God's image deviated from the Jewish neighbouring influences. For instance in the Ancient Near East Tradition (ANET), where the king alone enjoyed the image of God, no other person has right to the claim of *'Imago Dei'*. For the Jews, on the contrary every human being is created in the image and likeness of God and no more the king alone. Consequently the language "human dignity" was limited and understood in this sense as *'Imago Dei'*.

On the other hand the philosophical origin refers to the use made of the idea of human dignity among the stoics in the Greek city-state. The Stoics laid much emphasis on reason as the hallmark of humanness, and the ability of this reason to correspond with the natural law guaranteed the dignity of the individual. Here again, the language of human dignity had to be limited in this case only to reason. In the two great traditions we find a confluence in the famous Greco-Roman world, which emphasised the place of law in the polity. During that era, the rights of the feudal lords were protected due to the fact that they had *dignitas,* while the serfs had just *Pretium.*[638] It was the genius of Cicero the Roman legal luminary, to have granted this dignity to every reasonable, virtuous human being. For Cicero dignitas has a moral value. It became as it were a denominator for every individual and no more just for a specific aristocratic group – the feudal lords.

The Christian interpretation of human dignity evolved around the *Imago Dei* theology, emphasising virtuous and moral standards as signs of human dignity. With the enlightenment, reason featured once more in the interpretation of human dignity, thus going back once more to the stoics. A person as a rational being gets his or her full accentuation in the *autonomous subject* propounded by Immanuel Kant. He limited the dignity of human person to individual autonomy and moral imperative. Dignity for Kant qualified only as that which could have no other value placed on it.[639] In other words, dignity enjoys an absolute place in the ranking order of values. According to Georg Mohr, the whole edifice of the contemporary European concept of human dignity is based on the philosophies of Kant and Fichte.[640]

In sum, the West interpreted human dignity in two ways; heteronomy and autonomy. i) Heteronomy concepts refer to those interpretations that are based on the understanding of human dignity as an innate value given to man from birth or from above; and ii) Autonomy concepts refer to those interpretations based on the human functionality and reason.[641] Both forms of interpretation lay claim to universality.[642]

The concept of human dignity in the Igbo culture presents a different emphasis on life itself as a gift from *'chi okike'* (Igbo creator god) to the individual through the community. While dignity as a value enjoys an absolute position among the West, life is the absolute human value for the

---

638 Cf. Helmut Wegehaupt, Die Bedeutung und Anwendung von Dignitas in den Schriften der republikanischen Zeit 7.
639 Cf. Immanuel Kant, Grundlegung zur Metaphysik der Sitten 79.
640 Cf. Georg Mohr, „Grundlagen der Menschenwürde bei Kant und Fichte" 14.
641 Cf. Paul Tiedemann, Was ist Menschenwürde? 51.
642 See Paul Tiedemann, Was ist Menschenwürde? 2006.

traditional Igbo Africans, hence *ndu bu isi* (Life is paramount). First and foremost one notices a discrepancy in the notion of 'human being' (man) and 'person' between the two cultures. Ogbujah succinctly puts it this way: "The specific meaning of the concepts – 'man' and 'person' constitutes the diverging point between the Western and Igbo ideas of personhood."[643] Going further, he explains that the various conceptions of the person in the West were resultants of certain abstractions of some features of the lone individual, such as rationality, will or memory, while in the Igbo culture the idea of person is inextricably tied to the idea of a 'community'. Personal life issues from the communal life, and communal life gives credence to personal life. Under this setting, it becomes all the more clear that it is the community and not some isolated static quality of rationality, will or memory that defines the person as person but only that achieved in the community.[644] The concept of person in the Igbo perspective is limited only to those who have attained a certain stage in life through rites of initiation and achievement. Personhood ordinarily understood, is purely a process. For this reason, not every human being qualifies for the concept person in Igbo land. On the contrary, in the Christian West, the human being configured sacramentally to Christ remains a person from the beginning till the end of life. The only denominating factor for personhood in the Christian understanding is just the mere fact of being human.

Among the traditional Igbo African society, two languages are applied with almost the same meaning '*Nsopuru* and *Ugwu*' – respect and dignity. This dignity is purely a socio-anthropological construct. Construct in the sense of the society determining both the recognition and the withdrawal of dignity.

6.1.2 Dignity as an Interpretative Principle of the Human Person

The concept of human dignity acts as a limit concept of the person among the various cultures and religions of the world. It interprets this individual or this people in a particular cultural context. Consequently, a human im-

---

643 Ogbujah, The Idea of Personhood 176.
644 Ogbujah, The Idea of Personhood 177.

age obtainable in a culture serves as the definition of the person in that particular culture. If the human image is wicked and brutal, it would be concluded that the people are inhuman. Furthermore if a religious tenet is oppressive and suppressive, for instance against the women one concludes that such religion is inhuman. Logically, what ever that stands against the actualisation of human aspirations and ideals are tagged inhuman. The standard of this judgement is humanity itself. The human being is both unique in his world (limited by culture) and at same time extended by the mere fact of being human and sharing the same qualities of humanness, which we call here a *'shared human heritage'*. The Dignity of human person understood in its different and varied conceptions offers the anthropological key to the understanding of the person. The ideals of a person reside first and foremost in his nature as man or woman but further predicated by his or her experience in the environment (culture). This has a far-reaching implication in the understanding of a viable basis for human dignity, which is shared humanity.

The Ancient biblical question of the psalmist: "Lord what is man" found several answers in the course of time and history. However the most realistic theological approach remains that which views the human person as a unique person in his culture and context, but at the same time transcending these. Karl Rahner emphasised the role of anthropology in Catholic theology. For him, every attempt to 'do' theology involves anthropology. Rahner came to the conclusion that: "Every theology of course is always a theology which arises out of the secular anthropologies and self-interpretations of man".[645] Nonetheless, a complete understanding of the human person has remained a mirage in history, rather what has been possible are the identification of those anthropological ideals offered by human values in a particular environment and cultural context. The dignity of human person emphasises the sublime worth and value which every culture and religion accord human beings. Moreover it points to the value of human life; the respect for human life and the human person. For instance, our historical articulation of the hermeneutics of human dignity and rights in the West earlier in this inquiry reveals the

---

645 Karl Rahner, Foundation of Christian Faith. An Introduction to the Idea of Christianity, (Tans.) William V. Dych, New York 1978 7.

various efforts towards understanding the need for protecting the individual human person as an absolute moral value.

In the Traditional Igbo African culture, these anthropological ideals can be found in the structure of the individual in his or her community. This structure is inextricably joined so that the individual is nothing without the community and in a certain sense vice versa. Every person belongs to the community by a simply family affiliation. He or she emerges in the community through a process set up by the community itself. As we have said before, the status of personhood is not automatic. It is only achieved through a process or merit. All these expose the contextual nature of ideas and meanings as products of experience, which culminate into a culture through a complex process. In other words the human person shares a common heritage, but also limited in context.

In the light of the foregoing therefore, it becomes clear that even though humanity shares the same heritage namely: human ideals and the cravings to transcend these (that divine impulse in man to strive to the good and avoid evil in forms of moral norms) it is also limited in context by the mere fact of cultural differences. To respect these cultural differences and at the same time bearing in mind the shared heritage should be the goal of universal declaration of human rights. Against this backdrop, it is questionable whether any external cultural invasion or imposition on a people no matter in whatever pretext could be justifiable. The only way left for a cultural encounter remains that of dialogue and enlightenment of both parties. For the Igbo the ideals of the human person are contained in their complex pattern of thought enlivened by experiences in the environment, which in turn crystallizes in the way the people actually live their day-to-day lives. The Igbo call this norms and customs, *omenala*.

6.2 Social Moral Values and the Dignity of Human Person in the Society

Earlier in this inquiry human dignity has been identified as a moral value. Human values stand in relation to one another in a kind of a rank order. Human dignity as an absolute human value carries with it the foundation of all human social values and developments. The sense of community informs the necessity of morals among the people, in order to ensure value judgement on what is right and what is wrong. This value judgement leads to a just and peaceful coexistence in the community, which in turn guarantees the side-by-side recognition of the dignity in every person. Therefore the Western elevation of these moral values from the dignity of human person through a rational process of law to what we now know as human rights remains a remarkable development in the protection of human dignity.

However, it is also pertinent to say that transcending the experiences of a people creates cultures, which can be epitomised in their norms and customs. This ability to transcend one's self in relation to others and God ultimately is what many modern theologians will call the *Imago Dei* in man.[646] In the traditional Igbo African communities, the dignity of the human person was also protected according to the Igbo epistemological terms through their moral norms and customs known as the *omenala* which contains the rights and duties of the individual. *Omenala* is the embodiment of all the dos and don'ts of the community. Whether these social moral values are understood in terms of legislative code as we have them in the case of the West or as *omenala* in the case of the traditional Igbo African societies the basic principle remains the protection of the human person and his dignity. Therefore the social moral values are there to guide the human behaviour as well as guarantee the dignity and rights of the human person in every community. These norms and customs, even though basic to every human being are contextual and most often limited to the particular culture. Hence the English saying: "one man's meat is another man's poison". A certain custom that is obtainable in a particular community may not be in the other but that does not suggest a state of disorder or moral break down. It does not mean in practice that idea of evil in one place can be good in another. Rather, the concept of good and evil in different cultures remain what they are essentially. However, the conceptuality of evil, which finds expression in the laws and customs of different cultures remain as such. It is on the above note that

---

646 Modern theological approaches to the issue of Imago Dei emphasis, i) the substantival, ii) transcendental, iii) teleological as well as iv), The relational implication between human beings with themselves and ultimately with God. Scholars like Karl Rahner, Wolfhart Pannenberg, Karl Barth and Brunner; and Reinhold Niebuhr represent interests on the above approaches.

scholars argue over the viability of a universalised moral code, when every human being or group is unique in experience.

Bénézet Bujo argues for a more realistic idea of human right, which is linked with the cultural moral life of the people. Hence he insists: "The human rights are in the mouth of every person – they seem surely not realistic, if someone would want to make them into a collective ideal for the whole human race".[647] Bujo is thus conscious of the fact that rights are based on particular moral and ethical principles, which can only be realized in the context where they emanate, recognised, valued and therefore can make meaning.[648] It is pertinent to mention here, but quickly too that this does not in any way preclude the hidden danger of relativism. However he echoes among others the need to recognise the moral and ethical basis of rights before one talks of a universal right. Authors like Hans Maier insists that the correct understanding of universal human rights can only be achieved as a convergence of thoughts and ideas through dialogue among cultural values and norms. Hans Maier suggests in this case, a universal idea that must grow from below, not one dictated from above. And it must take with it all the suppressed and suspended "differences", in order to discuss and evaluate them so that nothing would be lost.[649] In his opinion the world ethos, as proposed by Hans Kung would not even suffice in the closing of the gaps created by cultural and ethical differences. Rather he hopes for a 'convergence in and between the cultures'; a cross pollination that would gradually result into oneness.[650]

---

647 Bujo Bénézet, Die ethische Dimension der Gemeinschaften 134.
648 For further readings on the limit of human rights to a particular culture see also, Stephen D. Krasner, „Sovereignty, Regimes, and Human Rights", in: Volker Rittberger (ed.), Regime Theory and International Relations, Baden – Baden 1997 139-169.
649 Cf. Hans Maier, „Die Menschenrechte als Weltrechte nach 1945: Universaler Anspruch und Kulturelle Differenzierung" 64
650 Cf. Hans Maier, „Die Menschenrechte als Weltrechte nach 1945" 64

6.2.1 Igbo Religious and Customary Norms and Laws – "Omenala" as Sacrosanct

Among Africans in general, religion plays a major part in their daily lives and activities.[651] In a culture where the presence of the divine is always felt and spurred customary norms and laws will definitely follow a religious pattern. Unfortunately, African religions were branded and denied in the past as no religion. However when we go by the nature of religion as part of culture, one would first need to deny a people of their humanity and culture in order to deny their religion. Hegel in 1830/31 in his public lectures in Berlin labelled the whole continent of Africa as not being part of human history. Hence he asserted:

> The peculiarly African character is difficult to comprehend, for the very reason that in reference to it, we must quite give up the principle which naturally accompanies all *our* ideas – the category of Universality. In Negro life the characteristic point is the fact that consciousness has not yet attained to the realization of any substantial objective existence-as for example, God, or Law-in which the interest of man's volition is involved and in which he realizes his own being. This distinction between himself as an individual and the universality of his essential being, the African in the uniform, undeveloped oneness of his existence has not yet attained; so that the Knowledge of an absolute Being, an Other and a Higher than his individual self, is entirely wanting. The Negro, as already observed, exhibits the natural man in his completely wild and untamed state. We must lay aside all thought of reverence and morality-all that we call feeling-if we would rightly comprehend him; there is nothing harmonious with humanity to be found in this type of character. The copious and circumstantial accounts of Missionaries completely confirm this, and Mohammedanism appears to be the only thing which in any way brings the Negroes within the range of culture .... At this point we leave Africa, not to mention it again. For it is no historical part of the World; it has no movement or development to exhibit. Historical movements in it-that is in its northern part-belong to the Asiatic or European World. Carthage

---

651 Cf. Mbiti, African religions and Philosophy 1969 1

displayed there an important transitionary phase of civilization; but arsis Nahoenician colony, it belongs to Asia. Egypt will be considered in reference to the passage of the human mind from its Eastern to its Western phase, but it does not belong to the African Spirit. What we properly understand by Africa, is the Unhistorical, Undeveloped Spirit, still involved in the conditions of mere nature, and which had to be presented here only as on the threshold of the World's History.[652]

This kind of prejudice against the people he preferred to designate as: salvage; and gross over generalization were the benchmarks of the colonial and missionary assessment of Africa, which has bedevilled the Western attitude to the continent till date. But on the contrary, the traditional Igbo African societies had and still have cultures and religions. At least Africa is recognised today as a deep religious people, whose religious thought and practices were embedded in their rich cultures. Therefore in the Igbo culture, *"omenala"* is the general name given to a stipulated body of tradition, customs and norms in the community. It is fundamentally a religious- divine compendium of what holds the community together and seriously held sacrosanct by all members. For the Igbo, the violation of this *omenala* has serious sanctions and could lead to calamity in the community when not appeased. These norms include; what one ought to do and ought not to do. In omenala there are prescriptions of rights and duties of the individuals towards one another, especially during certain ceremonies such as title taking, marriage and burial ceremonies in the community.

Even though it is arguable whether these rights were really human rights in the Western sense, but in so far as they satisfy the human ideals of the people about justice, equality, equity and responsible freedom they could be said to be one. Hence *Omenala* is the dictates and articulations of the people's thoughts; their *raison d' êtrè;* gaols and aspirations. It is believed by the Igbo that within the frame work of the *Omenala* a child grows to full maturity in the community. Moral norms and ethical codes contained in the *omenala* are like guides in the narrative of a particular community. When one searches for laws, rights and their protection in the

---

652 G.W.F. Hegel, The Philosophy of History, (trans) J. Jibree, New York 1956, 93 and 97.

traditional Igbo African society, these are to be sought in the compendium of *omenala*. Some of the dictates of the *omenala* are personally dictated and handed down by the gods and the *ndi iche-* the living dead, the ancestors; transmitted from one generation to the next. This is made possible through the family institution in its extended structure and the various agnatic groupings that make up the Igbo traditional society.

Omenala as ordinances of reason promulgated by the community with reference to their life struggles and survival in the community is analogical to the Western human right formularies, which stand as the fruits of the European struggles and survival in their own history. For instance in the traditional Igbo society the anecdote: *Egbe bere ugo bere* ... (Let the kite perch and let the eagle perch...) could be placed sides by side with the English, "Live and let live" or even the famous golden rule, *"do unto others as you would want them do unto you"*. Therefore, in the same vein *omenala* embodies the moral conscience of the Igbo guiding it assiduously with sanctions and penalties.

To illustrate further, it is an abomination to shed blood or take the life of another person in the Igbo community, such offences are punishable by death penalty and a sacrifice made to appease the gods of the land. Sleeping with some one's wife is against the rights of the individual and taking his properties by force are also trespasses against the *omenala*. One of the sacred functions of the *omenala* is the protection of the right to human life because of the dignity thereof; the propagation of the lineage and the community; and then the protection of right to property which is also necessarily to enjoy a peaceful and dignified life. It is through the observation of these moral laws and norms in the community that the dignity of the human person is guaranteed. Therefore one can assert that the *Omenala* exists actually for the sake of the dignity of human person in the society. Although customary courts of justice did exist, Legal proceedings so complex structured as we have them today did not exist, the traditional Igbo African moral norms have always been enforced through taboos, sanctions and punishments.

6.2.2 Taboos, Punishments and Sanctions protecting Human Dignity and Rights?

The Webster's New Encyclopaedia Dictionary defines taboo in two senses. a) "Taboo is a prohibition against touching, saying, or doing something for fear of immediate harm from a mysterious superhuman force". b) "A prohibition imposed by social custom".[653]

In the above definitions certain terms are worthy of note namely, prohibition, mysterious superhuman force and by social custom. These words portray the interconnectivity between the prohibition and the society responsible for their existence. Shorter in his definition approached it first from the point of view of etymology. He traced the origin of the word taboo from the Polynesian word, *tapu* designated as 'tied'. Shorter refers to this word as that "used culturally to inculcate practical attitudes, for instance religious respect, or human precaution, through dramatic symbolism".[654] Ferdinand Chukwuagozie Ezekwonna brings out the community aspect of the taboo clearly when he clarifies:

> It is a prohibition that is first contemplated by a group or community that has a common culture; before it is promulgated they had the intention that it would assist them in their moral, religious and social life.[655]

Taboo is not restricted only to the Igbo African cultures rather this can also be found in some other Western societies. It has nothing to do with primitivism as purported by some authors, but in the traditional Igbo African societies taboos are posited as protective guides to the articulations in the *Omenala* as the summary of the values of the society, of which rights and dignity of the human person are contained therein. To protect these values as a heritage it becomes necessary to use this measure as a veritable measure. According to Talbot:

---

653 Webster's New Encyclopaedic Dictionary, New York 1995.
654 Shorter Aylward, African Culture, Nairobi 1998, 42-43; Cf. Sarpong Peter, Ghana in Retrospect, Accra 1974 51.
655 Ferdinand Chukwuagozie Ezekwonna, African Communitarian Ethic: The Basis for the Moral Conscience and Autonomy of the Individual Igbo Culture as a Case Study, Frankfurt am Main 2005 120.

Certain *tabus* are almost invariably thought to apply to acts, which are displeasing to gods, jujus or ancestors and particularly to the earth Goddess. In fact among the Ibo, they are usually called *Nsaw ani*, the taboos of the earth, and through the country, the sacrifices of purification are generally offered to the goddess, if these prohibitions are not observed, the earth will be unable to give her increase and the women to bring forth children.[656]

Taboos such as: i) Stealing of yam seedlings a neighbour's yam barn or farm, ii) Homicide, iii) Incest of any kind, iv) Wilful abortion, v) A freeman having sex with osu, vi) Suicide, especially by hanging, vii) Poisoning someone, viii) Theft, ix) A woman climbing a palm tree or cola nut tree including others numerous to name here are regarded by the Igbo as very serious transgression of the omenala.

Others said to be minor taboos include: i) Adultery by a wife, ii) a wife throwing the husband down on the ground, iii) performing sex on a farm land, iv) disclosing a masquerade by a woman, v) a woman cooking food for her husband during her menstrual period, vi) a baby coming out of the womb with legs, vii) a woman giving birth to twins or triplets, viii) a child growing the upper tooth first and others still numerous to name here. These taboos are supposed to protect both the rights of the community to subsist by warding off calamity that can destroy the community life and that of the individual as well. There are so many other taboos guarding different groups in the community, these we cannot mention one after the other.[657] However, suffice it to say that offences against the taboos are viewed more seriously when the title- holders (the *nze na ozo* and the *oji ofo)* are involved. *Omenala* does not make any exceptions on the transgressor based on personality or statute, since every member of

---

656 P. A. Talbot, The People of Southern Nigeria, Vol. III, Oxford University Press, London 1926, cited in: Emefie Ikenga Metuh; African religions in Western Conceptual Schemes, Ibadan 1985 76-77.

657 See the following for more detailed list of taboos in Igbo culture; E, Ilogu, Christianity and Igbo Culture, London, 1974 125-127; See also Emmanuel Ifemesia, "Igbo Traditional Religion: A Cultural Means of Cultivating Discipline", in: Cahier des Religions Africaine, Vol. 19, no. 38, Juillet 1985 243-244; See also G. T. Basden, Among the Ibos of Southern Nigeria or Niger Igbos 60.

the community fall automatically under its rules just as in the case of a state constitution.

Punishment and sanctions are meted out to the transgressors of the *taboos* in different forms, but principally by what the Igbo call *ikwaala* meaning, the reparation, restoration, restitution and the appeasement of the earth goddess the *Ala*. There is always a communal ritual accompanying the *ikwaala*. It is performed publicly in the centre where the community gather for meetings and ceremonies in the presence of the young and the old. The elders of the clan often lead this ceremony. Offences against the taboos are punished according to the weight of the transgression. Some times, it would entail sacrifices, banishment into exile and in some other times simple restitution. The *ikwaala* ceremony is performed in the public, before all but not just to degrade the individual, but more importantly to restore him or her to the dignity, which the transgression of the *taboo* has severed.

It is pertinent to mention here, that some *taboos* became in the cause of time very odious to the dignity and rights of the human person they were meant to protect. Some deprive the human person the essence of living and happiness in living, especially in some cruel cultures where the gods are feared to the detriment of the living. For instance *taboos* placed over a woman who gives birth to twins or triplets were so odious to the dignity of life of the unborn and the mothers. The babies are exposed to an unspeakable torture until life is snuffed out of the unfortunate creatures, while mothers are chased away of their marital homes in shame.[658] There are also *taboos* placed on some human beings as untouchables- social out casts the *osu,* whose dignity among fellow humans are degraded through exclusion from social life of the community. Although the *osu* caste system of slavery still persist in small pockets among some parts of Igbo Land, Christian faith has succeeded to a great extent, in abolishing these sorry practices through her evangelical activities in the place.

---

658 Cf. Basden, Among the Ibos of Nigeria, 57; Okorocha, Meaning of Religious Conversion in Africa 105.

6.2.3 Human Violations as Affront on Human Dignity

Human violations refer to all acts inimical to a person as human; practices meted out to the human person, which eventually leads to the degradation of the values of his or her life. The moral prerogative of the human person stipulates some values and standards in every culture, which guarantee the dignity of the human person. When it occurs that the human person is debarred from achieving these set gaols and aspirations in the society due to share human factors, such as lack of freedom, oppression, suppression, impositions, enslavement, deprivation of justice, human sacrifices, dictatorship, hunger and all other forms of human degrading acts then one can speak of human violation. All human violations stand as affront on human dignity, just as we can see in the articulations of the UDHR of 1948, which has also become the fundament of state constitutions of our time: "The dignity of the human person is inviolable, to protect and safeguard it is the function and duty of every constituted government".[659]

Human rights stand as protection of the dignity of human person; human values, goals, aspirations and ideals of the person in the society. For every human person to develop in the society in line with his nature, certain rights are accorded to him to eschew all forms of derogatory attitude to his person, humiliation, which can lead to a violation of his dignity. It is freedom that allows this development as we have discussed earlier in this work. Therefore certain external impositions, exploitation, and some practice dehumanising the human person make one's life odious.

6.2.3.1 Alienating Elements in the Igbo Polity

The Igbo polity is divided into two main categories namely, the indigenous elements and the stranger (alienating) elements. Oliver Onwubiko distinguished the two categories in his book; *"Facing the Osu Issue in the African Synod (A personal Response)"* thus: The freeborn – the *di ala* – the indigenous population in Igbo community, can be grouped into three grades: The *Umuama* or *Umu-ilo*; the *Amala*, and *Ndi Okenye* or *Ndi Oha-ala*. While the stranger (alienating) elements comprised the resident

---

[659] Basic law for the Federal Republic of Germany Grundgesetz, GG, art. 1 (Human dignity).

aliens – the *Mbiambia* (may or may not be an Igbo person), the slaves – the *Ohu* and the outcast – the *Osu*.[660]

In his distinctions Onwubiko pointed out that the freeborn with the status of *di ala* stand as the *bona fide* members of the community with full rights and privileges, while the rights of those in the stranger (alienating) elements are restricted, each according to the level of his or her statutes in the community. This last group will occupy this part of the discussion.

A) The Resident Alien-Mbiambia

A resident alien in Igbo land is one who leaves his or her own community and cohabits among another community. There can be different reasons for this migration such as, trade, exile, security and safety. It will be recalled that earlier in this inquiry the Igbo have been identified as a 'person oriented' people with much emphasis on ancestral affinity. Each human being for the Igbo comes into the world belonging. The family, extended as it were and the agnates play veritable roles in the Igbo social anthropology. Therefore, no matter what the reason for this migration might be, the *mbiambia* – the alien in the Igbo thought and culture:

> "… Cannot be fully incorporated into the cults of the land of his sojourn and cannot, on that account, be 'a member' of that community because, as the Igbo ardently believe, either alive or dead, the stranger must one day go back to his people. This belief is so strong that the Igbo say: *'onye oso gbachaa oru ulo n'ihi na onye ije anaghi ato na mba'* (A fugitive must always return one day because a sojourner cannot forever stay away from home).[661]

The implication of the above information on the Igbo mentality on the alien – *mbiambia* is that the status of this individual affects the rights and privileges accorded this person in the community of residence. As long as one lives outside his or her ancestral home the status is restricted and limited. However this does not deny the Igbo hospitality and acceptance of the stranger. The emphasis here is rather on the Igbo restrictive element in the stranger status of not being fully incorporated in the community

---

660 Oliver A. Onwubiko, Facing the Osu Issue in the African Synod (A Personal Response), Enugu Nigeria 1993 10-34.
661 Onwubiko, Facing the Osu Issue in the African Synod 13.

simply on grounds of not being part of the community. In this case, one can contest the guarantee of the rights and dignity of this particular individual person – the *mbiambia* in the land of his or her sojourn. It is obvious that the Igbo African thought and culture do not support complete immigration, this is why most well meaning Igbo maintain double homes. There is the real ancestral home, which has so much religious and traditional importance and the alien home, the home of sojourn. This has a far-reaching implication in the Igbo relationship with her neighbours.

I find it so extreme, how the Igbo polity continue to hang on the traditional ancestral rights even though the modern economic pressure has created room for migration from rural areas to the cities. It is typical to see the Igbo in every part of the cities around them. They have a high docility to adaptation in foreign lands. However, the Igbo always find time in the year to return home for certain traditional ceremonies. For instance, in the south –south Igbo the people of Arochukwu popularly called the *Aros* will always return home for the *Ikeji* ceremony. This ceremony draws every sons and daughters of *Aro, obi na ulo na obi na ama* (both those living at home and those dwelling abroad). Onwubiko corroborated his findings with that of H.O. Eni on the significance of this home coming of the *Aros* that,

> During the *Ikeji* festival, the *Aro* Uzo (those abroad) has the opportunity to renew their filial ties with their brothers – *Aro* Ulo (those at home). Even in Ajali where the *Ikeji* festival takes place at a time different from the time it is celebrated in Arochukwu, the Ajali people visit their relatives in Arochukwu, and offer sacrifices to their ancestral ofo.[662]

The point at stake here is the effort by those outside, to make sure that their link with their ancestral home is not severed. Although they are living in their community of sojourn the inability of the stranger to possess an *ofo* – that means a lineage authority in that land of sojourn matters a lot in terms of dignity and rights. The stranger has the right to go home to his or her ancestral home any time but not the *ohu* – slave or the *osu* – outcast as we are going to see shortly.

---

662 H.O. Eni, The Ujari (Ajali) People of Awka District, Onitsha, University Press 1973 30.

B) Ohu – The Slave

Issue of slavery is not restricted only to the Igbo Africans. In the ancient societies slavery seemed to be an indispensable element of a household, especially of the rich.[663] Slaves were owned and used according to the whims of their owners. However in the case of the Igbo slavery, distinction is always made between i) the god- owned slaves *osu* and ii) the man owned slaves the *ohu*. Suffice it to say that it was this domestic slavery among the Igbo that the slave traders capitalized upon in their campaign to depopulate Africa in the trans-Saharan and trans-Atlantic slave traffic.

Among the traditional Igbo, slavery has two origins, i) religious and ii) economic. In the first instance slavery originated on religious grounds, due to the practice of human sacrifice in the belief system of the Igbo. During the burial of Chiefs human heads were sacrificed to accompany the rich chief in the land of the dead. These human offers were normally bought as slaves or war captives at inter tribal wars or simply kidnapped by a stroke of ill fate of the victim. Furthermore, children who had some abnormalities at birth and the never-do-wells were also sold as slaves.[664] On the other hand, the second group are bought by owners for purely economic reason, especially for farming in plantations. The *ohu* cannot leave his or her masters court unless redeemed. His freedom is disabled by the mere fact that he has been bought by someone as a personal property. Notwithstanding, the *ohu* enjoys the company of his owners without much discrimination against him or some sort of stratification. Be that as it may, an *ohu* could not participate fully in the ancestral rituals of the community, such as becoming the priest of a deity, for instance *Ala* the Earth goddess, pouring libation[665] to the ancestors or holding the *ofo* of

---

663 Cf. Onwubiko, Facing the Osu Issue in the African Synod 18.
664 Cf. Isichei, A History of the Igbo People 47.
665 Pouring libation is a traditional customary act of pouring wine, usually spirits as a sign of respect and link with the ancestral spirits of the kindred. Prayers and incantations, together with some aspersions warding off the evil spirits and evil persons from the community accompany the libation as sign of innocence and concordance with the ancestors or *ndi iche* as they are called in some Igbo communities. The eldest, the Opara of the lineage, usually performs this ritual.

the kindred where he lives.[666] In spite of the fact of his or her status, ohu remains a *di ala*, but of an alien status. This distinguishes the *ohu* from the *osu*, who does not in any way enjoy the *di ala* (indigene) status.

C) Osu – the Outcast

With reference to the alienating elements in the Igbo polity, the most dehumanising of them all is the *osu*- the outcast. Its phenomenon is the most misunderstood in the Igbo social reality and at the same time has continued to sustain the tyranny of ancient beliefs and ideologies on the minds of those communities and individuals in them, which stand as legacy of traditional religious beliefs and a reflection of inherited ancestral religious attitudes.

Starting with the nomenclature itself, *osu* is confusing, because some who do not fall under this stratification bear the prefix- *osu* to indicate a particular deity from whom favour was granted to them. Favours like child birth after a long period of barrenness could be attributed to the Igbo deity for fertility, the *igwe ka ala* of Umunoha in Mbaitolu LGA of Imo state Nigeria. In this case the child would answer, *Osuigwe*, meaning, dedicated to the *Igwe ka ala* deity. Other names such as, *Osueke*, dedicated to the deity Eke; *Osuala* dedicated to the earth goddess *Ala*; *Osuji*, dedicated to the yam deity-Ahiajoku; *Osuchukwu* or *Nwachukwu*, dedicated to the deity-*Chukwu* of Arochukwu and *Osuagwu*, dedicated to the deity *agwu* attest to this fact. These names inform the circumstances peculiar births different from the normal circumstance of one's chi.[667]

On a more contrasting note, whenever the name *osu* stands on itself in Igbo usage of the word, without playing a prefix as in the case of the analysis above it refers to a specific group of people, who have been stigmatised from time as social outcasts. This seclusion can be very dehumanising to the individual, who ordinarily supposed to integrate with the entire community. Regarding the precise origin of this ugly practice in Igbo culture, Onwubiko comments that, "No one can say clearly how the *osu* system came to have its present connotation. But as evidence

---

666 Cf. Uchendu, The Igbo of the South East Nigeria 88.
667 Cf. Onwubiko, Facing the Osu Issue in the African Synod 25.

available shows, the *osu* system has its roots in the practice of human sacrifice in Igbo land".[668]

Caste systems similar to the *osu* caste system have been found in some parts of the world other than the Igbo. Though different to some extent in character, it is still, a practice of singling out a whole race as a Lower case in contrast to the Upper case in one and the same society. Here the emphasis is on sense of superiority of the upper case over and above the inferiority of the lower case. It is a dangerous dehumanisation based on religious belief, which purports to create in the society an escape goat syndrome making the victims fit only for meagre services; as slaves of the Upper case, ritual functions and sacrifices in the society. Among the Indians the caste system is popular. The lower case are set apart to their fate, poor and suited only for messy jobs of performing burial rites and rituals in the ocean and for other ritual purposes. Apart from its religious origin *osu* in Igbo Land could be seen also as a system of slavery, when one enslaves an individual to an imaginary master, the deity. It is one of the most regrettable human violations in the traditional Igbo community from the point of view of the social isolation inflicted on the victims and their generations yet to come. *Osu* is a social stigma, which isolates the individual from other persons in the community. The victim becomes a reduced personality offered just for ritual sacrifice to the gods on behalf of the community. Because the *osu* has been offered to the gods, he or she becomes an "untouchable" in the society, an outcast having no contact with the members of the society. To go near an *osu*, or to have any thing to do with one is a taboo. Marriage between an *osu* and a *di ala* – free born is strictly forbidden. Who ever attempted to mix with an *osu* became automatically an osu. However, these restrictions have lost their valour with the passage of time, but the social stigma continues to endure.

There are so many prohibitions and denials of the rights and dignity of the *osu* against which the Church in Igbo land has spoken out in strong terms, but sad enough the *osu* syndrome seem to outlast all possible panacea. In as much as the *osu* caste system denies the freedom of the individual and his or her rights of free association in the society, it violates the dignity of the human person. Although the consciousness of this

---

[668] Onwubiko, Facing the Osu Issue in the African Synod 25.

practice seem to have waned in many parts of Igbo Land most parts still suffer under the shadow of its malignant ideologies.

6.2.3.2 Traditional Igbo Slavery and Transatlantic Slave Trade

Although slavery as a phenomenon was native to the Igbo society before the brake of the trans-Sahara and trans-Atlantic slave trade, it is pertinent to note from the foregoing, that the concept and practise of the man owned slavery in Igbo land before the coming of the white man differentiated itself greatly from the experience of the above mentioned form of slavery. It was a devastating factor in the history of Igbo civilisation. The trans-Saharan and trans-Atlantic slave trade of the 17th and 18th centuries have with them every dehumanising experience the Igbo person will ever experience. It rubbed the victim his or her humanity just for economic reasons, by agents, who never saw their victims as humans, but rather as salvage.

Authors like Equiano Olaudah, who eventually was a freed slave of the trans-Atlantic slave trade experience; and the account of G.T Basden attest to this fact. In his description of the experience of slavery in his own village before sold into the plantations in the West Indies, Equiano draws the distinctions thus:

> Those prisoners which were not sold or redeemed were kept as slaves; but how different was their condition from that of the slaves in the West Indies; with us they do no work than other members of the community, even their masters; their food, clothing and lodging were nearly the same as theirs, (except that they were not permitted to eat with those who were free born) .... Some of these slaves have even slaves under them as their own property and for their own use.[669]

Accding to this sharp difference in handling, G.T Basden mentioned in his ethnographical documentary of the Igbo he knew that slaves became the companion of their masters and was put in position demanding great trust and respect.[670] There is no gain saying that slavery repudiates the dignity and rights of the human person. But then, the way and manner in

---

669 Equiano Olaudah, Equiano's Travels, London, Heinemann, 1969 (1978) 10.
670 Cf. Basden, Among the Ibos of Southern Nigeria 109.

which the trans-Atlantic and trans-Saharan slave trade was carried out against the African continent; the malignant inhuman treatment meted out for those innocent souls by their European masters cries for vengeance.

6.2.3.3 Colonial Imperialism as Human Violation

Trade occasioned the first encounter between the West and Africa. This encounter was characterised by an experience of a superior trying to evade and conquer an inferior partner. Later, the constant craving for expansion of its might both economically and politically Europe started a massive conquest of the world around them. The birth of Imperialism as an ideology became the plague, which would bedevil the African continents in the coming centuries. European invasion of Africa left the continent different. Thus one can talk about the traditional Igbo culture as having existed before the European invasion of the Igbo society, while what ever remained during and after the invasion can be described as the modern Igbo culture. Today the Igbo society is being described sociologically, basing on this unprecedented division as 'pre' and 'post' colonial eras.

No matter in which ever way one considers the study of Igbo civilisation, either from historical or sociological point of views the event of Western colonisation will definitely feature. According to Emeka George Ekwuru,

> Thus seen and interpreted from both the sociological and historical points of view, the colonial event, in whichever way it is conceived and represented, occupies a significant cultural space in the Igbo history. In fact it occupies such a significant position that no serious scholarly study of the Igbo will be complete without its essential transformative role. Compared with the devastating experience of the trans-Atlantic slave trade, which considerably depopulated the Igbo, colonialism represents, for the Igbo, a higher and more disastrous form of slavery – the 'deculturisation' and 'depersonalisation' of a people within their own land.[671]

The effect of colonial imperialism on a people whose civilisation dated many years ago can be very difficult to describe. The famous African

---

[671] Emeka George Ekwuru, The Pangs of an African Culture in Travail, Uwa Ndi Igbo Yaghara ayagha (The Igbo World in Disarray), Totan Publishers Limited, Nigeria, 1999 11.

Novelist Chinua Achebe describes it aptly in his novel as: *"Things fall apart"* the centre can no longer hold.[672] Igbo Colonial experience was a shattering of the microcosm of the Igbo.[673] Colonialism ignored efforts of a people who have struggled for centuries to establish a polity based on their own experience. For that reason, the Igbo society started loosing her cultural values at different fronts. The imperial West started a massive and unprepared imposition of western culture. It was indeed a forced acculturation. First and foremost, the traditional cultural system were condemned and disassembled as native and primitive. The West carried their ideological weapons too far by a philosophy of history and culture that distinguished Europe as the only "civilised" culture, while all others were primitive. Therefore, to subdue these cultures was a great effort in the development of the salvage. The Africans on the whole, were denied of not having the capacity of thinking. Consequently, the following syllogism fits in this case: to deny one the capacity to think, that is, rationality is to deny one's humanity; to deny one's humanity is to destroy the basis for his dignity and right. Therefore, where then did imperial colonialists place the dignity of the Igbo person? The Igbo people were exploited, assaulted and reduced to a mere economic and political means. For this reason, colonial imperialism as a forceful and unlawful invasion of a people no matter under what pretext will remain a violation of the human person in his rights and dignity.

6.3 Understanding Human Dignity: A theological Dialogue

Hermeneutical approach to the issue of human dignity and rights has exposed the pitfalls in the various cultural conceptions, especially between the West as well as the Igbo Africans. Human dignity is in the mouth of every one, but nobody dares to say precisely what it is.[674] It remains a wonder that a culture, which respects and treasures life, allows human sacrifices at a different inference. For instance in the case of the

---

672 Cf. Achebe, Things Fall Apart, Title page.
673 Cf. Metuh, "The Shattered Microcosm" 11.
674 Cf. Spielmann, „Welche Menschenwürde?" 11.

traditional Igbo societies, people would offer human beings to deities for religious reasons; disrobe the person of his humanity; make the person loose all rights to social life and belongingness in the society as an out caste. While in the West, among others, enlightenment age granted reason only to the white; labelled others as people having no culture or inferior one for that matter; consequently having no sense of history or history itself; granted rights, liberty, freedom and justice to a few and denied humanity to a greater part of the globe. It was unfortunate that a culture with claims on high development failed through its ideologies to see the connection in the age long value of each person as related to humanity as a whole.

The slave trade, whether it is the traditional form of slave trading – *ohu* or the atrocious Trans-Saharan and the trans-Atlantic slave trade show the misplacement of values in the history of humanity. With the enlightenment, philosophy of culture ended up severing most part of the globe as uncultured, thereby presenting non-Western cultures ideologically as people in need of development from the so called developed world. Unfortunately, this ideology again created a monster in form of imperialistic colonialism.

The contradictions playing so far suggest the need for a deeper ground for understanding and interpreting the concept of human dignity. It is agreed as a principle that in hermeneutics history should not be judged with the newfound insights and this is fair enough, but a mere glossing over the mistakes of the past under this pretence would be a form of naiveté in the presence of a fast globalising world. Therefore what follows hereafter is a theological appraisal of the various events making up the history of human dignity and rights so far.

The theological concerns here is not to create an esoteric solution to the questions of human dignity and rights, but above all to highlight where and how this human being shows himself and who he is before the judgement seat of God. Theological appraisal goes beyond ethical judgement. Among others, it tries to uplift the Image of God formed already in the human being, helping the person to remain steadfast in the expectation and reflection of the Judgement of God.[675] A theological sensitivity of human beings and their dignity describes the contours of the events, in which the human beings remain in the expectation that God, who became man, will reveal himself to all cultures in their dignity.

---

675 Cf. Heuser, Menschenwürde 17.

Theological dialogue interests itself not just with what human beings by themselves have or can achieve but also with what the human beings can achieve through the promises of God.[676]

6.3.1 Religion: An Ambivalent Phenomenon

Religion as a phenomenon is ambivalent. Belief in a higher being other than man has two sides. It can be negative or positive, depending on the understanding and usage. This assertion can be historically verified in the fact that in every meaningful human development there is religious belief at the basis. While religion has given and still has the capacity to give orientation to the human person it is also true at the same time, that religion has also led and leads to human devaluation and violation. This is what is meant when one speaks of religion as being ambivalent.

Among the Igbo, the atrocious human violations were occasioned by religious beliefs on deities and spirits. Human sacrifice and the immolation of human beings to idle as *osu* are all products of religious convictions. It is a fact that most of the wars fought in Europe and America had religious motifs at their basis. Furthermore it is worthy of note that, it is usual with religion to link missionary activities with development of the people. This of course, makes their message find acceptance with little or no resistance among the people. Through developmental projects, the Missionaries gain credibility and thereby amass great influence on the social life of the people, just like Marshall Katherine explains:

> Wichtiger ist aber vielleicht die Tatsache, dass Religionen and religiöse Institutionen das Vertrauen von Milliarden von Menschen genießen, deren Handlungen und Verhaltensweisen formen und damit viele Entscheidungen beeinflussen, die mit sozialem Wandel und Modernisierung zusammenhängen.[677]

From the above explanation one can speak of religion, but with right, as being ambivalent. Religious missionaries, to their credit, built Churches,

---

676 Cf. Heuser, Menschenwürde, 18.
677 Marshall, Katherine, „Die Kluft überbrücken. Religion und Entwicklung – Eine alte Beziehung neu betrachtet", in: eins Entwicklungspolitik Nr. 7-8 (2006) 26-31 here 26.

started schools and hospitals in Igbo Land. While the Colonial masters concentrated on trade not excluding slave trade of course. However this monopoly enjoyed by religion was soon diverted and truncated by the civil organisations like the UNO. After the World war II. The United Nations through the Universal Basic Primary Education (UBE) stepped in for educational developmental projects in Igbo Land. School plants were renovated and new ones were built. Under health, hospitals and maternities were built. More rural healthcare services were offered. Although there were traces of friction between the religious agencies and the civil agencies, efforts were made to cooperate with each other for the achievement of the development of the people.

Nevertheless the Western concept of development was not limited to what has been described above. Ranger Terence acknowledged the difficulty involved with the notion of development when he wrote:

> What seems to me to be too much more difficult is the notion of "development". It is notorious that development specialists disagree about how to define development, how to measure it and how to achieve it.[678]

The development model operated by the Missionaries was limited by the above handicap in defining actually what development of Africa meant. On a sorry note, all that was Christian was developed while all that was not Christian remained undeveloped. This view posed and still poses a very big trait in the relationship or encounter between the West and the so-called "not developed world". During the missionary/ colonial era emphasis was placed more on cultural superiority and scientific prowess than on the human values. This was the case in Igbo land, where all the people needed to be cleansed and converted from their 'devilish culture'. This manner of apportioning a particular form of developmental pattern to a people, without taking cognisance of their history, culture and situations in life was dehumanising. Unfortunately, the whole history seems to have gone hand in hand with religious arrangement, which the Church regrets till tomorrow. Schools were the veritable instruments of putting through

---

[678] Ranger Terence, Religion Development and African Christian Identity, Uppsala 1987 29-55 here 29.

the relative change in behaviour among the 'underdeveloped'. Commenting on this epistemological flaw by religions Jack Goody concludes:

> While that command of schools was an important aspect of their spread throughout the world, it also placed limits on enquiry at various times, limits which in the European case were only transcended in a major way with the Renaissance and the return to 'pagan' classical precedents, appealing to a religion in which one no longer believed.[679]

Missionary activities especially that which took place in Igbo land, reveals a systematic attempt at globalization. Just like in every globalisation the missionary spirit was not free from those characteristic ways of expansion and imposition of foreign cultures and influences. Prof. Emefie Ikenga-Metuh, a renowned scholar of Comparative religions described the African missionary event as: "The Shattered Microcosm".[680] He argues among others, that the conversion process of the traditional Igbo person was a deep complex process; no single assumption can exhaustively explain it. It reveals missionary activities in this sense simply as a globalising process. The effort to supplant an existing culture (Igbo culture) with a foreign one (European Christian culture) whether intentional or not, was glaring. This he refers to as the shattered microcosm, which in turn violated the dignity and rights of the human person.

6.3.2 Missionary Proselytism: The Scramble for Igbo Land

The first group of French Catholic Missionaries to Igbo Land arrived in the year 1885. Their initial task was, in the first place to confront a very great rivalry created by the presence of another already existing missionary groups belonging to the Church of England. France had for several decades attempted to secure a political foothold on the Lower Niger (Igbo Land). Repeatedly, the British had foiled such attempts. But French firms, in spite of the objections of the United African Company succeeded in breaking the virtual monopoly of the company on the Niger. The Christian

---

679 Goody Jack, "Religion and Development: Some Comparative Considerations", in: Development 46 (2003) 4, 64-67 here 67.
680 Metuh, "The Shattered Microcosm" 11.

Missionary Society of England (CMS), therefore, saw Roman Catholic penetration into the Niger (Igbo Land) as a continuation of the French drive to challenge British interests. C.C Ifemesia confirms this rivalry that: "There are many adversaries; among these adversaries, Rome is conspicuous".[681] The whole missionary enterprise could be viewed as a continuation of French-British economic and political control of West Africa. On this note Ekechi F.K concludes: "Just as the two governments haggled for political and commercial advantages, so did the missionaries treat questions of religion as if they were a matter of politics".[682]

The unfortunate effect of religious Proselytism on the Igbo polity is a deep-rooted division among the people on account of confessional differences. Consequently, religion which suppose to guarantee the dignity and rights of the people end up making them hate each other; segregate, limit and abuse each other. Religious Proselytism and rivalries between the different confessions in Igbo Land have continued till date. Unfortunately, this division detracts from the basic communal value of Igbo unity. The above true documented story of the beginnings of missionary activities in Igbo land is just presented as a foretaste of the whole situation.[683] At the same time, this story reveals how ambivalent religion can be in the society.

6.3.3 "Imago Dei": A Standard Principle of Interpretation

Discussions on theological implications and relevance of *Imago Dei* in the different facets of life have formed a great catalogue. In the main, theologians try to show how useful a good understanding of the concept: "created in the image and likeness of God" (Gen. 1, 26/27) can lead to the answer of the age long question: what is man? In the field of interest of this research namely, theological anthropology one can not avoid coming

---

681 C. C. Ifemesia, British Enterprise on the Niger 1830-1869, London 1959 278.
682 F. K. Ekechi, Missionary Enterprise and Rivalry in Igbo Land 1857-1914, London 1972 86.
683 For more details on the subject, See F.K Ekechi, Missionary Enterprise and Rivalry in Igbo land 1857-1914.

back to this theme from time to time, not just because of its central significance in theological anthropology, but more so because of the fact that the theme has not yet been understood despite many efforts. Modern reformed theologians like Milliard J. Erickson, in his work: *"Christian Theology"*[684] divided theological view on *Imago Dei* into three Major groups namely, i) Substantive and transcendental views, already highlighted earlier in this research. The proponents are those who believe that every human being by nature is endowed with primordial spiritual quality, which the original sin could not extinguish. This group is represented by Irenaeus in the traditional Catholic view, Peter Lombard, St. Anselm and Karl Rahner in the contemporary era. Although clinching on the redeemed by grace theology Lutheran view and the traditional reformed view accept Christ's salvific act as the only chance of image of God once debilitated by original sin; ii) The Relational view is held by modern theologians who have interest in existential philosophy such as reformed theologians like Karl Barth and Emil Brunner. iii) Functional view of *Imago Dei* bespeaks of no other external interventions and is represented mainly by Leonard Verduin and Norman Snaith. Another dimension outside this ordering, but worthy of note will be the teleological dimension of the Imago Dei, which emphasises the human destiny, the end of man. This view is often associated with the Eastern (Patristic) Orthodoxy and contemporary Protestant and Lutheran theological systems, especially in the theologies of John Zizioulas (Orthodox) and Wolfhart Pannenberg (Lutheran).

In this inquiry an appeal is once more made to the concept of *Imago Dei* as a lender of last resort in the problem of finding genuine theological grounds for interpreting the dignity of human person in all cultures and religions. This decision is informed by the fact that by virtue of man's ability to transcend himself or herself in order to relate to himself; his fellows and ultimately to his God there is a better chance of establishing a more viable basis for understanding human dignity. This ability in human beings stands as the shared heritage of humanity. It does not matter wherever the human being is found; he tries daily to transcend his or her ideals as a human person. Based on the above argument this part of the discussion tries to extol this possibility in the human person of transcendence,

---

[684] Millard J. Erickson, Christian Theology, Grand Rapids, MI: Baker Book House, 1983, 1984, 1985, 495-517 here 496.

thereby seeking and making clearer the implications of such a gift from God for a better knowledge of oneself. In this vein Philip Heffner succinctly states: "Unless we perceive the human being's divinely ordained destiny, we have failed from the outset, to comprehend who and what *Homo sapiens* is".[685]

Some early Fathers of the church like Irenaeus of Lyon, in his emphasis on the primordial image of God after which the human being is fashioned, taught that the original sin could not extinguish the image of God in man.[686] Jesus the second person of the Trinity is the Logos, the incarnate word of God who is actually the image and likeness of God. This was the position of most of the early Christian fathers whose personal teachings on the *Imago Dei* for reasons of limitation will not be handled individually. However, with the scholastic anthropology, reason as the superior faculty assumes the role of image of God. The scholastic emphasis on reason created a dichotomy between it and other human faculties, presenting the intellect as the capacity that actually represents the image of God in human being. Thus understood, human being can reflect the image of God only through reason. Thomas Aquinas, but before him Peter Lombard and Saint Anselm were the proponents of this thought.

The scholastic teaching on *Imago Dei* had a lasting influence on the Catholic teaching right to the period when the modern theologians tried once again to dilute this lopsided trend with a theology of transcendence. The Modern theology clarified that the human being created with intellect and will remains open to the creator. This act of openness is transcendental as well as relational both to others outside the self and God.[687]

In modern and contemporary times, Jürgen Moltmann argues that the identity of man depends on what background information in combination with preconceived notions one has before attempting to answer the question: What is man? He acknowledges the complexities involved with such a question, also offers three possibilities namely; i) Man can compare

---

685 Philip J. Heffner, "The Human Being", in: Christian Dogmatics, Vol. 1, (Eds.) Carl E. Braaten and Robert W. Jenson, Philadelphia, Fortress Press 1986 324.
686 John F. O'Grady, Christian Anthropology. A Meaning for Human Life, New York 1976 16.
687 Cf. Scheffczyk, Einführung in die Schöpfungslehre 109.

himself with other creatures, ii) with other humans, or iii) with the divine. According to Moltmann, the best possible answer for man is in the comparism of himself with the divine. It is only then that the human being can see the crucified Christ who is both, the true God and the true man.[688]

Karl Rahner acknowledges the fact that man is both the object and subject of the inquiry in the biblical question: What is man? According to him, man in his infinite system cannot confront itself in its totality .... It does not ask questions about itself. It is not a subject".[689] A human being is fundamentally a transcendent being, whose realities of transcendental experience are subjectivity, personhood, responsibility and freedom experienced when a subject as such experiences himself. Even though the human being remains self reflexive, she is also conscious of his limitations: "Being situated in this way between the finite and the infinite is what constitutes a person, and is shown by the fact it is in his infinite transcendence and in his freedom that man experiences himself as dependent and historically conditioned".[690] Relying on the basic truth about his reality a human being comes to the real truth about himself or her self. Thus Rahner's anthropological theology could be summarized in this belief that the human person can find spiritual fulfilment only as a result of experiencing God's self-communication, or finding God for him or herself. Hence Rahner asserts:

> In the concrete order we encounter in our transcendental experience and as interpreted by Christian revelation, the spiritual creature is constituted to begin with as the possible addressee of such a divine self- communication. The spiritual essence of man is established by God in creation from the outset because God wants to communicate himself .... Man's transcendence is willed to begin with as the realm of God's self communication, and only in him does this transcendence find its absolute fulfilment.[691]

---

688 Cf. Jürgen Moltmann, Man. Christian Anthropology in the Conflicts of the Present. (Trans.) John Sturdy. Philadelphia: Fortress Press 1971 & 1974 x.
689 Karl Rahner, Foundations of Christian Faith 169.
690 Rahner, Foundations of Christian Faith 175.
691 Rahner, Foundations of Christian Faith 123.

Even though Rahner does not use the word *Imago Dei* in the above quotation as the underlying principle of man's communication with God, the teaching on transcendence based on what he referred always in his theological anthropology as "essence" point to the fact of *Imago Dei*. The expression used to denote the capacity in man, to say 'yes' to God was *Obidiential capacity*,[692] which points also to this image of God in man. For Rahner, "The history of salvation and grace has its roots in the essence of man which has been divinized by God's self- communication".[693]

Reinhold Niebuhr's theology of self-transcendence stands as the hallmark of his theological anthropology. Self-transcendence is the key to anthropological question, because the intellectual history centres on the same issue of mans destiny as *Imago Dei*. Man's capacity for self-transcendence is viewed by Niebuhr as the key to unlocking the meaning of the doctrine of *Imago Dei*. The ability for self-transcendence is an integral part of man's design as a creature created in the image of God. Even though he belongs to the natural order man transcends the nature in a kind of tension, just as Niebuhr opines:

> The Christian view of man emphasises the height of self-transcendence in man's spiritual stature in its doctrine of 'Image of God'. ... In its purest form the Christian view of man regards man as a unity of God-likeness and creatureliness in which he remains a creature even in the highest spiritual dimension of his existence and may reveal elements of the image of God even in the lowliest aspect of his natural life.[694]

Niebuhr's emphasis on the tension between man's creatureliness and his transcendence lays much credence to the theological works of Augustine and Kierkegaard, both of whom he referred to in his discussions on Imago Dei. Rahner and Niebuhr emphasised the fact of auto (self) tran-

---

692 Obidiential capacity is a word associated with the Thomistic theology of revelation designated with the expression capax entis. Because the human person is capax entis he is capax dei. Rahner uses this expression to explain the natural disposition in the human person to be open to God's revelation. This 'openness' to the divine is only possible through transcendence.
693 Rahner, Foundations of Christian Faith, 411.
694 Reinhold Niebuhr, The Nature and Destiny of man. A Christian Interpretation. Vol. 1, New York 1964 169-170.

scendence in the human person as a possibility created by the image of God in the person, however while Rahner concentrated on the 'dynamics' in other words, that which makes this self transcendence work, Niebuhr emphasises the signs of the presence of this image in the life of the individual and that of the society.

Pannenberg described the human being as part of nature, but "world open". Hence he asserts: Der Mensch ist nicht umweltgebunden, sondern weltoffen".[695] This openness distinguished the human being from other created beings especially from other animals. Human beings have unending ability to relate to things around them even to their creator. Therefore the human person can be said in this case to be 'God open' as well.[696] When we try to understand the human being as created in the image and likeness of God it refers to this teleological profile in the self-transcendence that only the human person alone can achieve. Through the auto (self) transcendence, which is occasioned as it were, by the 'world openness' the human being thinks of his relationship with God; even then think of life after death.

At this level of auto (self) transcendence the human being shares in the image of God. It is on this level that one can boast of relating to himself as a person and relate to others in the society. In this sense, *Imago Dei* understood, as auto (Self) transcendence in the human person can only be the secure basis for interpreting the human dignity, because it is a true heritage of humanity.

For this very reason *Imago Dei* is referred in this work as the standard measure of interpreting the dignity of human person in the modern theological understandings of the concept. Human beings in all cultures and civilisations share in the same capacity to transcend. The mere facts of life show that though separated by culture, colour and language, the ideals and aspirations of human beings remain the same namely, salvation which the Igbo conceive as *'Uju Ndu'* (The Fullness of life)[697]; *'Nka na*

---

695 Gunther Wenz, Wolfhart Pannenbergs Systematische Theologie. Ein Einführender Bericht, Göttingen 2003 40.
696 Cf. Wenz, Wolfhart Pannenbergs Systematische Theologie 40.
697 Cf. Michael Mozia, New Evangelisation and Christian Moral Theology, Cited in: Okorie, The Integral Salvation of the Human Person in Ecclesia in Africa 356.

Nzere' (Old age and life of virtue)[698] and '*Ezi Ndu*' (the good life).[699] Therefore, if we have to think about the possibility of a universal interpretation of human dignity and its attendant protective rights, we must think of *Imago Dei* as a concept that has the capacity of enunciating such an idea. This is because *Imago Dei* as a principle embodies auto transcendence as a unique quality in every human being as a shared heritage. However, it is sad to note, that historically speaking the doctrine of *Imago Dei* as the standard of all human interpretations has not yet been understood, or if at all understood has not been sincerely implemented.

6.4 Universal Declaration of Human Rights (UDHR) 1948: A Child of Circumstance

Historically speaking, issues concerning human rights were usually placed at the description of nation states before the UDHR of 1948.[700] Within the framework of human rights, authorities are expected to guarantee the well-being and security of their citizens. Acceding to the above fact Jack Donnelly clarifies, that human rights are profoundly national, not international issues, from both the point of views of international legal jurisdiction as with respect to the effective action to establish rights-respecting institutions.[701] It was in this sense that most former human rights' declarations on the rights of man came into existence. For instance, the Magna Carter of June 15 1215, the American declaration of Independence and Bills of rights (1776) and that of the French declaration of the Rights of Man and the Citizen (1789). On the contrary, the Universal Declaration of Human Rights (UDHR) 1948 was addressed to all citizens of the world, as if the world were just a nation. Was this a child of circumstance, since no historical instance before it could be found?

The UDHR 1948 was born as a mechanism to respond to the unique historical experience of discrimination and genocide against the Jewish

---

698 Nwoga, "Nka na Nzere" 1.
699 See Okorocha, The Meaning of Religious Conversion in Africa 204.
700 Cf. Stephen D. Krasner, „Sovereignty Regimes, and Human Rights" 139ff.
701 Jack Donnelly, Universal Human rights in Theory and Practice, Ithaca and London 212.

people during the World War II. As from thence, the UDHR will remain the international mechanism for humanitarian concerns, especially in the rescue service of those suffering in the hands of their own leaders. Some philosophers like Edmund Burke have earlier offered some philosophical basis for such actions when he thought, that states can intervene for the weaker states in times of suffering to "afford succour to the miserable sufferers" who happen to find themselves under "atrocious and bloody tyranny".[702] Immanuel Kant indicated that a global judicial system in times of emergencies is necessary, for the sake of global peace.[703] Consequently, the idea of a universal human rights instrument was born at the instance of human destruction of World War I &II. It was the first opportunity and effort at making the human rights universal.

Although the fathers of the UDHR did not make explicit reference to the universal basis of their claim of common humanity as self transcendence or common divine origin of mankind, the opening statement of the preamble make this intention obvious: "Whereas recognition of the inherent dignity and the equal and inalienable rights of all members of the human family is the foundation of freedom, justice and peace in the world …"[704] Therefore, to guarantee and protect these innate rights of human beings all over the world, to cling to their dignity as humans; and to fight for these rights when violated, the fathers of the UDHR opined: "… That human rights should be protected by the rule of law …"[705] The rule of law here refers to the application of genuine reason and regulations in the legitimate fight for innate rights of every one from the stand point of the fact of being human. By implication, the fathers of the UDHR did not invent these human rights, rather they acknowledged these rights as hav-

---

702 Edmund Burke saw the human proclivity to wickedness as a reason for ensuring the security of the weak globally. See Louis I. Bredvold, Ralph G. Ross (ed.), The Philosophy of Edmund Burke. A Selection from His Speeches and Writings, Ann Arbor, The University of Michigan Press 1967.
703 Kant insisted on the need for an international control and check on power drunk leaders who may rule with greed and ill will, and with other non-rational factors. See also, Reinhard Merkel, Roland Wittmann (Hg.) Zum Ewigen Frieden. Grundlagen, Aktualität und Aussichten einer Idee von Immanuel Kant, Frankfurt am Main 1996.
704 The Universal Declaration of Human Rights Preamble.
705 The Universal Declaration of Human Rights Preamble.

ing been fought for ages, but wishing it to be regulated and protected by the rule of law.

However, it is pertinent to note that before the UDHR of 1948 the dignity of human person never came in as law. It was only after the terrible human violation of the World War II that human dignity, as a moral law became a substantive part of legal lexicon. Records show that it only appeared in limited form before the twentieth century.[706]

Historically speaking, the concept of human dignity started to appear in the states constitutions from 1919 in article 151 of the *Weimar Reichsverfassung*. It was followed in 1933 fascist's constitution of Portugal, art. 6; and finally, appeared also in 1937 in the preamble of the Irish constitution.[707] It is pertinent to note here that the mention of human dignity in these constitutions was not in any form meant to raise this moral norm to the level of rights, or to enforce its observance legally but only to entrust in the hands of the state the care of a dignified form of living, which makes the dignity of human person shine out. Rather, human dignity was only understood in terms of the environmental and fair sharing of the economic goods; to maintain at least the barest minimum of human dignified existence in the state. Thus the concept of human dignity in these cases was merely normative as a moral obligation and never as a legal obligation neither of the state nor that of the individual. Human dignity as moral law only gained a constitutive status through its legal recognition after the event of the World War II as a child of circumstance. Since then, states have started including the clause of human dignity as fundamental norm as well as law in their various constitutions.

Against the backdrop of the universal declaration as a child of circumstance, several consequences have been noticed along the line of its operations. In the first place, the UDHR is fraught with many moral dilemmas, which have made its interpretation as a universal human dignity based on *Imago Dei*, though often preferred, but neglected. In the second place, as a consequence, a universal application of human rights has been truncated, limited, selective and most often hijacked by the strong and most powerful nations in the service of their national foreign policies.

---

706 Cf. Tiedemann, Was ist Menschenwürde? 12.
707 Cf. Tiedemann, Was ist Menschenwürde? 12.

6.4.1 Human Rights as a Case of Moral Dilemma

Dilemma occurs in the realm of ethics or morality when a given ethical theory or principle does no longer agree in actual practice. An obvious cause of moral dilemma or ethical dilemma is the relation of particular norms with the universal ones, which is often the case in modern and contemporary debates.[708] It is a common feature to hear human beings making general statements based on their personal moral standards.

A typical literary example is the case in the definition of justice as 'to give any one back what you owe him'[709] by the ancient poet *Simonides*. In the rhetoric, which played between *Cephalous, Polemarchus* and *Socrates* the dilemma by justice was significant because at the end of their discussion Socrates was able to convince his conversant that justice as giving one what is owed should not be taking on the face value but should be appropriated. Hence giving back to a mad person a dangerous weapon, which he or she handed over to a friend in the days of sanity, must not be given back in the days of insanity. The above example exposes the complexity of universal moral and ethical principles, from which UDHR is not exempted.

The ceremonial declaration of the universal human rights of 1948 after the human atrocities of the World War II was welcome with jubilation and hope, but that did not exonerate it from the particular historical ideology from which it was born. In reality it has been a world divided at different times by deep rooted anti human ideologies. The world was divided into the west and the rest with an idealism, which found a great resonance in the philosophy of enlightenment. In the famous ideology of 'clash of cultures' policies were formed to show the superiority of the Western culture over and above the other cultures. It was against this backdrop that slave trade and colonial ideologies were formed, justified and carried out as signs of the Western imperial supremacy. During the various sessions of the UDHR draft, such ideological differences reeled

---

708 For more information on „North-South Dialogue" See, Bujo, Die ethische Dimension der Gemeinschaften. Das afrikanische Modell im Nord-süd-Dialog, Freiburg, 1993.
709 Robin Waterfield (Trans. Ed.), Plato Republic, Oxford London, 2008 chapter 1, no. 321e p. 9.

off through some misunderstandings among the committee members as to what and which words are to be used for an appropriate formulation of terms of the declaration. For instance the words, *human personality* vis a vis *every human being* were debated of which the term *'every human being'* was accepted and endorsed. Of course this edition of his former suggestion of human personality did not impress the then South African president[710]. This position of the South African president will not be surprising looking at the apartheid regime in South Africa, which was based on the ideology of limited definition of human beings that included only the white settlement as the only human beings and the black settlers as sub humans.

Evaluating the successes and failures of the UDHR so far its projects seem to present an endeavour of self-evident and self-confirming virtue. But it is more complicated; it arrives in our time possessed of a past. The human rights project has served a variety of uses, often less altruistic than the humanitarian purposes with which it is now associated.[711] In line with this thought, Hasenkamp opines:

> With respect to the history of European colonialism in most African and Asian countries, Western diplomacy has had ambiguous effects in those post colonial states: Does it mean another import of Western imperialism or the real protection of people in need ... Western Human rights policies may be either viewed as political instruments with a strong degree of selection and inconsistency in order to serve its economic and security interests.[712]

Therefore, it is obvious that the old ideology of the West and the rest which was expressed in the colonial and imperials occupation of Africa and other peoples has been replaced with a pretentious body of universal human rights declaration to fight the Cold War between the Communist block and the Capitalist West. Today it is the emphasis on 'Globalisation' and the human rights as instruments of propagating human dignity and

---

710 Cf. Tiedemann, Was ist Menschenwürde? 14, 15.
711 Cf. Deborah M. Weissman, "The Human Rights Dilemma: Rethinking the Humanitarian Project", in: Public Law and Legal Theory Research Paper No. 13-8, htt://ssrn.com/abstract=462524 14.10.2011, 1-92 here 3, 4.
712 Hasenkamp, Universalization of Human Rights? 8.

rights through international interventions. Claims to higher civilisation, usually represented as a superior morality and the imperative of modernity, have long served as justification for colonial expansion. According to Deborah Weissman:

> Colonizers assigned to themselves the task of uplifting 'uncivilized' people who represent 'the negation of values', and set out to transform norms of the colonized cultures to correspond to the standards of morality as conceived in the world of the colonizer. In fact, however, the far-reaching normative disruptions resulting from the installation of colonial regimes inevitably compromised the efficacy of humanitarian projects and did little to obtain respect for human rights.[713]

International interventions have been argued and based on the need to rescue the suffering masses of a particular country. The suffering of humanity in form of genocide and ethnic cleansing, torture and mass murder, war and repression, are likely to involve the world at large, arousing the feelings and conscience of well meaning people every where. However, it is also true that these interventions are not global as some countries are exempted as beneficiaries, either because they do not qualify due to international interest of the super power and its allies or simply because they are classed as not hopeful future economic partners.

A typical example was the Nigerian Biafra civil war of 1966-1970, where the British government had a vested interest in the Nigerian crude oil. Even though the crude oil was located on the side of Biafra, Britain supported Nigeria in the war by supplying her with the remnant ammunitions of the World War II. Worse still, even when General Gowon led Nigerian administration imposed food blockage and starvation as a tool for winning the war against the 'rebellious' opponents the Biafra Britain supported the blockage of humanitarian aids to Biafra from the United Nations Organisation (UNO). It is sad to mention that America looked away in order not to hurt the interest of their big brother Britain. Even though the UN General assembly took place in the U.S.A within the time of this civil war, there was never a mention of this gross human destruction in

---

713 Weissman, "The Human Rights Dilemma: Rethinking the Humanitarian Project" 10, 11.

Nigeria against the Biafra. This is one of such examples of the dilemma of human rights as we have them today.

Therefore one can say with critics that human rights norms are subject to malleable standards and have been capable of advancing U.S. strategic and economic interests through coercive means, often at the expense of humanitarian concerns.[714] Suffice it to say that the universality of the declaration contradicts itself in the reality of the ideological interests and in the pretentious thought that the concept of morality can be generalised for every culture.

6.4.2 Selective Interpretation of human Rights and Dignity

A corollary to the above described universal human rights dilemma is the selective tendency in the interpretation and application of human dignity and rights. This tendency comes to manifestation in the foreign policies of some super powers in the West but especially in that of the United States of America in the events of international interventions. There has been a potentiality of the Western influence on issues pertaining human rights politics, particularly that of the United states as the sole superpower, to revise existing international law and thus decide the direction and content of international relation.[715] It boils down once more to the ideological understanding of ones culture in relation to that of others.

Culture as a dynamic complex whole has also been handled as something static by another form of ideological pride, so that some cultures always would remain on top while others must of necessity remain under. What has been experienced with the utility of the concept of culture as a source of coherence among people who share a general common worldview, has often prevailed through deterministic views of culture by confining some cultures to be static. The implication is that the stereotype of defining certain cultures with personal moral judgement; putting it through with powerful media coverage and super economic and military control, supports a selective interpretation of human rights and dignity.

---

714 Cf. Weissman, "The Human Rights Dilemma: Rethinking the Humanitarian Project" 4.
715 Cf. Hasenkamp, Universalization of Human Rights? 8.

For instance, the U.S policies on human rights have not only been selective but also contradictory, especially considering the source of such selective interpretations. The source can be seen in the Western ethics of comparison, whereby the Western cultures place themselves in comparison with the rest as a super culture, while the rest are undeveloped and therefore, must have to alien with this super culture. In the case of America, it becomes obvious that the countries or cultures who agree with their values and dictated policies would enjoy American friendship as well as their intervention power in times of humanitarian needs. These cultures are labelled 'hopeful cultures' while those outside these are 'uncivilized cultures' and candidates of neglect in times of intervention. Thus understood, the human rights project has been marred by a dangerous power-politics of dictatorship. Unfortunately the whole UN ideology run the risk of serving a selfish national interest of a particular world power instead of that of the universal interest that it set out to protect.

It is also a fact the some world powers namely, U.S.A are selective in their acceptance of certain UN charters and resolutions. The International bill of rights for women, the Convention for the Elimination of All Forms of Discrimination against Women (CEDAW) that was adopted in 1979 by the UN General Assembly was not signed by the US. The reason for this was the arrogant conviction that the treaty was incompatible with U.S traditions of motherhood and child- rearing customs in the United States.[716] Still on the point the Bush lead war in Iraq was not unanimously consented by the UN Security Council, but was still carried out by the USA and its allies, contrary to the will of the majority.

Nevertheless, this research work is not meant to be concerned mainly with the politics of human rights as well as international intervention, but because of its interest in the interpretation of the human dignity as seen in history makes it necessary to point out the weakness in the interpretation of human dignity and its operations so far, with the intention of proffering a more viable insight for an authentic interpretation. These few illustrations have been chosen to prove that human rights and dignity has been a victim of moral dilemma and selectively interpreted.

---

716 Cf. US Congress Rec. S. 1276 (March. 8, 2000)(Statement of Senator. Helms) Cited in: Weissman, "The Human Rights Dilemma: Rethinking the Humanitarian Project, 79.

6.5 Interpretative Openness A Way out?

The UDHR 1948 was a historical landmark. In this declaration, the recognition of the inherent dignity of the human person stands out clear as the basis of the declaration in the words of its preamble:

> Whereas recognition of the inherent dignity and of the equal and inalienable rights of all members of the human family is the foundation of freedom, justice and peace in the world .... Whereas the peoples of the United Nations have in the charter reaffirmed their faith in fundamental human rights, in the dignity and worth of the human person and in the equal rights of men and women and have determined to promote social progress and better standards of life in larger freedom, whereas member states have pledged themselves to achieve, in co-operation with the United Nations, the promotion of universal respect for and observance of human rights and fundamental freedoms ....[717]

One can already notice in the above preamble, a direct call on the human dignity, equality and rights of all mankind as the foundation of human rights, but at the same time will notice a no further effort to interpret the foundation of these human rights. Some authors suggest the problem of agreement among the various world views as the reason for this avoidance, while others project the conscious will of the declaration to leave the concept interpretative open for a better appreciation. Whatever the intention might be recent scholarship understands human rights as a universal concept in terms of "interpretative openness".[718] In this sense every worldview can be accommodated without minding from which angle one

---

717 The Universal Declaration of Human Rights, published by the United Nations Organisation (UNO).
718 Cf. Konrad Hilpert, „Idee der Menschenwürde aus der Sicht Christlicher Theologie", in: Hans Jörg sandkühler (Hg.), Menschenwürde. Philosophische, theologische und juristische Analysen, Frankfurt am Main 2007 41-55 here 49; cf. Elisabeth Gräb-Schmidt, „Würde als Bestimmung der Natur des Menschen? Theologische Reflexionen zu ihrem (nach-) Metaphysischen Horizont", in: Wilfried Härle, Bernhard Vogel (Hg.), Begründung von Menschenwürde und Menschenrechten, Freiburg – Basel – Wien 2008 134-168 here 157.

may choose to interpret human rights. Whether one chooses to interpret rights from religious or philosophical point of view the concept remains open. Interpretative openness offers the concept a kind of docility and dynamism, which make it possible for it to be approached from different angles. Above all, the decision to leave the interpretation of the concept of human rights in modern human rights' discussions interpretive open was intended to guarantee a concept of rights that would be universal, neutral and secular in character; one free from every religious perspective. To achieve this universality and neutrality, human reason was proffered and enthroned as a secure basis for interpretation. Reason as a human faculty was arrogated a great role to play in the interpretative openness of the concept so that it will not be confused simply, as an empty dimensionless formulary, instead as an invitation for every tradition and culture to contribute towards the understanding of the concept.[719]

Notwithstanding the above optimism, basic worries over the obvious pitfalls of human reason in practical terms were overlooked. For instance, the fact that opinions differ at times, which brings about arguments, misunderstanding and quarrels proves the precariousness of human reason. Even though rationality has the capacity to prove the rectitude of an ethical norm, it cannot by itself alone establish a substantive one; or stand as a self-founding instance.[720] Unfortunately, these basic truisms were virtually left out, so that one may ask whether this was simply a case of naiveté on the side of the modern human rights thinkers or a simple euphoria of the time. Therefore, the current problem of interpretation of human dignity has centred majorly on these questions: can reason exclusively qualify as a measure of interpretation of human dignity, bearing in mind that the reason talked about here remains a historically cultured reason? Or should there be need for a deeper transcendental religious interpretation?

When one considers the multiplicity of cultures, an idea of a universal interpretation and application solely on the pretext of reason creates a serious suspicion of dictation. It is pertinent to bear in mind the fact, that human dignity is a deep value attached to the status of the human person as such.[721] This implies all the qualities, faculties, characters that make up

---

719 Cf. Huber, Art. Menschenrechte/Menschenwürde, 1. 5, 581
720 Cf. Huber, Art. Menschenwürde/Menschenrechte, 5. 1, 591.
721 Cf. Hilpert, Art. Menschenwürde, 133.

the human person, of which reason is just a part. There are other aspects of the human person such as religion and culture which put together, make a person. As a matter of necessity, the historical, cultural and transcendental aspects of the human person should not be neglected.[722] Consequently, the adverse effect of this neglect became evident in the contradictory ethical standards for human rights that followed. Further more, experience has revealed that, the abandonment of the historical and cultural reality in the Western modern concept of human rights for the sake of neutrality and universality has not made it acceptable to non-Western cultures either. The abandonment of traditional historical interpretation cannot lead to the realization of the Western idea of universal human rights. Interpretative openness should be understood as a dialogue with other cultural concepts of human dignity and rights without past prejudices. Human reason thought to be the sole basis for any meaningful universal human rights can not guarantee a universal human rights idea without consideration of history.[723] Human beings are not only distinguished by the possession of rationality, but most importantly with the ability to transcend their world. Any assessment of the human person that does not consider these two aspects of man runs the risk of being lopsided. It is with both reason and transcendence that the human being becomes a being of history and culture. According to Gunda Schneider-Flume, a human being lives in histories, he is engolged in histories: he is also history himself, before he makes history.[724] Wolfgang Huber rightly opined that, the thesis that human rights can only be plausible on grounds of reason deviates from both the historical character of human rights and the historical character of human reason.[725] The effects of such presumptions have had long lasting effects both on religious and secular life, because any form of philosophy without history remains simply an ideology.

On the other hand, in the presence of some religious contexts such as, Hinduism, Confucianism Judaism, Islam, Buddhism, and some others outside the Euro-American hemisphere, such as African traditional religions any claim of a universal concept of human rights based on a single

---

722 Cf. Hilpert, Art. Menschenwürde, 136.
723 Cf. Huber, Art. Menschenrechte/Menschenwürde, 5. 1, 591.
724 Cf. Schneider-Flume, die Geschichte der Imago Dei 47.
725 Cf. Huber, Art. Menschenrechte/Menschenwürde, 5. 1, 591.

religious interpretations will be unrealistic. As we have mentioned before a theoretical concept or an idea of human dignity can be universal, because it is a common heritage of humanity, but as a universal practical human right or political foreign policy, its realisation remains questionable since universality is a normative concept.[726] For this reason except in the occasion of international human interventions in good faith human rights are largely from history left as a national concern.[727]

Interpretative openness creates a gap in the concept of rights leaving it lucid and fluid, so as to be relevant all the time. Most importantly, the purpose of interpretative openness is to enrich the concept with more perspectives and applicability. In this way different cultures and religious traditions will be enabled to contribute their own quotas in the debate on human dignity and rights. Interpretative openness offers theology the opportunity of filling the gap created by this opening[728]. In the first place however, it is pertinent to stress that the relevance of historically suitable interpretation of human dignity and rights does not becloud the fear of the possibility of every theological effort at interpretation being dependent on a particular religious tradition. The respect of divergent views and opinions is the first step to the acknowledgement of the interpretative openness of the concept. Differences among cultures, religions and opinions not only confirm the reality of human freedom, but also affirm man's capacity to self-transcendence. Interpretative openness calls also for a convergence through the acceptance of all suppressed differences among cultures, with the intention of bringing all together for dialogue.[729] Christian theology with its capacity to dialogue, acknowledges the fact of this man's self

---

726 Cf. Ramcharan, Contemporary Human Rights Ideas 56.
727 Cf. Stephen D. Krasner, „Sovereignty, Regimes, and Human Rights", in: Volker Rittberger (ed.), Regime Theory and International Relations, Baden-Baden 1997 139.
728 Cf. Hilpert, „Idee der Menschenwürde aus der Sicht Christlicher Theologie" 48-49.
729 Cf. Hans Maier, „Die Menschenrechte als Weltrechte nach 1945: Universeller Anspruch und Kulturelle Differenzierung", in: Michael Durst, Hans J. Münk (Hg.), Theologie und Menschenrechte, Freiburg – Schweiz 2008 50-67 here 64.

transcendence that links him to other fellow human beings and ultimately to his creator God.⁷³⁰

In the face of ideological impasse between relativism and pluralism in issues relating to the conceptions of dignity of human person theology stands a better chance of supporting a viable interpretation. Nonetheless, it is necessary from the outset, to stress the need for theology to remain inclusive and not exclusive in any approach to human questions and problems; it has to be historical, anthropologically based, interdisciplinary in approach and not ideological. In order to have meaning, the approach must not relegate any religion, culture or tradition as meaningless by a pretentious form of a dictated universalism, since the ugly fruits and consequences of such sinful attitudes would be regrettable.

Therefore the researcher supports the fact that interpretative openness of the concept of human rights should not lead to its abuse as an empty concept, unqualified for any interpretation, but rather lead to facing the challenge of filling up the gap created by openness of the concept with the intention to enrich it with many perspectives.⁷³¹ It is in this sense, that the real universal character of the concept can shine out as evident. Specifically, this research argues the fact that reason as it is historically projected before now simply as a limited heritage of a particular culture does not qualify as enough bases for interpreting human rights. On the contrary, the researcher insists on the need for a deeper transcendental basis which theology in the complementary role of reason can provide. It was in line with the above assertion that Martin Thurner made bold to say:

> Es soll hier die These vertreten werden, dass die Menschenrechte zu einer letztgültigen Begründung in der Dimension des Transzendenten und Unbedingten verankert werden müssen, also von ihrem Wesen her einen Bezug zu jener Dimension beinhalten, die Gegenstand der Religion ist. Wenn es zutrifft, dass die autonome Vernunft des

---

730 Cf. Huber, Art. Menschenrechte/Menschenwürde, 1. 5, 581.
731 Cf. Wolfgang Vögele, „Die Christliche Deutung der Menschenwürde im Kontext gegenwärtiger Debatten", in: Christian Thies (Hg.), Der Wert der Menschenwürde, Paderborn – München – Wien – Zürich 2009 63-74 here 63.

Menschen sich nicht selbst begründen kann, dann sind Menschenrechte und Menschenwürde prinzipiell begründungsoffen.[732]

Interpretative openness reminds of the short fall of reason as hegemony of a particular people or culture. Even though classifiable, reason remains a common heritage of humanity. Its variance from culture to culture makes it incapable of being the last instance of interpreting human rights and dignity. Just as Schneider-Flume asserted: «There are many reasons or rationalities.»[733] The best it could achieve is to recognise the concept as interpretative open, but cannot itself qualify as the last instance of interpretation.

6.5.1 Shared Heritage as the Basis for a viable Interpretation of Human Dignity

Human beings share much in common, the most basic of which is life. In the history of world religions and cultures measures are always taken to protect life. This is the reason for norms and morality in the society. World religions have the same basic principles towards the protection of individual rights and that of others outside the individual[734]. There is a central connection that is complex, which runs between the various religions. For instance, the sacredness of life and the golden rule: do unto others, as you would want them do unto you are always expressed in almost, if not all their moral and ethical codes. Positive contributions of the world religions includes; the affirmation of the unique value and dignity of the human person; ethical norms of justice and equity to govern interpersonal relations; condemnation of injustice and offences against man; norms for just government and institutions; social justice as an ex-

---

732 Martin Thurner, „Die Menschenrechte, die Menschenwürde und das Christentum", in: Richard Heinzmann u.a. (Hg.), Menschenwürde, Grundlagen in Christentum und Islam, Stuttgart 2007 80-91 here 83.
733 Schneider-Flume, Die Geschichte der Imago Dei 59.
734 Cf. Ramcharan, Contemporary Human Rights Ideas, 13ff; See also Leroy S. Rouner (ed.), Human Rights and the World's Religions, University of Notre Dame, Indiana 1988.

tension of individual rights; supremacy and integrity of the conscience as ultimate arbiter of right and wrong.

The above ideals have been pursued both by cultures and religions in the history of humanity showing that human beings share the same heritage, and contribute to the protection of both the individual and group rights. There has always being a respect for a common shared heritage in the different cultures and religions of the world. This common shared heritage upholds the dignity of the human person in every culture and religion through which the human ideals can shine out. It is on the basis of these human ideals, even though conceived in different ways that every human development in the society is built.

Therefore, the human person remains the centre of the understanding and interpretation of human dignity, but the concept of person varies among cultures this is why the interpretation of human dignity remains open.[735] At the basis of these conceptualities is the 'humanness' as a shared heritage in the both views. In every culture and religions, the goal, ideals and aspirations of the human person are the same but the way to achieve this may vary from culture to culture, religion to religion. Hence, the fight for rights is the same but the codifications may vary as in the case of the UDHR, which obviously is the brainchild of the Western humanism. While the Igbo Africans perceive the human person from the angle of his being only in consonance with the community, the West understand the individual person as a lone being needing the protection of the state from all human and natural aggression. It is pertinent to assert here that the interpretative openness of the idea of human dignity and rights is only valuable if it is actually maintained in praxis. On the contrary interpretative openness looses its meaning and relevance, when it occurs that in spite of its openness some cultural interpretations are dismissed[736] with the same old ideological "superior mentality" of the West

---

735 Cf. Hilpert, „Die Idee der Menschenwürde aus der Sicht Christlicher Theologie" 42-43.
736 The third generation rights on the equal distribution of the earthly goods proposed by the so called third world countries have not been accepted for ratification by the UNO. For this reason the united effort on the war on poverty or the so called hep for the third world or the developing nations seem to be pretentious.

while imposing personal ideas born of personal cultural and historical experiences. There is no gain saying that super powers like the United States of America usurp the idea for their own imperialistic foreign polices, which are most often biased and limited.

Therefore, the UDHR is not immune from the historical pitfall in a world synonymous with ideologies, where definitions of the human person have followed a rigour of cultural bias; a world where slavery and colonialism where backed with an imperialistic ideology of expansionism; a world where religion has become a global player and through the missionary activities of already divided Church scramble for dominance in innocent mission lands; a world that has experienced Cold war between two currents namely, the Communist East Bloc and the Capitalistic West bloc; a world with two ferocious political ideologies namely, the liberal and the conservatives with various national and international interests in their foreign policies; a world with a quest for globalisation through human rights instruments and interventions in difficult humanitarian cases, but at the same time faced with moral dilemma and selective interpretation of human dignity that corrodes the aim and objective of human protection.

In all, interpretative openness of human dignity seeks a deeper understanding, much deeper that the erstwhile ideologies we have enumerated above; an understanding deeper than the traditional Igbo African understanding of dignity comparable with antiquated Roman *dignitas* as status and title acquisition; a more human friendly interpretation, which does no longer permit human sacrifices as a sign of dignity and respect to the dead; an inclusive interpretation without segregating between the *osu* (out cast), *ohu-* (the stranger) and *diala-* (the indigene); an all round understanding of personhood that will embrace every human being as a person; an understanding of a community not only person oriented as it is in the Igbo African societies where those outside the family lineage are regarded as foreigners, but rather a more inclusive one; an interpretation of human dignity that is conscious of the protection of the rights of this individual here and now, who runs the risk of being subsumed by the *"we"* consciousness, but at the same time not one estranged by abstract ideologies; an interpretation of human dignity that is sensitive to gender equality but not confused with radical programmes of emancipation.

Theological dialogue in the whole discussion refers to a transcendental approach to the interpretation of human dignity, since humanity understands itself only when it aligns with its origin God.[737] On the above concern, one can rightly affirm with Martin Thurner, that it is pertinent to agree that human rights must be interpreted finally on the basis of transcendence. Such an interpretation must go with it, all the relevant aspects of Religion, which of course do not go contrary to the rule of reason, but objectively in line with its rules. For the fact that reason itself is not an end but a means to understand things, it has to be understood as well as contextual. Because reason is contextual the interpretation of human rights and dignity has to be "open-ended" among all cultures and religions of the world.[738] Christian theology in fulfilling its functions in the understanding of human beings in their transcendental nature succeeds in interpreting the dignity of human person from a universal point of the cherished human values as shared heritage, while respecting at the same time, the uniqueness of cultural and religious differences by leaving the interpretation of the concept "open". Above all, every interpretation of ethical norms must be ready to contest for recognition and acceptance; this applies to both religious and rational interpretations.[739]

The fruit of this endeavour will be an interpretation of human dignity devoid of anti human ideologies. For this reason, theological dialogue preoccupies itself with the subject human being, in relation to God and the world. Thanks to the modern anthropological brake through in the study of theology, through which the human being has been clarified as 'created in the image and likeness of God'. *Imago Dei* in this context is seen and principally understood in the ability of the human person to self-transcendence and also to transcend the world. This ability is a shared heritage of all human beings, and therefore qualifies as the stable foundation for the interpretation and protection of human dignity. I respect and recognise the other person because we all have a share in the God given capacity to transcend ourselves. Every human being is a person, through whose image we share, the real image and likeness of unseen God.

---

737 Cf. Pannenberg, Anthropology in the theological Perspective 11.
738 Martin Thurner, „Die Menschenrechte, die Menschenwürde und das Christentum", in: Richard Heinzmann (Hg.), Menschenwürde, Grundlagen in Christentum und Islam, Stuttgart 2007 80-91 here 83.
739 Cf. Schneider-Flume, Die Geschichte der Imago Dei 59.

General Bibliography

Primary Sources

LEXIKON FÜR THEOLOGIE UND KIRCHE, Dritte Völlig Neu Bearbeitete Auflage Walter Kasper, a.u., (Hgg.), BD. 1ff, Freiburg u.a., 1998ff.
NEW CATHOLIC ENCYCLOPAEDIA, W. J. McDonald u.a., (Hgg.), 15Bde. New York u.a., 1967.
THE NEW JERUSALEM BIBLE, Darton Longman & Todd, London.
THEOLOGISCHE REALENZYKLOPÄDIE, G. Krause/G. Müller (Hgg.), Berlin-New York 1976ff.
WEBSTER'S NEW ENCYCLOPAEDIC DICTIONARY, New York, 1995.

Historical Books

AUGUSTINE, Aurelius, De Libero Arbitrio-Vom Freien Willen. In: Theologische Frühschriften – Vom Freiem Willen – Von der Wahren Religion, Zürich und Stuttgart, 1962.
AUGUSTINE, Saint, The City of God, (trans.) DODS, Marcus, New York 1993.
CICERO, Marcus Tullius, *De Officiis 1*, 105.
CHRISTMANN, Heinrich Maria (Hg.): Thomas Aquinas, *Summa Theologica*, Völl. Deutsch-Latin Ausgabe, Bd. 3 Salzburg 1939.
THEOPHILUS of Antioch, Ad Autolycum: http:/www.ccel.org/fathers2/ANF-02/anfo2-40.htm (07.05.2010).
THOMAS, Aquinas, *Summa Theologica*, Völls. Deutsch-Latin Ausgabe, CHRISTMANN Heinrich Maria (Hg.), Bd.3 Salzburg, (1939), 1 question. 29.

Church Documents

CATECHISM OF THE CATHOLIC CHURCH (CCC), St Paul's Press Nairobi-Ibadan Nigeria, 1994.
DECLARATION ON RELIGIOUS LIBERTY, *Vatican II, Dignitatis Humanae*, (DH): 7 Dec. 1965: The Conciliar and Post Conciliar Documents, (ed.) AUSTINE, Flannary O.P. Dominican Publication Dublin, 1987.
DENZINGER, Henrici: Kompendium der Glaubensbekenntnisse und kirchlichen Lehrentscheidungen, no. 2730-2732.
DEUTSCHE BISCHOFSKONFERENZ, *Das Glaubensbekenntnis der Kirche*, Band.1 Katholischer Erwachsenenkatechismus, Freiburg, 2006.
DEUTSCHE, BISCHOFSKONFERENZ, De Iustitia in Mundo: Römische Bischofssynode 1971. Der Priesterliche Dienst. Gerechtigkeit in der Welt. Trier: Paulinus-Verlag, 1972 1-2.
PASTORAL CONSTITUTION ON THE MODERN WORLD, *Vatican Council II, Gaudium et Spes, (G.S)*: 7 Dec. 1965: The Conciliar and Post Conciliar Documents, (ed.) AUSTINE, Flannary O.p. Dominican Publication, Dublin 1987.

Encyclical Letters

JOHN XXIII, *Pacem in Terris* 11 April 1963: AAS 55 (1963) 257-304.
JOHN PAUL II, *Redemptor Hominis*, 4 March 1979: AAS 71 (1979) 251-324.
JOHN PAUL II, *Laborem Exercens*, 14th September 1981: AAS (1981) 577-647.
LEO XIII, *Human Liberty*, Paulist Press Version (P.P.V), New York, 1941.
LEO XIII, *Rerum Novarum*, November 1891: AAS 23 (1891) 640.
LEO XIII, *Libertas Praestantissimum*, August 1888: AAS 20 (605-608), Paulist Press Version, New York, 1941.
PIUS XII, *Nuntius Radiophonicus*, "Il Santo Natale e la Umanità Dolorante" 1943: AAS 35, (1943) 19-24.
PIUS XI, *Quadragesimo Anno*, 1931: AAS 23 (1931).

Secular Documents

BASIC LAW FOR THE FEDRAL REPUBLIC OF GERMANY, (Grundgesetz GG), Art. 1, *Human dignity*.
THE UNIVERSAL DECLARATION OF HUMAN RIGHTS (UDHR): http//www.un.org/en/documents/udhr/ (07.11.2011)
THE AMERICAN DECLARATION OF INDEPENDENCE July 4 1776. http//www.constitution.org/usdeclar.pdf (07.11.2011)

Secondary Sources

ABBAS, Hakima, Africa's Long Road to Rights, Reflections on the 20th Anniversary of the African Commission on Human and Peoples' Rights, Nairobi and Oxford 2007.
ACHEBE, Chinua, Things Fall Apart, Heinemann London, 1958.
ACHEBE, Chinua, Okonkwo oder Das Alte Stürzt (Things Fall Apart), HEUSLER, Dagmar, PETZOLD, Evelin (Hgs.), Bd. 138, Frankfurt am Main 1983.
ACHEBE, Chinua, „Chi" in Igbo Cosmology, in: EZE Emmanuel (ed.), African Philosophy: An Anthology, USA 1998, 67-72.
ACHEBE, Chinua, Arrow of God, Heinemann London, 1964.
ANGENENDT, Arnold, Toleranz und Gewalt: Das Christentum zwischen Bibel und Schwert, Aschendorff, 2009.
ARAZU, Raymond, The Supreme God in Igbo Traditional Religion, A Workshop paper: The State of Igbo Studies, Institute of African Studies Nssuka, June 1982.
ARINZE, Francis, Sacrifice in Igbo Religion, Ibadan-Nigeria, 1970.
AUER, Johann, Person, Ein Schlüssel zum Christlichen Mysterium, Regensburg, 1979.
AVNON, Dan, Martin Buber: The hidden Dialogue, Rowman and Littlefield Publications, London, 1998.
AYLWARD, Shorter, African Culture, Nairobi, 1998.
AZIKIWE, Nnamdi, Respect for Human Dignity: An Inaugural Address delivered by His Excellency, Dr. Nnamdi Azikiwe, Governor-General and Commander-in-Chief of the Federation of Nigeria, Government Press, Enugu, 16 November 1960.

BÂ, Amadou Ham pâté, Aspects de la Civilisation Africaine, Paris, 1972.

BASDEN, T. George, Among the Ibos of Nigeria, University Publishing Co. Nigeria 1982.

BENEDIKT XVI., Der Mensch-Herz des Friedens. Botschaft zur Feier des Weltfriedenstages, in: Amtsblatt der Österreichischen Bischofskonferenz 43, 2007, 10-16.

BENEDIKT XVI., Angelus am 1. Januar 2007 am Petersplatz Rom, Zitiert in: LEDERHILGER J. Severin (Hg.), Gott verlassen Menschenwürde und Menschenbilder, Frankfurt am Main, 2007.

BOUYER, Louis, Woman in the Church, Ignatius Publishers, New York, 1979.

BUJO, Bénézet, Die ethische Dimension der Gemeinschaften. Das afrikanische Modell im Nord- süd-Dialog, Freiburg, 1993.

BUJO, Bénézet Bujo,, Ethical Dimension of Community, Nairobi 1998

BUBER, Martin, Das dialogische Prinzip, Gütersloher Verlagshaus, Gütersloh 1986.

BUBER, Martin, I and thou, Edinburgh, 1937.

BUBER, Martin, Between Man and Man, Routledge Classic London, 2002.

BREDVOLD, Louis I / ROSS, Ralph Gilbert (eds.), The Philosophy of Edmund Burke. A Selection from His Speeches and Writings, Ann Arbor: The University of Michigan Press, 1967.

BROWN, Alan, On the Criticism of Being as Communion in Anglophone Orthodox Theology, in: KNIGHT, Douglas H, The Theology of John Zizioulas, England 2007, 35-78.

CORNFORD, Francis Macdonald, Plato's Cosmology: The Timaeus of Plato, (Trans. with Commentary) London, 1937.

DENG, Francis Mading, Human Rights in the African Context, in: WIREDU, Kwasi (ed.), A Companion to African Philosophy, Oxford 2005, 499-508.

DENZER, Horst, Moral philosophie und Naturrecht bei Samuel Pufendorf. Eine Geistes und Wissenschaftsgeschichliche Untersuchung zur Geburt des Naturrechts aus der Praktischen Philosophie, München, 1972.

DONNELLY, Jack, Human Rights and Human Dignity: An Analytic Critique of Non-Western Conceptions of Human Rights, in: *The American Political Science Review*, Vol. 76, No. 2 (Jun., 1982), 303-316.

DONNELLY, Jack, Universal Human rights in Theory and Practice, Ithaca and London, 1989.
DOVER, Kenneth (ed.), Plato's Symposium, Cambridge University Press, 1980.
DWORKIN, Ronald, Taking Rights Seriously. Cambridge: Harvard University Press, 1978.
DWYER, John C, Person, Dignity of, in: DWYER, Judith A./ MONTGOMERY, Elizabeth L. (eds.): The New Dictionary of Catholic Social Thought, Collegeville Minnesota 1994, 724-737.
EBOH, Simeon, Onyewueke, Human Rights and Democratization in Africa: The Role of Christians Enugu Nigeria, 2003.
EBOH, Simon O, Ozo Title Institution in Igbo land, Munich 1993.
ECHERUO, Michael, J. C., "Matter of Identity: *Aham Efula*", Ahiajoku Lecture Series 1979, Culture Division, Ministry of Information, Culture, Youth and Sports, Owerri, 1979.
EDEH, Emmanuel M. P., Towards an Igbo Metaphysics, Chicago, 1985.
EIGEN, Manfred, Stufen zum Leben. Die frühe Evolution im Visier der Molekularbiologie, München, 1987.
EJIZU, Christopher Ifeanyi, Ofo: Igbo Ritual Symbol, Ibadan Nigeria, 1986.
EKECHI, Felix K., Missionary Enterprise and Rivalry in Igbo Land 1857-1914 London, 1972.
EKWURU, Emeka George, The Pangs of an African Culture in Travail, Uwa Ndi Igbo Yaghara ayagha (The Igbo World in Disarray), Totan Publishers Limited, Nigeria, 1999.
ELLERBY, Jonathan Harold, Indigenous Integrative Phenomenology: Integrating Indigenous Epistemologies in traditional healing Research, Doctoral Thesis 2006 61-63. <http//www.gtfeducation.org/academics/OTL_Ellerby.pdf 06.12.2011>.
ENI, Humphrey O., The Ujari (Ajali) People of Awka District, Onitsha, University Press, 1973.
ENGLISH, M. C., An Outline of Nigerian History, London 1959.
ERICKSON, Millard J, Christian Theology, Grand Rapids, Michigan, 1983, 1984, 1985, 495-517.
EZE C. Osita, Human Rights in Africa: Some Selected Problems, Lagos Macmillan Nigeria, 1984.

EZEKWONNA, Ferdinand Chukwuagozie, African Communitarian Ethic: The Basis for the Moral Conscience and Autonomy of the Individual Igbo Culture as a Case Study, Frankfurt am Main, 2005.

FORSCHNER, Maximilian, Marktpreis und Würde oder vom Adel der Menschlichen Natur, in: KÖSSLER, Henning (Hg.), Die Würde des Menschen, Erlangen, 1997.

FORSCHNER, Maximilian, „Die Würde des Menschen ist unantastbar" – ein Plädoyer für ein Tabu, Ein Tagungsvortrag, der Katholische Akademie in München, *„Menschenwürde a.D.? Ein Grundwert im Wanken"*, 7/8 November 2008.

FOX, Patricia (ed.), God as Communion: John Zizioulas, Elizabeth Johnson, and the Retrieval of the Symbol of the Triune God, New York, 2001.

GANOCZY, Alexandre, Schöpfungslehre, Düsseldorf, 1983.

GEDDES/ WALLACE, Art. Person (In Philosophy): N C E Vol. XI, New York (1967), 166-168.

GORMALLY, L, Human Dignity: The Christian View and the Secularist View, Pontificia Academia Pro Vita, <http://www.academiavita.org/template.jsp> 11/09/2008.

GRÄB-SCHMIDT, Elisabeth: Würde als Bestimmung der Natur des Menschen? Theologische Reflexionen zu ihrem (nach-) Metaphysischen Horizont, in: HÄRLE, Wilfried/ VOGEL, Bernhard (Hgs.), Begründung von Menschenwürde und Menschenrechten, Freiburg-Basel-Wien 2008, 134-168.

GROSS, Walter, die Gottebenbildlichkeit des Menschen im Kontext der Priesterschrift, ThQ 161, 244-264 1981.

HARDING, Leonhard, Menschenbilder und Menschenrechte: Afrikanische Erfahrungen, in: SCHMIDT, Burghart (Hg.), Menschenrechte und Menschenbilder von der Antike bis zur Gegenwart, Hamburg 2006, 277-305.

HASENKAMP, Mao-ling, Universalization of Human Rights? The Effectiveness of Western Human Rights Policies towards Developing Countries after the Cold War With Case Studies on China, Frankfurt am Main, 2004.

HEFFNER, Philip J., The Human Being, in: Christian Dogmatics, Vol. 1, (eds.) BRAATEN, Carl E. / JENSON, Robert W. Philadelphia, 1986

HEGEL, Georg Wilhelm Friedrich, The Philosophy of History, (Trans.) J. Jibree, New York, 1956.

HEINZMANN, Richard, Der Mensch als Person-Verständnis des Menschen aus jüdisch-Christlichem Ursprung, in: HEINZMANN, Richard u.a. (Hgg), Menschenwürde, Grundlagen in Christentum und Islam, Stuttgart 2007, 45-56.

HENDRICKSON, Joy Mukubwa, Rights in Traditional African Societies, in: Zaccheus Sunday Ali, et al. (eds.), African Traditional Political Thought and Institutions, Lagos, 1989 19-39.

HERMES, Würde des Menschen, II Theologisch, in RGG^4 8 (2005), 1737-1739.

HEUSER, Stefan, Menschenwürde. Eine Theologische Erkundung, Münster, 2004.

HILPERT, Konrad, Theologische Begründung der Menschenwürde und der Auftrag der Kirche, Ein Tagungsvortrag der Katholische Akademie in München, „Menschenwürde a.D? Ein Grundwert im Wanken", 7/8 November 2008.

HILPERT, Konrad, Die Menschenrechte in Theologie und Kirche, in: DURST, Michael und MÜNK J. Hans, Theologie und Menschenrechte, Freiburg Schweiz 2008, 68-112.

HILPERT, Konrad, Idee der Menschenwürde aus der Sicht Christlicher Theologie, in: SANDKÜHLER Hans Jörg (Hg.), Menschenwürde. Philosophische, theologische und Juristische Analysen, Frankfurt am Main 2007, 41-55.

HILPERT, Konrad, Art. Menschenwürde, in: LThK 7, (^{3}1998) 131-137.

HIVES, Frank, Jaja and Justice in Nigeria, London, 1968.

HODES, Aubrey, Encounter with Martin Buber, Allen Lane/Penguin Press London, 1972.

HONNEFELDER, Ludger, Würde und Werte, in: THIES, Christian (Hg.), Der Werte der Menschenwürde, Paderborn 2009, 33-43.

HOOKER, Richard (Trans.), Pico Della Mirandola: Oration on the Dignity of Man, <http://www.wsu.edu:8080/~wldciv/world_civ_reader/world_civ_reader_1/pico.html> 10.05.2010.

HOUNTODJI, Paulin J., African Philosophy, London, 1983.

HUBER, Wolfgang, Art. Menschenwürde/ Menschenrechte: 1, in: TRE 22, Berlin-New York (^{3}1992), 577-602.

HUSSERL, Edmund, The Crisis of European Sciences and Transcendental Phenomenology: An Introduction to Phenomenological Philosophy. Evanston, III North Western University Press, 1989.

HÜNERMANN, Peter, Erlöste Freiheit, Dogmatische Reflexionen im Ausgang von den Menschenrechten, in: Zeitschrifteninhaltsdienst Theologie Ausgaben 1-6, Universität Tübingen 1985, 1-14.

IFEMESIA, Emmanuel, Igbo Traditional Religion: A Cultural Means of Cultivating Discipline, in: Cahier des Religions Africaine, Vol. 19, no. 38 Juillet, 1985, 243-244.

IFEMESIA, Chieka C., British Enterprise on the Niger 1830-1869, London, 1959.

ILOGU, Edmund, Christianity and Igbo Culture, London-New York-Enugu, 1974.

IROEGBU, Panteleon, Kpim of Personality: Treatise on the Human Person, Owerri, 2000.

ISICHEI, Elisabeth, A History of the Igbo People, London, 1976.

ISHAY, Micheline R. (Ed.), The Human Rights Reader Major Political Writings, Essays, Speeches, and Documents from the Bible to the Present, New York, 1997.

IWE, Nwachukwuike Sylvanus Sunday, The History and Contents of Human Rights A Study of the History and Interpretation of Human Rights, Frankfurt am Main, 1986.

IWE, Nwachukwuike Sylvanus Sunday, "Igbo Deities", in: The Ahiajoku Lecture (*Onugaotu)* Colloquium 1988, Culture Division, Ministry of Information, Culture, Youth and Sports, Owerri, 1988.

IWE, Nwachukwuike Sylvanus Sunday, The Dignity of Man as the Foundation of Human Rights, a Message for Nigerians, Calabar Nigeria 2000.

JABER, Dunja, Über den Mehrfachen Sinn von Menschenwürde-Garantien. Mit besonderer Berücksichtigung von Art. 1 Abs.1 Grundgesetz, Frankfurt am Main, 2003.

JACK, Goody, Religion and Development: Some Comparative Considerations, in: Development 46 (2003) 4, 64-67.

JORDAN, John P, Bishop Shanahan of Southern Nigeria, Elo Press Dublin, 1971.

KANT, Immanuel, Immanuel Kant, The Critique of Practical Reason, (trans.) PLUHAR, Werner S. Hackett United States of America, 2002.

KAPHAGAWANI, Didler Njirayamanda, African Conceptions of a Person: A Critical Survey, in: WIREDU, Kwasi (ed.), A Companion to African Philosophy, Oxford 2005, 332-342.

KASPER, Walter, Der Gott Jesu Christi, Matthias Grünewald Verlag, Mainz, 1982.

KATHER, Regine, Person. Die Begründung menschlicher Identität, Darmstadt, 2007.

KATHERINE, Marshall, Die Kluft Überbrücken. Religion und Entwicklung – eine alte Beziehung neu betracht, in: eins Entwicklungspolitik Nr. 7-8 (2006) 26-31.

KAUNDA, Kenneth, Spirituality and world Community, in: SHORTER, Aylward (ed.), African Christian Spirituality, Mary knoll-New York, 1980, 117-121.

KÖRNER, Bernhard, Art. Cano Melchior, in: LThK 2, (^{3}1994) 924-925.

KÖRNER, Bernhard, Melchior Cano. De Locis Theologicis Ein Beitrag zur Theologischen Erkenntnislehre, Graz, 1994.

KRASNER, Stephen D: Sovereignty, Regimes, and Human Rights, in: RITTBERGER, Volker (ed.), Regime Theory and International Relations, Baden–Baden, 1997 139-169.

KUHN, Helmut, Die Kirche im Zeitalter der Kulturrevolution, Graz, 1985.

KÜNG, Hans, Projekt Weltethos, München, 1990.

KUNZMANN, Peter Kunzmann, Die Würde des Tieres – Zwischen Leerformel und Prinzip, Freiburg-München 2007.

LACUGNA, Catherine, God for Us: The Trinity and the Christian Life, Harper One publishers, New York, 1993.

LADEUR, Karl-Hein/ AUGSBERG Ino, Die Funktion der Menschenwürde im Verfassungsstaat, Tübingen, 2008.

LANG, Albert, Die Loci Theologici des Melchior Cano und die Methode des Dogmatischen Beweises, München 1925.

LEONARD, Arthur Glyn, The Lower Niger and its Tribes, London 1956.

LIESENFELD, Stefan (Hg.), Alles wirkliche Leben ist Begegnung: Hundert Worte von Martin Buber, Verlag Neue Stadt, 2. Auflage München – Wien, 1999.

MAIER, Hans, Die Menschenrechte als Weltrechte nach 1945: Universeller Anspruch und Kulturelle Differenzierung, in: DURST, Michael, MÜNK J. Hans (Hgg.), Theologie und Menschenrechte, Freiburg – Schweiz 2008, 50-67.

MARGALIT, Avishai, Politik der Würde. Über Achtung und Verachtung. Frankfurt am Main, 1999.

MARITAIN, Jacque, Christianity and Democracy and the Rights of Man and Natural Law, New York, 1942.

MARQUETTE, Jacque, Africanity: The Cultural Unity of Black Africa, Oxford, 1972.

MBITI, John S., The Prayers of African Religion, London 1975.

MBITI, John S., African Religions and Philosophy, London-Ibadan-Nairobi, 1969.

MENKITI, Ifeanyi A., Person and Community in African Traditional Thought, in: WRIGHT, Richard A. (ed.), African Philosophy: An Introduction³, USA 1984, 171-181.

MENKITI, Ifeanyi A., On the Normative Conception of a Person, in: WIREDU, Kwasi (ed.), A Companion to African Philosophy, Oxford 2005, 324-331.

MERKEL, Reinhard/WITTMANN, Roland (Hgs.), Zum Ewigen Frieden. Grundlagen, Aktualität und Aussichten einer Idee von Immanuel Kant, Frankfurt am Main, 1996.

METUH, Emefie Ikenga, African Religions in Western Conceptual Schemes: The Problem of Interpretation, Jos Nigeria, 1991.

METUH, Emefie Ikenga, African religions in Western Conceptual Schemes, Ibadan, 1985.

METUH, Emefie Ikenga, Comparative Studies of African Traditional Religions, Onitsha-Nigeria 1996.

METUH, Emefie Ikenga, Comparative Studies of African Traditional Religions², Enugu, 1999.

METUH, Emefie Ikenga, The Shattered Microcosm: A Critical Survey of Explanations of Conversion in Africa, in: PETERSON, K. H (ed.), Religion, Development and African Identity, Uppsala 1987 11-27.

METUH, Emefie Ikenga/ OJOADE, O., et al: Nigerian Cultural Heritage, Jos Nigeria, 1990.

MOLTMANN, Jürgen, Man. Christian Anthropology in the Conflicts of the Present (Trans.) STURDY, John, Philadelphia: Fortress Press, 1971 & 1974.

MOHR, Georg, Ein „Wert, der Keinen Preis hat" –Philosophiegeschichtliche Grundlagen der Menschenwürde bei Kant und Fichte, in:

SANDKÜHLER, Hans Jörg (Hg.), Menschenwürde. Philosophische, theologische und juristische Analysen, Frankfurt am Main 2007, 13-39.
MOHR, Georg, Einleitung: Der Personenbegriff in der Geschichte der Philosophie, www.mentis.de/download.php?media_id=00000252.
MONDIN, Battista, Philosophical Anthropology, Rome, 1985.
MOORE, Edward, Origin of Alexandria (185-254 AD), in: Internet Encyclopaedia of Philosophy 02.05.2005.
MOZIA, Michael I., Solidarity in the Church and Solidarity among the Igbo of Nigeria, Rome, 1982.
MVENG, Engelbert, L'art d'Afrique noire: Liturgie cosmique et Langage religieux, in: APPIAH-KUBI, K. et al. (eds.), Libération au Adaptation? La théologie Africaine s'Interroge, Le Colleque d' Accra-Paris 1979, 167-173.
NIEBUHR, Reinhold, The Nature and Destiny of man A Christian Interpretation Vol. 1, New York 1964.
NIVEN, Rex Sir, A Short History of Nigeria, London 1948.
NJOKU, Jude Uzochukwu, The eastern Nigerian Women War of 1929 as a Model for the role of Women in the African Church, in: Journal of Inculturation Theology, Faculty of Theology, Catholic Institute of West Africa (CIWA) Portharcourt Nigeria, Vol. 7 No. 2, October 2005, 118-135
NKEMNKIA, Nkafu M., Il pensare africano come "vita logia", Rome, 1995.
NEDONCELLE, Maurice, Love and the Person, New York, 1966.
NTHAMBURI, Zablon, Making the Gospel Relevant within the African Context, in: *AFER* 25 (1983) 3, 162-171.
NWABARA, S. N., Ibo land: Century of Contact with Britain 1860-1960, London 1977.
NWAIGBO, Ferdinand, Church as a Communion: African Christian Perspective, Frankfurt am Main 1996.
NWOGA, Donatus Ibeakwadalam, „Nka na Nzere. The Focus of Igbo Worldview", in: Ahiajoku Lecture Series, Culture Division, Ministry of Information, Culture, Youth and Sports, Owerri, 1984.
NWOGA, Donatus Ibeakwadalam, The Supreme God as Stranger in Igbo Religious Thought, Enugu Nigeria 1984.
NYAMITI, Charles, The Incarnation Viewed from the African Understanding of Person, in: ACS 6 (1990) 1, 3-27.

NYERERE, Julius: Freedom and Socialism, London, 1968.
NYERERE, Julius Ujamaa: Essays on Socialism, London – New York 1971.
NZIMIRO, Ikenna, Studies in Ibo Political Systems. Chieftaincy and Politics in Four Niger States, London, 1972.
OBI, Chinwuba S. N., Law in Africa: Modern Family in South Nigeria, London 1966.
OBILOR, John, The Doctrine of the Resurrection of the Dead and the Igbo Belief in the Reincarnation, Frankfurt am Main, 1994.
O'DONOVAN, Connell (Trans. ed.), "Hen Ek Duoin": One out of Two, Aristophanes Speech from Plato's Symposium, (http//www.connelodonovan.com/hen.htm22.10.2011).
OGBUJAH, Columbus Nnamdi, The Idea of Personhood A study in Igbo (African) Philosophical Anthropology, Enugu, 2006.
O'GRADY, John F., Christian Anthropology: A Meaning for Human Life, New York, 1976.
OGUNBANJO, Bimbo M./IREWUNMI, Banwo, Human Rights and Culture in Human Rights Community: Beyond the Perspectives of Universality and Relativism, Department of Political Science and Sociology, Babcock University, Ilisan-Remo, Ogun State Nigeria, 2003.
OKERE, Theophilus, The Structure of the Self in Igbo Thought, in: OKERE, Theophilus (ed.), Identity and Change, Washington D.C. 1996.
OKERE, Theophilus, Odenigbo 1997 "Chibundu": *Ofufe Chukwu N' Etiti ndi Igbo,* Owerri, 1997.
OKORIE, George Maduakolam, The Integral Salvation of the Human Person in Ecclesia in Africa A case study of the theological implications among the Igbo in Nigeria, Frankfurt am Main, 2008.
OKOROCHA, Cyril Chukwunonyerem, The Meaning of Religious Conversion in Africa, The Case of the Igbo of Nigeria, Aldershot, u. a., 1987.
OKOT p'Bitek, The Concept of Jok among Acholi and Lango, in: The Uganda Journal, 27, 1 (March 1963), 15-29.
OLAUDAH, Equiano, Equiano's Travels, London, Heinemann, 1969 (1978).
ONWUBIKO, Oliver, African Thought, Religion and Culture, Enugu, 1991.

ONWUBIKO, Oliver, Facing the Osu Issue in the African Synod (A Personal Response), Enugu Nigeria, 1993.

ONWUMECHILI, Cyril Agodi, "Igbo Enwe Eze: The Igbo Has no Kings", Ahiajoku Lecture Series 2000, Culture Division, Ministry of Information, Culture, Youth and Sports, Owerri, 2000.

OSAGHE, Eghosa E., The Passage from the Past to the Present in African Political Thought: The Question of Relevance in: ALI, Zaccheus Sunday, et al. (eds.), African Traditional Political Thought and Institutions, Centre for Black and African Arts and Civilisation national Theatre, Lagos Nigeria 1989 53-75.

OSUJI, Cletus C., The Concept of Salvation in Igbo Traditional Religion, Rome 1977.

PANNENBERG, Wolfhart, Was ist der Mensch? Die Anthropologie der Gegenwart im Lichte der Theologie, Göttingen 1962.

PANNENBERG, Wolfhart, Anthropology in the Theological Perspective, (Trans.) O'CONNEL, Mathew J., Philadelphia-Pennsylvania, 1985.

PICO DELLA MIRANDOLA, Giovanni, Oration on the Dignity of Man, Washington DC 1999.

RAHNER, Karl, Foundation of Christian Faith. An Introduction to the Idea of Christianity, (Tans.) DYCH, William V. New York 1978.

RAHNER, Karl Rahner, Würde und Freiheit des Menschen, in: Schriften zur Theologie Bd. IV 247-277.

RAMCHARAN, Bertrand G: Contemporary Human Rights Ideas, Routledge New York 2008, 13-14.

RENDTORFF, Trutz, Menschenrechte als Bürgerrechte. Protestantische Aspekte ihrer Begründung, in: BÖCKENFÖRDE, Ernst-Wolfgang, SPAEMANN, Robert (Hgs.), Menschenrechte und menschenwürde. Historische Vorraussetzungen-Säkulare Gestalt-Christliches Verständnis, Stuttgart Klett-Cotta1987, 93-118.

RENSMANN, Thilo, Die Menschenwürde als Universaler Rechtsbegriff, in: THIES, Christian Thies (Hg.), Der Wert der Menschenwürde, Paderborn-München-Wien-Zürich 2009 75-92.

ROTIMI, Ola, The Gods are Not to Blame, University Press PLC Nigeria, 1971& 1990.

ROUNER, Leroy S. (ed.), Human Rights and the World Religions, Notre Dame, Indiana, 1988.

SANDAL, Michael J., Liberalism and the Limits of Justice, Cambridge u.a., 1982, 1998.
SANDER, Hans Joachim, Die Angetastete Menschenwürde-Ein Ort der Gegenwart Gottes, in: LEDERHILGER J. Severin (Hg.), Gott verlassen Menschenwürde und Menschenbilder. 8 Ökumenische Sommerakademie Kremsmünster 2008, Frankfurt am Main 2007, 33-51.
SANDER, Hans-Joachim, Macht in der Ohnmacht. Eine Theologie der Menschenrechte, Freiburg (a.u) 1999.
SANDKÜHLER, Hans Jörg, Menschenwürde und die Transformation moralischer Rechte in Positives Recht, in: SANDKÜHLER, Hans Jörg (Hg.), Menschenwürde. Philosophische, Theologische und Juristische Analysen, Frankfurt am Main 2007, 57-86.
SANSONI, Giulio Cesare (ed.), F. Battaglia, Classici del Liberalismo e del Socialismo (Le Carte del Dirriti) Seconda Edizione, Firenze 1947.
SARPONG, Peter, Ghana in Retrospect, Accra, 1974.
SARPONG, Peter, Growth or Decay: Can Christianity Dialogue with African Traditional Religion? in: Bulletin 69 (1988), 189-206.
SAUER, Hanjo/ RIEDL, Alfons, Die Menschenrechte als Ort der Theologie. Ein fundamental- und moraltheologischer Diskurs, Frankfurt am Main, 2003.
SCHEFFCZYK, Leo, Einführung in die Schöpfungslehre³, Darmstadt, 1987.
SCHEFFCZYK, Leo, Einführung in die Schöpfungslehre², Darmstadt 1975.
SCHILD, Wolfgang, Menschenrechte, in: WALTER, Rudolf a.u. (Hgs.), Handwörterbuch Religiöser Gegenwartsfragen (Sonderausgabe), Freiburg i. Br.²1989.
SCHNÄDELBACH, Herbert, Werte und Würde, in: THIES, Christian (Hg.), Der Wert der Menschenwürde, Paderborn 2009, 21-32.
SCHNEIDER-FLUME, Gunda, Die Geschichte der Imago Dei als Schutzraum der Menschenwürde, in: AMMER, Christian (Hg.), Herausforderung Menschenwürde; Beiträge zum interdisziplinären Gespräch, Neukirchener 2010, 37-60.
SCHÜTZ, Alfred, Phenomenology of the Social World. Evanston, III: North western University Press, 1967.
SENGHOR, Leopold Seder, On African Socialism, New York, 1964.
SHORTER, Aylward, African Christian Spirituality, London 1978.

SINGER, Peter, Animal Rights: The Right to Protest, in: *The Independent*, January 21, 2007.
SPAEMANN, Robert, Über den Begriff der Menschenwürde, in: BÖCKENFÖRDE, Ernst-Wolfgang, SPAEMANN, Robert (Hgg.): Menschenrechte und Menschenwürde: Historische Voraussetzungen-Säkulare Gestalt-Christliches Verständnis, Stuttgart, 1987.
SPENCER, Janet T, Achievement American Style: The Rewards and Costs of Individualism, in: American Psychologist, Vol. 40 (12) Dec. 1985, 1285-1295.
SPIELMANN, Renzo, Welche Menschenwürde?, in: Die Tagespost, Dienstag 11. Nr. 136, November 2008.
SUNDERMEIER, Theo, The Individual and Community in African Traditional Religions, Hamburg, 1998.
TALBOT, Amaury P., The People of Southern Nigeria, Vol. III, Oxford University Press, London 1926.
TEMPELS, Placid, La Philosophie Bantoue, Belgian-Congo-Lovania 1945.
TEMPELS, Placide, Bantu Philosophy^2, (Trans.) RUBBENS, A. Paris, 1959.
TEMPELS, Placide, Bantu Philosophie Ontologie und Ethik, Heidelberg, 1956.
TERENCE, Ranger, Religion, Development and African Christian Identity, Uppsala, 1987, 29-55.
THIES, Christian, Einleitung, in: THIES, Christian (Hg.), Der Wert der Menschenwürde, Paderborn-München-Wien-Zürich 2009, 7-19.
THOMPSON, Milford James, French Revolution Documents (1789-94), Blackwell Oxford, 1948.
THURNER, Martin, Die Menschenrechte, die Menschenwürde und das Christentum, in: HEINZMANN, Richard u.a. (Hgg.), Menschenwürde, Grundlagen in Christentum und Islam, Stuttgart 2007, 80-91.
TIEDEMANN, Paul, Was ist Menschenwürde? Eine Einführung, Darmstadt 2006.
TREVELYAN, George Macaulay, History of England, London 1960.
TURNER, Victor, The Ritual Process, Chicago, 1969.
UCHENDU, Victor Chikezie, *Ezi Na Ulo*: The Extended Family in Igbo Civilization, 1995 Ahiajoku Lecture, Owerri: Culture Division of Ministry of Information, Culture youth and Sports 1995.
UCHENDU Victor Chikezie, The Igbo of Southeast Nigeria, New York, 1965.

UZOR, Peter Chiehiura, The traditional African Concept of God and the Christian Concept of God Chukwu bu ndu-God is life (the Igbo Perspective). Frankfurt am Main u.a. 2004.

VOGEL, Bernhard (Hg.), Im Zentrum: Menschenwürde. Politisches Handeln aus Christlicher Verantwortung Christlicher Ethik als Orientierungshilfe. Germany 2006.

VÖGELE, Wolfgang, Die Christliche Deutung der Menschenwürde im Kontext gegenwärtiger Debatten, in: THIES, Christian (Hg.), Der Wert der Menschenwürde, Paderborn-München-Wien-Zürich 2009, 63-74.

WATERFIELD, Robin (Trans. ed.), Plato Republic, Oxford London, 2008.

WEGHAUPT, Helmut, Die Bedeutung und Anwendung von Dignitas in den Schriften der Republikanischen Zeit, Breslau 1932.

WEHRLE, Paul, In der Welt von Heute, Konradsblatts Nr. 50, 2005.

WEISCHEDEL, Wilhelm (Hg.), Immanuel Kant: Grundlage zur Metaphysik der Sitten, Werke BA 77, IV, Darmstadt 1975 (1785).

WEISCHEDEL, Wilhelm (Hg.), Immanuel Kant. Die Religion innerhalb der Grenzen der bloßen Vernunft, Werke in 10 Bänden, Bd.7, Darmstadt (2. Aufl.) 1983 (1794).

WEISCHEDEL, Wilhelm (Hg.), Immanuel Kant, Grundlegung zur Metaphysik der Sitten, Werke in 10 Bänden, Bd. 6 Darmstadt, 1983 (1786).

WEISCHEDEL, Wilhelm (Hg.), Immanuel Kant, Schriften zur Metaphysik und Logik 2, Werkausgaben Band VI. Darmstadt, 1977.

WEISSMAN, Deborah M, The Human Rights Dilemma: Rethinking the Humanitarian Project, in: Public Law and Legal Theory Research Paper No. 13-8, htt://ssrn.com/abstract=462524 14.10.2011, 1-92.

WENZ, Gunther, Wolfhart Pannenbergs Systematische Theologie. Ein Einführender Bericht, Göttingen, 2003.

WILLIAMSON, James Alexander, The Evolution of England (2nd Ed.), Oxford 1961.

WOJTYLA, Karol, The Person: Subject and Community, in: The Review of Metaphysics. A Philosophical Quarterly, Vol. XXXIII, No. 1 Issue no. 129, Sept. 1979 273-308.

WOJTYLA, Karol, The Acting Person, Vol. 10 Analecta Husserliana, TYMIENIECKA, Anna-Teresa (ed.): The Yearbook of Phenomenological Research, Dordrecht Holland, 1979.

WOJTYLA, Karol, Crossing the Threshold of Hope, London 1994.

ZIZIOULAS, John, Being as Communion: Studies in Personhood and the Church, St. Vladimir Seminary, New York, 1997.